"Clear and accessible, this book serves evangelical students and church people alike. McFarlane guides readers to help them to form their theological commitments and articulation, and—while he draws on a range of thinkers—he never deviates from conclusions and discussions which are textured by evangelical theological commitments and emphases. This is a good introduction for any evangelical wishing to think more about the faith in which they so passionately believe: it opens up the vast horizons of theological wisdom which can be explored in praise and love of God for all eternity."

—**Tom Greggs**, FRSE, University of Aberdeen

"Like the wise steward in Jesus's parable, Graham McFarlane brings out of the storehouse things old and new. *A Model for Evangelical Theology* presents the best insights from a wealth of theological sources, creatively woven into a fresh presentation that is a manifesto for the theological endeavor and, more importantly, a celebration of the high *vocation* of the evangelical theologian. McFarlane rehabilitates the Wesleyan Quadrilateral as an Evangelical Quintilateral, adding community to Scripture, tradition, reason, and experience, arguably bringing out what Wesley himself emphasized: that theology is only possible in the presence of God and of all others with whom we are formed and transformed. This is innovation on the theological tradition at its energizing best."

—**Andrew Stobart**, Wesley House, Cambridge

"At a time when the word 'evangelical' is increasingly misunderstood or politicized, McFarlane's comprehensive and systematic account of an evangelical theological method is a breath of fresh air. His writing is clearly the product of decades of teaching theology, allowing curiosity and questioning to shape his approach, engaging heart and mind in equal measure. McFarlane's proposal of community as a fifth dimension to the method of evangelical theology places theology right where it should be—at the heart of the church, and as the calling not of the academic elite but of all who are baptized into the body of Christ. This book will not only deepen your understanding of the foundations of your faith but also increase your love for the God of the gospel and his mission in the world today."

—**Hannah Steele**, St. Mellitus College, London

"A preoccupation with theological method has been described as clearing one's throat. If that is true, Graham McFarlane has accomplished this so well that those who read this book will speak with a more profound theological voice. McFarlane provides us with a truly evangelical prolegomena that goes further and deeper than anything that has been published, unpacking five dimensions of the theological enterprise in the company of a wide range of practitioners. He dissects, clarifies, and exemplifies the process of theological thinking that will assist us in remaining true to the Word and relevant to the human situation."

—**Dennis Okholm**, Azusa Pacific University; author
of *Learning Theology through the Church's Worship*

"McFarlane provides a much-needed critical-confessional model for evangelical theology revisited for the ecclesial realities of the twenty-first century. Thoughtfully engaging Albert Outler's descriptive Wesleyan Quadrilateral of Scripture, tradition, reason, and experience, McFarlane offers a systematic consideration of theology that is almost abandoned or at least overlooked in evangelical discussions. I highly recommend this book for students and individuals seeking a model for theology that is robustly evangelical and relevant for theological engagement today."

—**Joy J. Moore**, Luther Seminary

A Model for Evangelical Theology

Evangelical Theology

INTEGRATING SCRIPTURE, TRADITION, REASON, EXPERIENCE, AND COMMUNITY

GRAHAM McFARLANE

Baker Academic
a division of Baker Publishing Group
Grand Rapids, Michigan

Published by Baker Academic
a division of Baker Publishing Group
PO Box 6287, Grand Rapids, MI 49516-6287
www.bakeracademic.com

Printed in the United States of America

Library of Congress Cataloging-in-Publication Data
Names: McFarlane, Graham, 1959– author.
Title: A model for evangelical theology : integrating scripture, tradition, reason, experience, and community / Graham McFarlane.
Description: Grand Rapids, Michigan : Baker Academic, a division of Baker Publishing Group, 2020. | Includes bibliographical references and index.
Identifiers: LCCN 2019048618 | ISBN 9781540960351 (paperback) | ISBN 9781540962720 (casebound)
Subjects: LCSH: Evangelicalism. | Theology.
Classification: LCC BR1640 .M398 2020 | DDC 230/.04624—dc23
LC record available at https://lccn.loc.gov/2019048618

20   21   22   23   24   25   26   7   6   5   4   3   2   1

To my wife, Hilary

Contents

Preface

Lovers are the ones who know most about God; the theologian must listen to them.

Hans Urs von Balthasar, *Love Alone Is Credible*[1]

This is a book I have wanted to write for nearly three decades. It has taken me this long to understand why systematic theologians are advised to publish only toward the end of their lecturing years. It probably takes us this length of time not only to identify the issues facing the contemporary church but also to propose a mature solution. After all, we only get one shot per annum at giving our lectures, so we develop them, and then, in the busyness of academia, file them for the next year. I am a natural evangelical—I have too much energy for my own good, I like quick solutions, and I prefer action to reflection. Theological method was simply a distraction from getting on with the job! Indeed, being Scottish, I knew that there were superb faculties of divinity in my homeland that would earth a student in this skill for an entire first year of undergraduate studies, if this is what was desired.

My fascination with theological method began when I spent a research sabbatical at the hospitality of Asbury Theological Seminary in Kentucky. It was a privilege to spend time with Wesleyans and Methodists. In addition to discovering a gentle and deeply holistic spirituality, I was struck by their commitment to a theological method premised on John Wesley's approach. While Wesleyan scholars have now moved on from this position, on the whole, exposure to what has come to be known as the Wesleyan Quadrilateral did its damage to me! I became aware of *theological method permeating every aspect of faith*. As a result, I also became all too aware of the inadequacy of my own theological tradition and training in particular and, in general, the wider inadequacy of evangelical theology to address the mercurial nature of early twenty-first-century Western culture. Evangelicalism is, after all, a product of modernity and is ill fitted to the vagaries of postmodernity, let alone post-Christendom.

This awareness set me on a personal and professional inquiry: What might a specifically evangelical theological method look like? I quickly discovered just how difficult it was to convince others—in this instance my colleagues—that this was an issue worth putting in an evangelical theological curriculum. What galvanized my inquiry into the possibility of teaching an evangelical theological method was the challenge presented to the faculty at London School of Theology (LST) by the board of governors to come up with a new MA program. It became clear very quickly to me that there was no MA program in theological method for evangelical students. So, being in the position to pursue this trajectory, I convinced my faculty colleagues that an MA in evangelical theological method was worth developing. Over a period of several months, we pulled on our expertise and worked collaboratively—even joined by my colleague Conrad Gempf, whose Lutheran theology resists such approaches to theology—and eventually we created an MA in integrative theology. If this book ignites a theological flame, then know you can take it further at LST!

I am grateful, in turn, to LST for research leave during which time the back of this book was broken, and to LST's librarian, Keith Lang, for his meticulous professionalism. I am equally grateful to Baker Academic, especially David Nelson, senior acquisitions editor, for his faith in my proposal, and my editors Tim West and Eric Salo for their attention to detail. It is a particular honor to be able to partner with Baker Academic in this venture.

Closer to home, at LST, I have taught an introductory module for undergraduates, Introduction to Theological Method, in which I unpack what I call the "Evangelical Quintilateral." I have had the privilege of lecturing and exploring theology with the exceptional students who come to study at LST. I have seen the change that having a theological method makes not only to their studies but also to their praxis outside of lectures, whether in preaching, pastoring, barista-ing, or being husband, wife, daughter, son, parent, and disciple. The present book is a mature reflection on what I offer as a possible evangelical theological method with the aim of equipping Christians in their own *faith seeking understanding*, whether as ordinary believers or academic theologians. It is my hope that this theological method will provide the tools required to become mature and meaningful communicators of the gospel and its implications for the entirety of human life.

Finally, I honor a coterie of very important people who have journeyed with me thus far and without whom this study would not be written. First, my parents, Peter and Jessie McFarlane, who first introduced me to the gospel of our Lord Jesus Christ and who continue to live it out into their ninth decade. Then, to those at L'Abri Fellowship, Greatham, England—in particular, Richard Winter—who modeled a theological framework that made sense of this gospel. I am particularly indebted to the late Colin Gunton, who demonstrated a passion for theological engagement, whose legacy continues to this day in various theological faculties and pulpits around the world, and who introduced me to Edward Irving (thank you, Andrew Walker, for dropping this obscure theologian into Colin's mind!), whose passion and thought educated me into a deeper knowledge of the God and Father of our Lord Jesus Christ and their empowering Spirit. Max and Lucy Turner have embodied friendship, hospitality, and excellent food *coram Deo* in abundance—precious friends are an equally precious gift. Finally, I am especially indebted to my wife, Hilary, who more fully than anyone I know embodies what it means to be a lover of Christ. She, more than any book or theologian, has taught me what it means, costs, and looks like to inhabit Scripture, respect tradition, engage reason, enjoy experience, and love *coram Deo* and live out the *missio Dei* in community. To her this book is dedicated.

PART I

Evangelical Theology and Its Method

one

Framing the Skill
of Being a Theologian

Theology Is about Asking Questions

Questions lie at the very heart of human existence. Think about it: they are a way of life—human existence in all its complexity and struggles, as well as beauty and joys, demands questions. We ask questions about everything, from the simple (How are you? Can I help? What's your name? Where do you live? What's the time? Have you any milk? Now where did I put those keys? You said what? Didn't I give you the tickets? Are we there yet?) to the more complex (Why do we nod our heads to signify yes and shake them for no? What is time? Who am I? What's the meaning of life? Why do some people talk more than others? Is the brain different from the mind? Is there intelligent life anywhere else in the universe? Is there a God? What number do you get if you divide 40 by ½ and add 10?[1]).

Of course, questions are also highly practical. Questions come into their own when we are about to make a big purchase. We compare the price of one car and the value it has with that of another we may well be looking at—we ask questions about depreciation, energy consumption, and insurance brackets to find the best deal. We evaluate with almost every shopping purchase: Is something of better quality or value in another shop? We use comparison websites to determine the best deal for our purchases, whether a mobile phone, travel insurance, currency exchange, or appliances. The list is almost endless. And since questions intrude so much on just about every aspect of human existence, it is important that we recognize not only how ubiquitous this tool is—the universal drive to ask questions—but even more, how important it is.

Questions also lie at the very heart of human learning. They are the brain's way of "double-clicking" on a topic to get it to divulge meaning. Without questions, we would learn nothing new. So why is it, then, that when it comes to anything to do with our faith, we appear to be less willing to bring this way of life—this tool—to bear on what we believe, on our Christian life, or on our thoughts about God? Indeed, many of us are strangely uncomfortable when it comes to asking our questions about God. Shouldn't we "just believe"? Aren't we meant to have a "simple" faith? Who are we to ask questions of God? Surely this is sheer impertinence! Wasn't it because he asked too many questions that God slammed Job? Isn't it a bit irreverent to be critically thoughtful about what the pastor or teacher has taught or preached?

In addition to these more personal questions is the fact that our beliefs invariably have consequences: What if the church is wrong about something it believes? After all, aren't there some denominations that assumed that women being in leadership was untenable when they first started but are not so comfortable with this position today? And if Mother Church can get one thing wrong, who is to say that other things might not be similarly incorrect? How odd, then, that we ask questions in every other area of our lives but are less likely to do so when it comes to matters of faith, where a mindless piety can parade as an excuse not to engage in the messy business of human life and its transformation. Daniel Migliore captures this tension and the fear that asking questions can elicit when he points out that

> while we may be accustomed to raising questions in other areas of life, we are inclined to fear disturbance in matters of faith. We fear questions that might lead us down roads we have not travelled before. We fear disruption in our thinking, believing, and living that might come from inquiring too deeply into God and God's purposes. We fear that if we do not find answers to our questions we will be left in utter despair. As a result of these fears, we imprison our faith, allow it to become boring and stultifying, rather than releasing it to seek deeper understanding.[2]

There is little doubt that this kind of thinking would be ridiculed in any other contemporary discipline of human inquiry that is driven by the skill of asking judicious questions. For instance, without questions we would not enjoy the quality of life we do today, and most certainly we would not benefit from the many medical and scientific discoveries we take so much for granted. At the very heart of scientific discovery lies the discipline of asking questions:

How does this work? Is there a better way to conduct energy? Does the sun really go around the earth? Is the earth flat? Why do objects fall down rather than float up? What is a quark? Could human life exist on Mars? How can a wave and a particle exist at one and the same time together? Can medicine cure all illnesses? Is all artificial intelligence benign? Then, in response to some of the discoveries scientists make, other questions arise, ones that are more ethical in nature and have more to do with how a given discovery may be used: Which disabilities should genetic coding eradicate? Other questions are concerned about the economic implications of a given possibility: Should a government spend more on education and less on military defense? Others explore the political ramifications of a discovery: Who has the right to a limited vaccine, and thus the right to live, in the face of a fatal pandemic?

Of course, some of us ask more questions than others. For some, asking questions is as normal as breathing: we externally process, we are naturally inquisitive, we have thick skin! For others, whether due to temperament—we are shy or introverted—or because we process internally or have been conditioned to keep quiet or were raised not to speak unless spoken to, or our cultural values silence one gender and not another, or our religious upbringing told us to "just" believe—questioning is something that does not come naturally. However, whether or not we are aware of our questions, still we are involved in the activity of asking them throughout each day. Asking questions is like breathing: we do it without even necessarily being consciously aware of the activity. And yet, without it, we would be at quite a loss. Try going through one day without either asking or answering a question. Put simply, questions are ubiquitous!

Pause

Why not try a simple test that will enable you to discover how many questions you ask in any given day? Note on a tablet or smartphone every time you find yourself asking a question or answering someone else's question. Learn to recognize not only *how* you engage in this activity but also *when* you do it, *what things* cause you to ask questions, and *how regularly* you do this.

If questioning is such a basic instinct, why is it, then, that so many Christians, who in their everyday lives ask questions about everything and anything, are quietly reluctant to ask questions in relation to their faith or to what they believe about God, or Jesus, or the Holy Spirit, or about what the pastor, minister, elder, apostle, or bishop preaches or teaches whether from the front of church, or at home group, or in the weekly newsletter or church email? Why is it that church has become, for many, a place where our brains are disconnected and disempowered, set on "silent," like our smartphones? Why are people rendered "questionless" regarding what they hear or are taught within the confines of church? It's not as though what is being said is infallible! Why, then, does respect for church authority and what it teaches often necessitate unthinking allegiance? And while there are exceptions to the rule, on the whole, why does the physical structure of church buildings, as well as the way services are conducted, create socially constructed spaces and subcultures that render passive those who attend, disempowering them to question, explore, or externally process in any meaningful or participatory way? Would not the gains exceed any losses were time and space made within our church communities in which we could explore questions raised by a sermon or teaching and thus enable our faith to mature? Indeed, it is a rare church where the term "theology" is referred to in a positive sense. Consequently, and often in response, church becomes a place either of unhealthy notions of *mystery* that transcend any need for meaningful explanation or of unthinking *experience* that is to be entered into and enjoyed but never critically explored. As a result, for many, church is rarely an inviting space or place where questions can be asked and explored.

Why is the issue of asking questions such an important issue to raise here at the outset? What is the benefit in doing so? Importantly, the reason for raising this obstacle here is not to undermine the church. As we will discover later, the task of theology is impossible without the church. Rather, the reason is simply this: it is to highlight the fact that *the asking of questions and the subsequent ongoing task of finding answers to them lies at the very heart of theological inquiry!* There are two main reasons for this that come with their own significant challenges:

- The first concerns the matter of theology—God. As John Webster puts it, "Christian theology has a singular preoccupation: God, and everything else *sub specie divinitatis*,"[3] which is an old-fashioned Latin way of saying "from the perspective of divinity." In essence, what Webster is saying is that everything other than God has to be considered in the light of God's eternal existence. Put like this, theology does not immediately appear to be very clear. And perhaps this is the point that needs to be made here at the start of this book—the task of theology is not that easy or simple, because its subject matter is God. This being the case, the most natural and meaningful response to anything that is not immediately clear is to ask questions in the hope, by doing so, of discovering more information about it. This is normal procedure in every aspect of human life: when we want to understand something that is unfamiliar, unclear, uncertain, or even unknown, the first thing we do is to ask questions. Questions, in turn, hopefully elicit answers—good ones, wrong ones, half-baked ones, but at least they move us in the direction of discovery. What we call "theology" is simply the result of what Christian thinkers have discovered to be good (or bad) answers to the questions people have asked about and in response to hearing the gospel, being met by Jesus, or wondering about God.[4]

- The second reason for asking questions and finding answers follows from the first: not only is the subject matter of theology, God, not immediately clear, but by virtue of God's very nature, the subject matter of theology is also completely different from any other subject we can study or about which we can ask questions. Why?
  » Because God is not created: everything else we ask questions about is.
  » Because God is not directly observable: just about everything else is.

Therefore, the subject matter of theology raises its own peculiar and particular challenges not only in what can be said about God but also in terms of how we are even able to find out what can be said about God. This book is predominantly about the latter—how we go about the task of talking about God in any meaningful, thoughtful, and consistent manner. In essence, it is about how we go about the task of theology, how we go about asking the what, how, who, and when questions. We call this *theological method*.

Of course, we could be deceived at this point into thinking that the task of theology is perhaps not so difficult and should be a relatively simple and predictable affair; given that God does not change, our subject matter might be considered the most stable of all topics of inquiry. Sadly, however, we would be wrong to make this assumption. Such a theology would be one that fits all shapes and sizes; all social contexts and historical moments; every cultural, gender, age, and human condition. It would be a universal with no particulars. It would be "fundamental" in the wrong sense of the word: ungiving and inhospitable.[5] The reality is, as we will see, that we never know God in the abstract: we know God only within the context of our own life situations and histories and, in particular, in our places of brokenness, need, and impotence. Only to the extent that the questions we ask arise from the lives we and others live do we engage a living faith.

That this is the case means that the discipline of theology necessitates engaging in struggle and conflict—struggle with its subject matter, God, and conflict with its context, the good, the bad, the beautiful, and the ugly of human existence.[6] It means, too, that the setting within which theology takes place, where our questions are asked, will always be "a reality, which is inherently messy."[7] In fact, we could say that the task of theology should come with a health warning because of its spiritual and intellectual challenges, which militate against contemporary obsessions for order, control, and sanitized, bite-sized answers. So, be warned: "A theology which seeks always to smooth away life's rough edges is not likely to be a good theology."[8] Indeed, it is bad theology—and bad theology always damages people. So let's be honest in our starting point on the theological apprenticeship and take ownership of the fact that the nature of the reality in which we find ourselves is messy. We talk about God from this perspective of human brokenness rather than some heavenly idyll. What this means, of course, is that good theology engages with the here and now, with the issues Christians face in their own lives, personal and social—put bluntly, within the midst of our own and others' messiness. Consequently, I like how Colin Gunton hits the spot when he says that any theology that seeks "to transcend its temporal framework to a timeless realm above and beyond" is nothing other than religion.[9] That is, theology should not concern itself with religion; rather, its concern is always with God as God is known within the here and now of human existence in all its glory and brokenness.

By virtue of its subject matter—God—theology is a particular discipline in and of itself. Like any other discipline, be it medicine, carpentry, farming, engineering, hairdressing, and so on, theology requires its own set of distinct skills. Without them, it is not possible to master the discipline and practice well the theological craft: particular skills are required if theological inquiry is to be undertaken effectively. For example, when I have a toothache, I go to a dentist who knows how to treat teeth correctly; a woman about to give birth wants the help of a trained midwife or doctor who practices the skills of the profession with the necessary hygiene. The same goes for the task of theology. A trustworthy and dependable theologian is someone who can practice his or her craft correctly and engage wisely with the various questions that people have, that situations provoke, and that the messiness of human existence demands. Like a language, theology also has its own "grammar." Specifically, evangelical theology has its own "grammar," one that distinguishes it from other theological disciplines, Christian or otherwise. As we have noted above, theology cannot be separated from the church for the simple reason that theology is how the church throughout its history has expressed itself and given meaning to its beliefs and practices. Without the language of theology, there is no Christian speech. I like the way Robert Jenson, in particular, expresses the relationship between theology and the church in advocating that theology is the grammar of the church and that "the church is the community of the message."[10]

Theology Is about Our Worldview

This book seeks to offer a theological grammar—a theological method—that makes the contemporary task of being a theologian both possible and meaningful. It does so with the understanding that the discipline of theology has its own distinct set of skills, practices, and habits that enable Christians to articulate and communicate our knowledge of God consistently, first, in relation to each other: there need to be accepted norms and practices if we are to have any meaningful dialogue with our past and present. Second, theology requires specific and mutually agreed-on skills to engage with the complexities of human existence. Third, without some understanding of creation's meaning as well as human history, the task of making sense of the wider creation in which we live becomes so much more problematic. What the discipline of theology brings to the academic table is that it offers us the ability to transcend the particular in order to get a better vision of the whole, albeit from a particularly theological perspective. Umberto Eco captures the strangeness of such knowledge in his novel *The Name of the Rose* when he writes, "I am He who is, said the God of the Jews. I am the way, the truth, and the life, said our Lord. There you have it: knowledge is nothing but the awed comment on these two truths."[11]

Put this way, the task of theology is not so much to provide us with facts about God or with a technique to be learned that can be picked up and laid back down at will. Rather, the task of theology is to inform us how to engage in a particular way of living in the world—a *worldview*—without which meaningful life would not be possible. This worldview furnishes us with answers to the deeper questions of human existence. For example, sociologist Peter Berger pinpoints how our worldview manifests itself culturally as such: "Every human society has its own corpus of officially accredited wisdom, the beliefs and values that most people take for granted as self-evidently true. Every human society has institutions and functionaries whose task it is to represent this putative truth, to transmit it to each new generation, to engage in rituals that reaffirm it and sometimes to deal (at least in words) with those who are benighted or wicked enough to deny it."[12] Alternatively, apologist-theologian James Sire identifies a worldview as "a commitment, a fundamental orientation of the heart, that can be expressed as a story or in a set of presuppositions . . . which we hold . . . about the basic constitution of reality, and that provides the foundation on which we live and move and have our being."[13] Interestingly, each worldview itself is the sum total of all the answers men and women like you and me at various historical moments have asked of their own lives and the various worlds in which they have found themselves:

1. What is prime reality—ultimate being?
2. What is the nature of external reality—that is, the world around us?
3. What is human being?
4. What happens to a person at death?
5. Why is it possible to know anything at all?
6. How do we know what is right and wrong?
7. What is the meaning of human history?[14]

Our worldview is, thus, "the shared framework of ideas held by a particular society concerning how they perceive the world. . . . The worldview gives shape and order to the multitude of outward manifestations of a culture."[15] In general terms, then, a worldview achieves two key things. First, it provides the means by which we make sense of and hold together all the disparate elements of our various cultures, whether politics, religion, law, education, health, family, media, ecology, or the arts. Second, our worldview not only furnishes us with the necessary data by which we understand our world; it also enables us to live consistently within this world.

It is of tremendous importance, then, that we be able to identify the dominant worldviews around us—our own as well as others—a particularly important skill in our increasingly pluralistic contexts. It matters that we be able to locate the meaning of life in relation to each worldview since, if we think about it, each one acts like a "mental map" and attempts to "tell us how to navigate the world effectively."[16] N. T. Wright identifies four criteria for this task, all of which are pertinent to the task of theological inquiry:

• Worldviews provide the stories with which we understand reality.
• The worldview stories enable us to answer the basic question of human existence.
• We express our answers to such questions through cultural symbols.
• Our worldview provides ways of living in the world.[17]

On a grand scale, then, our worldview is a bit like glue—it acts as a unifying principle in what is, otherwise, a seemingly disconnected world. It is what unites belief and practice, faith and thought, and ultimately all of us together, for better or for worse. This has particular relevance for the theologian, for there is an intimate relation between how we live in the world with each other and what each of us believes (or not) about God. Since we believe that God is Creator and that Jesus presents himself to us as the source of abundant life, it follows, then, that what we believe about the God and Father of our Lord Jesus Christ should correspond to how we think we can live best in our world. Perhaps I can put it this way: the question is never "Do you have a worldview?" We all do.[18] Rather, the question is "Does your worldview work?" And for the Christian, the question is even more specific given our belief in God as Creator and Savior and can be posed as "How biblical is your worldview?"[19] This biblical worldview is expressed through the narratives of Scripture that outline the master stories of our Christian faith: creation, fall, covenant, re-creation, and consummation.

On a more particular level, our worldview is what comes at us every day through advertising—cultural aspirations are projected through a car, home décor, vacations, clothing. The media—newspapers, magazines, the internet, social media—filter what we read and what they want the public to read and know; entertainment media portray our worldview aspirations and beliefs. For instance, when on research leave at a seminary in the United States, I watched several TV sitcoms, and I was struck by just how central to the American worldview was the belief that everything is possible, problems are always solved, family disputes always get resolved well, and the good always win in the end. What struck me so forcibly was how, as a consequence, this threw light on my own British worldview and the fact that UK sitcoms are quite different: if it can get worse, it does; things don't usually get better, and good people get walked over. For one worldview, the glass is always half full, and for the other, it remains half empty. Each perspective, however, expresses a deeper, more unconscious worldview that the theologian has not only to identify and understand but also to engage.

Theology Is about Communication

The ubiquitous nature of worldviews means, obviously, that a specifically evangelical theology will have its own worldview too—its own way of doing things, its own beliefs and practices, its own way of living in the world, and, as we have already seen, its own grammar and language. On the one hand, the aim of evangelical theology is, as Kevin Vanhoozer and Daniel Treier describe, "to understand who God is, what he has done and why it counts as good news."[20] On the other hand, in order to go about this aim, as we have noted, we need a language and grammar. And like any other language with its own grammar,[21] Christian theology will be a very different speech, one that demarcates itself from other worldview languages. This being the case, we can say along with Jenson that "this grammar distinguishes Christian theology from all other theologies."[22]

As we have noted, Christians live differently from other people of faith and unfaith because their allegiance is to a worldview very different from others on offer. Craig Keener identifies one of the key consequences of embracing and living within the worldview of the Bible: it enables us "to view our own world in a different light (as opposed to primarily immersing ourselves in other narratives popular around us)."[23] That is, it is not merely others' worldviews that come under Scripture's scrutiny; it is also our own. Small wonder that Jesus likens living in the worldview of his Father's kingdom to a narrow path on which few are to be found (Matt. 7:13–14). Put like this, it is clear that an evangelical theological method is one that will be established on a particular view of reality, contoured by a theological understanding of creation—"By faith we understand that the universe was formed at God's command, so that what is seen was not made out of what was visible" (Heb. 11:3)—and a clear sense of where history is going. It will be expansive but equally grounded in the realities of human brokenness and the good news of the gospel.

Marva Dawn captures the contemporary glory of the biblical worldview rather pithily: "Scripture is the 'master-story,' the 'meta-Narrative' that offers meaning, identity, and hope to the channel-surfing postmodern society."[24] Consequently, the imperative for us as theologians is that we should be familiarly conversant with the grammar of our biblical worldview, because by it we speak its language and with it we are better able to engage the messy world that needs to hear good news. This biblical worldview sets Christian theology apart and allows it to be the lingua franca of the worldwide church. And, like all other languages, theology is best mastered by frequent repetition.[25]

Let's stop here for a moment. The point just made is important. Pause and try to work out what it might mean for you as a theologian to learn the language of the church and what it will demand of you. Here is what it means for me:

*To be a theologian is
to be bilingual.*

What is required to be a theologian, whether ordinary or academic, on the one hand, is the ability to speak, hear, listen to, understand, translate, and communicate what Karl Barth so beautifully describes as the "strange new world within the Bible."[26] On the other, it is to know how to communicate this strange new world within the Bible to our "old and familiar world of the here and now" as we experience it in our own particular context. Being a theologian, then, necessitates being so familiar with and so constantly listening to the contents of Scripture as to be able to speak it clearly, effectively, and consistently. It means the same, too, for each here-and-now context into which the theologian speaks and writes: to be listening to the context, the worldview, the issues, the hopes, the expectations both conscious and subconscious, and to be hearing the explicit as well as the implicit grammar and language of those to whom the gospel, with all its implications, is being proclaimed. What this means in practice is that the same kind of attention, time, and effort that is required in learning any new language is required of us in our own theological development. In the same way that the strange world of the Bible provides our new language of faith—a language that enables us to love God and follow Jesus Christ, to learn how to live with and to love the new and sometimes strange group of people who make up "church" or how to live as a disciple of Jesus in our own context—so, too, are we to learn similarly the language and grammar of the world in which our neighbors live. And in so doing, we "square the circle" between these two very distinct and different worlds that the Bible itself tells us cannot coexist.

Jesus Christ himself makes this point very clear in stating the impossibility of following two masters (Matt. 6:24), having qualified earlier a similar impossibility—namely, of serving God, and all that this entails, and at the same time serving "mammon," a word that embraces not simply the love of money but a much wider greedy intention to gain as much wealth as possible. However, simply "opting out" of the world and living in a Christian bubble is never an option for anyone who follows Jesus Christ, not least for theologians. Rather, while we belong either to the kingdom of God or to counterfeit nation-states, we are obliged to be in the world, but not of it (John 15:19; 17:14–15; Rom. 12:1–2; 1 John 2:15–17). The point will be made that theology is not an autonomous activity or entity but rather one that has meaning only in relation to exegeting Scripture. Theology serves Scripture. Any other is inadequate to the task.

Theologians, like anyone learning a new language, are only successful in learning and maturing in their craft to the degree they live in the text—indwell it—so that it comes alive with meaning and thus facilitates effective understanding and communication. Obviously, then, for this to happen, we need some kind of "tool kit," a specific means of constructing and maintaining our theology, so that it is *theology* and not anthropology, sociology, philosophy, or anything else we might wish to construct. Fundamental to creating that tool kit is understanding that to be a theologian is

- to identify and articulate the gospel of Jesus Christ;
- to master the discipline of understanding this gospel;

- to identify theology's way of going about its business;
- to handle theology's internal grammar;
- to read and speak theology's language; and
- to live with integrity within a specific worldview.

Theology Is about the Whole Person

It should be clear by now that theology does not "just happen." It is not the product of divine downloading that directly bypasses the mind of some suitably spiritual recipient or recipients. There is no "theology" folder on which to double-click in order to extract immediate and accessible answers to life's questions. Rather, because we are constituted as mind, body, and spirit, the task of theological inquiry requires specific realities to be honored. We are embodied spirits, enspirited bodies, and the task of theology engages all three aspects of our existence. It does so through what we can call *habits*—habits that are exercised by our physical, mental, and spiritual faculties. For these habits or disciplines to become working skills, they need to be identified, understood, handled correctly, practiced, repeated, allowed to mature, and, most definitely, mastered and loved. This sounds good in theory, but it is not so easy in practice, particularly when, for some of us, we are not all that comfortable with asking questions, let alone being disciplined in our habits.

However, even a cursory reading of New Testament texts shows that this theological task of learning new habits, of aspiring to certain virtues, is essential. Throughout the two Testaments, we discover an ongoing endorsement of disciplined habits that constitute a thoroughly holistic theological approach. First, there is the habit or discipline of using our mind effectively; second, there are bodily habits and disciplines that facilitate transformation; last, Scripture refers consistently to essential spiritual—that is, relational—habits that empower us in our calling to become the body politic of Christ.[27] Even a sample set of verses illustrates the point that our theological endeavors should embrace our entire being. Thus, when it comes to the mind, we discover exhortations that are really a radical call to develop new habits:

> Do your best to present yourself to God as one approved, a worker who does not need to be ashamed and who correctly handles the word of truth. (2 Tim. 2:15)

> Do not conform to the pattern of this world, but be transformed by the renewing of your mind. Then you will be able to test and approve what God's will is—his good, pleasing and perfect will. (Rom. 12:2)

Be made new in the attitude of your minds. (Eph. 4:23)

> For he is the kind of person
>> who is always thinking about the cost.[28]
> "Eat and drink," he says to you,
>> but his heart is not with you. (Prov. 23:7)

Then there are habits that specifically relate to our physical existence, our embodiedness, which demonstrate not only that our bodies directly influence *how* we know God (for instance, if I refuse the act of bodily worship, I clearly miss out on a particular corpus of knowledge) but also that our bodies are the *means* of knowing God. In other words, my knowledge of God comes via my body and is not external to it.[29] As Lance Peeler reminds us, "Brains are housed in bodies. . . . Thinking is more than just our brains—our whole bodies are involved in thinking, the same way that they are involved in eating, running, or resting."[30] Simply put, we come to a knowledge of the living God by virtue of what the gospel achieves in our individual physical bodies as well as in our wider social bodies:

> Therefore, I urge you, brothers and sisters, in view of God's mercy, to offer your bodies as a living sacrifice, holy and pleasing to God—this is your true and proper worship. (Rom. 12:1)

> For if you live according to the flesh, you will die; but if by the Spirit you put to death the misdeeds of the body, you will live. (Rom. 8:13)

> Put to death, therefore, whatever belongs to your earthly nature: sexual immorality, impurity, lust, evil desires and greed, which is idolatry. (Col. 3:5)

Last, there is what we can describe as "spiritual" habits and disciplines. Of course, these habits turn on what we mean by the term "spiritual." In some contexts, the spiritual is something that stands in juxtaposition to the mind, to the rational, and even to the body, the physical. For others, the spiritual is a purely individualistic concept: something that goes on between God and the believer. At this point, it may be more helpful to think of the spiritual as an aspect of human existence that works organically or holistically with the mind (soul) and the body to establish healthy relationships. It is clearly a powerful and leveling habit:

> On the last and greatest day of the festival, Jesus stood and said in a loud voice, "Let anyone who is thirsty come to me and drink. Whoever believes in me, as Scripture has said, rivers of living water will flow from within them." By this

he meant the Spirit, whom those who believed in him were later to receive. Up to that time the Spirit had not been given, since Jesus had not yet been glorified. (John 7:37–39)

So in everything, do to others what you would have them do to you, for this sums up the Law and the Prophets. (Matt. 7:12)

Pray continually. (1 Thess. 5:17)

Pause

Theological integrity requires proper use of words. This linguistic transparency is essential both to enable effective communication and to bring about clear understanding. Before you proceed, test your language skills on the three terms that we have been using: "body," "mind," "spirit."

- Write down your definition of each term in no more than two succinct sentences.
- You might want to clarify the terms by asking a variety of questions: Is the brain part of the body or the mind, or both? Is the mind different from the brain? What is "spirit"? Does my smartphone have "spirit"—if not, why not? If it does, what does it look like? How does spirit relate to mind? How does body relate to spirit?

Theology Is about Developing Habits

The task of theology is a "craft," and like any other craft it has its chief tools. One key tool is language, and in particular, words. After all, words make worlds: the Creator God simply speaks the command and creation comes into existence. Words destroy worlds too.[31] Trevor Hart points out that theology is made up of "words and the ideas to which they are related." Theologians, then, are "wordsmiths," but as Hart continues, "these words and ideas are inevitably finite: drawn from the available pool of human language and experience, handled by human thinkers and wordsmiths who can make no claim to have transcended their own finitude and sinfulness in the process, any more than can their readers in receiving the results."[32] What this means for the theological task is that our theology will always be constrained by our own humanity, history, and culture and require some help if it is to make sense to people outside of our own world of thinking and experience.

You might be realizing at this point that these habits, disciplines, and the skills they require remain an abstraction unless they are further clarified. For deeper understanding, in the next section I identify the various components necessary in any theological practice. These components are both *distinct* and *discrete*. They are distinct in that each one has its own particular function and therefore identity. They are discrete in that each one operates in a specific manner in relation to the others. Thus, to be effective theologians we must be able to identify each component as well as understand how it works, both in and of itself and in relation to others. Together, these components enable us "to do" theology—that is, they become the constituent parts of our theological method. And the degree to which we recognize and understand them will be the degree to which we are better able to undertake the task of being theologically minded. In essence, these various components "frame" the skill of being a theologian. This "frame" is, however, not rigid: the components have a liquidity, a flexibility, a fluidity about them because our theological inquiry is never abstracted from the variables of human existence, including history and culture. And these components enable us

to ask the right questions;

to engage the questions;

to respond to the questions; and

to construct answers to the questions.

There is a distinction to be understood at this point: while these components frame our theological endeavors, they are not necessarily, at the same time, the theological method itself. The tools of our theological method are quite different and will be the focus of our attention once the frame has been identified. What we can do here is explore what these various components look like and how they might help us construct our theological responses.

Knowledge

KNOWLEDGE THAT IS CONSTANT

A peculiar aspect of Christian theology is its nonnegotiable stance on Scripture. We will explore this in much more detail in the next chapter; for the moment I highlight four things:

1. The influence and authority of Scripture do not change—nothing can be added to Scripture, and no other writing has the same authority.

2. Most important, the belief that Scripture's source is God is nonnegotiable—which means that Scripture acts as the permanent constant in theological reflection.

3. The unity of the Bible cannot be separated from the God of the Bible.[33] Emil Brunner makes this last point well when he says, "The God of the Bible is the God who speaks, and the Word of the Bible is the Word of this God."[34] That is, whatever the historical and universal church believes, the credibility of its belief is the degree to which it corresponds with what God speaks in Scripture. Therefore, theological constructions are not necessarily relativistic; rather, they are merely the product of a specific culture, time, or thinker and, as a consequence, have no universal or objective application. Rather, because Scripture is God speaking, we can definitely argue that it is able to stand as truth, whatever the context, time, or circumstance.

4. Since Scripture cannot be separated from God's self-revelation and his goodwill for creation, including us, we cannot isolate Scripture from "its reception in the community of faith."[35] Why? Because Scripture does not exist in some kind of spiritual vacuum but rather has an authoritative place within the wider grand scheme of God's saving work—beginning with Israel and concluding with Jesus Christ—which is to unite the entire created order, both heavenly and earthly, in one great friendship with God.

Knowledge That Is Ongoing

Theology requires a body of knowledge, whether facts, data, information, thoughts, imaginations, poetry, aspirations, hopes, or beliefs. Without this body of knowledge, the task of theology is made more problematic. In turn, the kind of knowledge that engages theological construction is multifaceted, not one-dimensional. It comes to us through a variety of different media and rarely constitutes one single message. In addition, our theological reflections are the product of different contexts; thus, we need to differentiate the *contextual* from the *constant*. Colin Gunton comments that "all theologies belong in a particular context, and so are, to a degree, limited by the constraints of that context. To that extent, the context is one of the authorities to which the theologian must listen."[36] This kind of knowledge is also continually developing: it is dynamic rather than inert. Questions asked by one generation regarding a specific event elicit answers that may provide new information. In turn, this data is incorporated into what is already known. In addition, it may also raise new questions for which there might not be an immediate answer.

Thus, importantly, an evangelical theology will be marked out by particular beliefs that go against the grain of modern and postmodern cultures. It will hold to the belief that knowing the truth really is possible, and thus it will reject modernist and postmodernist notions of relativism, in which truth is a social construct and thus purely contextual and therefore something that can be different according to context. It will also hold to the belief that it is possible to know something directly or as a reality in and of itself, that objective knowledge is possible, and thus reject the idea that our knowledge is simply the result of language, culture, gender, or tradition.[37]

One of the most important examples of how theological knowledge develops is the way in which the earliest Christians wrestled with Jesus Christ's identity. They knew that he was human—they had lived, worked, eaten, laughed, and cried with him and were convinced that he was the Messiah of God, a prophet, a rabbi, a man worth believing in and following. They had seen him die; some had even embalmed his dead body and interred him in a rocky grave. Most definitely, his humanity was not in question. However, after his resurrection, this identity underwent serious thought. It would be quite strange had Jesus's disciples not asked a whole raft of questions once they met him three days after having seen him die agonizingly on a Roman cross. After all, when did you last see someone come back to life? This alone would be good enough reason to rethink who they thought Jesus was and ask an avalanche of questions. However, additional factors emerged after the resurrection that demanded that new questions be asked of Jesus. The risen and ascended Jesus was now Lord over God's Spirit; that is, Jesus now exercised authority over God's Spirit. The Spirit now made Jesus present to his followers scattered throughout Judea and the Roman Empire in the same way that, under the old covenant, the Spirit made God present to Jewish believers. In addition, Jesus was now identified with the God of Israel: God was his Father, Jesus was God's Son. One could not now be named without the other. Most importantly, the earliest Christians were at ease in worshiping Jesus alongside God (the Father) despite being monotheists, believers in one God.[38] These different experiences of the risen Christ were new and unprecedented realities that demanded that seriously searching questions be asked about his identity—about Jesus's relation not to his fellow humans but to the God of Israel.

Over a period of the next three hundred years, various answers were given to the question "Who is Jesus?" until finally, in AD 325, at a gathering of all the church's leaders, the church fathers assembled at Nicaea (Iznik, modern-day Turkey) to establish an official answer to the question, in response to one very clever but equally problematic solution offered by a theologian named Arius. They came up with a superb answer: not only is Jesus Christ fully human, like us in all ways except for sin; he is also the same nature or substance as the Father. As such, he is as much divine as the Father is. Therefore, in answer to the question "Who is Jesus?" Christians could affirm with confidence that Jesus Christ is everything it means to be fully human, and he is also everything it means to be fully divine. Problem solved!

> We believe in one God, the Father Almighty, Maker of all things visible and invisible.
> And in one Lord Jesus Christ, the Son of God, begotten of the Father the only-begotten; that is, of the essence of the Father, God of God, Light of Light, very God of very God, begotten, not made, being of one substance [*homoousion*] with the Father; by whom all things were made both in heaven and on earth; who for us men, and for our salvation, came down and was incarnate and was made man; he suffered, and the third day he rose again, ascended into heaven; from thence he shall come to judge the quick and the dead.
> And in the Holy Ghost.
> (But those who say: "There was a time when he was not"; and "He was not before he was made"; and "He was made out of nothing," or "He is of another substance" or "essence," or "The Son of God is created," or "changeable," or "alterable"—they are condemned by the holy catholic and apostolic Church.)[39]

However, once the "Who are you?" question of Jesus's identity was resolved, the answer itself immediately raised other, more problematic, questions. One concerned Jesus: "How is it possible for one person to be completely human and completely divine at the same time?" Another concerned God: "Who is God?" The God question was to become the next big theological challenge simply because if there is only *one* God, how can the Father and the Son both be God without signifying that there are two Gods, and in doing so jeopardizing the whole ability to maintain a monotheistic view of God?

The way in which the church's understanding of Jesus Christ developed in the first four centuries of its existence is a very helpful example of how theological understanding develops. What Christians believe is not derived from head knowledge alone. Whether it concerns Jesus Christ's identity or how God can be one in nature but also three divine persons, Father, Son, and Holy Spirit, the fact remains that the fluid and dynamic nature of theological understanding comes about because our questions arise from the fact that *we live in* the reality of Jesus being a Savior who has affected our lives in such a way that we are left asking questions about him. How can his death bring about my new life? What did he mean when he taught that I should give my life away rather than keep it? How did he enable me to break my addiction? What on earth is happening when we take communion? The list could be endless. Yet note this: the direction of questioning is not one way. Theology cannot be reduced to a purely human endeavor, as though the theologian is able to stand over and above the subject matter, God, ask the necessary questions, and objectively extract data. What Christians have discovered over millennia is that we are as much to be questioned as we are to question. The personal nature of theological inquiry means that the very task of theology opens us up to be questioned, challenged, even discombobulated, and sometimes silenced, ourselves. I like how Migliore puts it when he comments, "As a continuing inquiry, the spirit of theology is interrogative rather than doctrinaire; it presupposes a readiness to question and to be questioned."[40] Theological questions invite dialogue; theological dialogue invites questions. Questions undermine false beliefs and lead to greater understanding. Thus, they are dangerous!

And so, any form of specifically personal knowledge comes about not through reading a birth, marriage, or death certificate, or looking up a Wiki page, or even reading an autobiography. Rather, it comes out of personal engagement, relational inquiry. Thus, our knowledge of God as Father, Son, and Spirit is not something conjured out of thin air or the result of theological confusion. Rather, it comes about and continues to arise as a result of ongoing living in and for the God and Father of our Lord Jesus Christ, out of our obedience to our Savior and under the empowering agency of God's Spirit. Such living causes discussion by people like us, who, in declaring Jesus to be Lord, experience a very distinct and shared *lived-in* reality:

- The gospel of Jesus leads us to the Father and at the same time brings about a personal transformation that resembles what other believers experience and goes on to produce a way of life that has to be described in terms of being energized by God's Spirit.
- We can relate to God as Father only by virtue of having his life, his energy, his Spirit and having these through the intercessory work of Jesus Christ, his Son.
- When we become living temples in whom God's Spirit can abide (when we are filled with the Spirit), we discover that we start living out the life of Jesus and become active citizens of and participants in the kingdom of God the Father.

Can you see what is happening here? As a result, first, of reflecting on their experience of God, which came about as a response to Jesus Christ and his gospel, our Christian forefathers and foremothers began to ask questions, engage habits, establish disciplines of inquiry that ultimately led them to answers that resonate with the rest of the church and make the best sense, to date, of Christian experience. Second, they discovered that the face of Christian faith, as well as the identity of the One they were trying to understand, is always *trinitarian*. It always involves the undivided activity or presence of the Father, his Son, and their Holy Spirit, always together, never separately. I think Mark McIntosh puts the trinitarian face of theology most clearly when he points out that "both the practices of Christian life and the theory of Christian faith are human expressions of God's action within the lives and minds of the believing community."[41] And what we discover is the threefold manner by which the one God acts.

- At the center of our theological beliefs is "the formative and expressive power of Christ the *Word* provoking the church into reflective teaching."
- Our desire for understanding is driven by the *Spirit*, "pulling the church into an ever deeper sharing in its new identity in Christ."
- The *Father* is "at the unseen end of all theological endeavour . . . calling all things into the perfect fullness of their truth."[42]

This reflective element to the craft of theological thinking characterizes an important point—namely, that theology is not static but constantly moving; it is an event, a process, an ongoing conversation that enables us to sort out "the sound beliefs and practices from the unsound ones."[43] We can call this kind of knowledge *personal* knowledge—personal because it comes about as a result of living in the reality of the personal and triune God and the messy business of re-creation rather than standing apart from or above it objectively. As such, it is living, dynamic, fluid, and ongoing. And it is to be lived. We capture a sense of the "lived-in-ness" of this process when we look at what Paul says to Timothy as he learns his own craft in what clearly is an equally challenging historical and cultural context:

> If you point these things out to the brothers and sisters, you will be a good minister of Christ Jesus, nourished on the truths of the faith and of the good teaching that you have followed. Have nothing to do with godless myths and old wives' tales; rather, train yourself to be godly. For physical training is of some value, but godliness has value for all things, holding promise for both the present life and the life to come. This is a trustworthy saying that deserves full acceptance. That is why we labor and strive, because we have put our hope in the living God, who is the Savior of all people, and especially of those who believe. Command and teach these things. (1 Tim. 4:6–11)

History and Culture

A second habit for the theologian to develop is what we might describe as a "historical nose" and a "cultural sensibility"—that is, the ability to recognize, and a practice of recognizing, the historical situatedness of any given belief and its cultural expression. All human belief is a product of history—it originates at a particular time and in a specific cultural context, none more so than for Christian belief. What Christians believe is better understood as a social construct, one that spans several thousand years of human-divine encounter and reflection, belief and practice. It is *social* in that it only occurs within the various matrices of human-divine relationships and is then passed on to each subsequent generation through very regulated and controlled means in order to safeguard its content. It is a *construct* in that what we believe is more than information or technique: it constitutes a worldview, a way of living, which requires structures to function, whether legal, religious, financial, political, or economic.[44] This is the stuff of history! And as a product of history and culture, it is neither monochrome nor relativistic. Why? Because no moment in history is the same, and no two cultures are identical: each is dynamic and constantly developing, for good or for ill. Once again, developing an awareness of history and culture constitutes a habit that is necessary when we are engaging an ancient text spanning multiple generations and cultures. The relativistic nature of history and culture is tempered only to the degree we remind ourselves of the constants in theological construction and how these constants regulate our theological responses: the subject matter of theology— God—and the means of knowing God—Jesus Christ and Scripture.

One way I like to demonstrate the contemporaneity of this cultural and historical habit is to ask some of my international students to read out loud to the rest of the group a well-known verse to all, only this time the students read in their mother tongue and ask their colleagues what the verse is in English. For instance:

Imâk Gûdib sillaksoarmuit nagligivait, Ernetuane tunnilugo, illûnatik okpertut tâpsomunga assiokonnagit, nungusuitomigle inôgutekarkovlugit.[45]

Cristo nos rescató de la maldición de la ley al hacerse maldición por nosotros, pues está escrito: «Maldito todo el que es colgado de un madero». Así sucedió, para que, por medio de Cristo Jesús, la bendición prometida a Abraham llegara a las naciones, y para que por la fe recibiéramos el Espíritu según la promesa.[46]

De HERE is mijn herder,
dus heb ik alles wat ik nodig heb!
Hij laat mij uitrusten in een groene weide
en wijst mij de weg langs kabbelende beekjes.
Hij verfrist mijn innerlijk
en leidt mij op de weg waar zijn recht geldt,
tot eer van zijn naam.

Zelfs als ik door een donker dal moet lopen,
ben ik niet bang,
want U bent dicht bij mij.
Uw herdersstaf beschermt mij
en begeleidt mij heel de weg.[47]

Căci mie nu mi-e ruşine de Evanghelia lui Hristos, fiindcă ea este puterea lui Dumnezeu pentru mântuirea fiecăruia care crede: întâi a iudeului, apoi a grecului, deoarece în ea este descoperită o neprihănire pe care o dă Dumnezeu prin credinţă şi care duce la credinţă, după cum este scris: „Cel neprihănit va trăi prin credinţă."[48]

The effect on my students is usually one of complete silence—understandably so! However, the point is made with great effect. It is not about understanding the biblical text given in an unfamiliar language. Rather, it is to press home the point that our key beliefs are often encapsulated in iconic texts that, often unconsciously and uncritically, we think belong to us and thus become framed within our own language, our own time, and our wider culture or our specific Christian subculture. However, the simple act of hearing these familiar texts in a language unfamiliar to us alerts us to the fact that our understanding is indeed a linguistic, historical, and cultural expression, bound to our own context and time and our own way of seeing things.

Given, however, that the Majority World church is one that is growing predominantly where very little English is spoken, read, or thought, this theological habit takes on a deeper meaning: we need to learn the habit of being critically aware of our own situatedness, historical context, and cultural conditioning. Why? Because this habit equips us to realize that our histories and our cultures do not determine the theologies of other people groups. Our context, both historical and cultural, is ours, not theirs, and is a variable unique to ourselves, as much as theirs is to them. It is the result of the questions *we* have asked and the answers we have found most helpful. They might be of use to others; they might not. Thus, this habit enables us to be aware of Veli-Matti Kärkkäinen's truism: "It belongs to the essence of faith and worldviews in general that we often simply accept the tenets of our faith or worldview without much explicit reflection on them. But we also have a built-in need to make sense of what we believe."[49] Our task, then, is to ensure that we do not project our faith, theology, or worldview onto others but ensure, rather, that they remain as distinct as possible, and in doing so, better position ourselves for conversation. What we all hold in common, however, is that our historical and cultural constructs are profoundly *relational*, pointing to the fact that theology is itself a relational construct—it is the church's language of confession, communication, declaration, and, most importantly, worship in every cultural context and throughout its history.

Togetherness

Jesus Christ had a particular gift in being able to state the theologically obvious to devastating effect. He did this most effectively when he identified habits that militated against the central tenets of the Second Temple Jewish faith of his day. Here is one example. Every Jewish scholar, lawyer, theologian knew that the whole of Jewish Scripture hung on two foundational purposes: to love God with one's entire being and to love one's neighbor as oneself (Mark 12:30–31; Luke 10:27). Achieve this and you will have hit perfection. It was the complete fulfillment of Torah: the zenith points of righteousness, of abundant, full, complete human life and flourishing. This was the way of the good life for all and was intended to bring about a particular political and social community and provide the common good for all people. It comes as no surprise, then, that Jesus lambastes the theologians of his day for believing one thing (upholding Torah on these two points) while doing quite the opposite (exacting higher standards for others than for themselves). He takes them to task regarding these two great purposes of Torah, for their actions toward those who lived on the margins of Jewish society who were being excluded, for their xenophobic attitudes toward foreigners, and for the extortive practices of temple commerce. Anything that broke down this essential relational matrix and prohibited community was less than God's standard for the people of God. Such action militated against Jewish theology, which is hallmarked by a sense of togetherness—togetherness with God, with each other, and of each person with himself or herself.[50]

What might this same standard—of matching what we teach with how we relate—mean today for contemporary theologians? For many in the Western church, while we talk about community and the relational face of our faith, in practice we go about our theology in private, as individuals, and often disconnected from any wider social intercourse. In turn, we live this individualism out in church: as one observant friend once said, "We tend to bring our big gardens to church!" However, as we saw earlier when looking at the relation between history and culture, *theology cannot be anything other than communal.* We can identify four reasons that undergird this communal approach:

- First, Christians believe that theological beliefs are not mere intellectual statements for an elite to own. Rather, they are the church's collective response to what God has communicated in creation and in re-creation. As such, they are dialogical—that is, they address us as much as we address them.[51] They have an inclusive, communal character.

- Second, since the church is a collective group of people gathered together in Christ from different cultures and points in history, and theology is the language of the church as it seeks to make sense of this collective gathering—this kingdom with its politics and economics—our theology should represent the church in its entirety as a communal body, not merely our own individual or denominational positions.
- Third, since the purpose of theology is to equip the people of God in our calling, to help us be faithful, obedient, and believing—to love God with all our heart, soul, mind, and strength, and to love our neighbor as ourselves—theology should, of all disciplines, bring about a sense of togetherness, should be essentially communal in nature—relational rather than individual. It is not all about me.
- And last, what Christians believe is not premised on one single author's viewpoint: the Old and New Testaments span far too long a time for this to be the case. Rather, the sacred texts of both Jews and Christians constitute a communal reality—that is, one that is the shared and common experience of believers, Jewish (for the Old Testament) and Christian (for both Old and New Testaments) throughout their respective histories. And theology is the result of this experience. No surprise, then, that theology should reflect this sense of togetherness both in its content and in its consequence.

If I can borrow Schubert Ogden's distinction regarding how we have arrived at what we believe about Jesus Christ and apply it more widely to theology itself, we can say that theology is the product of two activities. First, it constitutes the collective *witness* of believers that has credibility regarding what they have experienced in relation to God: a body of data, events, gestalt, and so forth that requires some kind of processing to make any sense of what has occurred. This processing, second, takes place in the form of *reflection*, whereby the raw data, as it were, undergoes careful inquiry and thought, is discussed and turned over repeatedly, is pondered, undergoes debate and sometimes critical dissection, is argued about until—sooner or later—a sort of consensus is settled that is both appropriate to what has been witnessed and can be effectively communicated.[52]

Personal

We can identify two movements that together constitute the personal habit. One has to do with a movement from an encounter with the gospel of Jesus Christ—its transformative power and an ultimate new relationship with God as Father—to an understanding of God: theology. Perhaps it is stating the obvious, but it is good to remind ourselves that Christian theology is the product of the encounters of millions of individual people with the risen Christ and the command to live in unity with their new family. The other movement has to do with the fact that since our theology arises from personal encounter and personal engagement, its goal is to end in personal transformation.

Therefore, theology should not be an isolated and purely cerebral activity. Rather, it should cause spiritual transformation, if only because it comes out of our knowledge of God gained in worship, in doxology. Academic or ordinary, the study of theology renews our minds and is, therefore, transformational. And this is not a New Testament notion. As Craig Keener points out, "Jewish teachers expected the Torah to enlighten reason to provide power to overcome passions," and so for this reason we are able to understand the apostle Paul's concern that "the mind equipped with the law without the Spirit remains the mind of the flesh."[53] That is, information remains information, data remains data, until it becomes transformative. I particularly like the word that Ellen Charry has coined to express this very dynamic: "aretegenic." That is, Christian doctrines seek to be "conducive to virtue"[54] and are to be "good for us by forming or reforming our character; they aim to be salutary."[55] As we will see later, when we engage an evangelical view of reason, our minds and our reasoning were never meant to act as data depositories. Rather, they are the very means by which we can grow in maturity, change in character, flourish in thinking. Again, let's remind ourselves of what we have already noted: that Paul the apostle understood this same transformational process when he wrote to the Roman church, "Do not conform to the pattern of this world, but be transformed by the renewing of your mind. Then you will be able to test and approve what God's will is—his good, pleasing and perfect will" (Rom. 12:2), and likewise when he wrote to his convert and traveling companion, Titus, describing his own calling in a way that captures the transformational dynamic of theology, the "knowledge of the truth that leads to godliness" (Titus 1:1).

Cardinal Newman puts the transformational dynamic of theological belief wisely when he comments, "Those whose beliefs carry them into encounters with the reality of God will manifest signs that they are animated by love and humility in their bearing."[56] Put simply, theological knowledge is supposed to bring about personal transformation and character improvement. We don't expect a biologist studying bees to turn into a bee or exhibit bee-like characteristics since a bee is not made in the image of a human being, but we do expect a theologian studying God to become more like Christ since we are made in the image of God and are called to conform to Christ, who is the image of the invisible God (Col. 1:15).

It is not by accident, then, that theological construction, reflection, or study is transformational. It is the product of human engagement with the divine as it is made known to us through the gospel—with the God who self-identifies as love: a loving Trinity of Father, Son, and Holy Spirit. And we get to know this God in the process of being set free from the power of sin, through transformation, in redemption, by salvation. Thus, it is not by accident, either, that we refer to both God the Father and Jesus Christ as "Savior." This is not a surname—rather, it bears witness to the powerful change the gospel continues to have in people's lives. Many of us do not call Jesus "Savior" because he has rescued us from a future form of damnation. Rather, Jesus has—literally for many of us—*saved* us from lifestyles that were utterly chaotic, addictions that were lethal, relationships that were destructive, characters that were rotting from the inside. He really is our Savior! This is such an important point—our theological language expresses a *living* reality and is not meant to be rigid, inflexible, or dead. "Savior" and "Lord" are not dead terms similar to "foot of the mountain" or "muscle."[57] Rather, theology is a subdiscipline to the Christian evangel, the gospel, and serves the proclamation of God the Father reaching out to people in and through Jesus Christ and empowering them by his Spirit to live to their fullest potential in the here and now. It is not, as John Webster points out, "just the 'theme' or 'matter' of theology, as if the gospel were simply one more topic to which the inquiring human mind might choose to direct itself; rather, the gospel is that which brings theology into existence and holds it in being."[58]

Pause

Given that theology engages the whole person—body, soul, and spirit—and is transformative, why not take this moment to do two things.

- Identify the various ways in which the gospel has brought about personal transformation in your life. What difference does following Jesus bring to your mind, your body, your spirit?
- How would you express this change? What descriptors best communicate what *your* personal transformation says about who *God* is? Your answer will be *your theology*!

Can you see what you have just done? You have engaged in the practice of trying to understand your faith, what your experience tells you about God, and what might be the best language to communicate this to others, let alone make sense of it for yourself. You have engaged in the ancient, ongoing, and necessary theological craft of *faith seeking understanding!*[59] And with this insight we are able to summarize another aspect of theology:

> *Theology is personal, believing faith:*
> It is *faith* seeking understanding: it engages the *spirit*.[60]
> It is faith seeking *understanding*: it engages the *mind*.
> It is faith *seeking* understanding: it engages the *body*.

This seeking-understanding kind of faith engages our entire being as we express our trust in what God has declared in his incarnate Word and written Word, and through which we respond in obedience.[61] The result is human words about God—*theo-logia*, or God words—theology. Of course, once this process is underway, we discover that there is a second aspect to the personal. It is a movement from understanding to commitment, a movement from theological knowledge to theological praxis whereby we live by our new knowledge of God and develop a lifestyle of action. Jesus Christ himself expresses this reality when he describes God in terms of his kingdom, in which there is a very specific form of politics (love your neighbor as yourself, the least among you will be the greatest, the last will be first, the humble will be exalted) and economics (it is better to give than to receive, give and it will be given back to you, pressed down, running over). We are back to worldview living, where the role of theology has more to do with what Jeff Astley describes as "something Christian believers do with a view to producing something they can believe in and live by."[62]

If you think about it, this movement describes what lies at the heart of all human relationships. For example, I am married to a particular someone whom I first met in the very first lecture I gave as a lecturer. Before she was even seated at her desk I knew that I was going to marry her. However, I did not know her. I did not even know her name. Over time, as I stepped out of my own world and ways of doing things and "indwelled" her world, I got to know more about her as a person and discovered more about who she is. What made it a more personal relationship was the fact that my knowledge did not remain at the level of information about her. Rather, it moved from "data" to praxis, from knowledge about her to changed behavior for her. As a result, the relationship deepened, marriage ensued, and the movement of knowledge to praxis grew into a deeper dimension, one where two people start a new life together and create a lifestyle. That is, our knowledge of each other led to habits and beliefs about each other that created a way of life—something we both could believe in about and for each other as well as live by with each other.

The same goes for our knowledge of God—only it is God who does the chasing after us! We get to know God because, as John the apostle puts it so famously, he loved the world so much that he sent his only begotten Son—the One through whom all things were made—to make reconciliation possible (John 3:16). However, it is even more personal than this: the good news of the gospel is that God the Father chooses to step into our individual worlds and speak words of life to us through the proclamation of this gospel, inviting us to get to know him and believe in his declaration of love over us and find something to live by, live for, and live in. In Christ, God the Father has come to live in our world, stepping out of his world and choosing to discover our individual worlds and give us his transforming Spirit. In turn, we acquire personal knowledge of God the Father, of our Lord Jesus Christ, and of the Spirit who makes them real to each one of us.

We can illustrate the relational nature of Christian theology and the ebb and flow of theological understanding diagrammatically in this way:

Figure 1.1

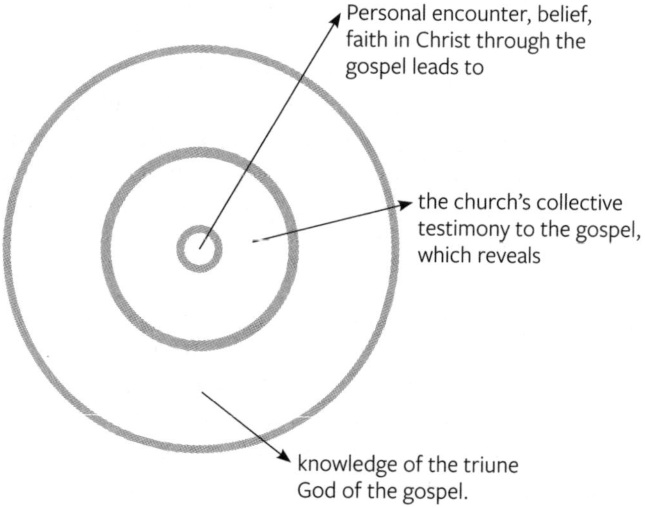

Personal encounter, belief, faith in Christ through the gospel leads to

the church's collective testimony to the gospel, which reveals

knowledge of the triune God of the gospel.

Unique

Theology has its own unique subject matter—God. It is unique for at least four reasons:

First is what makes theology similar to all other disciplines: it is a specific topic—God—not geometry, engineering, midwifery—and, therefore, like all other disciplines, theology has its own distinct approach, method, and tools.

The second concerns what makes theology dissimilar to every other discipline: its subject matter—God. Theology is unique among the entire corpus of human inquiry because its subject matter is God and therefore is distinct from all others in its very being and nature. In what way? First, because everything that exists is created—it is part of creation. God, on the other hand, is neither created nor part of creation. God is Creator.[63] All other living realities are creature. Second, Christian theology defies being pigeonholed as a discipline. It cannot be located as myth—that is, not quite truth, or as a product of the imagination that grasps human reality in narrative form in order to communicate or understand. Neither, however, is it reason—that is, the result of trying to make sense of reality. It is not even, argues Ingolf Dalferth, a combination of both. Along with Augustine, from way back in the fourth and fifth centuries AD, Dalferth argues that it is neither a form of natural theology nor a form of political theology. What it does, in fact, is critique all other kinds of theology.[64] More positively, however, Christian theology "is a sustained intellectual effort to understand everything in a new way from the point of view of the eschatological breaking in of God's creative presence in the human reality of this life and world in and through God's Word and Spirit."[65]

Third, the subject matter of theology presents us with unique challenges not only in terms of understanding, as the second reason highlights, but also in terms of how we communicate any knowledge we have of God. Unlike a doctor who can show an X-ray, or a painter who can paint a picture, or a chef who can create a meal as evidence of what they are communicating, the theologian is unable to "produce" God. And this is a particular problem for the contemporary church in that, on the whole, the metaphysical distinction we have noted between God and everything else is not much reflected upon in church circles. Popular worship and popular Christian thinking in church tend to portray God as an extension of the created realm, albeit unhelpfully invisible and much larger. It is more difficult, on the other hand, to imagine God in terms of being *no thing*, of not being at all created. However, when we do keep this distinction, it becomes clearer that God cannot be described in the same way that we describe that which is created. God has no material, physical, creaturely, or fabricated existence. God is *no thing*. Creation, on the other hand, and human beings, in particular, are *some thing*. Unlike God, we are created. We are a "thing"—and because we are *some thing*, we can distinguish ourselves from other "things" in the grand taxonomy of the universe. In so doing, we discover our unique identity and place within creation. Because we are *some thing*, we can be distinguished, also, from *no thing*—from God, who is not a "thing" but simply exists as pure being.

Note—we are able to self-identify in relation to God only inasmuch as we are creatures and he is Creator. This means that we tend to do so in negative terms. We are created; God is not. We can change; God does not.

We are limited by space and time; God is not. We are temporal; God is not. Can you see what the problem might be if this is the only way we can talk about God? God is not this, nor that, nor the next thing. All very good, but not very helpful. For example, an aardvark is not a rabbit, it does not fly, it cannot be in two places at once—but none of this information actually tells us anything positive about what an aardvark actually is. The same goes for God. It is one thing to state what God is not. It is an altogether different thing to say what or who God actually is. This is the great challenge we face as theologians, whether ordinary or academic: How do we gain, let alone communicate, any knowledge of God, who is not a part of creation? Once again, we have to ask questions in order to arrive at any meaningful answers. The first question, however, is how do we do this? An honest answer is that we do so with great difficulty.

Fourth, theology is unique in its greatest challenge: the very subject matter itself, God. As we have already discovered, theology is a very concrete, not an abstract, discipline. It arises out of the ongoing historical and worldwide experience of Christians who have heard and responded to the gospel; who, as a result, have experienced the saving and transformative power of a new relationship with the living God through the atoning life, death, resurrection, and ascension of Jesus Christ; and who are now energized by his Spirit. Like any other deeply affecting and transformative relationship, this evokes nothing short of a profound sense of mystery.

Enigmatic

This sense of mystery has to do, first, with *who* God is—Father, Son, and Holy Spirit—and with the fact that *what* God is—pure spirit—is an altogether different and unique reality. As such, both the who and the what of divine reality, God, are very different realities. In addition, knowledge of God is closed off to us. We cannot access divinity since it is not part of creation. Additionally, if to be a person is to be a bit of a mystery, in that we never really arrive at any complete and perfect knowledge of one another, how much more, then, must God be a mystery by virtue of the fact that God the Father, God the Son, or God the Holy Spirit is a person yet is not part of creation? Then, add to these the fact that our knowledge of God will never be the full story; it will always be approximate, never complete. Our language for God can never fully capture divine reality. In Augustine's words, if it can be understood, then it is not God.[66] This, however, is no excuse either to applaud ignorance or to advocate any sense of "blind faith" in response. Rather, it is helpful to quote at length the distinction Gabriel Marcel makes between a mystery and a problem:

There is this essential difference between a problem and a mystery. A problem is something which I meet, which I find complete before me, but which I can therefore lay siege to and reduce. But a mystery is something in which I am myself involved and it can therefore only be thought of as a sphere where the distinction between what is in me and what is before me loses its meaning and its initial validity. A genuine problem is subject to an appropriate technique by the exercise of which it is defined: whereas a mystery, by definition, transcends every conceivable technique. It is, no doubt, always possible (logically and psychologically) to degrade a mystery so as to turn it into a problem. But this is a fundamentally vicious proceeding, whose springs might perhaps be discovered in a kind of corruption of the intelligence.[67]

In brief, what Marcel is pointing out is that "a mystery is very different from a problem. While a problem can be solved, a mystery is inexhaustible."[68] A mystery is enigmatic. This term is apt for our subject matter: God is not a problem; God is a mystery! It also means that our knowledge of God is not a solution to a problem so much as the revealing of a mystery. God, then, is not to be considered a problem—a thing—but rather is to be viewed in terms of being a mystery—some "one"—the God of Abraham, the God of Isaac, and the God of Israel,[69] the LORD,[70] the Creator,[71] the Holy One,[72] and ultimately the God and Father who is revealed by Jesus Christ.[73] It is inappropriate, then, to approach theology in a clinical, objective, and abstract manner. Such an approach—such a theological method—misses the theological point. Theology, rather, is our human response to a profoundly personal and divine mystery, for which the only appropriate response is one that mystery alone elicits—namely, what we have already identified as "faith seeking understanding." An evangelical theological method recognizes that any dynamic engagement with such an enigmatic God occurs only when we seek to understand who God is in the light of the incarnation of the Son of God, Jesus Christ, or when we try to understand how the death of Jesus on a cursed cross can undo the problem of sin,[74] or when we articulate how the Holy Spirit can bring about transformation, or when we put into words how bread and wine act as the body and blood of Christ, or when we look forward to the new creation and wonder what "time" will look like if there is no sun but only the very presence of God himself with us (Rev. 22:5).

Let's remember, however, that this theology is not mere data or information. It is so much more than this. Rather, the kind of knowledge we are dealing with here is profoundly personal knowledge on two accounts. First, the information we have about this mystery, whom we call "God" and who is made known to us by Jesus Christ, is personal for the obvious reason that it refers both to God and to us, all of whom are persons. This account should draw out of us a sense of humility and, as Robert K. Johnston puts it, cause us to be "aware that what can be said pales in significance to what lies beyond and behind our words."[75] Second, this knowledge comes out of the deeply transformative impact the gospel has on our lives as we walk out our faith in relation to God, neighbor, and self. It is deeply personal knowledge, as a result, and very precious to those whose lives have been changed.

The second point should elicit love because of the kind of impact the self-revelation of God has on us. As Donald Bloesch illustrates, "God proves himself to us again and again as we believe and obey. Only as we increase in love do we become able to discriminate between the true and the false."[76] A similar example might be the way parents have to get to know and understand their newborn child in terms of his or her own unique body, personality, and gifting. That is, parental knowledge of a child is gained to the degree that there is interaction and disclosure between them as well as recognition of patterns of behavior that build up a composite picture of the little one's individual and unique personality. Only then is such knowledge personal and to some extent also mysterious.

How much more, then, concerning God, who is the subject matter of theology? The mystery we know to be God is made known to us in Jesus Christ's relation to the world in general and to the people of God in particular. He is a personal mystery: as Creator who moves creation to newness and as Father who brings people to new life through his loving and obedient Son and by means of his life, his energy, his Spirit. Without a doubt, an evangelical theology should be profoundly personal and therefore equally relational, whether in relation to God, to others, or to ourselves.

Pause

How relational is your theology? Take some time to reflect on the following task. Don't answer the wrong question: it is not about what you would like your theology to be or what you think might be the "correct" answer. Rather, this is another consciousness-raising exercise. Become aware of the strengths in your answer: those aspects you want to keep and strengthen. Try, also, to identify any areas of weakness that need to be addressed.

SUGGESTED READING

Astley, Jeff. *Studying God: Doing Theology*. London: SCM, 2014.
Harris, Brian. *The Big Picture: Building Blocks of a Christian Worldview*. Milton Keynes, UK: Paternoster, 2015.

McFarlane, Graham. *Why Do You Believe What You Believe about Jesus?* Eugene, OR: Wipf & Stock, 2009.

McIntosh, Mark A. *Divine Teaching: An Introduction to Christian Theology.* Oxford: Blackwell, 2008.

Migliore, Daniel L. *Faith Seeking Understanding: An Introduction to Christian Theology.* 3rd ed. Grand Rapids: Eerdmans, 2014.

Mouw, Richard J. *Restless Faith: Holding Evangelical Beliefs in a World of Contested Labels.* Grand Rapids: Brazos, 2019.

Porter, Stanley E., and Steven M. Studebaker, eds. *Evangelical Theological Method: Five Views.* Downers Grove, IL: IVP Academic, 2018.

Samples, Kenneth Richard. *A World of Difference: Putting Christian Truth-Claims to the Worldview Test.* Grand Rapids: Baker Books, 2007.

Treier, Daniel J. *Introducing Evangelical Theology.* Grand Rapids: Baker Academic, 2019.

Volf, Miroslav, and Matthew Croasmun. *For the Life of the World: Theology That Makes a Difference.* Grand Rapids: Brazos, 2019.

Webster, John. *The Culture of Theology.* Edited by Ivor J. Davidson and Alden C. McCray. Grand Rapids: Baker Academic, 2019.

two

Working Definition

The Ordinary and the Academic

I like the perspective that Mark McIntosh takes when he describes the task of theology as *an adventure*, taken from the Latin, *ad-venturam*—"towards the future."[1] This orientation toward the future helps us to understand that theology is pregnant with intention: God's desire for his creation, and for us in particular, is not random. Rather, it has a goal in mind, a telos that will be achieved through the worldwide and historical church, as this community of faith engages with and, as a result of this dynamic engagement, is shaped by ongoing encounter with Jesus Christ. It is what Emil Brunner describes as "believing thinking."[2] Not merely thinking about the Christian faith, it is the natural progression of the life of faith. Theology is not something that only an elite perform—it is the prerogative of all who follow Jesus Christ.

It should be becoming clear by now that the discipline of theology is something in which every follower of Jesus Christ engages. Eugene Peterson captures this superbly in his translation of Romans 12:1–2:

> So here's what I want you to do, God helping you: Take your everyday, ordinary life—your sleeping, eating, going-to-work, and walking-around life—and place it before God as an offering. Embracing what God does for you is the best thing you can do for him. Don't become so well-adjusted to your culture that you fit into it without even thinking. Instead, fix your attention on God. You'll be changed from the inside out. Readily recognize what he wants from you, and quickly respond to it. Unlike the culture around you, always dragging you down to its level of immaturity, God brings the best out of you, develops well-formed maturity in you. (The Message)

The contemporary feel of Peterson's translation draws out two fundamental aspects of theology, its ordinariness and its transformational nature, which is captured well by two authors as they express theological responses to their own everydayness.[3] Julie Canlis offers a stunningly simple yet equally profound "extended meditation" on the contemporary Western church's obsession with "greatness and being 'impactful.'" Particularly refreshing is her plea for a return to what she describes as the "holy ordinary" and her recognition of the theological necessity of understanding this in trinitarian terms since God is a trinity. Such a theology of the ordinary will be "marked by the benediction of the Father, the sacrifice of the Son, and the overflow of the Spirit." Most importantly, a "robust trinitarian theology of the ordinary will not undermine being passionate or sold-out but will ground and purify it."[4]

Alicia Britt Chole takes a different approach and offers deep wisdom in the face of today's obsession with speed. In *The Sacred Slow: A Holy Departure from Fast Faith*, Chole offers fifty-two experiences in unhurried honesty with God.[5] What a profound definition of "theology": she describes it in the purest of terms that convey the deeply relational bond that lies at the heart of the theological endeavor, which only the most intimate of relations can sustain— "unhurried honesty with God." I like Chole's desire to present a theology that offers an alternative to the heady and unsustainable expectations many of us face today in fast church—where everything has to happen now and knowledge of God becomes a commodity to exploit with immediate effect rather than a place where we recognize knowledge of God as something that matures over a lifetime of sanctified choices. The sacred slow, she clarifies, "is a holy departure from Fast Faith. It is a path that is both ancient (Enoch knew it) and holy (Jesus epitomized it)."[6]

Both Canlis and Chole offer us alternative vantage points from which to consider what theology is all about.[7] They describe the sort of theology Jeff Astley describes as "ordinary."[8] Astley teases out the different ways in which theology operates and identifies two parallel theological universes. The first is what he describes as *ordinary* theology. The second he distinguishes from the ordinary and is what we know as *academic* theology.[9] The life of Christian faith can operate at both levels, but it does so in quite different ways. Both theologies are responses to the way in which the gospel affects our individual and corporate lives and our understandings of the different worlds in which we live. Both have very distinct habits. Both have their own particular ways of going about their business. We can liken these habits to how we understand prayer to be a ritual: it can be ordinary—something we do as a daily habit in a quiet time—or it can be more formal, in the shape of liturgy. Both are equally important—only different.

So too with theology. It can be ordinary, with its own rituals. But equally it can be academic, which requires rituals of its own—a set time, a particular place, consistent note-taking. Both have their own ways of expression, their own rituals. They train the body and the soul, the mind and the spirit. In turn, the ritual "shapes individual life and the order of a community."[10] That is, what we believe will determine how we live out our beliefs. In essence, we—all of us—*do* theology, but only some of us *study* theology.[11] Each, however, is a way of thinking about Christian faith. Each can lift us up to new ways of seeing but, equally, shake us to our very foundations. For these reasons alone, we need the help of theological habits and disciplines.

Theology is a response to faith. Whether ordinary or academic, each has its own distinct posture. The distinction between the two is a helpful way of distinguishing one from the other. I like the way in which Astley draws on Hans Urs von Balthasar to identify the appropriate behavior of ordinary and academic theology. On the one hand, the theology every believer in Jesus Christ does—ordinary theology—has its own particular posture: *prayer*. Or, as Balthasar puts it, theology is done on one's knees.[12] On the other hand, the theology done in the university, seminary, or theological college also has its own particular posture, only this kind of critical thinking occurs at the desk.

In turn, Astley is quite right in emphasizing ordinary theology. It is primary. It arises directly from our faith, experience, and relationship with God through prayer and worship. It is framed by ongoing testimony, whether individual or corporate, and feeds our knowledge of God and who we are. Only when *this* foundational discipline and habit is in place does academic theology have any significance. The academic is an aid to the ordinary, not a replacement or upgrade, and it serves to clarify and critique ordinary theology "but can never wholly replace it."[13] Rather, because Christian faith "causes us to think,"[14] academic theology is the means by which we are enabled to do "hard thinking" about the questions that arise from our ordinary relationship with God through Christ. And while not all Christians pursue academic theology, they do face circumstances and situations in which a more critical and questioning season is necessary, and rightly so, since this kind of response "must always be a central strand of adult faith, as it is to being an adult."[15]

Craig Ott offers a helpful addendum to what we have identified as ordinary theology: he describes doing theology in terms of the local. That is, local theology will be determined, first, by the way people reflect and think theologically in a given locality and, second, in relation to the concerns of that specific locality. He then offers three "tools" that aid us in this task. The first is what he calls "mapping"—that is, our theology helps us to map the subject area of God, to make the complex understandable by mapping biblical truth in an accessible way. The local aspect of theology thus explains the differences in theological perspectives, in a way similar to how a driver in London will need a different map than a similar driver in New York. What stops theology from being completely relativistic is its conformity to Scripture, which is "the standard by which to judge the accuracy of a local theology, much the way the reality of the city is the standard for the accuracy of any given map."[16]

The second tool is improvisation—that is, building on what has gone on before, albeit sometimes in creative ways that are more a variation on a theme than a logical extension, something akin to jazz music. Ott makes his point very clear when he argues that "as the gospel moves into new cultural contexts—onto a new stage as it were—its performance must be improvised in ways suitable to the context while remaining faithful to the original story-line."[17] The French phenomenologist philosopher Maurice Merleau-Ponty captures this dynamic beautifully when he says,

> Rester fidèle à ce qu'on fut,
> tout reprendre par le début.
> Chacune des deux taches est immense.
>
> Remain faithful to what you were,
> Go over everything (again) right from the beginning.
> Each one of these tasks is immense.[18]

Last, Ott offers the concept of games to explain the task of theology. As he points out, it is for "nothing less than the theologically reasoned strategy for accomplishing God's purposes on the playing field of life that God has placed us [here]." Scripture sets out the "instructions" for play: it defines what God's purposes are; it sets out the boundaries and rules for playing; it makes clear the attitude required to play (and win)—namely, faith, hope, and love; it provides numerous playing strategies, particularly observing the skilled players in God's missional game.[19]

An important point bears repeating about these two kinds of theology, the ordinary and the academic. It is not a case of one or the other. Rather, both are necessary. Each is redemptive in that the ordinary and the academic should be ways in which we seek wholeness, healing, and the outworking of our salvation: we are transformed through the renewing of our minds, as noted above. In addition, each is a specific way in which our seeking-to-understand faith is an act of worship of God with the entirety of our minds. One, ordinary theology, is a response to faith lived out in the ebb and flow of life, relationships, sanctification, and becoming more conformed to Christ.

Canlis and Chole helpfully articulate what this kind of theology entails. The other, academic theology, is a critical endeavor where various ideas, opinions, and answers are tested in order to formulate the most appropriate response to any given issue, whether postapostolic, patristic, medieval, Scholastic, Reformed, Enlightenment, modern, postmodern, or post-postmodern. One is formative; the other is critical. And while we need both if we are to be effective theologians, it will be the latter, the academic, that will be our concern, on the whole, in this book.

What Is Theology?

We are now in a position to define more fully what we mean by "theology." In some senses, it signifies a very simple process that Elaine Robinson helpfully defines as a process of "meaning making."[20] That is, theology is the church's attempt at making sense of God. As such, theology can be described as the church's response to the God met in Jesus Christ and known as Father of *this* Son, enlivened by Holy (as distinct from created) Spirit. Theology, then, is the activity all followers of Jesus Christ engage in as they seek to understand their faith, as they experience their own and others' transformation, as they pray and worship God, and as they seek to live out and be obedient to God's Word. Robinson makes the very helpful distinction between

> *theology*, what we believe about God and our faith;
>
> *dogma*, more rigid, controlling principles or tenets; and
>
> *doctrine*, accepted and regulating teaching and learning.[21]

What I particularly like is her example of a fourth distinction, *opinion*, the personal belief of a person, distinct from the preceding three. I also like the picture Colin Gunton uses of a garden to describe the difference between dogma and theology. Dogma "is that which delimits the garden of theology, providing a space in which theologians may play freely and cultivate such plants as are cultivable in the space which is so defined." What is particularly significant is the important point that "theology ceases to be Christian theology if it effectively ceases to remain true to its boundaries."[22]

Academic theology, in particular, is the specific discipline where the daily faith, experience, belief, and practice of the church—and the questions each generates—are subjected to critical, believing faith with the intention of bringing understanding to the mystery we know as "God," now revealed in Jesus Christ. It is the theology of the academy—that highest level of learning, the university, with its own habits and posture. This kind of theology is not, therefore, the product of individuals. Rather, it is a corporate activity, originating in the intellectual monastic communities of faith and their centers of learning, later to become universities. This corporate aspect of academic theology exists today, whether in faculties, guilds, societies, or seminaries.[23] So, it is appropriate, at this point, to invite other expert voices to our conversation as we explore more fully what we are up to when we engage academic theology in particular.

To help us in this task, I would like to involve some conversation partners who identify specific, important aspects of academic theology. First, I particularly like the way Gunton holds the academic and the transformative together when he defines theology in the following way:

> By "theology" we mean, as a first approximation, the intellectual discipline of asking who God is and what the world is like in the light of the gospel of Jesus Christ, and consequently how we should live before God in the world. Theology is the hard intellectual work of asking what it means to believe that in Jesus Christ God the Son walked among us as one of us, died for our sins, rose again on the third day, ascended to the right hand of the Father, sent the Holy Spirit upon the church, and will return one day to bring in his Kingdom. If this story is true then it changes everything. Theology is the task of exploring that change.

This is possible because, as Gunton continues, "God has given himself to be known, and so we may dare to speak about who he is. Christian theology begins with the belief that human beings have looked God full in the face, so to speak, and so presume to speak with familiarity about God."[24] Can you see what Gunton is doing here? He articulates what we have been exploring: theology emerges from our lived experience. What I particularly appreciate here is the way in which Gunton draws out the personal and relational aspect of theology—this is not an abstract, ivory-tower activity. Quite the opposite: it emerges from the change people have experienced in response to the gospel of Jesus Christ, a change that brings closeness, even intimacy, into the academic, into the critical.

This combination of academic and deeply personal is perhaps best illustrated in the life of Karl Barth, a Swiss theologian of the last century. There is a (probably apocryphal)[25] story that, having given a lecture at the Rockefeller Chapel at the University of Chicago in 1962, Barth had a question-and-answer time. One questioner asked if Barth could summarize his entire theology in one sentence. Given that Barth is one of the most loquacious and precise theological minds of the twentieth century, the audience probably thought the questioner had Barth stumped! In response, however, Barth gave the simple answer: "Jesus loves me, this I know, for the Bible tells me so." Whether apocryphal or not, Barth's answer reflects very succinctly the point Gunton has just made—namely, the necessity of holding together one's mind and one's heart. It also very effectively reminds us that great theology does not necessarily need to be difficult to understand nor difficult to communicate. It is, as we have said, the unpacking of the gospel—Christ has died, Christ is risen, Christ will come again!

Our second interlocutor, John Franke, helps us understand that the task of academic theology involves overlapping, not independent, components. Franke's definition of theology is particularly helpful here in that it is not so much a definition as an overall approach to theology, one that has a degree of flexibility and fluidity about it, since each component resonates in some way with the others, and therefore safeguards the theologian from being fixed or fundamentalist in the practice of theology.

First, Franke calls our attention to the nature of theology. It is ongoing—we never exhaust its possibilities. It is a "second-order" discipline—that is, theology always serves Scripture: it is human commentary on divine revelation.[26] As such, as we have already noted, it is contextual—our theology is always framed by our culture, our history, our gender, our denomination, our own limitations.

Second, he identifies the task of theology. It is "critical and constructive reflection on the beliefs and practices of the Christian Church."[27] This is particularly helpful in that it reminds us that the theological enterprise is not about identifying abstract and timeless propositional statements denuded of any historical, cultural, or even ecclesial identity. Rather, our reflective task involves looking at the various ways in which we express our faith, whether intellectually, personally, corporately, or structurally as the church, and assessing the degree to which they are fit for the purpose of declaring the gospel, making disciples, and ensuring the ongoing mission of the church.

Last, Franke identifies the purpose of theology, in terms of its relation to the church in its "missional vocation to live as the people of God in the particular social-historical context in which they are situated."[28] That is, our task in doing academic theology is never an end in itself, but rather the means by which the people of God are empowered in living out their identity as citizens of the kingdom of God wherever they find themselves.

If Gunton reminds us of the *practical* and *personal* face of theology, then Franke here presents us with the *dynamic* face of theology, in which there is a continuous sense of engagement, whether in ensuring that we locate our theology under Scripture and the gospel or that we continuously audit the relevance of our practices in the service of the church and its gospel as it empowers Jesus's disciples to live gospel lives in the ebb and flow of their own respective situations.

Our final dialogue partner, Daniel Migliore, introduces us to the fact that theology is a form of interpersonal communication. Migliore's proposal reminds us that theology originates in God's self-communication to human beings and then continues in our responses to divine speech, whether we answer a divine question ("Where are you?") or articulate a new identity ("Your name will no longer be Jacob, but Israel") or a lament ("By the rivers of Babylon we sat and wept. . . . How can we sing the songs of the LORD while in a foreign land?") or we worship ("Praise the Lord, my soul; all my inmost being") or proclaim ("Prepare the way for the LORD") or narrate the gospel ("In the beginning was the Word, and the Word was with God, and the Word was God") or pray ("Our Father who art in heaven").[29] Put these different ways, theology is rightly understood as a form of personal narrative: its subject matter is always about persons, whether divine, human, angelic, or otherwise. And since it is personal, it should conform to the norms by which we understand that all other forms of personal knowledge are acquired. This is where I think Migliore helps us as we develop our understanding of the task of theology. He identifies five aspects of the dynamic of personal communication:

1. I disclose who I am through my *persistent patterns*, whether they be habits, characteristics, repeated actions, good or bad, chaotic or ordered, consistent or erratic. Knowing who I am requires giving attention to and identifying my particular patterns.

2. I am not reducible to these patterns: I am *free to do new and surprising things*. My *freedom* constitutes me as a person and not a thing.

3. If you want to know me, you will need to keep on accepting my invitation to trust as well as promises, and in doing so discover whether I keep my word, or am untrustworthy.

4. I often define my personal identity in narrative form, in story as opposed to facts. I am more than the sum total of my "data"—I have a history; I have my own self-narrative.

5. The Bible narrates God's own ongoing, *unfinished* self-disclosure. It is unfinished in that God is personal and eternal, and therefore there is more to God than the text can convey.[30]

Migliore reminds us that when we are doing theology, we are engaging in conversation with God, with our own self, and with one another. Like every other conversation we have with other people, it conforms to certain norms that make it a conversation rather than a list or schedule or equation or legal document. It is interpersonal—it takes place between persons. And it is communication—it invites a response.

What, then, is theology? Theology is essentially a twofold activity of the church:

- Theology is the church's personal and practical, dynamic, and interpersonal communication about the gospel—in particular, about the God people have met in and through the life, death, resurrection, and ascension of Jesus Christ, the God whom those people have come to know as Father of *this* Son, Jesus, the God who has enlivened and transformed those people by Holy (as distinct from created) Spirit. Theology is, therefore, always trinitarian in nature.
- Theology is "the self of examination of the Christian Church in respect of the content of its distinctive talk about God."[31] It is the activity all followers of Jesus Christ engage in as they
  » communicate with, pray to, and worship the triune God;
  » seek to understand their faith;
  » experience their own and others' transformation;
  » seek to live out and be obedient to God's Word in their own particular context.

A helpful way of considering this is, as David Clark puts it, *scientia*—that is, theology is *knowledge* of God, whose actions can be observed in creation and re-creation. As Clark goes on to elaborate, theology "is rooted in the Bible as its supreme authority. It focuses on Christ and his work at the cross. It operates by the power of the Holy Spirit. If it remains purely conceptual, it is fragmentary. It must continue to do its inward work until it transforms Christ-followers according to the image of Christ and reshapes Christian communities that follow the pattern of the inner life of the Trinity." Particularly helpful is the fact that Clark points out that theology does not remain at the level of knowledge. Once it has matured, it becomes "*sapientia*—the wisdom of God. This leads us to a passionate love for God, genuine worship of the Trinity, true community with fellow Christians, and loving service in personal evangelism and social compassion—all to the glory of God. That is what it means to know and love the true and living God. Absolutely nothing matters more."[32]

Pause

- Create a tweet-length response to this question: What is *your* definition of "theology"?
- Take time to reflect on the following question: How does your definition of "theology" affect the way you live?

Feel free to reject, edit, expand, or simplify the working definition above. The important point here is not only that you take time to construct your own definition of theology but equally that you own it for yourself and start thinking of ways you can apply it to how you think about your faith.

SUGGESTED READING

Canlis, Julie. *A Theology of the Ordinary*. Wenatchee, WA: Godspeed, 2017.

Cherry, Stephen. *God-Curious: Exploring Eternal Questions*. London: Jessica Kingsley, 2017.

Cole, Graham A. *Faithful Theology: An Introduction*. Wheaton: Crossway, 2020.

Kapic, Kelly M. *A Little Book for New Theologians: Why and How to Study Theology*. Downers Grove, IL: InterVarsity, 2012.

Robinson, Elaine A. *Exploring Theology*. Minneapolis: Fortress, 2014.

three

The Relational
and the Revelational

The Relational

I have argued thus far that the task of theology is relational both in its subject matter—the God we come to know through Jesus Christ as Father, Son, and Spirit—and in its habits, ones that facilitate and maintain personal encounter and transformation. I now want to develop this relational framework further in two ways: first, in how we engage with the mystery we call "God," and second, in the effect such engagement has on us as believers as we develop in our theological habit and mature as theologians. The teaching and therefore the learning of theology in any academic context has its own peculiar challenges, ones I have come to face annually as new students enroll in their theology program. These challenges are common to any discipline that is deeply personal or intrinsic to our own identity and lifestyle. Thus, for most people, the learning of mathematics, medieval and modern languages, or cybersecurity, for example, does not necessarily threaten their deeper identity and belief systems: these studies tend to reflect external interests rather than intrinsic aspects of the students' own personal identity. However, theology is unlike most other disciplines in that when it is taught in a confessional or denominational context, it invariably means that those students have a personal and deeply invested interest in the subject. This makes for potentially dynamic and deeply worthwhile engagement both in lectures and in private study. However, it also often has a downside: we come to our study already deeply invested in the subject matter and therefore with significant suppositions and beliefs. Some may be so intrinsic to our faith that we are unaware of their power until they are challenged or developed. One of the deepest challenges concerns how we perceive the content of theology, how we do theology, and what we think theology is. In previous tasks, I asked you to identify your theology at the moment and then to develop it and own what you have constructed so that you are more self-aware of these deeper influences, suppositions, and presuppositions. What did you discover? Is your theology first and foremost a relational construct? Or perhaps you discovered that you have been conditioned by upbringing and church influence into thinking that theology is primarily about what we believe—about doctrine, about data, about information download, about social (church) conformity in a way similar to how we should behave at a football match or a tennis club.

By now, however, you should be aware that theology is not reducible to doctrine or mere information. While both are essential to the task of theology, they are not primary. Rather, as we understand theology to be the *language of the church*, we discover that this language is both the result of communication—God self-communicating to us and our response—and the means of communication, how we express this divine communication.[1] It can be verbal (through words and song) or physical (through a burning bush, an empty tomb); it can even be metaphorical (a naked prophet, a rainbow, a bunch of roses) or even cyber (try living without your smartphone). Language, in whichever form it takes, is the most essential of human tools in relationship: without it, we are forever sealed within our own individual worlds. Theology, then, is communication: it is communication not of impersonal propositional statements, however true they may be, but of deeply personal encounter, impact, discombobulation, and transformation. It is the language of the church, the language of people who have been both met by the God and Father of Jesus Christ and changed by his Spirit as a result. Theology, then, is a relational activity and occurs in a global human theater—wherever there is human dysfunction; redemptive reconciliation through Jesus Christ; personal transformation as people walk by the Spirit; church witness; reflection or testimony; kingdom politics and economics that demonstrate the new creation—wherever and whenever the triune God encounters creation. The list is not meant to be exhaustive but reveals the breadth and depth of personal relationships theology expresses.

All this is to say that theology is both the articulation of our thinking about human-divine encounters and the expression of the faith that participates in and grows as a result of these encounters. And, like any other meaningful personal relationship, theology is generally a relationship that has a degree of content, and, as a relationship with content, it is not blind faith but rather "thinking faith."[2] Therefore, Cynthia Bennett Brown is right in pointing out that this thinking faith—both as noun (a faith characterized by thinking) and as verb (the action of "thinking one's faith")—leads to transformation of the knower.[3] Why? Because this is what happens when we relate to any person of personal significance! We change as we are encountered—as we are loved, known, challenged, understood, encouraged, accepted. So, too, with any encounter with the divine mystery we have come to know in and through our Lord Jesus Christ. It can never be mere head knowledge: encounter with the triune God leads to transformation—what we call "sanctification"—because we encounter a holy God.

This transformation starts with Jesus—whom we know as a result of being encountered by the gospel—and with the Father to whom we are related. As with any other deeply affecting relationship, we are driven, in turn, to reflect on this person, Jesus, and his God and Father as well as the new life and energy that empowers us by his Spirit. The degree to which a personal encounter causes us to change will be the degree to which it forces us to reflect on what kind of relationship it is. The result of this reflection is what we call "theology." This theology, however, needs some kind of clarification so that we can both understand it better and communicate it effectively, passing it on correctly to other people. This process of codification is called "doctrine" and always refers us back to our theology, which in turn refers us back to the gospel and takes us to Jesus. Since doctrine is living (not dead), flexible (not rigid), and contextual, it requires further interpretation to enable us to live it out, as opposed to merely believing it or giving mental assent to it. We call this interpretation "praxis," strangely, because the encounter we have with Jesus Christ, as we have already discovered, results in a new way of living, not just of thinking, a new worldview in which we live and have our being. We can illustrate it as shown in figure 3.1.

We have already seen that at the heart of Christian faith there is a profound mystery. God—the Creator—is not created. The Creator is not at all, in any way, like creation. We have also noted Gabriel Marcel's distinction between a problem and a mystery. While a problem is there to be solved, a mystery is not; it remains inexhaustible. If God could be "solved," he would be a problem, not a mystery! However, God is not a problem—God is indeed a mystery. Therefore, we can describe this as an *ontological* challenge: a challenge concerning God's being (Greek: *ontos*, "being"), simply because God's being is completely different from everything else.

This ontological mystery raises a more immediate challenge. We can describe this as an *epistemological* challenge (Greek: *epistēmē*, "knowledge"), the problem of how we know God. Put simply:

How do you know *nothing*?

Figure 3.1

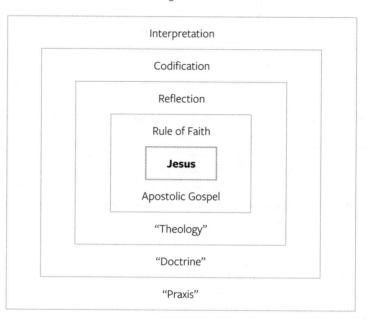

The Revelational

The mystery we have come to know as Father, through Jesus Christ, reveals himself by virtue of being an acting agent. That is, it is God who makes himself known to us, to that which God is not, to creation. Without this self-disclosing action on God's part, there would be no human knowledge of or relationship with God, since by our own efforts we are unable to penetrate the veil of divine identity and activity. The theological term for this self-disclosure is "revelation." This term can mean the *act* by which something hidden is made known, the *content* that is revealed, or the *means* by which revelation occurs.[4] This kind of divine revelation is different from all other kinds of revelation. Revelation that discloses hitherto unknown knowledge of God is to be distinguished from human revelation—knowledge humans have about themselves, their world, and how to live in their world. For example, in Romans 1 the apostle Paul constructs his argument premised on the belief that human beings have a moral code by which they know they should live. This does not need divinely inspired revelation. However, actual knowledge of and relationship with God is different: both require an act of disclosure, of revelation.

The concept of revelation can be approached either simply or dynamically. We see elements of the former in Jewish views of revelation, whether in creation, redemption, or revelation itself. Lord Rabbi Jonathan Sacks identifies creation as "the world that is: the wonders of nature, the vicissitudes of history, and the conflict within the human heart between duty and desire." Redemption, on the other hand, "is the world that ought to be: a world of justice, compassion, the dignity of the individual, and the sanctity of life, the world God had in mind when He created humankind and to which we are still travelling." And then there is revelation itself, which Sacks describes as "the word that decodes the world." For Jews, this is "the set of instructions—*mitzvot*— God has given us for reaching Him. Revelation is what happens when we put the world aside and listen to the will of God." Thus, from a Jewish perspective, "God is where the three meet and become one."[5] Catholic theologian Avery Dulles also represents the more simple approach to revelation when he identifies five different kinds of revelation. First is revelation as *doctrine*, more than likely the view of revelation most evangelicals might have today, where Scripture is understood as containing true facts about God. Second is revelation as *history*. Here, Scripture is understood as containing various witness accounts to revelation, but it is not revelation itself. In computer talk, while the first might be understood as "divine download"—double-click on the Bible icon and up pops divine information—the second is more to do with "human programming"—different apps that convey information. Third is revelation as *inner experience*. Here, revelation is derived from religious experience—experience that may or may not be based on Scripture or even Christian faith. Therefore, this is a quite different use of "inner experience" from that deployed in contemporary charismatic or Pentecostal theologies where religious experience centers on God and is subject to biblical support. Fourth is revelation as *dialectical presence*. Here, revelation is premised on the belief that what is being revealed is not God himself but only God as he relates to creation. God remains an utter mystery. In this way, therefore, Scripture witnesses to revelation but is not the revelation itself. Even with revelation, there is still the need to keep the means of revelation, Scripture, distinct from that which is being revealed: God. Last is revelation as *new awareness*. This model understands revelation more as a process than as information: it is the process of humanity moving toward fuller consciousness. Such a process is theological in that this human endeavor is enabled by God or by some transcendent agent.[6]

A more complex approach to understanding revelation is to understand it as a dynamic and oftentimes dialectical process whereby we are able to discern who God is by discerning God's "footprints in creation."[7] Hungarian philosopher of religion Balázs Mezei identifies ten dynamic pairings that give insight to the various dimensions of revelation, in which members of each pair are to be seen not in opposition but as a sometimes complex unity:

- *fact and cognition*—taking us beyond mere propositional statements to personal understanding that is to be acted upon and that engages our entire personality
- *creation and salvation*—holding together the original freedom regained through Christ and the context within which salvation makes sense
- *incarnation and resurrection*—where divine love is revealed in overcoming death through life
- *word and deed*—capturing the essence—namely, that what is revealed is to be acted upon and lived out
- *natural and supernatural*—underlying the "togetherness" of reality, the ordinariness of creation in which God acts in special ways (miracle)
- *experience and reality*—uniting the subjective experience of revelation with the objective world within which it takes place
- *private and public*—where the deeply personal and private is made known in the most public of manners
- *person and community*—reiterating the fact that revelation, while profoundly personal, is at the same time lived out in wider social intercourse, in the various communities in which we live
- *part and whole*—that revelation is contextual and therefore "in part" and seeks its fulfillment, its completeness, eschatologically
- *something and nothing*—not all revelation is tangible content: it can be silence, lack of revelation, or a privation that is only discerned within the context of the something that can be known[8]

What I like about these various couplings is that they remind us forcibly that revelation is not something that can be easily pigeonholed or tritely catalogued. They tell us, rather, that theology is only ever possible when God is revealed and that God is free to do so in whichever ways he chooses. Once this knowledge is acquired, the hidden becomes visible, and only then is the veil of ignorance replaced with the table of presence. Post-revelation everything can be seen in a new and very different light. William Abraham describes this in terms of a "threshold concept"[9]—that is, a concept that "can be considered as akin to a portal, opening up a new and previously inaccessible way of thinking about something. It represents a transformed way of understanding, or interpreting, or viewing something without which the learner cannot progress."[10] A threshold concept is multifaceted in what it brings about. It can be:

- *transformative*: the knowledge it provides brings about personal change;
- *troublesome*: it can undo previously held convictions;
- *irreversible*: once the threshold to the concept is crossed, it is not possible to "unknow" the concept or return to a previous state of knowing;
- *integrative*: it can pull hitherto disparate things together;
- *bounded*: it sets a frame around what is known;
- *discursive*: it will expand vocabulary;
- *reconstitutive*: it brings about a subjective change that others will notice;
- *liminal*: it involves to-ing and fro-ing until mastered.[11]

Divine revelation, then, is the unveiling of what is hidden in order that what was previously unknown can become known. The agent of this act of unveiling is God—not humans—and thus our theology is always in response to God's initial act toward us and is never the cause of it. Thus, this kind of revelation is deeply personal: it is relational.[12] It is personal disclosure—intimate and response-creating. It reveals the very nature of God's relationship to a very particular creation—one created to be faithful or unfaithful to divine desire and pure goodwill—and in so doing, lets us know who God is. As Colin Gunton points out, "The conception of God as triune is meant to express a view of the one God who is various in his being and is, therefore, able to be seen as relating himself to the world in a variety of ways."[13] We can identify two aspects of revelation:

1. Revelation is intentional. It occurs with very good reason and intention—namely, to give knowledge of God with the aim of restoring creation and in particular the divine image bearers—men and women—to what they were created to be. It is not merely "information download," a sense of conveying information about God. Neither is it arbitrary or mere coincidence.
2. Revelation is relational. It is relational, first, in its initiation. It is a personal, free, and volitional act of God undertaken with the specific intention of making himself known. It is relational, second, in its intention. God chooses to make himself known in the encounter of revelation in order to bring about personal, collective, national, and ultimately universal transformation, of people and creation as a whole.[14] I like the way John Webster describes revelation as "the communicative fellowship-establishing trajectory of the acts of God in the election,

creation, providential ordering, reconciliation, judgement and glorification of God's creatures."[15] What an immense and broad way of unpacking what we mean by this term—quite far removed from any notion of divine download to passive humans!

However, we can go further in clarifying what we mean by revelation. Revelation, for instance, can be understood in terms of gift.[16] Like all other forms of personal knowledge, we know to the extent that we are allowed to know, especially when it comes to knowledge of other people.[17] P. T. Forsyth makes the point simply and clearly when he comments that "our neighbours know us in our act of knowing them: and it is this reciprocal knowledge that is the kind exercised in religion."[18] Gunton goes on to add that "we come to know both others and ourselves as we enable ourselves to be known, as we reveal ourselves and are granted revelation in return."[19] Quite simply, all personal knowledge requires a degree of self-disclosure.[20] The question here is not so much whether we need revelation but rather which kind of revelation is needed. When it comes to knowledge of God, such knowledge is knowable, first, only to the degree that God acts in relation to us and the world and, second, only to the degree that such action is observable. It is God who takes the initiative as acting agent in self-revelation; it is for humans to see and understand this "event" as distinct from "information download." As Esther Meek argues persuasively, the pattern of Christian theology will always be one of descent,[21] a movement from the one revealing to those being informed. In God's case, the act of revelation will always be one that "descends" from the realm of the divine, God's habitation, to ours, whether it be in the act of creation, the act of incarnation, the act of revivification (Pentecost), the act of resurrection, or the act of complete restoration (new heaven and earth). It is gifted to us. As such, this kind of knowledge is not something human beings discover, create, construct, or produce by virtue of their imagination. It is not, as Gunton points out regarding the theology of the nineteenth-century father of liberalism, Friedrich Schleiermacher, a purely human construct.[22] To understand Christian theology in this way is to lock theology within creation, within the confines of human interpretation, within space, time, and history.[23] To do this is to render the mystery of God forever unknowable.

It is important, then, that we understand the primacy of divine agency and acting first in revelation. With it, we confirm a biblical way of doing theology—a divine modus operandi regarding creation in general and human beings in particular. Neither humans nor the rest of creation are able, in and of themselves, to reveal the mystery: they can only carry or be a medium of the revelation. Isaac Massey Haldeman, a turn-of-the-twentieth-century

Baptist pastor in New York, captures a sense of this: "For six thousand years [a] break in the faith relationship has been written in human history. For six thousand years man has continued to eat of the tree of knowledge. Six thousand years he has battled with the problem of good and evil. Six thousand years he has studied and thought, searched and investigated. He has attained to much knowledge. [But] by wisdom he knows not God. He knows good and evil."[24] Haldeman nails the issue here clearly: only God can reveal God. Revelation is the Creator's gift, and it happens in the theater of creation, the theater of God's glory, which has profound implications for how we understand, engage with, and tend creation. By virtue of being the location for divine revelation, creation—everything that is not God—is given great dignity as a result, fallen or not.[25] Gerard Manley Hopkins understands this relationship only too well as he articulates it so beautifully in his poem "God's Grandeur":

> The world is charged with the grandeur of God.
>   It will flame out, like shining from shook foil;
>   It gathers to a greatness, like the ooze of oil
> Crushed. Why do men then now not reck his rod?
> Generations have trod, have trod, have trod;
>   And all is seared with trade; bleared, smeared with toil;
>   And wears man's smudge and shares man's smell: the soil
> Is bare now, nor can foot feel, being shod.
>
> And for all this, nature is never spent;
>   There lives the dearest freshness deep down things;
> And though the last lights off the black West went
>   Oh, morning, at the brown brink eastward, springs—
> Because the Holy Ghost over the bent
>   World broods with warm breast and with ah! bright wings.[26]

On the other hand, revelation finds expression in words. While it is God who descends with the gift of revelation, "it is human beings who give this revelation its words."[27] Theology—written and proclaimed—is our response to revelation, our speaking of God. Gunton describes this as one of "the most perilous of all theological enterprises" because there is the temptation to forget that our knowledge of God is a gift and so "run the risk of 'objectifying' God: of turning him into a static and impersonal object to be subjected to our unfettered intellectual control."[28] What we discover when we allow God to be God, however, is that our knowledge goes beyond mere information: it has a purpose, it has an end, it has a terminus point that is located in the future fulfillment of creation.

This purpose is relational. We can describe the relational dynamic of theological inquiry in the following way:

- God reveals himself to persons through Jesus Christ, the one who discloses in human form the fullness of divine being. This brings about a relationship between God and human beings.
- The individual responds in "obedience—in-trust" (faith), thus completing the encounter in fellowship. And Scripture witnesses to this.[29]

Revelation, therefore, is neither an abstract nor even a solely rational concept. It is profoundly relational in its origin, its content, and its purpose. It is divine personal disclosure with the aim of bringing about human response and transformation. It comes about as a response to the gospel and is shaped through our individual and corporate following of Jesus.[30] Theology apart from this kind of personal transformation in and to Jesus Christ is as useful to the church—and to the world—as a picture of bread is to a starving man or woman.

This purpose is also eschatological: there is an openness to a future dimension to it. Think how we relate to each other in and with hopeful expectation. If all our knowledge of each other was known in that first epiphany of relationship, there would be little of interest beyond the here and now. There would be nothing more to discover. Friendship would be no different from owning a particularly precious object—desire fulfilled but no hope of anything more. However, it is in the nature of personal relating, of becoming and being known as a person, that there is openness to the future, to things developing, to desire being fulfilled, and to growth in togetherness.

It is for this reason that death is so tragic—the termination of hope and the conclusion to the beloved's existence and identity. Thus, while we live in the now, in all our personal relationships we are also living in anticipation of what can still be. A *thing* may well be known just about fully, but it cannot change except, ultimately, to deteriorate. However, knowledge of another human being is driven by the hope that the best is yet to come, however good the present may be. Similarly, we live in the same tension with God: for now, we see through a glass dimly, but one day our knowledge will not be limited. We will know, as we are fully known (1 Cor. 13:12). One day, faith will be superseded by sight: we will see God and experience a quite different kind of personal knowing. Donald Bloesch carefully distinguishes this kind of knowledge from the certainty of the natural sciences when he affirms that "we look forward to the public revelation of the mystery of God's marvelous condescension in Jesus Christ at the end of the age rather than look within to innate ideas or universal truths that have only to be drawn out into the open."[31]

We can say, then, that Christian faith and belief will be fulfilled in personal union with the object of our faith, the subject matter of our theology. Until then, there will be the constant challenge of ensuring that our theology matches our gospel, that our praxis reflects our knowledge, and that our lives demonstrate personal transformation to the degree our minds are renewed (Rom. 12:2). Here the ordinary and the academic coincide in the sense that theology is a very practical discipline: it observes how the gospel affects and transforms dysfunctional human beings who are alienated from God, themselves, and their neighbors into people who can be active participants in the kingdom of God—in loving God, neighbor, and self—and can thus live out the gospel. In this sense, our theology is not primarily about what we believe or hold as dogma but rather about how much our lives have been transformed by the gospel, through faith in Christ and the empowering work of the Holy Spirit. Theology expresses this change and provides ways of understanding it, as well as answering the questions it raises as a result.

Pause

Reflect on the differences between the following:

- Knowing God
- Knowing about God
- Being known by God

How do you express these different ways of knowing in your own understanding of God, in your own theology?

Concluding Remarks

Knowledge gained through the gift of divine self-revelation is not to be read like an instruction manual or dictionary of timeless propositional truths. To do so only upsets its true purpose. Rather, revelation knowledge is personal, intentional, and eschatological. It is personal in that such knowledge cannot be known apart from Jesus Christ (there is no other name by which human beings can be saved) and the Spirit of God (it is he who pours God's love into our hearts and transforms us at the level of our personality and personal relationships). It is intentional in that it is the love-seeking and love-finding of a Creator God who loves his creation so much that he master-planned his Son's rescue package. It is eschatological in that its hope lies not in the present but in what can be and is thus replete with all the characteristics of personal expectation. It seeks to engage with each person gifted with the privilege of such knowledge. It desires personal response: whether of awe or wonder, of fascination or worship, of reverence or fear, of fidelity or trust. But God, in revealing himself to us, ultimately desires people who demonstrate their fullest response in faithful obedience to God's good and perfect will for his creation, his will for each one of us.

The task of academic theology will always be to question faithfully, discern prayerfully, recognize corporately, codify critically, and communicate clearly this divine self-disclosure in such a way that its meaning is clear for human life, in thought and praxis. To achieve this, certain theological tools need to be appropriated. These tools are to be mastered, whether they be Scripture; creeds that set boundaries and establish understanding of God and Christ; various traditions of the historic and universal church, along with our own denominational ways of doing things; human experience; or the call to live under the love of God and to take the gospel to our respective communities. For all this to be living and effective, theology—the ordinary and the academic—is to be lived in and lived out in relation to Jesus Christ, and we must do so in such a way that our lives become evidence of the veracity of the gospel. In this way, our lives also act as sacraments of revelation, means of revealing who God is.

The task before us, therefore, is twofold: the professional and the personal. On the one hand, we must be able to identify the necessary tools of our profession in becoming theologians and know how to use them properly. On the other hand, what we produce professionally is only meaningful to the degree it is evidenced personally in our individual and corporate lives as we live out our response to the call of the gospel and demonstrate its power—the righteousness of God, what Paul proclaims in Romans 1:16–17—as people who not only have received the gospel by faith but also evidence ongoing lives of faith.

SUGGESTED READING

Gunton, Colin E. *The Christian Faith: An Introduction to Christian Doctrine*. Oxford: Blackwell, 2002.

Kreider, Glenn R., and Michael J. Svigel. *A Practical Primer on Theological Method*. Grand Rapids: Zondervan Academic, 2019.

four

Theological Method

The Evangelical in Theological Method

My own experience from teaching theology for nearly thirty years has helped me to realize that students undertake the expensive and challenging task of studying academic theology for a variety of reasons. However, one major reason is what David Ford, in his Very Short Introduction series on theology, talks about as "inappropriate knowledge."[1] By this, he refers to what we might call "bad theology." What students struggle with often are overly simplistic approaches and answers to life's very challenging questions that they have been given by others, often in authority. That is, they choose to study theology on the back of their own experience of being on the receiving end of inappropriate or bad theology. As we have noted, ordinary theology is what sustains us as believers. Inappropriate knowledge has no place in our ordinary theology—in any theology. Inappropriate knowledge is indeed inappropriate theology; it is also inadequate theology, soul-numbing and spirit-crushing theology—the answers offered are too shallow and ultimately too weak to sustain any form of abundant life in the midst of life's messiness.

We know that we are dealing with inappropriate knowledge when our questions cannot be asked at church, when our spiritual leaders are unable or unwilling to engage the difficult questions or do so with very unsatisfactory answers, when our questions threaten others, or when our unanswered doubts and questions gnaw away at the very heart of our faith. If you are anything like me in these situations, you are unable to rest until your questions are respected with answers that are satisfying. The temptation in all this is to think that if only we can discover "the info," be told the "answer," then we will be satisfied. However, this is not necessarily how things pan out in reality.

I want to offer at this point a somewhat counterintuitive proposal—namely, that it is not the *content* of our theology that overcomes the temptation "to just get the facts." Rather, it is the *method* of our theology that enables us to do this. What we have been doing up to this point is spending much time exploring different aspects of theology. Possibly without realizing it, you have been engaging with various aspects of the task of theology, what we can call "theological method." This has been deliberate in that it is better to walk through this process with various gobbets of information and engage in reflective exercises than to be overtly prescriptive with a list of "how-tos" regarding theology that may or may not scratch the itch that caused you to ask your questions in the first instance. The place of method, therefore, is important—but often it is presented in off-putting ways. This is unfortunate, especially because to excel and be proficient at any discipline it is necessary to have proper method. The surgeon in the operating room needs to follow set procedures that ensure safe hygiene and proper practice. The tennis player succeeds to the degree she develops correct tennis habits, whereby she knows that the position of her feet determines her success in placing a ball precisely, and so she practices, practices, practices until her muscle memory allows her instinctively to place a particular shot.

Every profession has its own method. As theologians from the apostle Paul onward have come to appreciate, the Holy Spirit does not bypass the faculties of our mind. Rather, it is by the mind that we change. Contemporary neuroscience only serves to confirm the centrality of the mind in any human transformation. I am suggesting here, therefore, that the imperative has to be as much on our theological method as it is on our theological content. Interestingly, liberation theologian J. L. Segundo captures the essence of this fact—namely, that "it is not content but method that determines liberative character of theology."[2] In reality, the same goes for any kind of theology, including a specifically evangelical theology. I deliberately do not spend much time here on the purely evangelical nature of theology, mainly because the subsequent chapters of the book will delineate the specific nature of evangelical theology in terms of its own particular theological method. However, by the term "evangelical," I refer simply to a mainly Protestant, conversionist movement, as distinct from any specific denomination,[3] a movement that stresses the high authority of the Bible[4] and identifies its entire raison d'être around the death and resurrection of Jesus Christ, what the New Testament describes as the "gospel" or the "good news"—in Greek, *euangelion*, "evangel," from which is derived the term "evangelical." Kevin Vanhoozer and Daniel Treier define "evangelical" similarly as a "movement" with three distinctives:

- it is a *renewal* movement—and as such is transdenominational;
- it is a *retrieving* movement—it returns constantly to Scripture; and
- it is a *reviving* movement—it encourages personal response to God's authoritative Word.[5]

They further define this movement via two principles, substance (its content) and style (how it goes about its faith). The former they identify in terms of "orthodox" (it conforms to the early Christian creeds), "catholic" (it spans time and place), and "Protestant" (it holds to the Reformation *solas*).[6] The latter they identify in terms of being "radical" (it is rooted in the gospel of the triune Word that confronts the world), "irenic" (it takes a wide variety of people to appreciate the wealth of the gospel), and "joyful" (it is energized by God's Spirit).[7]

At this point, it suffices to agree on one of the most concise summaries of a specifically evangelical theology—namely, that offered by Roger Olson. Evangelical theology, he argues, is constituted by four nonnegotiable theological commitments:

- the supremacy of the Bible
- a supernatural worldview centering on the living Creator God
- a conversion experience of God through Christ
- the imperative for mission and service[8]

To these four I add a fifth "nonnegotiable," one that is more an outworking of the other four, but one that nonetheless conveys the character and culture of evangelical theology. To a very large extent, the focus of an evangelical theology is on practical theology: there is a gospel that has to be preached, and there are converts who have to be discipled, congregations that need to be pastored and taught. In this sense, the focus and attention of evangelical theology are robustly ordinary.[9] However, Christianity is also a thinking faith, and therefore these various criteria concern not only the ordinary but also the academic in evangelical theology. Thus, an evangelical theology will also be committed to integrating the ordinary and the academic. As David Bebbington has pointed out, the *evangelical* in *theology* embraces four cornerstones, each of which, I may add, can be both ordinary and academic:

- *conversionism* (a positive and faithful response to the gospel concerning Jesus Christ)
- *biblicism* (the centrality and utter authority of the Bible in all things)

- *activism* (taking the gospel to the here and now rather than being a Christian couch potato)
- *crucicentrism* (the centrality of the sacrificial and atoning death of Jesus Christ on the cross in all things)[10]

An Integrated Theological Method

It might be helpful at this point to summarize what we have learned thus far about theology, for the church and for the academy, as well as how it affects how we live and think:

- We understand that theology is about asking questions. There is something about Jesus, God, ourselves, the messy business of life, the transformation that comes through believing faith, that demands inquiry.
- We appreciate the complexity of these questions. They cover the entire spectrum of human existence.
- We acknowledge that the answers support the different ways we understand our world and ourselves. They provide ways of living with their own polity and economy. We contest that for our theology to be personal it should be the result of knowledge built up through identifying patterns of behavior and consistency in these responses. Our answers, and therefore our theology, need to be the result of "genuine engagement and disciplined judgment."[11] Without the quality of thought, what we think will always be prey to the vagaries of fashion at best, ignorance at least.
- We distinguish between ordinary and academic theology while recognizing that each has its own set of questions about God and our faith.
- We observe that theology can be identified alongside our worldview—it is something that is lived in. Theology provides answers to our worldview questions: it reflects on every aspect of creation in relation to God.

What remain outstanding are two aspects of our theological method. The first has to do with how we ask questions and answer them in the first place. Put bluntly, What are the right questions to ask? Should they be a "standard set of questions," or should they "arise from the contemporary context"?[12] How might we distinguish a good question from the inadequate or the bad? And, in turn, how do we determine the usefulness and truth of any subsequent answer? Like a worldview, the issue is not whether or not have a theological method: we all have one. The challenge, rather, is in being able to identify *what* our theological method is. I want to suggest that whatever your theological method might be, it should be able to connect with the entirety of human life since theology covers every aspect of how creation, and human beings in particular, relate to God. In this sense, then, theology can be considered in terms of worldview. And since it covers the entirety of human existence, Simon Oliver is correct in reminding us that theology cannot be considered "just like another discipline alongside others."[13]

The second remaining issue develops this last point and constitutes what will be the remainder of the book. Since theology is different from other disciplines due to its subject matter, which is God and all things that relate to God—that is, everything—how we go about the task of theology, our theological method, will also be different. What is required, here, is a theological method that does justice to the discipline of critical inquiry regarding God and our faith, both of which are complex phenomena rather than simple. The task, then, demands a similarly complex (as distinct from one-dimensional) method. In the remainder of the book I argue that this is best done in an integrated manner—by developing an integrative theological method.

Integrative Theology versus Integrative Theological Method

At this point, we need to clarify the difference between an integrative theology and an integrative theological method. Integrative theology describes *what we believe* and is a form of theology that seeks to draw different disciplines together in order to create what we might call a holistic entity. An integrative theological method, on the other hand, describes *how we believe*.

Integrative Theology

We can identify four different iterations of integrative theology. The first example of integrative theology is illustrated by its main proponents, Gordon Lewis and Bruce Demarest, and their three-volume theological approach to Christian doctrine, which combines biblical theology, historical theology, apologetics, and practical theology.[14] This integrative theology draws together various viewpoints from historical and contemporary theology using six criteria to determine the best response:

1. Define, distinguish, and identify the problem.
2. Look at historical responses to the problem.
3. Go to primary sources.
4. Order findings in a coherent manner.

5. Defend your position.

6. Apply what has been established to the Christian's life-situation.[15]

This integrative approach to theology, however, is no recent phenomenon. Perhaps one of the greatest Anglican theologians, the sixteenth century's Richard Hooker, produced *The Laws of Ecclesiastical Polity*[16] and sought to find a middle way—a *via media*—at a time of great transition in the English church, in the age of Elizabeth I. On the basis of the belief that God had put a natural law in creation, Hooker argued for a holistic and integrative theology that was built on Scripture, an intrinsic reasonableness, the judgments and traditions of antiquity, and the ongoing practice of the church.

The second iteration of integrative theology consists of more recent integrative theologies. One example of the Anglican tradition, albeit with less middle ground than Hooker, is found in the internet journal *The Theologian*, which offers an Anglican, evangelical, and Reformed position on contemporary matters. Its aim is "to integrate biblical studies, doctrine, and pastoralia in creative and useful ways avoiding the over-specialized nature of theological college education in order to produce more rounded and effective theologians and preachers in the 21st century."[17] More globally, the South African Jurgens Hendriks has sought to develop an integrative practical theology that meets the needs of South African churches in the training of their clergy, one that seeks to bridge the academic and the ordinary, recognizing that the latter is not always what the local church needs.[18] Both of these approaches consider the purely "academic" as being insufficient for the needs of the local church. However, an excellent example of a contemporary exercise in integrative theology that is both academic and relevant can be found in *Transforming Spirituality*, by LeRon Shults and Steven Sandage, who combine the various disciplines of psychology, theology, and spirituality in their study of relational spirituality.[19]

Third, there is what we might describe as a more loosely constructed integrative theology, one that organizes, systematizes, or integrates theology around a particular construct or concept that holds the theologian's theology together or by which it is systematized. Thus, for Martin Luther it was the theme of "justification by faith"; for John Calvin it was "the glory of God"; for John Wesley it was "responsible grace"; Friedrich Schleiermacher's was "human religious experience"; Karl Barth systematized his theology around "the nature of revelation of the triune God"; and for Stanley Grenz it was "the community of God."

The final iteration, though not so explicitly methodological, has more to do with the desired outcomes of theological education. That said, these desired aims control the manner in which the theological education is constructed, and therefore a theology governed by these aims acts in an implicitly methodological way. Thus, a theological program may well desire that its students not only learn various skills essential to the academic task of theology but be able to integrate these skills, whether they be knowledge, critical thinking, application to real life, or spiritual formation. More generally, the desired outcome may be to integrate "faith" with "learning," or its aim may be more on different learning pairs that need to be integrated rather than learned in isolation; thus, "knowledge and skill" are integrated with "spiritual formation and moral integrity."

Integrative Theological Method

In contrast to the *what* of integrative theology, an integrative theological method is concerned with *how* we believe. More specifically, it expresses a desire to find a way of integrating various independent aspects used in theological construction and knowing how to use them. It seeks to serve better the contemporary church as it moves away from historic Enlightenment forms of individualism in a desire to develop more holistic forms of theological expression. Most importantly, it recognizes that a resurgence in the priority of Scripture has taken hold of the academy and the church. In essence, an integrative theological method moves away from a prescriptive *what to believe* approach to a more descriptive *how to believe* approach. Given the complex nature of the discipline, as we have noted, an integrative theological method will require a multidimensional approach.[20] James Packer suggests five guiding principles:

- Maintain trajectories—Christian virtues, historic supernaturalist Christian orthodoxy.
- Maintain the organism—keep theology intact by combining Scripture with praxis.
- Maintain constant dialogue with the Bible—"To evangelicals . . . the to-and-fro of searching Scripture and finding in it answers to their questions is the heart of theological life and work."
- Maintain constant dialogue with the culture—theology is used to "persuade the world."
- Maintain constant dialogue with non-evangelical theology.[21]

However, to achieve any modicum of consistency, this kind of maintenance requires specific skills and a particular approach, or method. For instance,

Stanley Grenz and Roger Olson offer three "tools" for theology: the biblical message, the theological heritage of the church, and the thought-forms of contemporary culture.[22] Alister McGrath adds another in his understanding of how we go about our theological construction:

> Christian theology, like most disciplines, draws upon a number of sources. There has been considerable discussion within the Christian tradition concerning the identity of these sources, [and] their relative importance for theological analysis. . . . Broadly speaking, four main sources have been acknowledged within the Christian tradition:
>
> 1. Scripture (also known as "the Bible")
> 2. tradition
> 3. reason
> 4. religious experience
>
> Though not regarded as being of equal importance, each of these sources has a distinct contribution to make within the discipline of theology.[23]

These four sources—we could call them "tools" or "criteria"—constitute what has come to be called "the Wesleyan Quadrilateral." This term was first coined by Albert Outler to describe John Wesley's theological method.[24] The quadrilateral was more recently made widely known by Don Thorsen's *The Wesleyan Quadrilateral*,[25] in which he outlines how each of these four aspects of Wesley's theology can be used to produce a specifically evangelical theological method. Admittedly, Wesley never used this description about his own theology, and, probably for this reason, a number of contemporary Wesleyan denominational seminaries distance themselves from this definition. More importantly, this method dates back to early modernity or beyond and has, therefore, a very specific understanding of Scripture—namely, Wesley's—as well as a particular take on "experience," which does not translate easily into evangelical churchmanship, let alone charismatic or Pentecostal expressions.

However, while the four sources for theology given by McGrath illustrate what a multidimensional approach might look like, my concern in this book is to develop this approach in the belief that this fourfold approach to theology is inadequate to the contemporary task. Rather, what I propose is a theological method relevant to an evangelical sensibility and persuasion. Given that the central focus of evangelicalism is its passion for the gospel, a fifth dimension to our theological method is required, one that addresses this fundamental concern. It does so through a twofold understanding of *community*: the internal and the external. The internal is a *didactic* tool of the church and is concerned with how we communicate, teach, and learn our faith. It focuses on what it means for us to do theology as a community of believers living our faith *coram Deo*—that is, in the *presence of God*, before the *face of God*, to the *glory of God*. The external is a *curative* tool of the church and is concerned with the reconciling, healing, and transforming power of the divine mission toward creation in general and humanity in particular. It focuses on what it means to do theology as a community of believers living our faith *missio Dei*—that is, in the light of God's mission to the world and the church's participation in this mission. When we add this to our four established sources, we have what we can name "the Evangelical Quintilateral": Scripture, tradition, reason, experience, and community. What we have, as a result, is a revision of a well-used theological method that is able to revive contemporary theological inquiry. It is an integrative theological method that

- respects the authority of Scripture;
- recognizes the historical construction of Christian thought;
- is the result of considered, rational, and critical thought;
- is evidenced in the gestalt or experience of the believer;
- is acknowledged by the witness of the church as it makes the gospel known and nurtures disciples.

What this model is *not* is a *unilateral* with four additional components. That is, Scripture does not stand alone. Nor do these different components operate independently of each other or individually in relation to Scripture. Rather, they are integrated. We can present this method diagrammatically thus:

Figure 4.1

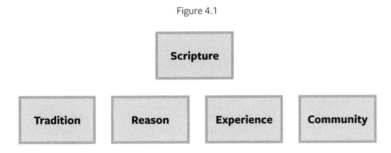

We are now in a position to explore this Evangelical Quintilateral and its application. We rightly begin with Scripture, for it is here that we locate the primary means of answering our questions. It is Scripture that enables us to identify what Mary Veeneman describes as the "orienting questions and starting point."[26] It is Scripture that furnishes us with the trajectories. Scripture is where the story of our faith unfolds and reveals. It is to Scripture, then, that we now turn.

SUGGESTED READING

Kidd, Thomas S. *Who Is an Evangelical? The History of a Movement in Crisis*. New Haven: Yale University Press, 2019.

McGrath, Alister. *Christian Theology: An Introduction*. 6th ed. Oxford: Wiley & Sons, 2017.

Veeneman, Mary M. *Introducing Theological Method: A Survey of Contemporary Theologians and Approaches*. Grand Rapids: Baker Academic, 2017.

PART 2

An Integrated Model for Evangelical Theology

five

Scripture

The Supremacy of Scripture

We are now in a position to start looking in more detail at "the theologian's tools." To some extent, the first—Scripture—is not so much a tool like the others—tradition, reason, experience, community—but more the actual bag in which the rest are located. What is important at this point to understand is the priority that Scripture has over every other element in the Quintilateral. Let's remind ourselves, once again, of this priority diagrammatically:

Figure 5.1

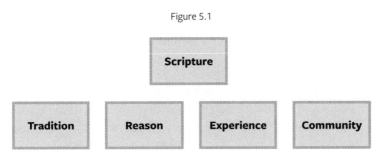

We can see quite clearly that the Bible is located in such a position that it very deliberately functions, as Trevor Hart points out, "as the church's primary authority for the formation of Christian identity at every level" and should do so since this is "basic to a properly Christian treatment of it as Scripture."[1] This priority given to Scripture is the golden thread that ran throughout part 1. It is the reason the discipline of theology is understood to be a secondary and subordinate task in relation to Scripture. Indeed, our ambition as theologians is that we should be known as "Masters of the Sacred Page," a rather ancient term going back to the thirteenth century but one that still has meaning for today. To be a theologian, you have to know your sacred texts: to be a Christian theologian, you have to be intimately familiar with the Bible. Only then can you ever hope to be a theological expert. And, of course, when this happens, something very dynamic and potent takes place—personal understanding of our faith as it is located in Jesus Christ and articulated in Scripture.

We discover this relationship between great theological thinking and a deep knowledge of Scripture in those men and women who engage the Bible in search of answers to their respective situations. It is their answers, rooted and grounded in Scripture, that make them the most lasting of Christian theologians, whether in the writings of the church fathers in the first millennium of the church, or in that of later thinkers like Anselm of Canterbury, who gave us the term *fides quaerens intellectum* (faith seeking understanding), or in Martin Luther's battle cry, or in John Calvin's attention to biblical detail, or in Karl Barth's quest for theological rootedness in writing a commentary or two on Paul's epistle to the Romans as he (Barth) rejected the theology of his own day and returned to a faith seeking (biblical) understanding. More recently, we can look to people like Charles Spurgeon, D. L. Moody, John Stott, Kwame Bediako, Martin Lloyd-Jones, F. F. Bruce, and Francis Schaeffer. Then there are contemporary speakers who influence hundreds of thousands of people via satellite TV, such as Joyce Meyer, Beth Moore, Jentezen Franklin, Pat Robertson, Creflo Dollar, Kenneth Copeland, and Alistair Begg; and the list could be expanded significantly. However controversial you might consider some of these to be, and whether or not you particularly approve of the names cited, my point is that each would agree that, whether ancient or contemporary, they all hold something in common. Whether as archbishop, tenured academic theologian, religious, church minister, pastoral minister, or satellite TV host, in their different ways each of these Christian thinkers understands that there is a relation between Scripture and what they teach or preach. Each evidences a basic understanding that "theology serves the reading of the text"[2] and should never be read in any self-serving way.[3]

Like our theological foremothers and fathers, we face a similar, if not the same, challenge. It is the challenge to create, engineer, construct, and communicate a way of doing theology that maintains, upholds, and secures this fundamental and irreplaceable disposition concerning what we say and the source from which we say it. As John Franke comments, "Theological construction ought never proceed apart from a careful exegesis of the biblical texts."[4] That is, we simply do not go about our theological inquiry and reflection, as well as our responses, without their roots being firmly in the ground of Scripture. In the same way that a doctor does not do medicine apart from her understanding and deep knowledge of the human body, so the theologian speaks from a similar expertise: an intimate grounding in and knowledge of Scripture. Indeed, the very center of any evangelical theology is this biblical priority. As Robert Jenson comments, "Theology is a long, inextricably interpersonal series of elaborations on the gospel."[5]

There are, then, two nonnegotiables to a specifically evangelical theological method. The first is the priority it gives to the gospel. Whatever "theology" is, one thing is certain: the controlling mechanisms for doing theology are both the content of the gospel and the act of living in the gospel. In essence, theology is what happens when the people of God step back from and reflect critically upon the *lived-in-and-worked-out-ness of the gospel concerning Jesus Christ*. The second nonnegotiable to a specifically evangelical theological method is its rootedness and its to-ing-and-fro-ing with Scripture.

- We ground ourselves in Scripture and take root in it.
- We connect through Scripture with the God of Israel and the Lord Jesus Christ.
- We give testimony through Scripture to its transformative potency.

Scripture is both the primary content and the nonnegotiable authority in the theological task.

Pause

This is a good point to stop and think about your own approach to what you think about your faith, God, and Jesus—that is, your theology. This is a purely personal and individual reflection—no two will be the same.

- Write a two-to-three-sentence definition of what you believe is the gospel.
- How much of what you believe can you trace back to this understanding of the good news? Is what you believe an unpacking of your gospel?
- How much of what you believe can you trace back to Scripture?

Scripture Speaks and Acts with Authority

Scripture communicates as a voice speaking. Voice—to be heard—requires both content (words) and power of expression (breath/spirit). It is with very real intention that Christians refer to Scripture in ways that parallel the dynamics of our own human expression. As voice speaking, Scripture can be understood as the dynamic relation between divine Word and Spirit, a beautiful image of how the triune God communicates—as agent (Father) whose Word (Son) is made audible and fulfilled by his Breath (Spirit). And since human beings reflect God's image, we should not be surprised to find that this understanding of Scripture as voice speaking resonates with our own human words and spirit, given that our knowledge of God elicits worship and praise as a response and generates a desire to communicate this knowledge and live it out.

Scripture is not only voice speaking; it is also voice acting. The authority of Scripture is attested by its ability to bring about what it says, what it declares, what it purposes. Let's face it, there's no point believing in, let alone trying to live out, words that cannot achieve anything, that are impotent to bring about what they declare. Scripture, after all, is not fake news, nor is it a dull and boring sitcom or play. Rather, Scripture invites us into the dynamic interplay between word—spoken, breathed, and empowered—and agency, which is both willed and lived out or enacted, which in turn creates history that is narrated and experienced. Once again, we see Loving Will, Word, and Breath all working to create a history of God relating to creation and creating what we call "history"—one that has to be experienced, reflected upon, recorded, passed down, celebrated, lamented, and lived. Of course, all this centers on the transforming work of Jesus Christ.

Pause

Why not pause at this point and write out a summary of what *you* think is the reason for the Bible. Since this is a bit of a consciousness-raising exercise, there is no right or wrong answer in this personal reflection. Rather, before we continue, it might be helpful if you spend a little time reflecting on this question—and your answer—so that you are more aware of your own view on the purpose of Scripture. If you think about it, whatever you think is the answer, it will color your approach to the Bible, whether you are aware of it or not.

The point of language is that it is effective—it does something. So, too, with Scripture. Its authority lies not only in its source—God—and what the pages of text reveal to us but also in the way the content of these pages comes alive as each of us lives it out. As this happens, we discover, of course, that the same thing is happening to each one of us, that we are being transformed in the same way, reflecting the same glory, cultivating the same characteristics, and so we discover that the best way to test the truthfulness of these words is simply to live them out. They are to be lived out, and in so doing we are transformed. Indeed, we might say that the "greatest test of Scripture is the ways in which it has the power to shape faithful lives."[6] This only occurs over time, which allows for things to change and thus the veracity of Scripture to be proven. Of course, this can happen only to the degree we demonstrate faith-filled obedience: *faith* in that we start without the evidence of it having happened and *obedience* in that our faith has to be put into practice in accordance with what the text says and not our own inclination.

How we view Scripture, therefore, determines how we relate to it. For instance, a car manual interests me only when something goes wrong—it's my go-to when there is a problem. However, it would never occur to me to sit down and read it through so that I might be more intimately and more knowledgeably informed about it because I am so interested in it. But some people would, because they are passionate about cars and how they work, and so they want to know all that they can about their car just because they like—sometimes love—their car. The same could be said for cookbooks. Now here I am different. I like making food, so I read cookbooks to find out more about how flavors work, which herbs or spices to use, what ingredients work. Added to this, my wife can eat only a very limited range of foods, and so I like reading around to find out ideas that make meals more interesting and enjoyable. Why? Because I love her, and I appreciate food! The same goes for Scripture: it is something to be loved, as the psalmist who wrote Psalm 119 loved it, repeatedly stating that he loved God's precepts because he loved God and because God's precepts contained such wisdom.

So when it comes to Scripture, it is important that we bring to the surface any subliminal notions we have about Scripture that might not be helpful. For instance, if it is a rule book, then we are not going to read it with passion. Rather, we will read it not to fail, or not be caught, or for ways in which we might be able to "get off the hook" if we are caught. If it is a history book, then we will read it from a historical perspective, focused on the past with no expectation of the same events affecting the present. On the other hand, if we see it as a devotional book with blessed thoughts to cheer us on our way, then we will engage with it in an entirely different way than do those who understand it to contain the key texts that confirm their particular theological or denominational positions.

Recalling the primacy of Scripture and of the gospel message in evangelical theology, we approach the Bible from a positive perspective: it is the grand story or narrative telling us good news. It also has an authority to deliver on its good news. What does this authority look like? Take, for example, a police officer who stands at the center of a busy interchange because the traffic lights are out. Drivers stop when he signals and move on only when he instructs them. However, if we were to try to direct traffic at a busy interchange, it is unlikely that anyone would stop at our command. Most likely we would get injured in the process. Yet, think about it. The officer is no different from us except that when he is directing the traffic, he does so with the full authority of the law supporting his actions and authorizing him to penalize anyone who does not comply with his instructions. So, on what grounds do we say that Scripture is the authority that allows us to talk truthfully about God and the good news we have experienced through Jesus Christ?

Scripture Is Inspired

When we ask, "What gives Scripture its authority?," the first and foremost answer is given by the Bible itself. Scripture's authority is God himself, Father, Son, and Holy Spirit.[7] The reason we describe this authority in terms of inspiration is, first, that Scripture itself attests the fact. For instance, Old Testament authors have their own vernacular to communicate divine speech, which of course requires *spiration*, "breath." Gerhard Hasel points out that the Old Testament authors had their own shorthand for what the New Testament calls "inspiration." Terms such as "the hand of God," "the Word of the Lord," "thus says the Lord," "thus declares the Lord," and even "the hand of God" are "the OT's way of saying that it is God-derived and 'God-breathed' and, as such, intrinsically 'canonical.'"[8] I like this because once again Scripture authenticates its own testimony about God—it is about God, and it comes from God, and it is given by God—and God does this as a voice speaking—by Word and the Spirit/Breath of God.

We see this when Paul encourages his mentee, Timothy, stating that "all Scripture is God-breathed and is useful for teaching, rebuking, correcting and training in righteousness, so that the servant of God may be thoroughly equipped for every good work" (2 Tim. 3:16–17). Thus, an evangelical response to the question of authority is that Scripture has authority simply because it is divinely given and inspired. While Scripture may well be human responses to the divine, its authority lies in who does the revealing—not in who does the writing. Put simply, Scripture's authority is its divine, not merely human, origin. Scripture is above all divine communication mediated through human communication. This credo is very much an evangelical fundamental. Because Scripture is the Word of God, it has God's authority.

I find it helpful to think a little more deeply about what we mean when we say something is "inspired." We are stating something about its ability to lift us up out of the mundane here and now and make us feel like we've just experienced a fresh *breath* of air, a new *wind* in our sails. For example, some people might describe a person's solution to an almost impossible problem as being inspired. Others call the music of Bach or Mozart inspired. The way a football player performs a particular move on the field might also be termed as inspired. When people say things like this, they are really using a kind of shorthand to communicate what they have experienced. In the case of Bach and Mozart, for example, to say that their music is inspired not only expresses the impact the music has had on the listener but equally says something about the source of the music, since it has the ability to lift its listeners out of their own situation in a way that "ordinary" music cannot and therefore must have a source outside of the composer. Of course, when impact and source come together so powerfully in this way, the music, the football player, and the solution stand apart from the ordinary and take on an authority that sets the gold standard from then on.

When we turn to consider what we mean in declaring that Scripture is inspired, we recognize similar shorthand being used. More importantly, this shorthand occurs within the language and grammar of an evangelical theology that holds theory and practice in intimate union. Consequently, the impact Scripture has on the people of God as we faithfully and obediently live it out helps us recognize not only that it is altogether different from any other text but also that it confirms its own message and is, thus, completely different from any other narrative. The sheer transformative impact Scripture has on those who live it out in faithful obedience forces us to ask questions, once again, about its source and to recognize that its power is only possible if the source goes beyond the human with all its contextual and historical situatedness and is located in God. Isn't it interesting, therefore, that the shorthand expressions we use in our own communications—breath of fresh air, a new wind in our sails—are the very words Scripture uses to describe the Holy Spirit: the breath of God—dare we say, the fresh breath of God's Spirit? Or might we even speak of perceiving the Spirit as the constantly new wind in God's sails? The language of Scripture itself is replete with meaning, whether the Hebrew *ruach* or the Greek *pneuma*—both contain what we mean when we say that Scripture is inspired. An evangelical theological method, therefore, will uphold a belief and understanding of the divine origin of Scripture as communication that comes into being as the divine breath of God moves over divine vocal chords to utter divine words. It is communication breathed by God, as the divine wind of God bringing history to its divinely ordained fulfillment. Therefore, we can say that Scripture is inspired on several levels:

- It lifts us up out of our messy lives. As we trust in and live out its precepts, principles, and teaching, we discover that we change. We are transformed to the degree that we renew our minds (Rom. 12:1–2). What this means, in practice, is relatively straightforward even if it is more difficult to implement apart from God's enabling Spirit. That is, the degree to which our minds focus on what Scripture says and the extent to which we live it out will be the level of personal transformation that occurs. After all, we are what we think—and our thinking is expressed most powerfully in spoken words—and words create worlds! Therefore, it is only when we indwell and live out Scripture that we discover that *we* change, *things* change, and *history* changes. Much more significantly, we find ourselves more in union with other believers, changing more into the "family likeness" of those who are active participants in the kingdom of God.

- As we live out the text, we discover it has the power to transform other people's lives too. When this happens, we discover that they, like us, experience the same power and the same Spirit and begin to change in ways similar to our own experience. Surely, this is the determining reason Jesus commanded his disciples, and us, to take the good news of how God loves his creation and how he has made it possible to achieve its rich and fertile end. For this reason, we are so passionate about spreading the gospel of Jesus Christ—it really is good news! It is not merely about "saving people from hell." Rather, it has the power to change people's lives for the good, the very good.

- As we are transformed to the extent that we are living out the text, we also discover that something truly amazing must be happening. We discover that we are in touch with and are being changed by a very different power, energy, *breath* (the fundamental essence of life) and *spirit* (relational energy that enables us to transcend the mess). The apostle Paul makes sense of this dynamic when he writes about how we change status once we declare Jesus is Lord and believe that God has raised him from the dead (Rom. 10:9–11). As the newly born baby draws breath, changing status upon emerging from her mother's womb, so the new birth—the being born again of John 3:16—is possible only because we draw breath from God's Spirit. The history of the church universal is that we instinctively describe this new birth by referring back to the power of the gospel contained within Scripture's pages.

- Ultimately, we detect in the various texts of Scripture not only the same Spirit of God who is changing us and growing us into the family likeness of Jesus Christ but also the same Spirit of God, the same Energy, the same Power, the same Breath that brought about the sacred texts of Scripture. When we realize this, then the circle is squared: the power that transforms us is the same power that creates Scripture.

An evangelical theological method, therefore, will always uphold the foundational belief concerning the inspiration of Scripture. It is, indeed, God-breathed. Therefore, this stance provides us with one foundational aspect of the role Scripture holds as an authority—namely, its divine origins. However, if the concept is left like this, there is a possible danger worth noting: to put all the "authority eggs" in the one "basket" of divine inspiration is to ignore the contextual nature of Scripture. What we might then miss about Scripture's authority is the wider picture that takes into account the fact that our knowledge of God comes about as a result of God's saving actions toward us. This knowledge is not in abstraction from the life, death, resurrection, ascension, and glorification of Jesus Christ and the ongoing transforming and sanctifying work of the Holy Spirit as each works in harmony to fulfill the Father's good will for his creation. It is rooted in concrete reality.

We see the centrality of this Jesus-dynamic, this gospel-dynamic, operating in the way the canon was recognized and subsequently closed to any additions. As we have seen above, one criterion for including a text in the canon was the apostolic authorship of the candidate text (either directly or by association). Thus, to be included within the New Testament, the text not only had to be inspired—have a *divine* origin; it also had to be written by an apostolic eyewitness to the gospel events—that is, it must also have a *human* origin.[9] Of course, the human dimension also comes out of our own response to the gospel and how it changes us. There's almost a sense of joy in one of Colin Gunton's sermons where he expresses his own understanding of what it means to say that Scripture is inspired: "It so represents God's reality and love before our minds that it makes them real, mediates them to us, and the book becomes the inspiration for our lives. Inspiration means the action of God the Spirit, and the Bible is thus the means of the Spirit's action because by it, and through Christ, we come to God the Father, creator and redeemer of all."[10]

Consequently, not only is there a divine aspect to Scripture's authority; there is also a human dimension to Scripture's authority. Our task is to ensure that each is equally understood and upheld. The authority of Scripture is grounded in the triune God—Father, Son and Holy Spirit—as it is mediated through the human beings in their cultural and historical contexts. Our understanding of authority, therefore, should not divorce Scripture from its human context simply because its authority within the church, within communities of faith, is grounded in the gospel of Jesus Christ, who himself was conditioned by his own specific culture and history.

To say, therefore, that Scripture is authoritative solely because of its divine origins is potentially to divorce God's communication to us from the context within which the good news was given, as well as from the contexts for which it is intended. It is to suggest, first, that because God can relate to us abstractly, he does not need the created order to make himself known or bring about his will. Second, it is to suggest that *our* world is secondary at best, irrelevant at worst. This perception undermines a biblical worldview that asserts that what we see, feel, touch, and experience all around us matters to God and should therefore matter to us. Finally, this approach separates the text from its divine and human authors. When this happens, the authority of Scripture shifts dramatically from the divine to the human, to whatever a leader, movement, or even denomination wants it to say. Of course, this is no recent phenomenon—the apostle Paul contests a similar issue with the Galatian church in the first century, so it is worth referring to what he has to offer on the topic, especially as he hardly minces his words or pulls his punch:

> I am astonished that you are so quickly deserting the one who called you to live in the grace of Christ and are turning to a different gospel—which is really no gospel at all. Evidently some people are throwing you into confusion and are trying to pervert the gospel of Christ. But even if we or an angel from heaven should preach a gospel other than the one we preached to you, let them be under God's curse! As we have already said, so now I say again: If anybody is preaching to you a gospel other than what you accepted, let them be under God's curse! (Gal. 1:6–9)

In our own day, sociologist Peter Berger has identified the danger of what he describes as "different gospels": "*this false preaching denies ministry to those who desperately need it.*"[11] It is a watering down of the church's message and thus "a betrayal of Christ and a betrayal of the gospel" as well as of the church's mission.[12] And since a church's entire identity is formed around its "gospel," the net result of false preaching and bad theology will always be an aberration of what the true gospel promises and, therefore, damaged lives.

This evangelical posture may well be offensive to contemporary Western sensibilities in that it is making a truth claim, one that overrides other worldview claims to divine revelation. We can identify two major stumbling blocks: the cultural, as seen in conceptual ideologies, and the ecclesial, as seen in the current penchant for spiritual independence.

- *Conceptual ideologies.* We have already commented in part 1 about our postmodern Western worldview, but one element of it is particularly relevant at this point. It is the belief that secular human knowledge will suffice in aiding the human race to find its fulfillment. However, an evangelical position challenges what Bruce Ellis Benson describes as "graven ideologies"—that is, conceptual ideologies[13] or philosophical belief systems that have become the contemporary idols of the West. Sure, we are too sophisticated to give our allegiance and our lives to a graven *image*. Only primitive cultures stoop this low. Rather, with the rise of the Enlightenment and the humanism it espoused, Western culture developed its own alternative belief systems—its ideologies. These, in turn, required political and economic expressions, giving rise to capitalism and communism. Either way, authority moved from the divine to the secular, whether this be the self-made autonomous capitalist or the totalitarian state. The scandal, therefore, of a specifically evangelical theological method that gives its allegiance to the God and Father of Jesus Christ as revealed in Scripture is in declaring that personal knowledge of God is found only through the gospel of Jesus Christ.

- *An independent Spirit.* The evangelical stance toward Scripture may even be somewhat scandalous to contemporary Christian culture, within which there is a growing assumption that not only is there more revelation to be had (true) but also it can be discovered apart from the gospel, that it can be directly downloaded, as it were, by the Spirit, as if the Spirit could work independently of the Father and Son. Not so—it is no more possible for the Holy Spirit to act separately from the Father and Son than it is for you to think independently of your brain. Your head is part of your body and cannot be removed from it without serious consequences. So also concerning the Holy Spirit—he is as much God as are the Father and Son. Therefore, to isolate the Spirit and make him an independent agent is both to do great harm to our knowledge and experience of God and to hold to an altered gospel and altogether different revelation. In a similar manner, then, divine speech is always located within the context of the gospel. To be honest, it is not even a very attractive kind of authority—a "do as I say because I say it" kind of authority. Daniel Migliore communicates the dynamic feel involved here when he declares,

> The authority of Scripture has to be understood in relation to its central content and its particular function within the community of faith. Scripture is the unique and irreplaceable witness to the liberating and reconciling activity of God in the history of Israel and supremely in Jesus Christ. By the power of the Holy Spirit, Scripture serves the purpose of mediating the good news of the astonishing grace of God in Christ that moves us to greater love of God and neighbor and calls us to the freedom for which Christ has set us free.[14]

Consequently, whatever we understand the Bible's authority to be, an evangelical theological method will always understand that it is an authority invested not only in the Bible's *power* to achieve what it says it will do but also in its *ability* to do something that no other texts are able to do. That specific and unique reality is the gospel, for it alone is good news, it alone is the power of God unto salvation to everyone who has faith, for only the gospel reveals the righteousness of God (Rom. 1:16–17). No other text does this. No other text claims this. No other text delivers on this. Migliore captures a sense of this authority when he writes, "To speak of the authority rightly is to speak of its power by God's Spirit to help create, nourish and reform this new life in relation with God and with others."[15] That is, Scripture has, in some way or other, a vitality, a power, a dynamic that is able to bring about God's intentions for his creation, which, of course, are both demonstrated and communicated in and through the gospel. Therefore, I like how N. T. Wright captures the meaning of "authority" as it is applied to Scripture when he reminds us that the authority of Scripture is delegated from God himself and the risen Lord Jesus Christ and that the word "authority" is shorthand for speaking about "the authority of the triune God, exercised somehow *through* Scripture"[16] to achieve what it says it will do.[17]

Of course, any authority requires some kind of authentication; otherwise it can be easily denied. Scripture is no different. Its authentication is "canon," a term often bandied around but with little understanding. What the term means is of immense importance given the role it has in establishing the authority of the Bible in general and the New Testament in particular. It might be helpful, therefore, to look at this term from two perspectives: criteria and chronology.

Criteria

What we know as the Bible today, both Old and New Testaments, is the result of very intentional reflection by Jewish and Christian believers. It did not arrive at its final form by accident or without intent. Rather, it is the product of thoughtful conviction. The challenge, however, is to identify why certain texts were recognized as authoritative and given a place in the Bible while others were not. What were the criteria used for establishing a specific text as being worthy of inclusion in the canon? John Peckham identifies three key criteria applied to guide this procedure:[18]

- The text must evidence divine commissioning as prophetic and/or apostolic: it should be "a written record of covenantal prophetic and/or apostolical testimony written either by a prophet/apostle or a close contemporary associate thereof."[19] It comes to us through people who have been chosen either to hear or to see the "real thing."

- The text must be consistent with previous revelation: it should be consistent with other canonical texts. God speaks with one mind. Therefore, Scripture reflects an interconnectedness and consistency despite its historical, authorial, and cultural diversity.
- The text must be self-authenticating: it must evidence that its own writings have a divine and not merely human origin and therefore authorship. Of course, the litmus test for this evidence is its power to bring about God's purposes for creation and for humanity.

Chronology

In addition to identifying the criteria used to determine the text's place in the canon—the "Why is it here?" question—it is helpful also to understand the "How did it get here?" question. John Goldingay, in *Models for Scripture*, offers a two-stage time line for this authentication:[20]

- Stage 1 concerns the core story that is contained within the Pentateuch. The rest of the Old Testament extends Israel's core story. By the first century AD, the Old Testament had been authenticated—that is, it had been canonized; the standard of authority had been decided. John Morrison points out that until the second half of the second century AD, "Scripture in the *official* sense referred to the Old Testament, with rare exceptions." However, when Marcion stated that there was a canon within the canon—that is, some texts were not really authoritative—the church was forced to think about the identity of the canon and thus clarify the basis of its authority. By AD 144, an *implicit* Christian canon was determined for use within the church's belief and practice—that is, the use of the Old Testament and New Testament as divinely authoritative.[21]
- Stage 2 continued in the first and second centuries, when the majority of the canon was established. As is the case in much Christian thought and belief, it was heretical disputes in the late second century that brought clarity. By the third and fourth centuries, the church had arrived at the "official standard." However, this standard reflects the different opinions of the church's three main traditions, which can be summarized as follows:
  - » Protestant: sixty-six books
  - » Roman Catholic: sixty-six books plus seven deuterocanonical books: Tobit, Judith, Wisdom of Solomon, Sirach (Ecclesiasticus), Baruch, 1–2 Maccabees

» Orthodox: same as Catholic plus 3 Maccabees, Psalm 151, Prayer of Manasseh, 3 Esdras (although note that there is some variation among different branches of Orthodoxy)

Despite the differences between the Protestant, Roman Catholic, and Orthodox canons, there is a universal acceptance of a core set of sixty-six books that make up the Bible. Debate occurs over whether other books should be included in the canon.[22] Thus, what we know as Scripture constitutes the "one revelation that virtually all Christians agree on as the 'canon,' or measuring stick, for all other claims to revelation."[23] This is a significant and important theological shibboleth, something that defines a specifically Christian theology—namely, that the standard for assessing any revelation is Scripture itself. It means that anything not corresponding to what is in Scripture is to be taken cautiously and with care.

We catch a glimpse of this dynamic when we look at how the early church went about developing its own theology in response to various questions being asked of Jesus and the One God. Here we discover that it took the early church around three centuries to debate the identity of Jesus, after several insufficient attempts by various theologians. Only after very careful debate did the church finally affirm that Jesus is everything it is to be human and at the same time everything it is to be God, and both occurring in one person, the incarnate Son of God, the Christ. However, once the Jesus question was answered, it immediately raised the God question: If Jesus is fully God, how can we believe in one God? Again, it took the early church well into the fourth century before its theological leaders were able to affirm something that was not directly stated in Scripture, and the church even needed a few heretical ideas on the subject to bring this about. The church finally arrived at its understanding of God as a Trinity of Father, Son, and Holy Spirit only after considerable reflection and debate on what Scripture says about God and what they were experiencing.

Scripture Today

The priority we give to Scripture as the supreme location for knowledge of God means that every other kind of revelation has to conform to the principle that Scripture is inspired, apostolic—has divine authority—works through human agents, but must be self-authenticating. This sounds good in theory, but within the contemporary church there is a growing belief that there is "extra revelation" in addition to that which is given in Scripture. Increasingly, Christians seek special words of knowledge not found in Scripture and give these words authority that is often set above Scripture. In some instances, this looks more like Christian clairvoyance since it is not grounded in or brought under the scrutiny of Scripture and, worse, it becomes authoritative in decision-making or living. Am I against words of knowledge? No! There is truth to be discovered beyond Scripture: the apostle John affirms this when he says that Jesus did far more miracles than are recorded in his Gospel, and the apostle Paul talks about spiritual experiences in which he gained understanding. There is more to the truth than the Bible can convey, simply because the Bible is not the final word: Jesus alone is Truth, whom we are yet to know fully. Only through indwelling Jesus Christ, through personal obedience to his expectations of us, will we inhabit a truth that cannot end, because he is the beginning and the end; all things exist in him.

Rather, whatever revelation John, Paul, or any other New Testament writer received, it was always tested against the Scriptures of the day and was found to have the same authority to make God known and to transform the lives of people who lived them out. So there is a warning here—how much easier it is for someone else to tell me what God thinks of me than for me to have to spend time before God, being marinated in Scripture and acting obediently in relation to what it says! Instant guidance, instant revelation—no need for studying to show ourselves approved by God in order to handle the Word of truth correctly, when the Holy Spirit can bypass all that effort and download special news, information, and guidance directly to us, apart from the Christ, apart from the people of God, and apart from Scripture.

At this point, it might be helpful to articulate your own approach to Scripture and the kind of authority you think it has, as well as being able to describe the kind of relationship you have with this authority. For instance, while I do not agree with John Barton's more open-ended stress on the Bible as human rather than as a text that is also divinely inspired, it is interesting to note where he locates the authority of the Bible when he offers three perspectives on the matter:

- Scripture is authoritative as evidence. It provides us with the earliest data on Christian faith through the events it records, as well as providing evidence of the faith of Israel and of the early church.
- Scripture is authoritative as the source book of correct theology and doctrine.
- Scripture is authoritative as a classic of literature (where classic texts possess a certain authority, whether by Plato, Aristotle, Shakespeare, or Hawking).[24]

These are some ways in which we can understand Scripture's authority. You may well have others. At this point, then, pause to take time to answer the questions below especially in the light of what you have read.

Pause

- Why do you believe Scripture is authoritative?
- If you believe Scripture is authoritative, do you believe so because you have been told to, or for another reason? If the latter, what is that reason?
- What does the authority of Scripture look like in your life?

It should not surprise us that the authority Christians give to Scripture is problematic for moderns, postmoderns, and other contemporary Westerners. In various ways, our current culture subscribes to what might be called "the ugly ditch of history." This is manifested in two forms. First, there is the modernist assumption that it is not possible for us to go back to the past and gain any knowledge with certainty. Rather, there is an "ugly ditch" forever separating now from then. Thus, the eighteenth-century Enlightenment philosopher G. E. Lessing writes, "Accidental truths of history can never become the proof of necessary truths of reason," and he goes on to describe this reality as "the ugly broad ditch which I cannot get across, however often and however earnestly I have tried to make the leap. If anyone can help me over it, let him do it, I beg him, I adjure him. He will deserve a divine reward."[25]

Second, there is the more contemporary attitude that tends to express what C. S. Lewis calls "chronological snobbery," which Lewis describes as "uncritical acceptance of the intellectual climate common to our own age and the assumption that whatever has gone out of date is on that account discredited."[26] Here, the snobbery comes to the fore regarding ancient texts: put simply, why would any intelligent person give his or her life over to some ancient document written by people who have no connection with either our culture or ourselves today? Richard Hays captures what this means today when he makes the point that in

> postmodern culture the Bible has lost its place, and citizens in a pluralistic, secular culture have trouble knowing what to make of it. If they pay any attention to it at all, they treat it as a consumer product, one more therapeutic option for rootless selves engaged in an endless quest to invent and improve themselves. Not surprisingly, this approach does not yield a very satisfactory reading of the Bible, for the Bible is not about "self-help" but about *God's* action to rescue a lost and broken world.[27]

Of course, the problem here is that many of us do indeed read the Bible in this way. Instead, it is to be read solely as a means of getting to know God and his loving will as well as to know how to love God through our obedience, which, of course, is what the Bible defines as *love*. Think about it—what woman would date a man who only wanted to date her because it would be good for him—because it would be a way for him to become a better person? No—any person with healthy self-worth would not be attracted to such a narcissistic person. Apply this, now, to God and Scripture: How guilty are we of doing the same thing when we come to the text "for a blessing" or for "guidance" or even for "self-improvement" and not simply to know and love God and his will for our lives? The blessing, the guidance, and the self-improvement are all by-products, consequences that come about as a result of the relationship with God. When Scripture and the God of Scripture are the priority and passion, everything else grows in response.

Joel Green warns of an additional consequence of the "elevated" assumption that this chronological snobbery takes, one that ultimately concludes that "if all age is historically grounded, as has been increasingly recognized, then we moderns should not be governed in our own knowing by someone else's history (e.g., by the Christian tradition)."[28] However quaintly this thinking expresses itself in the name of political correctness, since one should not be seen to be arrogating oneself above another people group, the underlying message remains: no one in their right mind chooses to live by an ancient text.

In addition, there is also an underlying subtext—namely, that people in a free society who choose to live by an ancient text should be politely ignored at best, marginalized at worst. Green helpfully articulates a key characteristic of our contemporary world, the "hermeneutic of suspicion." We all have a "hermeneutic" in that all knowledge is in some way "interpreted" knowledge, and the dominant hermeneutic of our time is one governed by "suspicion" in that this kind of chronological snobbery is undergirded by a deeper "chronological skepticism" regarding the possibility of any kind of certainty. Thus, we have suspicion of an agenda, suspicion concerning a person's ulterior motives, suspicion of the God of Scripture, suspicion of any ancient text. Rather, we prefer to believe the anecdotal, one-dimensional, and usually biased information that we get on our phone or hear in the news, a one-sided monologue with very little opportunity for dialogue. All this, of course, is at odds with how human culture and thinking develop, how our legal and financial institutions operate.

However, I think it is important to point out the dangers of reading the Bible through the lens of an overly suspicious and critical mind. Walter Moberly helpfully identifies three problems with suspicious readings of Scripture. First, in assuming this approach to Scripture, the reader makes it impossible to indwell "the narrative world in its own right" and thus to know the reality about which the text speaks. And, as we have already discovered, unless a reader indwells a text, it is not possible to take its narrative seriously. Second, Moberly argues that this approach to Scripture lacks any meaningful appreciation of what it means to encounter God. I like the window he gives us on this: "It is one thing to criticize those who stress a narrowly defined personal piety at the expense of any critical understanding of, or engagement with, the social, economic, and political dimensions of institutional, not least religious life. It is another thing to undervalue the realities of personal encounter with the living God or dismiss its foundational nature for human existence." Last, such a suspicious positioning in relation to Scripture means that the reader loses a sense of how Scripture constantly recontextualizes its own texts for new historical situations.[29]

We can draw two conclusions from the above. First, let's not miss the significance of this "recontextualizing" dynamic that we discover within Scripture. It means that within the Bible itself, there is both an open-endedness and progression in understanding and a flexibility in divine communication, as it were. If this is the case, then, we should expect some kind of continuity between what Scripture declares and how the church lives it out. Second, if we think about it, we do not live as though events or observations from the past, whether recent or ancient, cannot be trusted. Rather, we accept them without thought and then build upon them. Consequently, we gain wisdom and develop culturally to the extent we are familiar with the past, are cognizant of other cultures, and are appreciative of previous answers to similar questions. It is all well and good to disparage the past; it is an altogether different matter to live as though it is irrelevant. Here's how C. S. Lewis establishes not only the relevance but also the need for this kind of disposition:

> Most of all we need intimate knowledge of the past. Not that the past has any magic about it, but because we cannot study the future, and yet need something to set against the present, to remind us that the basic assumptions have been quite different in different periods and that much which seems certain to the uneducated is merely temporary fashion. A man who has lived in many places is not likely to be deceived by the local errors of his native village. The scholar has lived in many times and is therefore in some degree immune from the cataract of nonsense that pours from the press and the microphone of his own age.[30]

Why Scripture Does What It Does

Set against our contemporary backdrop, Scripture offers a significant antidote to the nonsense Lewis describes, much of which we have to process daily on social media, in the tabloid press, in news feeds, in magazines, or on TV and radio. Scripture is able to critique and to challenge other worldviews:

- It can do so, first, because of its vitality in connecting us with other thinkers, different cultures, histories alternative to our own. As with the experience of the scholar above, Scripture has the ability to vaccinate us against other ideologies. Remember what we looked at in part 1? Scripture advances an altogether alternative worldview within which we live and out of which we critique others.

- Second, as we have seen earlier concerning "the-lived-in-ness" of Scripture, its reality is to be entered into, not merely explored, discussed, or objectified. We could put it this way: Scripture has a "more than" dimension. That is, what Scripture tells us cannot be reduced to mere data or information. Green interestingly comments on this aspect of Scripture as literature, drawing on Umberto Eco when he argues that "texts like those in Scripture are characterized by the invitation for readers 'to make work' together with the author so that texts might achieve a vitality that cannot be reduced to the cognitive domain. Rather, they are rendered meaningful in personal and communal performance."[31]

Can you see, then, that Scripture does not contain deposits of knowledge that we excavate at will, but rather invites our engagement in order that its truth can be unlocked and we can experience what it reveals to us? Donald Bloesch defines this as "revelationalism," which he describes as "the living God personally addressing us in the moment of decision."[32] Thus, Scripture demands of us a particular stance, what Bloesch calls "fideistic revelationalism"—where, as he puts it, "the decision of faith is as important as the fact of revelation in giving us certainty of the truth of faith." This stance he distinguishes from several other options: *revelational positivism* (revelation is true whether or not we experience its truth for ourselves), *presuppositionalism* (we start with certain givens in our thinking even though we cannot prove them), *foundationalism* (we start with strong but unprovable assumptions that are taken as completely true), *evidentialism* (we derive certainty from what is demonstrably true), and *coherentism* (we see proof of something in its unity with other beliefs).[33]

What this scriptural engagement means is best expressed in the words of Michael Polanyi: it is to be "indwelt"—it is "to be lived in."[34] Polanyi argues that we make new discoveries and acquire deeper knowledge only to the degree we are passionate about the process of knowing an object. It is this passion that drives the scientist to pursue her intuition that received wisdom on her subject is wrong. It is this passion that causes scientists to believe that they may have a better answer or solution—like Marie Curie, Sir Isaac Newton, or Albert Einstein, for example. Because of their passion, they are willing to be heretics regarding the accepted norm or truth and challenge it with an alternative. What Polanyi is pointing out to us is that all discoveries, especially the scientific ones, start out as acts of heresy to begin with. It is only the rebels who make new discoveries! The genesis of any new discovery, of a better answer, starts when the scientist suspends her belief concerning what is the accepted and acceptable and pursues an altogether different trajectory. To be so engaged is, as Polanyi puts it, to be driven by a deep conviction that "we know more than we can tell."[35]

What is so interesting and important is that this kind of scientific discovery really is no different from its theological counterpart. Like the theologian, the scientist seeks new knowledge as an act of faith. The difference between the scientist and the theologian is that the theologian's "heresy," relative to a secular materialist worldview, is to believe that what is seen, what can be touched, what can undergo empirical study is not the whole truth—perhaps not even anywhere near the truth. In this sense, then, theology is indeed a science, the queen of the sciences. We should not be duped, therefore, into thinking that science and theology are like oil and water, ice and fire—incompatible. Rather, while taking Bloesch's earlier point that theology is different from science,[36] we can agree with theologians like Wolfhart Pannenberg and Alister McGrath that there is indeed a commensurability, some sense of compatibility, between science and theology.[37] However, both the scientist and the theologian take a series of faith-seeking-understanding steps into the unknown, to go further and show, hopefully, that there is something more. Polanyi terms this kind of intuitive and passionate thinking "tacit knowledge." Here is how Polanyi describes the process:

> To hold such knowledge is an act deeply committed to the conviction that there is something there to be discovered. It is personal, in the sense of involving the personality of him who holds it, and also in the sense of being, as a rule, solitary; but there is no trace in it of self-indulgence. The discoverer is filled with a compelling sense of responsibility for the pursuit of a hidden truth, which demands his services for revealing it. His act of knowing exercises a personal judgement in relating evidence to an external reality, an aspect of which he is seeking to apprehend.[38]

The understanding we gain from this, in turn, becomes "personal knowledge." We can describe this "lived-in" character of Scripture in three ways that draw from the world of theater:

- It can be helpful if we understand the way God exercises his authority through the Bible by means of *narrative*. N. T. Wright takes us to the theater, as it were, and compares Scripture to the script of a play that tells its story through five *acts*. Think of the works of Euripides, William Shakespeare, Henrik Ibsen, Anton Chekhov, Tennessee Williams, Lorraine Hansberry, Agatha Christie, Harold Pinter. It is not the actor, nor even the playwright, who is the ultimate authority—it is the written and finished text of the play that holds this honor. The same is true of Scripture: it holds authority over the church (we who live out the text) and over its human authors (the divine Author is the one who inspires the text). And like a playscript, Scripture has its own acts, as it were. These are creation, fall, Israel, Jesus, and "act 5," in which the New Testament is the first scene and we go on to create the subsequent scenes as we participate in this final act ourselves.

- Green talks about the lived-in nature of Scripture in a similar vein to Wright when he describes Scripture as being there in order to be *performed*.[39] Again, this dynamic understanding of our relationship to Scripture invites us to engage personally with the text, to make it our own, but always as *under* the text, always being true to what the text says.

- Kevin Vanhoozer also draws from the world of theater when he describes the entire history of God's saving activity in his creation as a drama—in fact, a *theo*drama, *God's* drama. Like Wright, Vanhoozer identifies five acts, albeit slightly differently from Wright's five stages: creation, Israel, Jesus, church, and eschaton. The Bible, then, is the authoritative script of this drama, the drama of our being reconciled to God, a drama that must be performed—one that demands participation—in order to be lived out and experienced. I like the way Vanhoozer holds script and performance so closely when he says that "script and performance are equally necessary, though not equally authoritative. Biblical script without ecclesial performance is empty; ecclesial performance without biblical script is blind."[40]

I hope that you can grasp how this understanding of Scripture enables us to see the Bible as something that requires our participation to indwell it, to perform it, to discover its narrative world.[41] In so doing, we discover that Scripture really is alive and active and why it is able to have such a transformative impact on our lives (Heb. 4:12). Scripture is there to be performed, to be lived out not only in the theaters of our individual lives but also in the grand theater of the world, as church. We live—perform—in relation to this biblical text. In the same way that a playscript is authoritative in that it narrates and thus provides an authoritative and consistent flow for the actors to perform, or in the way that a ballet's dance notation is authoritative because it ensures dancers perform together consistently and flawlessly, or in the way that a soccer team's set pieces are authoritative in that they enable the entire team to work toward scoring a goal, so Scripture is authoritative for living authentically and fully both as person and as the church. The particular character of our performance, like any other, is hallmarked in terms of how obedient we are to the text: the actor follows the script, the musician the score, the dancer the notation, the soccer player executes or plays the set piece. Thus, Christians affirm that this "lived-in-ness" is "performed" most truly through the grammar and action of "obedience."[42] I think Craig Keener gets it completely right when he points out that "affirming God's Word as truth means submitting our lives to it more than it means the sorts of issues that Christian scholars *sometimes* divide over."[43] Thus, through

> submitting to Scripture
> indwelling Scripture
> obeying Scripture

the people of God find the grammar, vocabulary, direction, content, and benefits of their transforming faith in Jesus Christ. For this reason, therefore, we should understand and protect Scripture's proper place as the church's primary authority in its declaration to bring about human transformation at every level.[44]

Reading Scripture as Indwelling Scripture

I like the idea of "indwelling" as a metaphor for describing what Christians mean by "obedience." Can you see the way in which this approach liberates the notion of obedience from the cage of dos and don'ts, from the restrictions of rules and regulations, to a more dynamic understanding? Rather than a sense of having to "come under" a text, it is more a sense of being freed to engage with and participate in a story, what Bloesch describes as "glad acceptance of the message that saves and transforms."[45] This is particularly important in a culture where the dominant hermeneutic, as we have seen, is one of suspicion. In this culture, if the text is perceived as being something we are obliged to come under, then people will be loath to submit themselves willingly to the alien authority of a text, especially a strange and ancient text. Add to this a growing sense of relativism within Western culture, where there can be no authority except the authority that says that there can be no authority(!). It is clearly problematic to expect such obedience from our contemporaries. They rightly ask why they should obey the Bible rather than any other text, and they understandably question the right of anyone to claim that the Bible is the only source of truth about God, let alone about ourselves. Rather, because of the popular narratives of contemporary Western culture, they assume the premise of their secular worldview, that truth is a relative construct—relative to each historical or cultural context—and not an absolute, remaining the same regardless of historical era or cultural context. Put bluntly, it is all too arrogant a claim to make on truth to believe that its truest and fullest expression is to be found within the pages of the Christian Bible.

However, when our relationship to Scripture is defined in terms of indwelling, a very different posture can be taken and a more dynamic response elicited. Indeed, the notion of indwelling neutralizes any passive or blind assent and opens up possibilities for personal engagement, even play. Perhaps it is this that the psalmist has in mind when he exhorts us to "taste and see that the LORD is good," and then goes on almost to unpack a particular dramatic posture, "Blessed is the one who takes refuge in him" (Ps. 34:8). See how the text invites participation—we have to be active, intentional, hopeful—all of which are demonstrated in the act of going to God for security and safety in times of trouble. The idea of indwelling, then, invites active participation, or, as we have already seen from Umberto Eco, it requires the reader's engagement. The question, however, is, Which kind of engagement? As with any other text that we approach, this engagement itself is identified by the expectations we bring to it. These expectations help shape how we read the text. As Keener reminds us, "Expectations shape how we approach any text. . . . Expectations help shape our reading of Scripture."[46] When we come to the Bible, we inevitably bring our expectations, usually in the form of our theology, even when we are reading it with a view to quarrying answers to our questions.

Specific to Scripture, then, we read it expectantly—as the narrative, the storied record, of how Jesus and his God have acted redemptively—with future anticipation. This redemptive content that Scripture itself offers to us invites personal response, response that is expressed in faithful commitment to Jesus and the God he tells us is our Father. I like the way Katherine Sonderegger captures this dynamic relationality:

> Christians do not read the Bible in order to learn about God, though, of course it can be done in this fashion! Rather we read Holy Scripture in order to enter into the Divine Presence, to walk before Him, to draw near. This is the *dearness* of Scripture, its intimate charisma, its lovely familiarity. Christians do not understand or embrace or rest at ease with every last verse of Scripture; it remains a strange book, sometimes an alien and terrible one. But to hear the history and song and parable and law book of Holy Scripture is to come in the penumbra of a welcome Light, to touch a lovely garment, well-worn, and to love a token, a remnant and a sign, of the One who irresistibly calls us to Himself.[47]

Scripture as Revelation

The collective testimony of the people of God is that in the commitment of indwelling Scripture and living it out in faithful communal and individual obedience, the same people discover in the process that Scripture is the reliable site of God's own self-communication and revelation. And since this self-revelation is personal rather than abstractly detached from human social interaction, it follows that this self-disclosure is best understood in terms of "an unveiling, an act of disclosure, in which the human subject is an active participant rather than a passive observer."[48] What this means, in practice, is that the knowledge we gain from God's self-revelation in and through the life, death, resurrection, ascension, and glorification of Jesus Christ is not given as "data" but as personal communication that, in turn, elicits personal response. The communication has a purpose. For example, the communication you give to your bank is given so that you can open an account, get a credit card, take out a mortgage. The information given is in relation to the goal desired. It is usually also, within the context of a bank, either in person or online. Similarly, the information God reveals about himself is intentional; it is in order to achieve something. In addition, this information is given in a specific context—namely, our need of reconciliation with God, neighbor, and self, our need of wholeness, personal and communal. Therefore, there are some very important points to grasp about the divine self-revelation we have in Scripture:

- God discloses himself to us within the context of our own and the world's brokenness.
- God discloses himself to us solely with the intention that we be reconciled to him.
- God always self-discloses within the spectrum of brokenness and wholeness, alienation and reconciliation.

Pause

- What do you do with any knowledge you discover about God?
- Do you treat it like fact (like applying to the bank for a loan) or do you treat it like personal communication (such as with friends, or lovers, or family)?
- What effect does knowledge of God have on your day-to-day life?

We can see, then, that an evangelical theological method engages with Scripture on several levels. On the one hand, it engages our spirit in that it elicits from us a personal commitment and brings about a new relationship, a new vitality. On the other, it engages our mind in that it causes us to reflect personally on what we discover about God, as well as about ourselves, our neighbor, and our world. As with what we learned earlier about theological habits, we can say also that we need to develop habits in relation to Scripture, that "we come to know and recognize and to discern," Peter Leithart points out, "through ritualized action" and that through these rituals—which for many are practiced during a daily disciplined time set apart to read, think about, and pray through parts of Scripture—we discover the reliability of Scripture.[49] Last, an evangelical theological method engages our wills in that it only "kicks in" to the degree we are obedient and faithful. After all, if we remind ourselves of the distinction made in part 1 about ordinary and academic theologies and their "postures," we can go on to develop this and say that Scripture, too, demands a particular posture—namely, faith. Why? For three significant reasons:

- To access the narrative world of Scripture, we have to believe and trust in certain things that are both unseen—as Paul reminds us in 2 Corinthians 4—and also only hoped for, with unshakable certainty in their fulfillment.
- The truth that Scripture talks about cannot be likened to the content of a folder: we can't simply double-click on the text, as it were, and expect its content to appear crystal clear and ready for understanding. Faith in the divine Author as well as in the truth and veracity of the text is required. It is by faith that we believe the text. It is with faith that we span the hiatus between what the text says and when the text delivers.
- Since Scripture discloses the gospel, the good news about Jesus Christ and God's kingdom, the most natural response to Scripture is one that resonates with a similar gospel disposition.

When we combine all these reasons, we discover that what we have here, as a result, are all the components required to establish personal communication and thus personal relationship. There is a speaker, there are words, there is an invitation to engage the good news contained in these words, and, last, there is the necessity to trust the words in living faithfully and obediently to what they say in the certainty that they will indeed come to pass. All that is required to bring about personal relationship is present. One thing, however, is missing, to which we now turn.

Scripture as a Living Text

Christians believe that Scripture is more than the sum total of its individual historical parts. As we have already noted, in it is contained the grand narrative of God's relationship with his creation in general and his covenant people in particular, culminating in the life, death, resurrection, ascension, and glorification of Jesus Christ. It is an ongoing divine-human narrative. It is a *living* text. For any words to exist, let alone be seen to be living—for any set of words to have verve and transformative power—there must be breath to breathe the words into existence as well as to bring them to life each time they are spoken. It is not surprising, then, that the Bible talks of the Spirit of God in terms of "breath."[50]

If the Bible were not in this sense a living text, there would be little defense against the charge we noted earlier: that those who put their trust in such an ancient text are credulous. What this means for Christians is that the sixty-six books of the Bible are not embarrassing ancient ruminations of antiquated religious cultures and are not the product of human religious imagination. Rather, Scripture is the product of the following:

- The authors and the wider people of God have encountered and experienced the God of Israel—the Father of Jesus Christ—and Jesus Christ himself, and they have reflected on these encounters and experiences and written down eyewitness accounts of them.

- These encounters took place in historical time and are, therefore, verifiable by the same criteria that enable us to verify other historical data—for example, regarding Julius Caesar, Boadicea, Sitting Bull, Robert the Bruce, Saint Francis of Assisi, Abraham Lincoln, Queen Nefertiti, Anne Frank, and others; the list is endless, the historical method the same.

- Millions of people continue to give their testimony, which is preserved through narrative tradition—oral and written—and reveals how they have experienced the transformative vitality of God's covenant faithfulness and the power of the gospel, about which Scripture attests, in their own lives and communities.

- The same power narrated in Scripture continues to transform our lives today—the lives of those who indwell Scripture through faithful commitment. As a result, our lives bear witness to the vigor of both God and Jesus: a power, energy, a liveliness, a spirit—Holy Spirit—who both brings about our own personal transformation and presences God to us with a sense of get-up-and-go!

Scripture, therefore, not only informs Christians but also empowers them to hear what the Spirit of God is saying to the church. Theology, in this dynamic, assists in this process by helping us not only to understand better but also to convey the message of Scripture better. Theology achieves this best to the degree that we are faithful indwellers of Scripture who consistently and faithfully "perform" Scripture, in all its cross-cultural complexities. We are to read Scripture through the interpretive lens, the hermeneutic, of faith and praxis, belief and application. This, of course, involves a kind of "regulating circle"—that is, Scripture requires subsequent interpretive tools such as creeds, confessions, and doctrines, all of which are determined in their veracity by Scripture. We will look at these in more detail when we turn to tradition in our next chapter, but at this point it is important to understand the regulating role that Scripture should play in all our theology.

For most Protestants, including evangelicals, this regulatory role understands Scripture as being the *norming norm*—that is, the theological standard by which everything else is regulated. It is the standard, the norm, by which everything else is determined (the *norma normans*, or "norming norm") and as such is never determined by anything else (the *norma normata*, or "normed norm"). Roger Olson puts it this way: "Scripture is our norming norm and tradition is our normed norm and . . . in a doctrinal controversy Scripture alone has absolute veto power while The Great Tradition (orthodox doctrine) has a vote but not a veto."[51] Consequently, Orthodox theological method has much to offer us regarding how to go about our theology, being "the conscious memory and the life-experience of the historic church" and that it is here, in Scripture, "that the fullness of the revelation, in all its richness and abundant dimensions, dwells."[52] What I like about this understanding is that it resonates with a thoroughly evangelical appreciation of Scripture. Scripture is the "mindset" of the living church. If this is the case, then we can agree that there is a *holy tradition* within a specifically evangelical theological method that prioritizes Scripture and is centered in the gospel of Jesus Christ and informs us of Jesus Christ in terms of both who he is and what he achieves for us.

We will look at what this tradition might be and how it informs our theological method in the next chapter. For now, I think it is possible to describe the manner in which evangelical theology prioritizes Scripture by saying that for evangelical theology, Scripture is a *rule of faith*. "Rule of faith" is the term used for an authority that sets the bar on what is authoritative, the gold standard by which everything else is determined. Of course, this phrase is historically applied to what is called the "apostolic tradition" or to specific creeds of the early church. Interestingly, one of the earliest theologians in the late first century, Clement, gives a clear and simple definition of the apostolic tradition in his epistle to the Corinthians:

> The Apostles received the Gospel for us from the Lord Jesus Christ; Jesus Christ was sent forth from God. So then Christ is from God, and the Apostles are from Christ. Both therefore came of the will of God in the appointed order. Having therefore received a charge, and having been fully assured through the

resurrection of our Lord Jesus Christ and confirmed in the word of God with full assurance of the Holy Ghost, they went forth with the glad tidings that the kingdom of God should come. So preaching everywhere in country and town, they appointed their firstfruits, when they had proved them by the Spirit, to be bishops.[53]

What is so interesting here is that the priority and authority evangelicals give to the gospel and Scripture resonates with Clement's understanding of apostolic tradition. That is, the authority of the apostolic tradition is located in Scripture and particularly in the gospel given by Christ to his apostles. An evangelical theological method, too, is located in Scripture. This distinguishes it from a Roman Catholic or Orthodox understanding of the rule of faith. We have already noted that all the major and most ancient of Christian expressions give priority to Scripture. However, both the Orthodox and the Roman Catholic churches believe that tradition, especially that of the early creeds, has a higher priority than that given to it in an evangelical theology, and so those other churches call tradition a rule of faith and distinguish it as such from Scripture. Indeed, we would expect a more Protestant rule of faith to focus only on Scripture: Scripture interprets Scripture. Thus, what I want to propose is that while an evangelical theological method must, as we will see next, give place to the historic and contemporary traditions of the universal church, it will be Scripture alone that has priority; Scripture alone is the gold standard for all Christian belief. Therefore, it is appropriate to designate Scripture as a specifically evangelical rule of faith.

Concluding Remarks

We have covered much ground in this chapter, looking at the foundational nature of Scripture—what it is, why it has authority, and how that authority functions. Fundamental to any Christian theological method is the central place given to Scripture. It acts as our norming norm, our rule of faith, the go-to for every theological and practical question regarding our faith. We have seen, too, that in a specifically evangelical theological method Scripture is not some kind of tool we pick up when the occasion demands but is, rather, a strange world that we are called to live in faithfully and obediently. It is not extrinsic to the task of theology. Quite the opposite. It is the most intrinsic aspect of an evangelical theological method simply because we constitute a social construct—church—whose authority is Scripture. The theologian, therefore, whether ordinary or academic, is someone who not only reads Scripture but also indwells Scripture and is faithfully obedient to Scripture.

The theologian is also someone who lives out all three in company, not in isolation: as a body politic, church, and not as an autonomous individual. What this means, of course, is that the theologian reads Scripture as truth—truth that at times awaits its consummation—but truth all the same. In this way, the strange new world of the Bible continues to seep into and transform the familiar but tired world of our own stories.

Pause

Before you begin reading the next chapter, I suggest that you summarize in your own words your understanding of the role Scripture should have in your theological method. Once you have identified this role, it would be good then to identify its strengths and weaknesses. Then set some goals on how you might build on your strengths as well as how you can improve on the weaknesses. Finally, share these goals with someone to whom you give permission to check up on you and see how well you are achieving your goals. Remember—a medical student is accountable to her tutor for how familiar she is with the human body. The theologian is no different regarding the human soul and the means by which this is healed, Scripture!

SUGGESTED READING

Castelo, Daniel, and Robert W. Wall. *The Marks of Scripture: Rethinking the Nature of the Bible*. Grand Rapids: Baker Academic, 2018.

Franke, John R. *The Character of Theology: An Introduction to Its Nature, Task, and Purpose*. Grand Rapids: Baker Academic, 2005.

Goldingay, John. *Models for Scripture*. Grand Rapids: Eerdmans, 1994.

Gorman, Michael J., ed. *Scripture and Its Interpretation: A Global, Ecumenical Introduction to the Bible*. Grand Rapids: Baker Academic, 2017.

Gunton, Colin E. "The Bible (2 Timothy 3.16)." In *Theology through Preaching*, 23–28. Edinburgh: T&T Clark, 2001.

Lamb, William. *Scripture: A Guide for the Perplexed*. London: Bloomsbury T&T Clark, 2013.

Morrison, John Douglas. *Has God Said? Scripture, the Word of God, and the Crisis of Theological Authority*. Eugene, OR: Pickwick, 2006.

Peckham, John C. *Canonical Theology: The Biblical Canon*, Sola Scriptura, *and Theological Method*. Grand Rapids: Eerdmans, 2016.

Stanglin, Keith D. *The Letter and Spirit of Biblical Interpretation: From the Early Church to Modern Practice*. Grand Rapids: Baker Academic, 2018.

Vanhoozer, Kevin J., and Daniel J. Treier. *Theology and the Mirror of Scripture: A Mere Evangelical Account*. Downers Grove, IL: IVP Academic, 2015.

Webster, John. *Holy Scripture: A Dogmatic Sketch*. Cambridge: Cambridge University Press, 2003.

Wright, N. T. *Scripture and the Authority of God: How to Read the Bible Today*. London: SPCK, 2011.

six

Tradition

Tradition Defined

There is a select group of theological terms that have what we might call the "Marmite effect"—Marmite being a particularly salty, tar-like British yeast product with its own very distinct and powerful flavor that has the ability to polarize people's opinions.[1] "Tradition" is one such word. For some, it is a theological shibboleth,[2] a term that polarizes people: some hold it to be an essential aspect of their faith in terms of both content and how it is expressed. Others view it as an unnecessary and unhelpful restriction, one that stifles innovation by tying the contemporary church to the past: after all, if it is not in the Bible, why believe it? Of course, with this viewpoint comes the counterargument that to hold such a position is nothing short of what C. S. Lewis calls "chronological snobbery." In addition to these various views, the word itself means different things to different people, thus creating confusion and misunderstanding. At this point, then, it may be beneficial to pause for a moment in order to reflect on what the word "tradition" means for you.

> ### Pause
> - What do you mean when you use the word "tradition"?
> - Identify various examples of "tradition" in your own church and theological tradition.

When theologians talk about "tradition," they are referring to a word that acts rather like an icon folder on your laptop or desktop—double-click it, and what looks like a single entity reveals much more. In fact, the folder can be as complex as its designer needs it to be. Similarly, when we talk about tradition, we are referring to something that is rich both in meaning and in content, something that has been handed down from the past with the purpose of safeguarding the present. On the one hand, its Latin origins tell us that *traditio* is a term that means "handing down" or "handing over," and, on the other, the New Testament Greek words that refer to the handing over of tradition—the noun *paradosis* and the corresponding verb *paradidōmi*—convey a sense of ritual and of a body of precepts as well as other things that we mean by tradition. Tradition, thus, serves as the "icon folder" that holds together some kind of collective wisdom esteemed by the people of God, be it in word or in practice. However, just in case the impression has been given that tradition is some kind of *static* construct that never changes, something that you have to dust off before using, we should also note the equally important point that tradition is also *dynamic*—an ever-present reality, having a life of its own that stretches from Scripture to the week's Sunday church service.[3]

All this may sound rather odd to an evangelical ear. After all, evangelicalism, on the whole, is known more for its contemporaneity, its ability to make the gospel relevant to each contemporary context, and not for its overt upholding of church tradition. Alister McGrath identifies three reasons. Evangelicalism, he says, typically

- understands tradition as a human construction in opposition to Scripture;
- perceives tradition as "traditionalism"—as dead formality;
- is suspicious of patristic writers, who do not share the commonsense values of the Enlightenment or a propositionalist view of revelation.[4]

The oft-quoted distinction that Jaroslav Pelikan makes between tradition, on the one hand, and traditionalism, on the other, is worth repeating at this point since it helps convey the dynamic in tradition that distinguishes it from traditionalism:

> Tradition is the living faith of the dead; traditionalism is the dead faith of the living. Tradition lives in conversation with the past, while remembering where we are and when we are and that it is we who have to decide. Traditionalism supposes that nothing should ever be done for the first time, so all that is needed to solve any problem is to arrive at the supposedly unanimous testimony of this homogenized tradition.[5]

Thought of in this way, therefore, the term "tradition" can be seen as holding together a wide range of meaning and intention. Perhaps this is why Greek has both a noun meaning "tradition" and a verb meaning "to pass on a tradition." On the one hand, as a noun, "tradition" refers to a very specific set of data and practice that function in a regulatory manner. That is, this tradition has been identified by the church as a means of making sure correct belief is maintained. On the other hand, "tradition" can also refer to an action, that of passing on that set of data and practice; thus tradition plays an ongoing, dynamic—almost living—role in the present. As with a worldview, it is not a question of whether we have a tradition or not—we always do, even if we cannot articulate it. So the question is never "*Does* tradition play a role in your theology?" but rather, "*Which* tradition controls your theology?" as well as "*How* does this tradition control your theology?" Admittedly, it may well come across as sounding somewhat arrogant or presumptuous to assume tradition operates in this way, especially if our churchmanship or denominational allegiance is Free Church (that is, not affiliated to any state or historic church). However, in this chapter I want to explore a number of points germane to the place tradition should play in an evangelical theological method:

- First, the biblical witness itself attests to the fact that the biblical writers were aware of tradition as a constructive entity, both as a corpus of belief to be passed down the generations and as the ongoing and developing dynamic of authority.
- Second, tradition is neither ad hoc nor extemporaneous. Rather, there are very specific criteria—we might even describe them as rules or regulations—for safeguarding the content of tradition and how it is to be used, and these rules or criteria are broken at one's peril. They have something to say to us today in terms both of encouragement and of challenge.
- Third, the task of faithful believing—theology—requires both awareness of and familiarity with what we call "the Great Tradition" as well as understanding its relation to Scripture. While the content of this particular tradition may well be unfamiliar to many, contemporary evangelical theologians should be aware of its importance in maintaining healthy theology and, as a consequence, the life and vibrancy of the local church.
- Fourth, it should not be very surprising that when we refer to tradition we connect with a complex, not a simple, reality that begins, as we will see, in Scripture and continues over two millennia. Tradition is primarily written—whether as creed, doctrine, book, article, or tweet. However, it can also be spoken, as in liturgy; sung, as in liturgy, hymn,

or contemporary song;[6] painted, as with an icon;[7] used in architecture, as in the great cathedrals of Europe;[8] or performed.[9]

- Fifth, when differences in biblical interpretation occur, as they do, tradition can act as a wider framework of reference.[10] In so doing, tradition not only has a constructive role but can act in a mediatorial one too: it unites our various denominational and theological differences.

- Last, tradition plays a hermeneutical role, of which every theologian should be aware. We all have a tradition of sorts, whether it is explicit or implicit, and whether we can consciously articulate it or not. As a result, our own tradition or traditions influence how we read Scripture.

At the heart of all the various ways in which tradition functions in our theology, the basic assertion is that our tradition is the means by which something of theological importance is being passed on from one point of reference to another, from one person to another, from one generation to another. Of course, if you think about it, this kind of communication is fraught with potential difficulties, especially if it is not itself regulated in some way. Anyone who has played the party game known as Telephone or Chinese Whispers[11] will know just how easy it is to mishear, mistake, and thus miscommunicate what is being said. What makes this game so hilarious at times are the bizarre and often unrecognizable variations that occur at the final "whisper." It would appear, therefore, that very clear guidelines, checks, and procedures are required if we are to preserve the original meaning throughout the period during which our tradition is handed down—however brief that period is, as in a party game, or however long, as in cultural, historical, or religious narratives. In Scripture's case, this period of transmission was in some instances considerable before the spoken tradition being passed down was put in written form. To the contemporary mind, the very idea of a tradition being passed on solely by word of mouth spanning a long period of time could only mean one thing: that mistakes were made frequently. However, as we will note, this is not necessarily the case. Cultures that preserve their traditions by memorization use clearly regulated forms of communication to avoid errors happening in the process. This being the case, as we will see below, the manner in which tradition came to be passed down from one generation or period to another was never the prerogative of the hoi polloi. Rather, only the guardians of the tradition—those who had possession of the tradition itself and who were skilled in the ways by which it could be communicated safely—held this right. That is, very clear regulatory procedures were maintained in the process of passing on a tradition.

What can we say, then, at this point about tradition? First, it bears repeating that every one of us is involved in the dynamic of engaging with tradition, whether we are aware of it or not. We are dipping in and out of tradition every time we engage a body of knowledge from the past that we consider to be authoritative in some way, whether it be small or large, oral or written, narrative or creed, doctrine or story, mental or physical, sung or spoken. Second, whether we can articulate it or not, we engage with our own traditions according to certain rules. Some we follow explicitly—it is unlikely that we give the Apocrypha the same degree of authority as we do the Protestant Bible. Some are more implicit, such as the frequency of taking Communion or the Lord's Supper. Christians celebrate regularly—whether that be daily (as do some high-church Episcopalians, Anglicans, and Roman Catholics), weekly (Plymouth Brethren—for example, at their weekly Lord's Supper), monthly (every third Sunday of the month for Baptists), quarterly (as do some Presbyterians), or only annually (the Free Church of Scotland).

Pause

Another consciousness-raising activity—there are no right or wrong answers here! This is an opportunity to stop, reflect, and become aware of your own traditions.

- What traditions can you see operating in your church?
- How are they regulated?
- What traditions do *you* keep?
- Why?

Tradition in Scripture

We now turn our attention to how tradition operates within Scripture itself. To begin with, let's remind ourselves that the content of the Bible did not fall out of the sky. Neither was it the product of divine dictation. Rather, what we read on the pages of the Bible finds its genesis in some historical event. This event may be that of an individual's encounter with the living God, an encounter that has profound social consequences (we see this most clearly concerning the various Old Testament patriarchs—for instance, the call of Moses in Exod. 2:11–3:22 and the call of Abraham in Gen. 11:27–12:20). Equally, it can be a social event of the magnitude of the Hebrews' divinely executed exit from Egypt (Exod. 2:23–14:31). Either way, it is a historical event that is pregnant not only with human experience but also with divine significance. The divine-human nature of this experience, in turn, is such that it requires some kind of reflection for it to be understood. This reflection is embedded eventually in a text or some form of communication, which, in turn, needs socially agreed-on structures that safeguard both its content and its interpretation,[12] all of which takes place over a long time.[13]

Therefore, the question of the integrity and reliability of tradition is important. We get a hint of this in the injunction of Deuteronomy 32:7, "Remember the days of old; consider the generations long past. Ask your father and he will tell you, your elders, and they will explain to you." Here there is both content (the days of old) and form (go to your elders). Something of great importance from the past continued to affect and influence life in the Hebrew present, a tradition of such magnitude that it informed every aspect of Jewish identity and life. We see its importance in a late Old Testament book, Ezekiel, where we read: "I will bring you into the wilderness of the nations and there, face to face, I will execute judgment upon you. As I judged your ancestors in the wilderness of the land of Egypt, so I will judge you, declares the Sovereign Lord. I will take note of you as you pass under my rod, and I will bring you into the bond [tradition] of the covenant" (Ezek. 20:35–37). What is being referred to here is the ancient covenant that God made with Abraham. It was the various covenants God made with Israel that encoded their most basic and fundamental traditions. In this sense, it is not unnecessarily unusual that the actual word "tradition" occurs only once in the entire Old Testament: the living tradition that was to be handed down, taught, believed, and practiced was encoded in this covenantal documentation. We will see below how certain "rules" are in place regarding this great tradition.

The Prodigal Son

It is when we turn to the New Testament, however, that we are able more easily to identify various ways in which tradition operated both as noun (a content to be passed on) and as verb (the manner by which it is passed on). Admittedly, the socially constructed manner in which tradition developed within what was a predominantly oral culture is lost on us today. Therefore, to see more clearly how tradition may well have developed in relation to the teaching of Jesus Christ himself, let's take one of Jesus's best-known parables, popularly known as the parable of the prodigal (or lost) son, in Luke 15:11–32, and use it as an example.

> Jesus continued: "There was a man who had two sons. The younger one said to his father, 'Father, give me my share of the estate.' So he divided his property between them. Not long after that, the younger son got together all he had, set off for a distant country and there squandered his wealth in wild living. After he had spent everything, there was a severe famine in that whole country, and

he began to be in need. So he went and hired himself out to a citizen of that country, who sent him to his fields to feed pigs. He longed to fill his stomach with the pods that the pigs were eating, but no one gave him anything. When he came to his senses, he said, 'How many of my father's hired servants have food to spare, and here I am starving to death! I will set out and go back to my father and say to him: Father, I have sinned against heaven and against you. I am no longer worthy to be called your son; make me like one of your hired servants.' So he got up and went to his father. But while he was still a long way off, his father saw him and was filled with compassion for him; he ran to his son, threw his arms around him and kissed him. The son said to him, 'Father, I have sinned against heaven and against you. I am no longer worthy to be called your son.' But the father said to his servants, 'Quick! Bring the best robe and put it on him. Put a ring on his finger and sandals on his feet. Bring the fattened calf and kill it. Let's have a feast and celebrate. For this son of mine was dead and is alive again; he was lost and is found.' So they began to celebrate. Meanwhile, the older son was in the field. When he came near the house, he heard music and dancing. So he called one of the servants and asked him what was going on. 'Your brother has come,' he replied, 'and your father has killed the fattened calf because he has him back safe and sound.' The older brother became angry and refused to go in. So his father went out and pleaded with him. But he answered his father, 'Look! All these years I've been slaving for you and never disobeyed your orders. Yet you never gave me even a young goat so I could celebrate with my friends. But when this son of yours who has squandered your property with prostitutes comes home, you kill the fattened calf for him!' 'My son,' the father said, 'you are always with me, and everything I have is yours. But we had to celebrate and be glad, because this brother of yours was dead and is alive again; he was lost and is found.'"

This parable is a great example of the living nature of tradition, both in how we understand a text—remember, theology is exegesis—and also in how a tradition maintains the integrity of a text, as well as how the intended meaning of the parable can subsequently be lost. Kenneth Bailey highlights aspects of tradition that operated at the time of Jesus and that continue to do so up to the present.[14] The first has to do with how the text comes to us. If we think back on what we discovered about Chinese Whispers or Telephone, then the most obvious question we want to ask is how what Jesus taught came to be written down with any degree of proximity to what was originally heard. How could his teaching be passed on without being corrupted, however unintentionally, along the way? After all, we are referring to a time when there were no newspapers, no internet, no smartphone recordings—only memory and speech. What I appreciate so much about Bailey's attention to this parable is that he situates the parable in its own cultural setting and in so doing offers us a window into the precise manner in which the Gospel parables and stories came to us as they did. And so Bailey introduces us to the well-honed social mores of the Near Eastern Palestinian oral culture, where the narratives and stories that held the collective identity of a village, a family, a tribe, even a nation, were recorded in human memory and retold by human speech.

First, there is how the text comes to us intact and with integrity. Here we confront the relationship between the how and the what of communication, between the appropriate form—structure or medium—necessary if the content is to be communicated effectively. Toward the end of the last century, Neil Postman appositely wrote, in an almost prophetic sense, concerning the paucity of knowledge in Western culture. Postman identifies the predominant contemporary form or medium of communication as being television—a medium through which Western culture is literally "amusing itself to death," and he claims that, as a form of communication, television is incapable of communicating content with any depth. What I find so interesting about Postman is his basic thesis: not only does content depend on an appropriate *form*—or medium—for it to be communicated effectively; the form taken will also determine the kind of *content*—knowledge—we can acquire. The medium really is the message! Postman's insights have significance in relation to what we are discussing about tradition. What is required, if Postman's insights are correct, is a proper medium to carry the spoken words.[15]

This is where Bailey helps us. Remember, when we engage the world of the Gospels, we enter into the strange and alien world of an honor-shame, oral culture where the family, or more likely the village, would informally gather in the evening for the *haflat samar*, a storytelling gathering around the campfire—the *medium*—where the stories that carried their history, their values, their identity—the *content*—would be retold. The way in which this was done—the medium—was of equal importance. First, the telling of the story was controlled in two ways: on the one hand, and most importantly, by authority figures with social standing and, on the other, by the seated listeners who exercised control through group rules that preserved how the tradition could be told. Second, this storytelling privilege took place within a culture where honor and shame were formidable social constructs as well as deterrents. There was honor in telling the story correctly. Forget who has the biggest house or the most sheep; the ultimate social status was to be a person of honor—in this case, someone who could retell a story correctly. Conversely, no one wanted to be shamed in front of their kith and kin. Therefore, there was a profoundly strong deterrent against narrating wrongly—the entire family, clan, or village called you out and shamed you! Only those who have experienced profound embarrassment or shame know the power of such a social and interpersonal construct. It can be quite devastating and humiliating. On the other hand, we all know how good it feels and the energy that is created, when we do something that gains the respect of those important to us. In this way, parables like that of the prodigal son were told repeatedly and correctly, reinforcing a theological point that was intrinsic to the new Christian communities' identity.

Bailey describes this process as an *informal controlled oral tradition* at work, one that continues to this day in the Middle East.[16] By means of this method the entire village is involved in preserving its store of tradition and, in doing so, avoids the equivalent to what we call today "fake news." On the one hand, it is informal in that there is no teacher or tutor, only an informed elder who knows the story. On the other, it is controlled through various levels of flexibility that ensure the integrity of the story. Bailey identifies three levels:

- No flexibility—psalms and proverbs that cannot be changed without incurring shame.
- Some flexibility—parables and recollections. Here there is a core that is to be passed on and that does not change. However, certain slight embellishments can be added, such as emotion, for effect.
- Total flexibility—jokes, local news, basically anything that is irrelevant to the village's identity.[17]

What we have here is a complex social construction for preserving the stories that narrated the history and identity of a particular family, village, or clan. It was only when the Romans destroyed Jerusalem in AD 70, with all the social upheaval this entailed, that the *haflat samar* was destroyed and the informal controlled oral tradition was jeopardized. As a result, what had previously been passed down orally was now written down.[18] And, of course, by this time, while different communities told the same stories, the way in which they were told would not necessarily be identical, because some stories could be embellished by the narrator to make a point relevant to the particular community, while others had no flexibility in transmission and thus were passed on with much more control.

I want to highlight three important points here before applying them to the parable of the prodigal son. First, what Jesus taught was safeguarded by the specific way in which it was subsequently passed on within the earliest Christian communities. The significance of this very specific way of doing things was that it safeguarded against the inevitable negative consequences of corruption were this not in place, as we will see later. Second, a central place was given to a specific authority figure whose role it was to preserve the tradition not only by maintaining the tradition's integrity for the community but also by maintaining the community's integrity in mediating the stories to subsequent members, thus safeguarding their wider identity. Last, the tradition was made up of distinct data that could not be altered and that separated it from other traditions. For instance, Richard Bauckham argues that we have the Gospels today because the oral Jesus tradition that preceded them was passed on for its own sake and was not absorbed into any other traditions. The same can be said about Paul's experience: "The mere fact that Paul speaks of a formal process of handing on the Jesus tradition (1 Cor. 11:23) requires us to support that it had an existence in its own right and was transmitted as such."[19]

Important points to remember:

- The tradition consists of an unchangeable core.
- There needs to be an authority figure whose authority is recognized by the community and who thus safeguards the integrity of the tradition's narrative.
- There is an intended meaning to the tradition.

What this means, in relation to the *content* of Jesus's parable, is that the message of the parable is intentional and very clear. This message conveyed something intrinsic to the community's identity in terms of what it means to be accepted by God the Father, whatever one's history, and thus the parable related to the community something about God the Father's character. We can also see that the parable has its own DNA, as it were, that is altered only at significant cost to the original story. In addition to this, the *form* by which the parable is handed down, as shown in the conditions of the original setting of the *haflat samar*, suggests that the tradition is to be passed on through an authority figure who has the skill to safeguard its transmission and whom the community respects and has confidence in, so that it trusts him to do so.

This safeguarding role is as important today as it was then, especially because of our contemporary unregulated hyperinformation technologies, which allow for unprecedented amounts of teaching that is often disconnected from the past, unregulated, and not accountable to any greater authority. I suggest that it is the guild of theologians—the theologically trained and accountable, whether ordinary or academic—who are best positioned today to fulfill this role. And last, the context within which tradition is passed on should always be the community of faith itself—in our case, within the context of the wider church, whose identity is formed by such traditions and which therefore has a vested interest in keeping its traditions living and dynamic. In this sense, then, I also suggest that the traditional or "normal" ways by which we hand on our traditions—for example, someone at the front of church communicating information to passive recipients—are inadequate to this task. Rather, there should always be some form of ebb and flow within the community that ensures accountability—safeguards against any notion that a single personality or leadership group has sole access to the traditions that constitute the wider group's beliefs and therefore its identity. It is only this kind of ebb and flow between the guardians of tradition and those to whom these traditions are being passed on that safeguards against eventual manipulation and error.

When we turn to the present, it is rather obvious that many contemporary evangelical churches generally do not operate in this way. This omission has resulted in diminishing the role of tradition both in terms of its content and in terms of how it is regulated. A quick look at the parable of the prodigal son suffices in providing us with an apt example. Traditional interpretations of this parable have usually taken the shape of interpreting the core story as that of a selfish son who squanders his inheritance to such an extent that he is reduced not only to feeding pigs but to eyeing what they eat, due to hunger. Of course, it is only at this low point that he comes to his senses, repents, and decides to return to his father, who, on seeing him, rushes to him in joy and throws a big party to celebrate. Remember, theology is primarily and supremely exegesis of the biblical text. So this interpretation of the parable will result in a specific theological understanding derived from the text. In this case, the message will be that it is only when we get to the very end of ourselves that we are able to embrace the gospel in our wretched situation. Such an understanding will then determine what we emphasize when we present the gospel, and it well explains why so much evangelism may be described as "crisis" evangelism, which turns on demonstrating the utter hopelessness of our case in order to bring about a much-indebted response.

However, this is not the parable the original hearers would have heard. Rather, what Bailey so helpfully points out is the cultural framework that would be part of the community's understanding of such a parable—much of which is lost on us today.

- To ask for your inheritance before your father's death would be most dishonoring and tantamount to wishing that he were dead.
- Since this is clearly a wealthy landowner father whose house and land would dominate the village, the son's actions would not go unnoticed by the locals. They would interpret it, rightly, as a highly dishonoring act and would know that their task was to protect the father's reputation were the son ever to return.
- The son does not repent at the pig sty. He is far too calculating. Clearly, he does not realize the extent to which he has dishonored his father.

Instead, he comes up with the ridiculous notion that by returning home and working as a servant he can pay back his inheritance.

- News of the son's return would inevitably precede his arriving at his village—this being the potential mother of all showdowns. Villagers would know their responsibility in such a situation: it was to prevent the son from getting anywhere near his father's house and thus adding insult to injury. Consequently, every piece of rotting vegetation, in fact, rotting anything, along with any available "produce," would be thrown at the lad as he tried to make his way home. Even if he managed to evade their aim in stopping him, at least they would have thoroughly shamed and completely humiliated him.

- The father, of course, knows what is in store for his son and the inevitable outcome. His is not the only son who has shamed his family and tried to come home. It is at this point that we arrive at the central scene of the parable, the nonnegotiable point of the tradition: to save his son from unmitigated shame, the father takes the shame onto himself. In a culture where the older you got the slower you walked, in running to the son and accepting him, the father shamed himself, first, in accepting the son and, second, in running to the son and, in doing so, probably also exposing rather more than was socially acceptable.

- It is only when the son sees how the father takes his shame on himself that he "gets it," and in the face of his father's love he realizes his true state and truly changes his agenda.

- It turns out that the other son is equally lost since he no more understands who his father really is than does his younger brother.

It would appear, then, that this is not so much a parable about a prodigal son as it is a parable about two lost sons. More probably and most emphatically, it is a narrative intended to communicate what God the Father's love, grace, and forgiveness look like. In turn, it is also a story that encapsulates beautifully what the community believes about God—its theology—as well as its understanding of the nature of true forgiveness. As such, the parable communicates a very particular tradition, one that focuses not so much on what human repentance looks like but, much more gloriously, on what God the Father's love, grace, and mercy look like, and ultimately, therefore, what the gospel that forms the people of God looks like.

The importance of this example is what it tells us about not only how traditions operated in the earliest church but also what can happen when a tradition is not regulated. Of course, this is problematic in today's Western church, where so many of us are influenced by the ideology of the Enlightenment and of modernity, which advocates the supremacy of progress. This has had devastating implications on how contemporary Christians view tradition, especially since the pressure today is to prioritize "the new" and "the innovative" over the past and the well-worn. Like the consumerist culture around us, we are constantly egged on to buy into (consume) the latest megachurch praise music, the best-selling celebrity author publications, the internet guru podcast. Undoubtedly, evangelicalism overall has done well out of this momentum while it has been on the ascendency. However, as with all things cultural, as the Western worldview and its consumerism begin to wane, perhaps today we are at a better place to recover the old ways, especially once we recapture the colorful and dynamic means by which they were first communicated.[20]

It should not surprise us that when we turn to the rest of the New Testament, we find further evidence of a tradition already being passed on within the texts themselves. For instance, the apostle Paul alludes to this when he writes to the church at Thessalonica, "Hold fast to the teachings we passed on to you" (2 Thess. 2:15). He exhorts his mentee, Timothy, "What you heard from me, keep as the pattern of sound teaching" (2 Tim. 1:13). And he encourages Titus to appoint elders who "hold firmly to the trustworthy message as it has been taught" (Titus 1:9). However, Paul also alludes to the way in which these traditions and teachings are passed on and does so in a very clear manner that corroborates what we have noted above—namely, that there is an accepted way by which tradition is passed on. For instance, Paul writes to the church in Corinth, "Now, brothers and sisters, I want to remind you of the gospel I preached to you, which *you received* and on which you have taken your stand. . . . For what *I received I passed on to you* as of first importance: that Christ died for our sins according to the Scriptures" (1 Cor. 15:1, 3, emphasis added). What we read here contains much more than the words themselves actually convey to us today. There is a subscript, as it were, operating here. Can you see what it is? (The clue may well be in the italicized words.) The text is replete with a sense of gravitas and authority. Paul is not communicating something along the lines of the weather. Rather, the words used are those of an authoritative figure who is passing something on of such importance that it constitutes both a tradition, which they are to safeguard, and an identity, which they are to live out. This same interplay of authority and tradition can be seen at work elsewhere:

> For *I received* from the Lord what *I also passed on* to you: The Lord Jesus, on the night he was betrayed, took bread . . . (1 Cor. 11:23, emphasis added)[21]

> As we have already said, so now I say again: If anybody is preaching to you a gospel other than what *you accepted*, let them be under God's curse! (Gal. 1:9, emphasis added)

So then, brothers and sisters, stand firm and hold fast to the *teachings we passed on to you*, whether by word of mouth or by letter. (2 Thess. 2:15, emphasis added)

Richard Bauckham, in his *Jesus and the Eyewitnesses*,[22] is helpful at this point in identifying what he describes as a *tradition dynamic* at work in Paul's various communications. We can see this in the language that he uses repeatedly, language that parallels what we have already noted above—namely, communication from, through, and to.

Paul—From Whom

1 Cor. 15:3–7; Gal. 1:18–19

Paul was able to get information about his new faith from his two-week visit to Jerusalem, three years into his conversion. He met only with Peter and James, the brother of Jesus. Thus, Paul himself is the recipient of a tradition, one that derives from two of the most important disciples, now apostles, of Jesus.

1 Cor. 11:23–32

What Paul writes finds a parallel with Luke 22:14–23, suggesting that there is some kind of Lukan-Pauline tradition that Paul is, in turn, passing on to the church at Corinth. Bauckham suggests that Paul's "I received from the Lord" is not probably so much a direct revelation as a euphemism for referring to a unit of Jesus tradition that has been passed on through authoritative figures, such as his meeting in Jerusalem with Peter and James.

Paul—Through Whom

Rom. 12:7; 1 Cor. 12:28–29; Gal. 6:6; Eph. 4:11

In the same way that the Pharisees passed on traditions from previous teachers, so Paul also passed on the traditions he had received. Thus, Paul would be constrained by the rules of oral transmission, as would any other local source of authority who was recognized as having a teaching role and holding teaching responsibilities in the early church.[23] Of equal importance is Paul's responsibility in passing on what he had received to someone of the same teaching authority. In doing so, Paul ensured that "designated persons in each Pauline community knew the Jesus traditions through a chain of only two links between themselves and Jesus himself, namely Paul and the Jerusalem apostles."[24]

Paul—To Whom

1 COR. 11:2; 15:2; 2 THESS. 2:15

Here Paul adheres to one of the key principles that Bailey has highlighted from the *haflat samar*—namely, that whatever is being passed on (the tradition) is a process of community control. What Paul is doing here is of profound significance for our understanding of tradition and how it comes to us, given its apparent current demise. By addressing the entire Christian community, Paul is affirming the tradition's role in how the early Christian communities maintained their identity, belief, and purpose. It most certainly came through recognized authority figures, but equally, if not more so, the processes by which tradition was communicated, learned, and lived out were controlled, on the whole, by the community. Bauckham puts it nicely: "The retaining and maintaining of the tradition is always represented as a responsibility of all Paul's readers."[25] This, of course, has quite significant implications for an evangelical theological method.

In addition, this tradition process also works negatively in terms of what the community is to avoid. We see this when Paul writes to the Galatian church, "If anybody is preaching to you a gospel other than what you accepted, let them be under God's curse!" (Gal. 1:9), and to the church at Colossae, "See to it that no one takes you captive through hollow and deceptive philosophy, which depends on human tradition and the elemental spiritual forces of this world rather than on Christ" (Col. 2:8). And Jude writes, "I felt compelled to write and urge you to contend for the faith that was once for all entrusted to God's holy people" (Jude 3). And Paul urges Timothy to follow "the truths of the faith" and the "good teaching" that he received from Paul, as well as to avoid "godless myths" (1 Tim. 4:6–7). Obviously, if there is a true gospel, a true tradition that is to be passed on, then it follows that there are also false traditions that can be passed on too. Take time to read 1 Corinthians 11:23; 15:3; 2 Corinthians 11:3–4; Galatians 1:9; 2:2, 9; 2 Thessalonians 2:15; 3:6; 1 Timothy 4:6; 6:20; 2 Timothy 1:12–14; 2:2; 4:3; Titus 1:9, 15; Hebrews 3:1; 4:14; 10:23. These various texts reinforce the necessity of being able to discern the true from the false—and following this regular practice is also required of us if we are to be in line with Scripture.

In conclusion, what we see in the New Testament—as a continuation of the Old Testament—is that a tradition dynamic is at work on two levels. The first has to do with the content of tradition. Here we are concerned with teaching that needs to be preserved, taught, proclaimed, and passed on. It appears to consist primarily of the gospel (also referred to as "the faith") and the teaching of the apostles. The second has to do with the method by which this material, instruction, teaching, good news, or practice is preserved, taught, and passed on. It is passed on through an authoritative figure and passed on to the community of faith, who take possession of it. Put simply, tradition involves both a what and a how. Without both, it is unlikely that the tradition will remain positive for long.

Continuing the Tradition: Gospel Tradition Process

We can see, then, that there is what we might call "a gospel tradition process." This process preserves not only the content but also the manner in which this content is communicated. It safeguards the content as it is being passed on. It is on such grounds that the apostle Paul appeals to his own Pharisaic training in theological tradition for being responsible in preserving this tradition (being a repository for it) and then in passing it on to the community. We can summarize this process as follows:

Content	Knowledge/practice
Guardian	Authoritative figure
Recipient	Community of faith

Once the early church began to expand in numbers and reflect on its faith, controversies developed on the path to orthodoxy. Of interest here is the way in which the early church resolved these matters. Anthony Lane describes the approach as the "coincidence view," where the content of the apostolic tradition coincides with the content of Scripture.[26] Or, as Bauckham puts it, "The purpose of apostolic tradition is not to add to Scripture but to show how it is to be interpreted. Apostolic tradition in this context means the Rule of Faith, a basic outline of beliefs that later grew into the Apostles' Creed. Thus, there is harmony or *coincidence* between Scripture, tradition, and the teaching of the church."[27]

Perhaps the best example of how tradition works in relation to Scripture for the good of the community of faith is seen in the way the second-century bishop Irenaeus of Lugdunum (present-day Lyon, France) handled a particular problem in his day. Recall from part 1 that theology is the church's answer to a specific problem—in this case, it was the problem of Gnosticism. In brief, the Gnostics argued for a body of truth to which only an elite (the Gnostics) had access—a "secret tradition" (at the time oral and unwritten) by which correct understanding and interpretation of Scripture could occur. Now, since theology includes first and foremost the exegesis of Scripture, to make this claim is to say that only a select few have the means of understanding Scripture correctly. The same tradition process is at work here, only this time the content consists of secret knowledge, a secret apostolic tradition that goes beyond what the early church holds. The guardians, in this instance, are the Gnostics themselves; the recipients remain other Christians. At stake was the very identity of the second-century church, if not the universal church. What we have here, then, is a clash of traditions, and it was for the Gallic bishop Irenaeus to respond to this secret tradition by defending a "public truth" made known to and accessible by the entire church, not a specific elite. And what we see, once again, is evidence of a tradition dynamic at work.

What Irenaeus does is to continue the same tradition process we have seen at work elsewhere—namely, locating the content of truth in the message of salvation (the gospel) and in teachings that have been publicly preached and taught. In turn, Irenaeus locates the authority for this content in the apostles and their teaching since they are the guardians of the message, having been eyewitnesses to it. Finally, Irenaeus establishes a rule of faith—a *regula fidei*—for the community of faith, the recipients. By this rule, correct belief, correct faith seeking understanding, can be identified, established, taught, and defended. As a result, the church guardians, as it were, identify publicly the truth—the rule of faith—as received from the apostles. I think that an important point is being established at the very start of the life of the Christian church—namely, that whatever theology is, it is not innovation for its own sake, or divinely inspired original thinking. Rather, what makes theologians significant is their fidelity to and "faithful recollection" of a tradition that came through the apostles from Christ himself.[28] Irenaeus talks of this as "the rule that is the truth,"[29] and for Irenaeus, this rule acts "as an *authoritative* norm of doctrinal truth."[30] Of course, Scripture is always the superior source. Therefore, the rule is not a freestanding truth but rather one in which Scripture is always the source of the rule's doctrines. What resulted from this debate was a recognition of the intimate bond between Scripture and the rule of faith, so much so that "'the rule of faith' becomes synonymous with the faith."[31] I think New Testament scholar F. F. Bruce catches the essence of what is going on here when he comments, "If at times [the rule of faith] is formally distinguished from Scripture in the sense that it is recognized as the interpretation of Scripture, at other times it is materially identical with Scripture in the sense that it sums up what Scripture says."[32] However, let's allow Irenaeus to present his argument in his own words:

> The truth is to be found nowhere else but in the Catholic Church, the sole depository of apostolical doctrine. Heresies are of recent formation, and cannot trace their origin up to the apostles.
>
> 1. Since therefore we have such proofs, it is not necessary to seek the truth among others which it is easy to obtain from the Church; since the apostles, like

a rich man [depositing his money] in a bank, lodged in her hands most copiously all things pertaining to the truth: so that every man, whosoever will, can draw from her the water of life. For she is the entrance to life; all others are thieves and robbers. On this account are we bound to avoid *them*, but to make choice of the thing pertaining to the Church with the utmost diligence, and to lay hold of the tradition of the truth. For how stands the case? Suppose there arise a dispute relative to some important question among us, should we not have recourse to the most ancient Churches with which the apostles held constant intercourse, and learn from them what is certain and clear in regard to the present question? For how should it be if the apostles themselves had not left us writings? Would it not be necessary, [in that case,] to follow the course of the tradition which they handed down to those to whom they did commit the Churches?

2. To which course many nations of those barbarians who believe in Christ do assent, having salvation written in their hearts by the Spirit, without paper or ink, and, carefully preserving the ancient tradition, believing in one God, the Creator of heaven and earth, and all things therein, by means of Christ Jesus, the Son of God; who, because of His surpassing love towards His creation, condescended to be born of the virgin, He Himself uniting man through Himself to God, and having suffered under Pontius Pilate, and rising again, and having been received up in splendour, shall come in glory, the Saviour of those who are saved, and the Judge of those who are judged, and sending into eternal fire those who transform the truth, and despise His Father and His advent. Those who, in the absence of written documents, have believed this faith, are barbarians, so far as regards our language; but as regards doctrine, manner, and tenor of life, they are, because of faith, very wise indeed; and they do please God, ordering their conversation in all righteousness, chastity, and wisdom. If any one were to preach to these men the inventions of the heretics, speaking to them in their own language, they would at once stop their ears, and flee as far off as possible, not enduring even to listen to the blasphemous address. Thus, by means of that ancient tradition of the apostles, they do not suffer their mind to conceive anything of the [doctrines suggested by the] portentous language of these teachers, among whom neither Church nor doctrine has ever been established.[33]

What the Gnostic challenge revealed was the need for a publicly recognized and authoritative tool that would establish the boundaries for biblical exegesis. From this point on, therefore, as Alister McGrath explains, only those doctrines or teachings that were historically connected to the apostles' teaching could claim to be authoritative,[34] and as a result, the "apostolic tradition safeguarded apostolic teaching,"[35] which, of course, had been passed down from Jesus Christ himself. There now existed a yardstick by which to assess the correctness, the orthodoxy, of any exegesis of Scripture, an objective dynamic regulated by an apostolic faith. In this sense, then, the *regula* is not Scripture but rather acts as a doctrinal and interpretive standard that sets the boundaries for Christian thought, beyond which Christian reflection and teaching must not go. I like to compare it with the rules of soccer: the pitch, or field, marks out the boundaries within which the game is played; beyond them you are out of the game. And as in soccer, which has a limited number of players, so the *regula* has a limited number—in the case of the *regula*, it is always *triadic*. That is, any teaching that follows the rule of faith will also conform to the identity of God revealed in Scripture, whom we have come to know as the Father; his Son, Jesus Christ; and the Holy Spirit. We see this trinitarian framework at work as early as the second century in what is known as the "Old Roman Creed," which, by the eighth century, had morphed into what we now know as the Apostles' Creed, though very close forms of it existed in the fifth century. Finally, it was given official church recognition in the ninth century, when it became part of the Catholic Church's liturgy.[36]

> I believe in God, the Father almighty,
> creator of heaven and earth.
>
> I believe in Jesus Christ, his only Son, our Lord.
> He was conceived by the power of the Holy Spirit
> and born of the Virgin Mary.
>
> He suffered under Pontius Pilate,
> was crucified, died, and was buried.
>
> He descended to the dead.
> On the third day he rose again.
> He ascended into heaven,
> and is seated at the right hand of the Father.
> He will come again to judge the living and the dead.
>
> I believe in the Holy Spirit,
> the holy catholic Church,
> the communion of saints,
> the forgiveness of sins,
> the resurrection of the body,
> and the life everlasting.
>
> Amen.[37]

And so, for the early church, it was the "rule of faith," which could be traced all the way back to the apostles and their association with Jesus Christ, that regulated Christian belief. We can see, then, that at every stage of the tradition process, content is passed on through an authoritative medium to the desired recipients. The gospel was passed on by Jesus Christ to his apostles;

the apostles passed on what they had seen and heard to the early church. This content, in turn, is passed on by the early church with the intention of preserving correct Scriptural interpretation for the church universal. Can you see the rhythm of theological development here? A very clear ebb and flow is taking place as this standard is both established and passed on. And what is rather humbling in all this is that the likes of you and me, unlikely theologians, are responsible for continuing this tradition dynamic today. To the theologians remains the task of speaking, teaching, and safeguarding the faith, delivered once and for all to the saints. Theologians are guardians of the church and ensure that the church interprets Scripture correctly, as she alone should do. It is this theological guild—whether in the church, the academy, the workplace, in hospitals or in prisons—to whom this honorable responsibility has been given and whose task it is to speak it out.

This, then, is the place that tradition should hold in an evangelical theological method if it is to remain faithful to the gospel that has taken hold of the church catholic as well as to the great cloud of witnesses cheering us on in this task. It serves solely as a standard for determining truth and thus ensuring faithful obedience to Scripture and the God who so graciously speaks to us through it.

> The apostolic witness serves as the standard by which we gauge what is central to personal encounter and therefore true, and what is peripheral to faith and thus not theology's priority. This measure is what [Emil] Brunner calls the *principle of contiguity* according to which all doctrine is to be weighed. This principle facilitates such questions as, How closely related is X doctrine to the word of God in Christ? To what extent does the doctrine guide our attention to God and away from itself as the truth? The purpose of the principle is that "the more . . . the testimony about God enables one to hear His address, so much more immediate is the something, the doctrine, connected with the primary concern of the Holy Scriptures."[38]

What does this mean for us today as we develop our own theological method? Let's explore four points of engagement:

- First, since Scripture and the earliest theologians, who either had been in direct contact with Jesus Christ or were mentored by those who had been so themselves, all follow a very clear tradition process, a contemporary theological method surely bears considerable responsibility to evidence the same dynamic.
- Second, *sola scriptura* is shorthand for the unequivocal centrality of Scripture in all things pertaining to salvation and the things of God.

Therefore, even the church must be open to being corrected by Scripture as the final authority. In addition, the early church recognized the need for a *regula fidei* that both ensured and safeguarded correct interpretation of Scripture. What this means, in practice, is that an evangelical theological method does not function as though we need only Scripture and Scripture alone, what we might describe as *solo Scriptura*, stripped of every other contact, *nuda Scriptura*. Rather, an evangelical theological method will hold to the wider notion of *sola Scriptura*—Scripture alone—in relation to where our theological authority lies. It lies in Scripture alone. That said, however, this does not mean that we read Scripture alone. Rather, Scripture and a tradition that is rooted in the historical belief of the church universal go hand in hand.

- Third, since the purpose of Scripture is to reveal God's intentions for his creation, and since these intentions are revealed in and through the incarnation of the Son of God, Jesus Christ, and through proclaiming the gospel, whereby the Holy Spirit sustains these intentions in the here and now, an evangelical theological method will always be triune in its structure if it is to remain faithful to the historical faith.

- Last, since Scripture and the early church demonstrate, on the one hand, the need for a recognized authority figure whose expertise ensures the integrity of the content being passed on and, on the other hand, the responsibility of the wider community to own what has been passed on to them and live out the tradition that has been passed on, an evangelical theological method, similarly, will demonstrate both. This means, first, that those in authority who have the responsibility for passing on the tradition of the church are not autonomous free agents but are themselves accountable to others and are regulated. Second, there are implications for the community of faith itself—namely, to establish ways that facilitate active, not passive, participation in the passing on and reception of tradition, thus requiring a significant restructuring of how we "do" church today.

Pause

Why not take a moment to reflect on each of the above points in relation to how *your* theology develops. Consider the following questions:

- Identify the various ways your theological tradition has been passed on to you. Can you identify a tradition process at work? If so, what does it look like?

- What theological traditions do you bring to your own reading of Scripture? How do they influence how you read the text?
- How trinitarian is your reading of Scripture? Is the effect of your belief in the Trinity something you are aware of when you're reading Scripture? How might you read Scripture as communication from the God who is Father, Son, and Spirit?
- Who is the authoritative guardian of tradition in your church or denomination? How much congregational participation takes place in the passing on or teaching of tradition in your church or denomination? Do you think this is a good thing to have? If not, why not? If so, why?

Continuing the Tradition: Tradition and Orthodoxy

This tradition process was particularly active in the first millennium of the church's existence. For the first five hundred years or so, the church was identified in two forms, generally identified in terms of geography and language. One was the Latin-speaking Western church, and the other was its Greek-speaking Eastern counterpart. The latter became known as the Orthodox Church—a blanket term for several different expressions of the same church, not all Greek-speaking. The term "orthodox" means "correct glory," which is a lovely way of communicating that when we get our theology right, we are aligning with God's glory! Here we see an interesting marker for understanding truth. Truth is not so much something that is to be believed as it is something that gives God glory. Truth relates to God and honors God—it gives due worth to God and says something about God's "style," his way of doing things. As we have also noted earlier, "orthodox" implies "unorthodox" or "heterodox." That is, to make a claim about orthodoxy is to draw a line, to set a boundary on what can be said that conveys the truth about God. It is both belief and action, which Andrew Walker describes rather colorfully as "*true worship*, which is the overflowing of God's personal love into the church. This overflowing is like abundant wine brimming in the cup from which we must drink deeply if we want new life, and drinking is both a physical act of opening our mouths and a spiritual act of surrender, of opening our hearts."[39]

Think about this—the notion of there being a line, a boundary, a limit to what can be said that is true about our faith. This slaps the face of today's relativism, where there appear to be no lines or boundaries,[40] whether regarding truth, sexuality, or identity. However, what we have learned in part 1 is that an evangelical theology will be hallmarked by certain very clear lines and boundaries—what were once described as "fundamentals"—regarding God, Jesus Christ, salvation, Scripture, and mission. We might even go so far as to posit that these various evangelical criteria constitute an evangelical "orthodoxy." In this, evangelicals have something to learn from their older Orthodox counterparts, even as they realize what we have in common.

Stanley Harakas summarizes the importance of orthodoxy when he points out that for the Orthodox Church, there is only one tradition—holy tradition—one that incorporates the teaching of Scripture, the apostles, and the church fathers. Now, while the typical evangelical may well be able to say "Amen" to the first two, there might be problems with the third. After all, surely *sola Scriptura* precludes further additions? Let's identify four helpful responses to this matter.

- First, we gain here an insight into how tradition serves Scripture. This notion of holy tradition safeguards what the church came to believe about Jesus Christ, his gospel, and God's identity during the church's transition from the time of Jesus Christ, through the apostles, and into the early church. It recognizes, then, an organic flow in how the church came to establish its boundaries on correct belief.

- Second, what we see here is a similar tradition dynamic at work: recognized authority figures passing the church's identity on to the community of faith through the content of its tradition.

- Third, these authority figures recognize the authority of Scripture and the role that tradition plays in subsequent theological debate. This is where I think we can identify a coalition between an evangelical theological method and a more ancient Orthodoxy: evangelicals hold robustly to two fundamental doctrines, both of which are not found explicitly in Scripture but which act as definitive narratives for an evangelical identity as well as theology. The first is the doctrine of the Trinity—the belief that God is Father, Son, and Spirit at one and the same time, but only one God. The second is the belief that Jesus Christ is fully human and fully divine at one and the same time. Both beliefs are foundational to evangelical belief and identity, but neither can be read directly out of Scripture. Rather, they are the result of centuries of theological debate that refused to settle until the church arrived at an answer that did not compromise or contradict the content of Scripture.

- Fourth, these doctrines were developed by and accepted by the universal church. What this means is that the church speaks with one voice on the identity of God and of Jesus Christ and does so as a direct consequence of the gospel. Once again, here we see the power of tradition at work, this time in securing the unity of the church concerning its identity, both in the East and in the West. On these fundamentals, the Western church cannot be played against the Eastern church and vice versa. And so here we are able to identify the same dynamic operating in our own evangelical theology: every time we uphold the doctrines of the Trinity or the two natures of Christ, we recognize the place that the tradition of the church fathers has in our own theological method.

What Harakas highlights so helpfully is how the Orthodox talk of tradition as the mindset of the Orthodox Church, describing the canon of faith, the rule of faith—tradition—as "the conscious memory and life-experience of the historic Church, that the fullness of the revelation, in all its richness and abundant dimensions, dwells."[41] Of equal interest for us is his insistence that tradition is not some kind of protogospel that preceded what we have in the Gospels but is, rather, the very means by which the Holy Spirit is present in the church. Of course, what this means is that through the inspired Scriptures, the passed-on teaching and tradition of the apostles, and the safeguarding canon of faith of the church fathers, not only do we have an unbroken process of understanding with regard to the gospel, but we also have a way of describing how the Holy Spirit himself worked within the church then and continues to work now—through the content of that which has been delivered once and for all to the saints. As we will see later when we consider the role of experience in an evangelical theological method, this has profound implications for the contemporary evangelical church.

Here's a simple test to see if you hold to *sola Scriptura* or to *solo Scriptura*. Matthew 14:22–33 records Jesus walking on water. Read the passage below and then take time to engage in the reflection.

> Immediately Jesus made the disciples get into the boat and go on ahead of him to the other side, while he dismissed the crowd. After he had dismissed them, he went up on a mountainside by himself to pray. Later that night, he was there alone, and the boat was already a considerable distance from land, buffeted by the waves because the wind was against it.
>
> Shortly before dawn Jesus went out to them, walking on the lake. When the disciples saw him walking on the lake, they were terrified. "It's a ghost," they said, and cried out in fear.
>
> But Jesus immediately said to them: "Take courage! It is I. Don't be afraid."
>
> "Lord, if it's you," Peter replied, "tell me to come to you on the water."
>
> "Come," he said.
>
> Then Peter got down out of the boat, walked on the water and came toward Jesus. But when he saw the wind, he was afraid and, beginning to sink, cried out, "Lord, save me!"

Immediately Jesus reached out his hand and caught him. "You of little faith," he said, "why did you doubt?"

And when they climbed into the boat, the wind died down. Then those who were in the boat worshiped him, saying, "Truly you are the Son of God."

Pause

Here's a question:

- Does Jesus walk on the water because he is divine or because he is human?

Give reasons for your answer. Identify the various sources you draw from to answer the question.

Whichever status you opted for, divine or human, for you to engage the question and arrive at your own answer, you will have needed to draw on sources outside the Bible. If human, how did he do it? If he could do it, therefore so should we. If divine, then his humanity is quite different from ours. And with this we come full circle regarding the initial point made about tradition—there is no question whether we have traditions; the question is which ones are at work in our theology. We can identify four different components of tradition:

- **The apostolic tradition**—This refers to Scripture and the gospel (what is sometimes referred to as *kerygma*). This constitutes the authentic faith of the church, which can be traced back to the apostles, who were eyewitnesses to Jesus and his teaching. In this sense, then, Scripture is "seen as the concrete manifestation of the divinely authoritative apostolic tradition."[42]
- **The patristic tradition**—This tradition is perhaps best referred to as the tradition that the Logos gave, the apostles preached, and the fathers safeguarded.
- **The seven ecumenical councils**

Nicaea	AD 325	refuting Arius regarding the Son's (divine) nature
Constantinople	AD 381	refuting Apollinaris regarding the Son's human nature
Ephesus	AD 431	refuting Nestorius regarding how the two natures unite

Chalcedon	AD 451	refuting Eutyches and affirming two natures
Second Council of Constantinople	AD 553	refuting residual Nestorian sympathizers
Third Council of Constantinople	AD 680–81	affirming that Christ had two wills
Second Council of Nicaea	AD 787	affirming the validity of venerating icons

- **The living tradition of the Eucharist**—By means of this final element, the Eucharist (Lord's Supper, Communion), Christ is united with his church. The significance of this particular tradition is the way in which it demonstrates how "tradition" is living and contemporary, that it is something dynamic in believers' lives up to the present.

This tradition dynamic is best articulated in the following maxim: *The rule of faith is the rule of worship*. Put simply, it is a reminder that what ultimately defines our theological identity is not mere propositional statements, however true they are, but rather that identity is located in the content of our worship as well as in the actual act of worship. These are not dead and ossified beliefs and actions. Rather, they are deep expressions of what is of utmost and primary importance in our individual and collective lives. It is in the act of worship that I am truly myself—transparent, intimate, honest—and it is in the object of my worship that I declare who I am and hope to become. The Scottish bard captures the human face of worship in his famous poem about human love: "Oh my Luve's like a red, red rose."[43] Here, the worship of his beloved has a life all its own—it is dynamic and living, not dead and ossified, and expresses what generation after generation of Scots feel deeply.

In a similar manner, while the initial idea of tradition may sound quite strange to the contemporary evangelical, who is more used to the new with a touch of entertainment thrown in for good measure, it is not perhaps so far-fetched to consider serious engagement with past and even ancient creeds. After all, we all stand on the shoulders of giants who have preceded us and who have passed on traditions of various kinds, be they notions of gravity, relativity, mathematics, language. What has been passed on to us from previous generations as well as what we will hand on to subsequent generations is transmitted through recognized authorities, be they scientific, economic, political, linguistic, industrial, or artistic. And equally important, we treasure these various traditions because they have the power to construct and constitute our very identities, such is the power we invest in them. This power, of course, is what makes traditions so potent and valuable. Therefore, the tradition dynamic is to be treasured and protected. It operates at a very deep level of human identity construction, both personally and corporately. Alasdair MacIntyre perhaps expresses best the way in which the power of tradition operates, and in so doing he shows the universal and ubiquitous role that tradition plays in human society, thus demonstrating that tradition is not merely a religious artifact but in fact a basic social construction of human culture.

> But the traditions through which particular practices are transmitted and reshaped never exist in isolation for larger social traditions. What constitutes such traditions? . . .
>
> All reasoning takes place within the context of some traditional mode of thought, transcending through criticism and invention the limitations of what had hitherto been reasoned in that tradition; this is as true of modern physics as of medieval logic. Moreover when a tradition is in good order it is always partially constituted by an argument about the goods the pursuit of which gives to that tradition its particular point and purpose.[44]

And, of course, the contemporary media capitalizes on this with great skill—just look at a magazine stand in a major supermarket and take in all the different "traditions" on display, each pulling at our deeper instincts and needs for identity, whether they be youth and beauty, perfect bodies, hair or clothes, house and car, food and drink—the list is almost endless but the intent is the same. The same "tradition dynamic" operates on the magazine stand—each magazine claiming to be the recognized publication with authority on the matter and thus aiming to convince us that it should determine what we should wear or eat or drive or inhabit and thus to enable us to construct the "right" identity until eventually, often unconsciously, we give them worth—begin to worship them—by purchasing the magazine, believing its content, and unknowingly becoming a fashion victim. Such is the power of tradition.

What I want to propose is that an evangelical theological method will resist the temptation to go over to the dark side of tradition—manipulative, ersatz, and misleading—but will, rather, recognize the necessity of tradition as well as its power for good. I conclude in concord with Georges Florovsky, who, in speaking for the Orthodox, describes tradition rather beautifully and enticingly: "Tradition is not a principle striving to restore the past, using the past as a criterion for the present. Such a conception of tradition is rejected by history itself and by the consciousness of the Orthodox Church. . . . *Tradition is the constant abiding of the Spirit and not only the memory of words.* Tradition is a *charismatic,* not a historical, principle."[45]

Continuing the Tradition: Tradition in the West

The Western church also developed its own understanding of "tradition," albeit one different from its Eastern counterpart. Although both parts of Christendom affirm the same creeds, on the whole, there are a couple of significant differences between the two. We have seen how the Eastern church advocates boundaries to orthodoxy, best described by John of Damascus in the eighth century: "We do not change the everlasting boundaries which our fathers have set but we keep the Tradition, just as we received it."[46] This understanding of orthodoxy parallels how the Orthodox church understands its leadership—namely, that all bishops are equal, going back to the apostles themselves. And if they are all equal, then they speak with a united voice and do not contradict each other. Consequently, tradition was regulated by a strict hermeneutic premised on the priority of *precedence*—theological development bound by conformity to what had taken place and what had been spoken and agreed on by guardians of the past. Innovation was anathema. It should be clear that tradition in the Eastern sense operated somewhat similarly to the way we have seen described earlier regarding the *haflat samar* (what Anthony Lane describes as the supplementary view—as in the *haflat samar*, there was room for innovation as long as it did not change the "core," the "rule of faith"). In all this, there is a strong imperative to maintain tradition, as John of Damascus tells us.

The Western church, on the other hand, developed differently. It would be false to say that Western theology was not constrained by its own strict criteria, but its major peculiarity lay in the fact that in giving authority to one particular bishop—the pope—it allowed tradition to develop more along the lines of the supplementary, rather than the ancillary, view—that is, tradition could be added to, and was not necessarily subordinate to, Scripture. As a result, the way in which tradition developed and was used, both in its content and in its process, was now the responsibility of the church. Of course, "the church" is an abstraction: the real location of this interpretive authority was the magisterium—the teaching authorities of the church. And so, as Steven Cone points out, "If we want to know what is true, the place [where] that is maximally located is in *what the Church magisterium teaches today*."[47] For the Roman face of the Western church, its official teachers are the guardians of Scripture and tradition. In this sense, then, this is a development from the tradition dynamic we have noted at work in Scripture and the early church, as well as that operating within the Eastern church.

If we look at the Protestant face of the Western church, we should not be surprised to discover tradition assuming a different kind of operation. Here, the priority of Scripture as the ultimate and final authority is emphasized much more. Yet when we look at this Western expression, we discover a parallel understanding that Scripture requires interpretation and that this interpretation needs to be monitored in some way.[48] Despite their clear differences, each of the various historical expressions that we have looked at recognizes the necessary role an apostolic tradition plays in both interpreting and safeguarding Scripture. Equally so within the Protestant West, where the priority of Scripture is maintained and the historical apostolic tradition and its creeds are given their proper place. In addition, an informal, unwritten tradition is equally at work, with its emphasis on preaching the gospel and on teaching that can be traced back to the gospel message. This Protestant understanding of tradition deserves to be highlighted for its relevance to a contemporary evangelical theological method. It does seem to me that at a practical level, certain elements within the evangelical constituency today have increasingly disconnected the historical link between Scripture and tradition, and they have done so for one of two reasons.

First, as D. H. Williams points out, the notion of tradition is "antithetical to the absolute authority of the Bible," and the "longstanding and prevalent conception among evangelicals is that *sola scriptura* is compromised by any acceptance of extracanonical authority."[49] More traditional evangelical approaches to Scripture tend in this direction. However, in doing so, they end up cutting themselves off from one of the major means by which the Holy Spirit not only engages with the church but also renews the church.

Second, in experiential, personality-driven approaches to doing theology, tradition is smothered by the stronger drive for relevance and contemporaneity, resulting in a more *solo Scriptura* than *sola Scriptura* approach being adopted. As a result, Scripture is handled as though it is some freestanding entity, an end in itself rather than divine communication that requires thought, reflection, interpretation, and application. And when this happens, a vacuum is created, one historically filled by tradition, playing its interpretive and regulatory role in relation to Scripture. The contemporary church then opens itself up to two consequences that tradition safeguards against. On the one hand, various forms of theological amnesia occur that result in the mistakes of the past being repeated unnecessarily. On the other, theological ignorance fills the space vacated by tradition, ignorance that manifests itself in various counterfeits that are a short hop, skip, and jump from downright gobbledygook at best, or lunatic fringe material at worst. Williams alerts us to a very real problem that arises once tradition no longer functions in the way it should—as a means of safeguarding biblical interpretation. We are left with either the tyranny of the magisterium—as was the case at the time of the Reformation—or, closer to home, the tyranny of the individual, in which "every evangelical conscience feels free to speak *ex cathedra*."[50]

That said, it seems to me that the internet and digital television pose significant alternatives to a robust evangelical theological method. On the one hand, they serve only to exacerbate this tyranny in facilitating the proliferation of generally unaccountable individuals speaking *ex cathedra*—that is, as though their theological position and scriptural interpretation trump all others. On the other, the limitations of the institutional or human ego are unable to support the weight of Scripture and thus result in an inevitable lack of integrity. Jesus himself calls it out beautifully in Matthew 23:27: "Woe to you, teachers of the law and Pharisees, you hypocrites! You are like whitewashed tombs, which look beautiful on the outside but on the inside are full of the bones of the dead and everything unclean." What I would like to advocate is that we rediscover the ancient ways of the historic church that seek to avoid a falling short of the mark in terms of how the evangelical constituency handles Scripture and that we thus undercut the growing sense of "celebrityism" that encroaches on the contemporary evangelical church. Inevitably, this kind of easily accessible, personality-driven ersatz approach to Scripture betrays the true function of theological method, one that is based on the historically tested and affirmed integrity and relevance of Scripture. Thus, the accompanying celebrity culture that replaces tradition's tried and tested historical role results, eventually, in Scripture itself being subordinated to the manipulations and needs of an individual personality, a church organization along with its salaries and pensions, a Christian network that has to raise millions of dollars in order to run, or the latest trend that makes fashion victims out of the contemporary church's "fad addicts." This is not cynicism. Rather, it is commentary on the unstoppable consequence when the teachers and guardians of the church's apostolic tradition fail to maintain their proper role, in like manner to the way the religious leaders failed the people of God under the old covenant. All this is to say that tradition is as necessary to Scripture as oxygen is to lungs, and a contemporary evangelical theological method will ensure that this relationship continues.

Concluding Remarks

In summary, these key features characterize the role of tradition in a healthy evangelical theological method:

- Tradition functions both within Scripture itself and beyond by means of a tradition dynamic—a body of identity-forming knowledge passed on by an authoritative figure to a person or community who takes responsibility for its integrity and its praxis.

- Tradition's function is to keep a check on how we interpret Scripture. In doing so, tradition reminds us that "faith is to be checked, is to be understood."[51] An evangelical theological method knows that our interpretation of the Bible requires boundaries in order to safeguard against the hegemony of human ego or denominational bias.
- Tradition has a mediatorial rather than a magisterial role. Tradition is the means by which Scripture is preserved.
- Tradition helps us differentiate the important from the interesting: "In the end, a reception to the ancient tradition enables a believer to determine where the centerpoints of the faith lie and how to distinguish the essential aspects of the faith from the more ephemeral."[52]
- Tradition is an important historical tool by which the Holy Spirit renews the church. Timothy George points out that in

> the history of the church, theological renewal has frequently involved the recovery of a forgotten past. Spurgeon fell in love with the Puritans, Wesley drank deeply from the Fathers of the East, Luther and Calvin were Augustinians with a passion, and the Doctor of Grace himself recovered an authentic Paulinism for his own day. None of these are mere repeaters of the past. No, they looked to the past in order to find the answer to the question, "What will be?" This is also the task of faithful evangelical theology today: it anticipates and illuminates the future while remaining faithful to the scriptural pattern of divine truth.[53]

- The Spirit safeguards the apostolic teaching of the church—which includes the gospel—from being reduced to a private and personal rather than a historical and communal faith.
- Tradition has a ministerial role rather than a magisterial role.[54]
- Tradition's relationship with Scripture means that tradition does not service our theology but rather theology services our tradition. Ellen Charry correctly states that the "overarching regulative task of theology is to keep the Christian tradition resilient."[55]
- Tradition contextualizes the present. As Walter Brueggemann reminds us, "When we have completely forgotten our past, we will absolutize the present and we will be like contented cows in Bashan who want nothing more than the best of today."[56]
- Tradition safeguards us against what Williams describes as the disease of "an ahistoricism and spiritual subjectivism" that dumbs down the content of Christian faith to accommodate to the culture.[57]
- Tradition is not the prerogative of an elite but, rather, is the responsibility of the entire community. Therefore, a specifically evangelical

theological method will construct relationally engineered processes that engage not only the guardians of the faith—its theologians—but also the wider community of faith.

- Tradition reminds the church that its Christian teaching is vastly superior to the intellectual fashions of our secularized culture, and tradition challenges the church to regain this awareness.

SUGGESTED READING

Bailey, Kenneth E. *"Poet and Peasant" and "Through Peasant Eyes": A Literary-Cultural Approach to the Parables in Luke.* Grand Rapids: Eerdmans, 1983.

Bauckham, Richard. *Jesus and the Eyewitnesses: The Gospels as Eyewitness Testimony.* 2nd ed. Grand Rapids: Eerdmans, 2017.

Bruce, F. F. *The Canon of Scripture.* New ed. Downers Grove, IL: InterVarsity, 1988.

Castleman, Robbie F. *Interpreting the God-Breathed Word: How to Read and Study the Bible.* Grand Rapids: Baker Academic, 2018.

Cone, Steven D. *Theology from the Great Tradition.* London: Bloomsbury T&T Clark, 2018.

Fairbairn, Douglas, and Ryan M. Reeves, *The Story of Creeds and Confessions.* Grand Rapids: Baker Academic, 2019.

Holmes, Stephen R. *Listening to the Past: The Place of Tradition in Theology.* Grand Rapids: Baker Academic, 2003.

Humphrey, Edith M. *Scripture and Tradition: What the Bible Really Says.* Grand Rapids: Baker Academic, 2013.

McGrath, Alister. "Faith and Tradition." In *The Oxford Handbook of Evangelical Theology*, edited by Gerald R. McDermott, 81–95. Oxford: Oxford University Press, 2010.

Ortlund, Gavin. *Theological Retrieval for Evangelicals: Why We Need Our Past to Have a Future.* Wheaton: Crossway, 2019.

Pelikan, Jaroslav. *The Vindication of Tradition.* New Haven: Yale University Press, 1984.

Williams, D. H. *Retrieving the Tradition and Renewing Evangelicalism.* Grand Rapids: Eerdmans, 1999.

seven

Reason

Setting the Scene

It will be clear by now that the gospel and the God we come to know through it draw from us very specific questions. We have also noted that we come to know about the God and Father of our Lord Jesus Christ through *what* he does—his good news—and *how* he does it: through the life, death, resurrection, ascension, and glorification of his Son, Jesus Christ. In this sense, God is what he does—he does who he is. Theology is exegesis of this gospel. We have also noted that this process of understanding involves careful unpacking and application, following tried and tested, recognized and established habits of various sorts. These procedures constitute our theological method and ensure the consistency and truth of Christian reflection about the God and Father of our Lord Jesus Christ. They are necessary if our exegesis of the gospel—our theology—is to be the result of *faith seeking understanding*. That is, there is something about the gospel and the God of the gospel, as well as the way in which the good news has been executed, that requires not only faithful response but also ongoing inquiry and thought. As we have already noted, whether this faithful response is that of the ordinary theologian at prayer or the academic theologian at study, both have a specific place for reason. An essential part of faith seeking understanding is having confidence in being able to communicate, either as gospel or as teaching, what we believe. As Trevor Hart reminds us, "We commend the Christian gospel to others because we believe that it is a truth which genuinely pertains to their objective situation."[1]

It is rather obvious, therefore, that in order for our theological method to equip us in this task, we need to be able to think carefully about the revelation itself, what it might mean, and then how we communicate that effectively. As we have noted, the task of theology has its own specific challenges:

- There is the sheer incongruity of the discipline. God, the unknowable but for revelation, demands serious scrutiny and thought.
- The nature of faith—an act of assurance and conviction—demands reasoning if the end point of faith is to be achieved. Faith both elicits and requires reason.

This coupling of faith and reason should be a natural union in any theological method and the theology it produces, whether ordinary or academic. Admittedly, it has not always been a happy marriage. The history of Christian thought and reflection reveals an altogether different story: an uneasy tension, if not outright breakdown, in the relation between faith and reason. After all, what has Athens (the seat of philosophy) got to do with Jerusalem (the seat of faith), reason to do with faith? Indeed, the history of modern Western thought can be summarized as the uneasy relationship between faith and reason coalescing in the Enlightenment dualism between pure Reason (knowledge through objective, empirically observable thought), on the one hand, and high Romanticism (knowledge through experience and the senses), on the other. It does not help that Christian thought feeds into this troublesome matter. Scripture appears to vilify the place of reason. The apostle Paul himself appears almost disingenuous in how he parodies "reason" in the face of the gospel. For instance, in his letter to the Corinthian church and its "super" apostolic tendencies, it is almost as though Paul is ridiculing the place of reason when he writes,

> For the message of the cross is foolishness to those who are perishing, but to us who are being saved it is the power of God. For it is written:
>
> > "I will destroy the wisdom of the wise;
> >   the intelligence of the intelligent I will frustrate."

Where is the wise person? Where is the teacher of the law? Where is the philosopher of this age? Has not God made foolish the wisdom of the world? For since in the wisdom of God the world through its wisdom did not know him, God was pleased through the foolishness of what was preached to save those who believe. Jews demand signs and Greeks look for wisdom, but we preach Christ crucified: a stumbling block to Jews and foolishness to Gentiles, but to those whom God has called, both Jews and Greeks, Christ the power of God and the wisdom of God. For the foolishness of God is wiser than human wisdom, and the weakness of God is stronger than human strength.

Brothers and sisters, think of what you were when you were called. Not many of you were wise by human standards; not many were influential; not many were of noble birth. But God chose the foolish things of the world to shame the wise; God chose the weak things of the world to shame the strong. God chose the lowly things of this world and the despised things—and the things that are not—to nullify the things that are, so that no one may boast before him. It is because of him that you are in Christ Jesus, who has become for us wisdom from God—that is, our righteousness, holiness and redemption. Therefore, as it is written: "Let the one who boasts boast in the Lord." (1 Cor. 1:18–31)

I am not going to present any historical survey of the relationship between faith and reason in this chapter. This has been stated more than sufficiently by historians, philosophers, and theologians. At times, it will be necessary to "touch base" with this historic narrative since it locates the ongoing context within which Christian theology has been formed, on the whole. However, and more importantly, an evangelical theological method goes beyond this historical straitjacket and seeks to establish its own epistemology and rationality. Given the centrality of Jesus Christ's own claim to being the Truth (John 14:6), and given that reason is a key means by which we discover, judge, critique, and understand any claim to truth, let alone this core belief about Christ, it should not be too surprising to discover an intimate bond between truth and reason. After all, as Colin Gunton reminds us, "Christian Theology is a discipline which seeks to speak the truth, to tell things as they are. It is the church's intellectual discipline, but one which is at the same time spiritual, because it can be truly itself only through what the Holy Spirit gives."[2] With regard to our theological method, we can make two points regarding a specifically evangelical attitude to reason and its place in how we come to know.

First, such an approach is premised on a specific doctrine of creation, one that is determined by Scripture itself. The significance of the opening chapters of Scripture for the entire task of theological thought should not be dismissed. Whatever our take on the creation narratives of Genesis 1–3, the Genesis theologians understood there to be an intrinsic rationality to creation, one that is demonstrated not only in how the Creator orders creation—day follows night, seasons follow in an established order, living creatures exist according to their own kind—but also in the Creator's own critical reasoning in response to what has been verbally commanded into existence: it is very good.[3] This reasoning, in turn, extends in the way the divine image bearer, Adam, uses reason to name all other living creatures—the first example of human taxonomy. However, this is not a mechanical process—the execution of pure reason on creation. Rather, we are offered an intimate window into the primal relation between what is all around us and how we make sense of it: knowledge comes by relationship. In naming the animals, an act carried out by the first biologist—a student of living organisms—Adam had first to get to know, to indwell, the reality of the various creatures so that he could both identify and name them. We miss an exceptionally important insight if we assume that this act of naming was random. Rather, from the very beginnings of human reason and the knowledge it facilitates, it is possible to detect an intimate bond between thought and relation. Knowledge comes about via relationship with that which is hitherto unknown and through the execution of reason. It is faith seeking understanding.

Second, and following on from our first point, an evangelical theological method will distinguish different forms of knowledge. On the one hand, it recognizes with J. P. Moreland that *we humans have the power to 'see,' to be directly aware of, to directly experience a wide range of things, many of which are not subject to sensory awareness with the five senses*—what he describes as *rational awareness*.[4] I want to suggest that this notion of rational awareness very helpfully establishes an anthropological norm here—namely, that reason is not to be reduced to rational criteria alone. Rather, for Moreland, this kind of knowledge is positioned within a wider understanding of "soul" and its awareness of various universal laws (mathematics), beauty (aesthetics), moral laws (ethics), and abstractions (what it is to be human, wisdom).

On the other hand, an evangelical understanding will also recognize and respect the wider cultural and worldview mindset each of us has, which provides each of us with our own understanding of reason and how knowledge is acquired. That is, not everybody thinks and reasons in the same way, for the simple reason that our reasoning is itself a social construct, something we are taught through our local and national social conditioning. It will differ from civilization to civilization, culture to culture, generation to generation, person to person. This kind of reason requires our theological method to be both missional and apologetic, on the grounds that Jesus Christ has established an imperative: to preach the gospel and make—teach and mentor—disciples (Matt. 28:19), starting at home and going out to the farthest and consequently unknown ends of the earth (Acts 1:8), to people as far removed from our own ways of thinking and understanding as fire is to ice. Thus, while for most of us our own calling is to inhabit the gospel and make sense of it within our own context, for others there is a wider *missional* challenge of communicating what we understand about the gospel to different world contexts in order to make disciples. In addition, both engage an additional challenge, as the apostle Paul demonstrates in his Areopagus speech in Acts 17. Here, Paul had to give an account for what he believed in the face of other religious and philosophical alternatives. This "defense," or "apologia," was the *apologetic* challenge of rational and reasoned engagement about his faith.

To proclaim the gospel in contexts very different from our own and face both challenges, we need transformed characters. That is, we are not downloading abstracted notions of truth. Rather, we communicate something that is transformative. We do so as people whose lives evidence their own encounter with the power of the gospel and the God who gifts it—and with well-trained minds—as people who exercise intellectual muscle through rigorous study and who, as a result, can rightly handle the word of truth. In a nutshell, we communicate as men and women who have applied themselves to faith seeking understanding due to the transformative nature of this faith and who do so in such a way that what we communicate also expresses the very DNA of Christian reason—that is, not information for information's sake but information for transformation's sake.

Pause

This is a good point at which to stop and identify some of the issues you face today that require serious thinking.

- What are the ones that matter most to you?
- Why?
- How does your theological method enable you to engage them meaningfully?

Engaged Reason

Although Moreland's perception is helpful here, in the light of what we have noted earlier concerning Michael Polanyi—that we come to know through indwelling—I suggest that a specifically evangelical theological method is better served when it situates reason within a wider *personal* framework whose end is to bring about wisdom. Ellen Charry describes such knowledge as *sapience*:

> Sapience is engaged knowledge that emotionally connects the knower to the known.[5]

Such an approach elicits questions from those who are encountered by the gospel and, through it, by the God of the gospel. These questions are faith-wrestling questions and cannot be dismissed superficially without doing damage to what we believe as well as how we live out our beliefs in our personal and collective lives. Even to acknowledge the need to ask deeper, more penetrating questions is itself to recognize that our believing faith requires not only knowledge as facts and data, as mere information, but also skills that enable us to recognize, gather, collate, judge, critique, and review with the goal of understanding our faith more fully—to evidence God-approved thinking, as the apostle Paul puts it (2 Tim. 2:15). More importantly, asking deeper questions requires a form of reason that brings about not only personal transformation but also social-ecclesial flourishing: what Jesus Christ calls life in all its abundance, what Paul describes as church.

This, of course, covers a plurality of issues, each raising its own questions: What kind of person am I seeking to become through following Christ? What does it mean to say that God's own Spirit indwells me? How is it possible for the created to know the Uncreated? What does "uncreated" even look like? How can Jesus be at one and the same time both everything God is and everything humans are when "God" and "human" are not the same thing? Surely this a form of ontological schizophrenia? How can Father, Son, and Spirit be one God when there are three persons? How much does God love me? Why do we worship Jesus when Scripture tells us to worship God alone? What is the soul? What is "spirit," let alone *Holy* Spirit? How many angels can dance on the head of a pin? How can a decomposed body be resurrected? What will the new creation look like if there is no sun and therefore no time as we know it? What is the fate of those who have never heard the gospel and been able to respond to it? If the righteous are saved through faith for faith, where does the mind fit in? What's the place of reason? And of course, you may well add the questions you identified in the Pause above.

Here we can expand a little on the "knowing process" that Douglas J. Hall describes in three stages:[6]

1. First, there is the kind of initial information we gain from the gospel. The God to whom we are introduced through the gospel provides us with what Hall describes as "knowledge." That is, by virtue of the gospel, we come into the possession of certain knowledge. At this stage, however, this knowledge is not necessarily self-explanatory. It is a sort of "hangs in the air" kind of "information" without any real personal impact.

2. It is only to the degree that we respond to this knowledge and appropriate it to our own lives, whether singularly or corporately, that this "information" becomes a form of "acknowledgment." That is, we acknowledge that it has potential personal importance, that there is something about it that is of significance for us. And since there are many of us, there are also as many reasons why it does so. The important point

here is that it stops being a "hanging-in-the-air" piece of information and starts becoming more personal—what we might describe as a kind of "sticks-to-us" sort of knowledge.

3. Last, it is only when we engage at a volitional and personal level—when the information gleaned and acknowledged as having some significance is then embraced in an act of trust—that it becomes "part of us" knowledge. Harking back to an earlier point: it is "thinking faith."[7] For Hall it becomes the means by which we make choices, what Polanyi describes as "personal knowledge." This process of coming to know shows us that there is a dynamic at work that requires us to process the information provided in the gospel to arrive at the point of acting trust that is an ongoing expression of the life of faith. This process demands more than mere information, as Hall shows. It demands, rather, the kind of knowledge that we have had to think about, reason with, and then indwell if we are to live by faith and not merely by sight.

There may well be some who contest this process by arguing, rightly, that our response to the gospel is not a long, drawn-out process but a decision made in response to hearing the good news of Jesus Christ. For many, this is indeed the case. For others, it develops more gradually, until a decision is made or a lifestyle is formed that evidences a changed life in response to Jesus Christ. It is helpful to remind ourselves that this dynamic is what was argued in part 1: the gospel is primary; theology is secondary. That is, our faith in the God of the gospel of Jesus Christ and what he offers should always be primary, and any attempt at understanding what this means—our theology, whether ordinary or academic—will always be subordinate to the gospel. John Frame expresses this in a pithy and exact manner: "Faith is the foundation of knowledge, not a conclusion of it."[8] We respond to the gospel and then spend the rest of our lives working out what it means for our lives, whether individually or corporately, as we follow Jesus Christ in the different avenues of life.

This is what theology is—a here-and-now gospel—which is why it requires its own set of rules and habits, its own methodology. Thus, it is in response to the goodness of God that our reasoning takes place. Put like this, our "thinking faith" is as much the product of faith that has been proved as it can be the product of trust still waiting to be proved, fulfilled, actualized—something akin to what the psalmist captures in Psalm 126, where, as Ian Stackhouse points out,[9] we are left to wonder whether the final verses are testimony or hopeful thinking:

> When the LORD restored the fortunes of Zion,
>   we were like those who dreamed.

> Our mouths were filled with laughter,
>> our tongues with songs of joy.
> Then it was said among the nations,
>> "The LORD has done great things for them."
> The LORD has done great things for us,
>> and we are filled with joy.
>
> Restore our fortunes, LORD,
>> like streams in the Negev.
> Those who sow with tears
>> will reap with songs of joy.
> Those who go out weeping,
>> carrying seed to sow,
> will return with songs of joy,
>> carrying sheaves with them. (Ps. 126:1–6)

Of course, it is not possible to arrive at this high point of faith, as expressed by the psalmist, without serious reflection and thinking on our own life experience in the light of what Scripture reveals to us about God and his own self-communication. Our response to this is the voice of lived-in theology. It constitutes the very heartbeat of Scripture—the response of God's people to his own self-disclosure in the mess of their personal and national lives. Therefore, it is important to affirm that the highest and most praised form of reason extended to us in Scripture, whether as psalm, proverb, prophetic speech, or, especially, through the gospel, is not pure fact, highly polished propositional data, or refined knowledge. It is, rather, a profound relational form of revelational reasoning. As Jesus Christ himself puts it, the end point of his gospel is not to gain information but rather to live *coram Deo*—that is, to live under the love of God. It is to love God with our entire being and reflect this in loving our neighbor to the same standard as we do ourselves (Mark 12:30–31).

How we reason and think has not only *personal* implications—we are what we think—but equally, if not more so, profound *political* implications. The human capacity to reason influences how we live with one another, whether as a city-state—the original meaning of *polis*, from which the word "political" derives—or as various communities,[10] nationally or internationally. Of course, human beings reason individually, but we also reason as a *polis*, as a body politic, whether as a democracy or as a totalitarian regime. We all inhabit a social context that affects the way we think and reason in our everyday lives. The question to ask, then, is, Which kind of corporate reasoning is operating? John's Gospel offers a frame through which we can see what a specifically christological form of reasoning is intended to bring about in terms of the polis. First, the goal of this political reality is actualized in bringing about unity, and, second, the evidence of the success a polis achieves in pursuing this unity is proved in the flourishing of the polis. John makes quite clear that Jesus Christ intends a very specific polis. Unity! As a consequence of faithful thinking, of believing faith, in his own gospel manifesto Jesus expected political and social—relational—unity: "My prayer is not for them alone. I pray also for those who will believe in me through their message, that all of them may be one, Father, just as you are in me and I am in you. May they also be in us so that the world may believe that you have sent me" (John 17:20–21). And what is the evidence of this unity? The most extreme form of flourishing—eternal life! "Now this is eternal life: that they know you, the only true God, and Jesus Christ, whom you have sent" (John 17:3).

Of significance here is John's insistence that the unity and the flourishing come via the act of believing—faithful trust premised on a considered, thoughtful, and reasoned response. This relational dimension is significant regarding how we perceive the place of reason in our theological method. Daniel Treier has recently offered what he describes as "a brief theology of human reason" that helpfully develops the points argued above. He identifies three criteria:[11]

- The first concerns rationality's personal character. In our increasingly artificial-intelligence-oriented world, it is important to defend a basic anthropological maxim: "Reason is an activity of persons, not of machines geared for either the most efficient results or the most complex understanding."[12]
- The second, rationality's communal practice, encompasses the points made above. As Treier puts it, "Character and practice affect both theological reception of revelation and societal employment of reason."[13]
- In describing the third, rationality's cultural products, Treier, again, reiterates what we have explored above. I particularly like his summary: "In short, the activity of reasoning depends on testimony, so it produces 'culture' or 'cultures' (depending on theoretical preferences for emphasizing the singular or the plural). Such cultural activity involves not just static products but dynamic feedback loops, as texts and institutions shape the concepts, ideas, and beliefs of persons through their communal practices."[14]

In chapter 8, we will pick up this communal dimension of our theological method, but suffice it to say that an evangelical theological method will embody, not deny, a central element of Jesus Christ's teaching—namely, neighbor love. For our theological method to possess the very DNA of Jesus Christ's mission, it will need to go beyond the purely individualistic methodology so engrained in the evangelical psyche and incorporate the wider social constructs that we inhabit and that mold us. As we will see, we need to work out how we think as a corporate entity (church) first, and then as individuals.

Implications for an Evangelical Theological Method

Contrary to the predominant view held in the West for over three hundred years, an evangelical theological method will move *from* Scripture *to* understanding. That is, the truth claims of the I AM and of Jesus Christ determine how we come to understand. The personal and therefore subjective reality of our faith—that is, what it means for "me"—can be considered and understood only with reference to the social and thus objective criteria of that faith. Such an endeavor requires the proper use of reason: the ability to think, to understand, to argue logically and arrive at an informed judgment and consensus. As Ingolf Dalferth puts it, "Theology cannot unfold the internal perspective of faith in a critical and systematic way while ignoring the external perspectives."[15] The question then becomes "Which perspective do we assume when applying reason to our faith?" In relation to Christian faith in Christ, the answer to this question turns on our understanding of truth and how we determine its veracity—that is, its trustworthiness and integrity. Dalferth identifies four possible responses:

1. The exclusivist position: only Christ is truth (John 14:6).
2. The dualist position: what is true for faith is not necessarily true for reason.
3. The pluralist position: truth comes in many different forms, and it is only our lack of knowledge that holds us back from recognizing this.
4. The inclusivist position: truth is not necessarily reducible to Christ, but it is best defined in Christ.[16]

Clearly, our understanding of the gospel dictates the position we hold regarding our understanding of truth. An evangelical theological method will hold to the centrality of Jesus Christ's own claim to being Truth—a thoroughly personal and, therefore, relational reality that is fulfilled not in abstract knowledge but in transformational relationship with God the Father. Peter Hicks reminds us that truth is not simply a thing, a body of knowledge; it is also an action—it is also something we love, and because we love it we desire to do it.[17] I appreciate the way Hicks pulls together three essential strands of theological drama: it involves what we believe (orthodoxy), what we do (orthopraxis), and our affections—what we love, value, empathize with, and emote (orthopathy). I, too, like the way Edward Foley describes what this integrative challenge looks like in terms of "juggling" as well as his assessment of how it operates in reality—namely, that "it is somewhat problematic to treat orthodoxy, orthopraxis, and particularly orthopathy separately."[18]

> ### Pause
>
> Sometimes it is good to stop and reflect.
>
> On a scale of 0 to 10 (0 being the lowest, 10 the highest), score the following in their significance regarding how you go about your theology:
>
> - What you believe
> - What you do
> - What you love
> - How much you integrate your belief and practice
> - How much you integrate your belief and practice with your affections
>
> How might you better integrate your belief, practice, and affections?

I have always believed that the mind has an important place in Christian faith, not because I think Christians are supposed to be particularly clever but because my own theological foundations have been established on two realities. First, the Bible shows profound respect for the human mind. The creation of the mind is, for me, the apex of divine creativity: God made the brain an organ of great complexity, something so small and yet so utterly beautiful— our own individual human-hardware—with one hundred million cells, each cell having the capacity of a single laptop; and the human mind appears to be facilitated by the brain and to become the brain's software, with its own fecundity and seemingly endless possibilities. And then, in the light of the fact that in responding to the gospel of Jesus Christ, each of us receives the mind of Christ, this brain appears to have the additional capacity to engage with its Designer. For this reason, as we will note below, Scripture itself reminds us of the importance of the mind, of wrestling with the bricks and mortar, as it were, of our faith. For this to happen, some form of meaningful thinking and reasoning must take place.

Second, I believe that the mind has an important place for a thoroughly *practical* reason. As a child and youth, I sat each Sunday listening to relatively unschooled men, on the whole, open the Word of God and engage with it, preach from it, admonish by it, and encourage through it. This form of reasonable engagement with things pertaining to faith was both regular and habitual. Although many were not particularly educated, the esteem in being able to teach with wisdom and integrity and thus build up the local church was significant: much respect gained from handling Scripture properly. Yes, education is important in Scottish culture. Yet, it was more than this—a dynamic similar to what we saw earlier in the *haflat samar* was operating: it was important not only to think deeply about one's faith but also to ensure that it was taught and passed on properly. This cultural appreciation of having a working mind, however, is not one necessarily shared by all Christian traditions today. Ironically, the historical evangelical stress on conversion and the more contemporary elevation of experience has resulted in what J. P. Moreland describes as a form of increasing anti-intellectualism within the wider evangelical church, which, he argues, affects the contemporary church in five different ways:[19]

- *A misunderstanding of faith's relation to reason.* There is something very appealing about the way Moreland perceives the proper relationship between the two: "Faith is a power or skill to act in accordance with the nature of the Kingdom of God, a trust in what we have reason to believe is true."[20]
- *A separation of the secular and the sacred.*
- *A weakened sense of world mission.* Cross-cultural communication requires significant thinking time for the different cultural context to be understood, the gospel to be preached effectively, and the Bible to be translated correctly.
- *An irrelevant, if not false, gospel.* The gospel challenges our theological, cultural, social, and personal suppositions with its significant implications that require careful consideration. The pathway to theological orthodoxy is pitted with the law of unintended consequences, the most insidious being those that distort the gospel, whether those made by Arius or Apollinaris or contemporary distortions of the gospel.[21] After all, whatever we make of the apostle Paul's fourteen years of relative anonymity, it took him around three years in Arabia (Gal. 1:17)[22] to make sense of the resurrection of Jesus Christ from the dead before he went up to Jerusalem for just over two weeks to speak with Peter and Jesus's brother James (Acts 9:26–29; Gal. 1:18–19).[23]
- *Fear in confronting our cultural worldview "idea structures."* Fear results in an ineffective Christian witness.

Clearly there are significant obstacles in the way of consolidating the place of reason within a contemporary evangelical theological method. They are, however, not the only impediments we need to overcome. Treier describes the regime of reason as a "technique" and identifies three negative consequences on Christian thinking that, I add, have noteworthy impact on how we go about our theology. First, he refers to the effect that the technique-ing of reason has on Christian scholars and public intellectuals. Citing Stephen Evans, he says that we face the fear of making any "Bible- or tradition-based claims in the public square."[24] The second area of impact is on evangelical biblical and theological scholars who have accepted the way in which this regime of reason now regulates Scripture, reducing it to merely another set of texts, like any other, with the "assumption that genuine scholarship must now appeal to procedural reason as neutrally as possible."[25] Last, reason exerts its tyranny on pastors and laypersons who long for training and preaching that can be applied in both their congregations and their everyday lives but receive from the academy only abstractions.[26]

Treier highlights yet again important consequences, albeit unintended, from the evangelical legacy of constructing an evangelical *academic* theology on a view of reason determined not by evangelicalism's own worldview values but by an understanding of reason premised on a worldview whose rationality is increasingly at odds with the intimate relation Scripture presents between faith and reason. Yes, evangelical theology will conform to the mores of reason—after all, we follow the Word who became flesh, the very Logos of God, the living, dynamic Reason of God in flesh. However, an evangelical theological method will resist the pull of alternative, *different* forms of reason, ones that create dualisms between faith and reason and that reify reason to a solely intellectual, rational category and ignore the affective and character-forming characteristics of reason so valued in both Testaments, what Charry has called sapience, wisdom. As a result, although contemporary evangelical theology has knowledge in abundance, at the same time it suffers from significant *sapiental* emaciation in terms of Scripture's transformational and relational understanding of reason, described in terms of wisdom. And as at every other point in Christian history, this sapiental detritus fails to deliver. Mark Noll, Cornelius Plantinga Jr., and David Wells express it well, commenting about much evangelicalism that

> has been cognitively bartering with modernity and has come away impoverished—in fact, has been taken to the cleaners. Voyages of self-discovery, the desire to get rich or get happy, the neglect of old arts like reading and thinking, the professionalization of the clergy so that they are no longer ardent students of Scripture and its interpretation but rather ersatz managers and therapists—all

of these moves garnished with a D.Min. degree, so that, as a minister's social prestige drops, the number and kind of his advanced degrees rises to compensate; the loss of appetite for great, stately hymns and their replacement by pop songs from the Christian Billboard's Top Ten Singles; the democratizing of the church to such a degree that learned opinion is immediately suspect as an elitist putdown—these and similar unhappinesses make serious theology in the church uphill work. We evangelicals have to face the fact that we are going through a time when we are suffering a serious trivializing of the Christian faith and a serious diminishment of interest in its theological expression. To paraphrase Carl F. Henry, we are going through a time in which, in too many settings, "a high five for Jesus" has taken the place of the Apostles' Creed and "Five Ways to Pump Up Your Ego Whenever It Loses Pressure" has supplanted reflection on the nature of God.[27]

One particular reason for the demise of a specifically evangelical appreciation of reason is the way in which we have pitted knowledge against faith. There was a time in recent evangelical history when, in order to give weight to a particular sermon point, reference would be made specifically to the fact that "even scientists" believe this to be true. Implicit in this allusion is the underlying assumption of a plethora of takes on reason which, when stripped back to its most practical understanding, reflects a deeper and more unconscious perception of knowledge itself. Esther Meek, in writing of this additional and equally unhelpful set of suppositions that Christians often unwittingly hold regarding the place of knowledge in relation to their Christian faith, helps us identify these suppositions with what she calls "a daisy of dichotomies":[28]

- Knowledge is opposed to belief.
- Knowledge equals facts and is opposite of values/morals.
- Knowledge and facts equal reason, and reason is opposed to faith and emotion.
- Knowledge, facts, and reason equal theory. Theory is different from application and action.
- Knowledge, facts, reason, and theory are the essence of science. Science is opposed to art, imagination, religion, and authority.
- Knowledge, facts, reason, theory, and science are objective realities. The subjective is deemed inferior to the objective.
- Knowledge, facts, reason, theory, science, and the objective are neutral and belong to the public sphere. Everything else is private.
- Knowledge, facts, reason, theory, science, the objective, and the public align with the mind.

- Knowledge, facts, reason, theory, science, the objective, the public, and the mind "align with *the way things are (reality)*, to be distinguished from *the way things appear (appearance)*."[29]
- Knowledge, facts, reason, theory, science, the objective, the public, and the mind are identified with the male.[30]

We are engaging here with a deeper worldview set of attitudes that not only pervades Western culture, of course, but has crept insidiously into contemporary church thinking, too, and invades our theological method often without our being aware of it. Sure, the current postmodern Western context has brought some of these values to the fore, as a result of which we are better informed of our epistemic history and what to avoid. However, as much as this is the case, our contemporary theological context continues to operate under their influence. For this reason, I particularly appreciate Meek's prescience in identifying three consequences of the above way of thinking. In turn, I believe that an evangelical theological method must consider each, since they affect the very possibility of both communicating the gospel and doing theology.

- The first is the existential result in assuming that knowledge is solely about information—resulting in boredom for any divergent, visual, or verbal thinker!
- The second is a sense of hopelessness, not only in the sense that we cannot know everything but, I would add, also in the sense that this perception of reason excludes all those who have not had the privilege of education or who feel and think that they are not particularly "bright" intellectually. The learned response, as Meek points out, is an inevitable skepticism—How is it possible to know anything?—resulting in the opposite of all that human beings are created to experience. As Meek puts it, "Skepticism is a hopelessness unsuited to humanness and to the abundant world in which we live."[31]
- The third consequence resonates with what we learned earlier concerning knowledge as indwelling: boredom, hopelessness, and skepticism result in a sense of betrayal. Again, as we have already argued, human beings are made for relationship, the kind of relationship that comes with expectations. We see this immediately as the first pages of Scripture are opened—the one made in the image of God is given the task of naming the rest of creation. What a phenomenal honor! And human beings have been doing this ever since—taxonomy after taxonomy, seeking to name new discoveries, even to the farthest visible parts of the whole

created order. Without reason—what William Butler Yeats describes as a "baptized imagination"—this is not possible. Our knowledge comes from indwelling the "other" and discovering its, his, her, their own reality. This is both an IQ and an EQ (emotional quotient) issue—it involves the rational as well as the affective. What it is *not* is a passive bypassing of the mind.

Of course, we can identify other causes for the demise of reason in our theological reflection. For some, their indifference is purely practical: it is the responsibility of paid churchmen and women to do all the hard thinking. The professionalization of the clergy and consequences thereof have created a need to raise an entire generation of ordinary theologians trained to engage not only their own faith but that of others, whether secular, religious, or atheistic. For others, their indifference is more theologically—more specifically, *pneumatologically*—driven: it is the Holy Spirit who provides us with all the understanding required. Consequently, there is little need to think deeply, if at all. Just believe! The net result is that there is little or no incentive to follow Paul's injunction to Timothy—namely, to study so that he can show himself approved by God and able to handle Scripture properly (2 Tim. 2:15). I think, too, that Peter makes a profound statement about the importance of reason in 1 Peter, a letter addressed to those "exiles scattered throughout the provinces of Pontus, Galatia, Cappadocia, Asia and Bithynia" (1:1)—that is, most of modern Turkey and the Greek Mediterranean islands. "In your hearts," he urges in 3:15, "revere Christ as Lord." And then, "Always be prepared to give an answer to everyone who asks you to give the reason for the hope that you have." Thus, having asserted to this diverse and scattered community that Jesus is Lord, he immediately links this statement to the ability to give a defense—an apologetic, a reasoned argument and explanation—for their hope and faith. And the same applies to followers of the Lord Jesus Christ today.

Others, for more denominational reasons, hold to a very high view of spirit and the Spirit, which unfortunately consigns the mind to a lower place regarding their faith. Most certainly, the strong emphasis that evangelicalism has historically placed on conversion has not been followed through in the contemporary scene with a similar emphasis on mind-transforming discipleship. It is all too facile to appropriate the dynamic process of sanctification to the Holy Spirit without the imperative of cognitive input. However, as the Puritan divine John Owen, in his classic tome on the Holy Spirit, argues, the Holy Spirit does not bypass the faculty of the mind in our growth in Christ.[32] More importantly, not only are we commanded to love God with our minds, as we have already noted, but it is through the renewing of our *minds* that we are transformed (Rom. 12:2). A theological method that gives primacy to Scripture, therefore, will put the ability to reason theologically in its rightful place.

Others have quite different, *cultural* reasons for their understanding of how reason is applied to their faith. Here, the concept of reason is understood within a wider worldview perspective in which the mind and its ability to reason are viewed very differently from how they are viewed in the West. For instance, those of us who are educated in a Western context or method are used to thinking analytically and logically and are well accustomed to abstract thinking. However, for those of us educated within non-Western contexts, this kind of Western rationality is quite foreign. Rather, thinking takes on a more holistic and experiential frame of mind, in which a more dialectical form of reasoning occurs.[33] This reminds us that language and culture significantly influence the way we think. It appears that while thinking is a universal human phenomenon, the actual way in which we think is very much specific to our culture and language. This, of course, should not be surprising. Recall the worldview questions in part 1—the way in which we answer these questions will act as underlying, unconscious, and precritical filters that, in turn, influence how the brain constructs its neural pathways, literally framing how we view the world and therefore how we engage, or reason, with it, consciously or unconsciously. Given that evangelicalism is a world movement, two significant corollaries follow from the above:

1. We do not all think the same way. The importance of this point should not be underestimated. Whatever this means for a specifically evangelical theological method, we should note that the Western church cannot impose its own form of reasoning on others, especially given that evangelicalism is growing most in the Majority World church, with its many different ways of thinking and reasoning. The need for wider dialogue and intercultural awareness, therefore, becomes a necessity rather than a niche point of interest.

2. Western rationalism itself is currently under scrutiny as the tectonic plates of its own modes of thinking shift significantly. Given that reason operates on the assumption that there is a truth of some sort to discover, the fact that truth itself is now perceived as a relativized construct within the post-postmodern West, the ramifications for knowledge and the place of reason are significant. With all the talk of fake news, Western reasoning now incorporates the notion of "truthiness"—"the quality of seeming or being felt to be true, even if not necessarily true."[34] Of course, the implications for any Christian truth claim are staggering: the battlegrounds are no longer drawn at the boundaries of relativism,

which at least suggests a shared belief in truth as a reality to be engaged. Rather, the line now distinguishes between truth as a reality in itself (whether or not it is believed) and the existential notion of truth as a subjective and temporal construct whose veracity and plausibility rest not on any objective reality but, rather, on a particular state of cognition wherein a statement is believed to be true at the time. The former attests to a reality that exists whether or not I believe it; the latter attests to one whose reality is determined by my own subjective decision and thought. Therefore, a contemporary evangelical theological method must engage not only with the understanding of reason that theologians have historically held in theological development but also with contemporary changes.

What, then, can we take forward as we explore the tool of reason in our theological method? First, that Christian theology is peculiarly a gift. We know the subject matter—God—only to the extent that God chooses us to know. Because this divinely sourced knowledge is personal knowledge, it will always be what Stephen Bevans describes as "tentative"—it is not to be understood as "proof" but rather as "understanding," not "certainty" but faith.[35] This knowledge, itself, is given most supremely in the gospel—the gracious gift of salvation procured for us through the incarnation, life, ministry, crucifixion, death, resurrection, ascension, and glorification of the Son of God himself. *No* thing became *some* thing in order that we might become everything the Creator intends for his image bearers. This event requires serious thinking—intentional *faith seeking understanding*—whether in the sense of ordinary theology, with its posture of worship and prayer on our knees, or in the activity of academic theology, with its posture of study at the desk, where truth, the goal of reason, surely is, as Peter Hicks describes, in terms rather similar to Ellen Charry's "sapience," personal communication from God to us that requires both our personal understanding and personal commitment.[36]

Reason and the Church

I hope that it is clear by now not only that reason holds a profoundly important place in an evangelical theological method but also that a specifically evangelical understanding of reason should be different from simple rationalism. It is, rather, the "understanding" part of *fides quaerens intellectum*, of faith seeking *understanding*. And when it comes to answering the question "What has Athens (the seat of reason) to do with Jerusalem (the seat of theology)?"[37] the answer must be—unlike that of the original speaker,

Tertullian—"Everything!" However, as we have argued, this union of mind and faith is not one consummated at the expense of Scripture. There is a worldview premised on Scripture that allows faith and reason to kiss.

In similar manner to there being false gospels to contend against, there are also false philosophies, false ways of reasoning, that are to be challenged. Paul, the first apostle to the gentiles, sets the tone: "See to it that no one takes you captive through hollow and deceptive philosophy, which depends on human tradition and the elemental spiritual forces of this world rather than on Christ" (Col. 2:8). Here again we evidence the reality of a particular view of reality—a worldview—where reason is given a place of significance.[38]

In many senses, the entire history of Christendom can be interpreted as one long bickering between faith and reason. Sometimes the former triumphs, often the latter. Each, however, influences the wider worldview for good or ill. We can highlight some significant illustrations to show the importance of how we reason and thus know and understand. As we have noted, Tertullian in the second century held strongly to the belief that philosophical inquiry was the source of heresy. However, he was not against reason itself, taking the view that Christian faith is a gift to everyone, and so reason was used more along the lines of what we have termed "ordinary" theology. The Cappadocian fathers championed the Christian doctrine of the Trinity and could not have achieved this high point in Christian thinking without serious training in philosophy. And although the philosophy they studied would have been predominantly pagan—that is, non-Christian—it was used carefully and circumspectly.[39] Yet, at the same time, the use of reason, for them, was always subordinated to the habits of faith, particularly prayer, since reason, like all other human attributes, is fallen and therefore incapable of providing any assurance concerning the invisible, however well it may provide understanding. Faith and reason remain distinctly separate.

We have already noted in relation to the identity of Jesus Christ that Scripture does not provide a ready-made descriptor. Rather, it took nearly three centuries to arrive at what now constitutes Christian orthodoxy regarding what Christians believe about Jesus Christ—that he is both everything God is and everything we are—two distinct realities, human and divine, and one person. Similarly, when it came to the identity of God—the Father of our Lord Jesus Christ, his only begotten Son, and the Spirit of God given at Pentecost—the church fathers not only wrestled with providing an understanding of God that honored Scripture but also faced the demanding challenge of reframing the meaning of key words so that they might have a vocabulary that was up to the task of carrying and communicating their faith seeking understanding. The fact is that the church's greatest theologians of this period, whose responses have become the very cornerstones of evangelical theology—namely, the doctrine of the two natures of Christ and the doctrine of the Trinity—received the best education in their day, which included the art and skill of thinking critically using the philosophies of Christian and—predominantly—non-Christian thinkers alike.

As a result of their faith seeking understanding, these patristic thinkers set the foundations for subsequent thought. By the Middle Ages, AD 500 to 1500, there were serious attempts at combining faith with reason, the specific impetus to this being the challenge facing Christian thinkers in the eleventh and twelfth centuries, when a Muslim worldview collided with Christendom in the form of commentaries on Aristotle that had been discovered to have been translated into Latin. These exceptional examples of reason incentivized the Christian church, rightly or wrongly, to step up to the challenge of Aristotelian rationalism. Admittedly, elements of pride were involved, but nonetheless, these endeavors brought about the founding of universities in Bologna, Paris, Oxford, and Cambridge. What we can see happening around this time illustrates the power of a worldview, and particularly its question "How do we know anything?" What emerged was the establishment of a common rational language—mathematics—which became the lingua franca of Europe and, in turn, led to what Lesslie Newbigin identifies as a paradigm of certainty.[40] This, of course, had significant repercussions regarding the place of faith in Western thinking.

At this point, the gauntlet was thrown down in the form of the philosophers' challenge and was picked up most significantly by a medieval scholar and expert in Jewish and Muslim thought, Thomas Aquinas. Which God is true? The God of the philosophers and natural theology? Or the God of the Bible and revelation? It was Aquinas who championed the place of reason in relation to faith in the form of a synthesis of Aristotelian philosophy and biblical tradition. For Aquinas, reason aids faith in that it enables us to understand what he describes as "the articles of faith" taught by the church. Of course, Aquinas put high value on the role of human reason, but it is always as a handmaiden to Scripture. More recently, Colin Gunton captures Aquinas's approach well in observing that "Aquinas also believed that reason operates in the service of faith in addition to providing a philosophical foundation for theology. *Its function is to penetrate into the meaning of the articles of faith taught by the Church in order to show how they should be understood.*"[41]

Of course, the compass has been set, as it were, by the role reason would play within this Catholic worldview,[42] one that would eventually give rise to misuse that, in turn, resulted in sixteenth-century Reformers like John Calvin and Martin Luther being suspicious of the role reason played in leading believers away from Scripture. As indebted as we are to the protest against baser practices of the church, the worldview in which faith predominated was entering its final chapters. Rather, what was to emerge was a worldview that increasingly deconstructed the worldviews prevalent in Scripture and in the patristic and medieval eras. It was a worldview where "enlightenment"—the quest for certainty (epistemology) and freedom (anthropology)—was sought at the expense of biblical revelation. Thus, from the mid-sixteenth to the end of the eighteenth century, a series of proposals would emerge that were to change Western rationality and its culture significantly. Again, we are privy to the tension between Christian faith and the demands of reason. Thus, René Descartes sought for certainty of thought, not objectively in God but in each human knower, who would establish true knowledge based on universal and indubitable foundations—that is, unquestionable facts that could be understood as "foundations." As Bruce Ellis Benson summarizes, "Foundationalism is the ideal of achieving epistemological certainty by providing a ground or 'foundation' for one's thought."[43] For this to occur, of course, the notion of an objective reality as well as the authority of religious belief had to be rejected.[44] In doing so, however, Descartes bequeathed to the West a dualism that remains with us to this day—namely, a dualism between the subjective and the objective, between mind and matter.[45]

John Locke, who also held to a Christian faith, built on Descartes's legacy, seeking to establish criteria for Christian faith that were drawn from outside the sphere of faith itself while allowing for some kind of "extraordinary communication."[46] To some extent, this was a worldview form of having your cake and eating it too! Given our preliminary argument—namely, that such knowledge is unknowable outside the realm of revelation and is only afforded via the gospel of Jesus Christ's life, death, resurrection, ascension, and glorification and the giving of the Spirit at Pentecost—Locke simply exacerbated Descartes's dualism in separating divine from human understanding in this way.

However, it was with Immanuel Kant in the eighteenth century that an Enlightenment view of reason assumed the role that would determine what Benson describes as the "modernist manifesto"[47] that was to determine how modernity and its successors perceived the place and role of religious faith. First, for human knowledge to be "mature," human beings, in essence, have to grow up. Thus, for Kant "enlightenment" was a thoroughly human endeavor—a movement from immaturity in not being able to think independently. Second, like Locke, Kant argued that we never know a thing directly, in itself, but only in its appearance to us. The consequence of this understanding for reason was to be far-reaching.

On the one hand, reason results in the subjectivity of truth. That is, truth is no longer "outside of us, something we discover and receive and submit to; it is something inside us, private, subjective."[48] One significant consequence of this was that theology was no longer understood in terms of exegesis of a gospel lived and practiced. Rather, it came "to be thought of as the intellectual justification of the faith, apart from the practice of Christian life,"[49] resulting in the reification of "natural" as opposed to "revealed" theology since the former, alone, complied with the rationality of the Enlightenment. That is, as Robert Jenson argues, the plausibility of the church's teachings and practices came "to depend on the general culture" and did so with devastating consequences for our understanding and use of reason.[50]

- We no longer have any access to truth—only our language about it.[51] And, of course, whoever controls our language—that is, what and how it communicates—wields power.
- Knowledge of God becomes a natural human capacity. Therefore, there is no need for "special revelation" since all knowledge is equal.[52]
  » Church thinking came to prefer a specific theological method—the historical-critical method. As we have already noted, "a method . . . is a self-conscious way of going about doing something."[53] Jenson's theological acumen comes to the fore in his critique here in highlighting two elements of this hermeneutic of suspicion and their consequences for our confidence to reason faithfully.
  » This kind of thinking has no teleology—that is, it does not necessarily mean that a statement intends anything. Of course, we see this aspect of Western reason coming to maturity in notions of "fake news" and "truthiness," where meaning is mercurial and where statements can be made to mean whatever those with the influence desire.
  » Such thinking has a particular historical "take" on what *really* happened. Thus, it has its own set of questions and beliefs.[54]

On the other hand, and as a result, for Kant and his successors the objectivity of knowledge, and thus our reasoning, is grounded in our own individual subjectivity. That is, "all of us see the world in a particular way."[55] It is not a very long hop, skip, and jump from this understanding of reason to the contemporary postmodern position, where reason determines truth, a subjective determination premised not on "facts" but on their interpretation, at best, or their fallacious construction, at worst. Understood from this perspective, the notion of "fake news" can be perceived as simply the consequence of separating faith in an objective reality from the reason required to discover and comprehend it. The phenomenon of "fake news" reveals more deeply the power of worldview and its answer to the question of how we know and, thus, the place of truth and reason. Brian McNair argues that fake news is itself "one expression of a wider crisis of trust" in the "long-standing structures of power and authority" of the architects, designers, manufacturers, and propagators of contemporary liberal democracy whose power is being challenged.[56] He especially captures the degree of power operating here when he comments,

> Great power rivalries play out in many arenas, but in the crucial aspect of communication, the competition to define what is and is not "fake news" is one of the most visible to global publics. It goes to the heart of what is meant and understood by concepts such as Truth, Trust, Objectivity, and is a central strand in the information warfare deployed by political actors within and between nation-states.[57]

At a more popular level, this shift in perspective concerning one of the most basic building blocks of reason—truth—is reflected in the fact that in 2005 the word "truthiness" was voted word of the year by the American Dialect Society,[58] and in 2006 it was so designated by the *Merriam-Webster's Dictionary*, both merely reflecting a cultural shift that would be further reflected in 2016 when "post-truth" was voted the Oxford Word of the Year.[59] By then the term had over a decade of use, having first been introduced in 2004 as a descriptor of contemporary social dishonesty and deception, only to be picked up in 2010 and applied to journalism.[60] It is a short hop, skip, and jump from "truthiness" to "fake news." Thus, journalists may operate from "truthiness" while the White House response will be "fake news."

This linguistic development reveals that, at a deeply cultural level, our notions of reasoning itself are up for grabs. The changeable nature of language and the words we employ allow for profound shifts in understanding to be made. This is a positive, in some ways, since it reflects how language develops. As we have seen, the patristic authors recognized this and used it to the benefit of the Christian faith in changing the word "person" to express something stable about the triune God. However, the opposite is happening today. In light of the ideological movement we call "modernity,"[61] where the authorities of Scripture, church, and tradition were replaced by the authority of the subjective self, it follows that the number of subjects who reason in this manner can quite plausibly equal the number of perceived truths. Of course, this has profound implications for how we communicate and talk reasonably concerning our faith. T. S. Eliot expresses this tension perhaps supremely when he writes,

> Words strain,
> Crack and sometimes break, under the burden,
> Under the tension, slip, slide, perish,
> Decay with imprecision, will not stay in place,
> Will not stay still.[62]

Ironically, rather than truth being liberated from all authorities bar our own, subjectivism results in truth being trapped in the reasoning of our own individual private opinions, whether they be truth or post-truth in nature. Matthew d'Ancona rather hits the nail on the head when he comments, "Our Own Post-Truth era is a taste of what happens when a society relaxes its defence of the values that underpin its cohesion, order and progress: the values of veracity, honesty and accountability."[63]

What we see today is the eclipse of a Christian worldview in the West. The worldview that has predominated for nearly two thousand years—namely, the Judeo-Christian worldview—is now superseded by one that has sought emancipation from this worldview. Secularization has finally come of age. Whereas the meaning of words once relied on a stable view of reality furnished by God, now this stability has been removed, with inevitable consequences. Graham Ward identifies these consequences in terms of "the implosion of secularism," by which he means two things:

1. What was once understood to be governed by divine fiat is now "governed by its own values, its own internally conceived laws."
2. This internalized worldview has no reality by which to regulate it other than itself and consequently "over shoots it." Part of the "over shooting" explains our contemporary dismissal of objective and therefore fixed realities or truth. It involves the deconstruction of reason, which postmodernism—the later flowering of modernism—affords. The result is "truthiness" rather than "Truth."[64]

Linda Hutcheon anticipates current phenomena when she observes that "postmodernism is a contradictory phenomenon, one that uses and abuses, installs and then subverts, the very concepts it challenges."[65] However, it does so with a very clear agenda—to control the ways in which we understand and express the world in which we live. And it does so because to control these "representations" is "to wield power," and to attack them "is to attack power."[66] To attack the powers that control what and how we think is to liberate humanity from the tyranny of external authorities. Of course, this is nothing other than the maturation of Enlightenment ideology, where human reason is hermetically sealed within its own delineations. It is a trade-off between publicly recognized authority—whether king, pope, God, Bible, or church—and, in Ingolf Dalferth's words, the "purely private character of religious and ideological convictions" of the individual:

> This ideology means not only that the individual is released from public accountability in matters of religion and left with the illusion that in this sensitive

realm we are responsible to no one but ourselves. To this ideology belongs also a patchwork of mentality that systematically fails to recognize religion's relation to reality and the perception of reality that belongs to faith. In connection with a constructivism that considers itself radical, we might read that "because reality is simply our creation and the product of our fictions," so too religion, faith and prayer "are rehabilitated as autosuggestive reinforcers of these fictions." . . . The slogan is clear: "I determine what God is!" No one asks whether what is determined this way is really God and whether God really is this way. These questions play no role because they are not thought to have any answer that would be more than a new (or old) mixture of opinions. In matters of religion and faith, public opinion now appears to recognize, at most, questions of taste.[67]

I propose that the contemporary challenge exposed in this cultural shift should be perceived not negatively, as something to bemoan, but rather as a clarion call to an evangelical theological method to respond positively and faithfully to the challenge this shift poses. We know that theology is exegesis of the gospel and that the gospel seeks to engage its contemporary context in order that it might be best heard, understood, and received in faith. We know, too, that the task of evangelical theology is to give understanding to our faith so we can move forward in our biblical faith and reasoning. In terms of "ordinary" theology, this is the point at which most Christians arrest their thinking. However, if we are to achieve this task, we must also recognize the necessity of a theological method appropriate to the charge. This means that we cannot let our theological understanding rest at the level of individualistic, privatized, uncommitted, self-opinionated chatter. Otherwise, evangelical theology becomes as fragmented as the postmodernisms around it.

Therefore, the gauntlet needs to be picked up regarding the place and role of reason in our theological method if we are to engage the gospel with this particular worldview. Here is where the prophetic nature of theology comes to our aid. Remember, the role of the theologian is not only to be a faithful conduit of the church community's beliefs to each new generation but equally to be aware of the present challenges the church faces and to anticipate the future. Only in this way are we able once more to speak faithfully into the way things are or are about to be. To do this, language, neural pathways, thought structures—forms of reason—need to be established to empower the people of God to remain faithful to the gospel, whatever might come.

In terms of where this leaves us now in relation to an evangelical theological method, I think Craig Carter articulates the good news and the bad news clearly. On the one hand, and to some extent, "the original Enlightenment is over." That is, "the naïve faith in reason as an adequate source of morality and truth has run its course and is dissipating into the acids of postmodernism."

That's the good news. The bad news, on the other hand, is that it "continues to exert a malign influence" over us. It would appear, in turn, that this malignancy pervades not only our culture but increasingly evangelicalism too; that is, "the cult of the autonomous individual unfortunately continues without diminishment in the romanticism and postmodernism that followed the Enlightenment."[68] If unabated, the endgame might simply be that just about every evangelical will end up speaking solely for him- or herself—simply because, as David Tracy diagnoses, "Most forms of postmodernity are explosions of once-forgotten, marginalized, and repressed realities of Enlightenment modernity: the other, the different . . . the fragments that disallow any totality system by demanding attention to the other, especially the different and the marginal other."[69] While I am not fully in agreement with Tracy's own counterproposal, I fully endorse Carter's proposal of a return to what he posits as a premodern way of reading and interpreting Scripture.

Now, this notion of "fragments" is important. It acts as an interpretive key to just about everything we can observe today in our daily, individual, corporate, private, and public lives. Our cityscapes reflect the fragmentation of architecture, with individual construction vying for unique status. News media copy daily fragments of disparate news for mindless consumption. Art galleries hang visual fragments of color or texture or shape or artifact, all signifying that the world in which we live has no essential cohesion.[70] What was marginalized in the outgoing Western worldview is celebrated in the new: the yearly Oscars reify social, relational, sexual, political, and economic fragments supported by various forms of political correctness that silence and thus marginalize once mainstream voices and viewpoints.[71] Such is the contemporary success of secularization that even those voices that once championed the secular trajectory are now dismissed for not being sufficiently secular.

An Alternative Evangelical Reason

Intrinsic to an evangelical theological method is the belief that its purpose is to facilitate interpretation of the gospel for the here and now. This, in itself, is an act of reason—of faith reaching out for understanding, communication, and application. Faith requires understanding for it to be communicated to others; understanding requires faith in that it is a critical expression of what is often "hoped for," "unseen," "tacit," "liminal." Understanding is "a self-conscious way of going about doing something," as Jenson proposed in a text cited above. Yet, the potency of this act is not always immediately understood. The power of our theological method does not reside in its constituent parts, important as they are. Rather, that power is in the method's *metaphysical* integrity—that is, the degree to which our theological method corresponds with reality—that is how we ascertain its true impact.

As we have already noted, every human being exists within a wider and often unrecognized worldview. Its significance is located in how well it enables us to live meaningfully in our respective worlds—the questions it asks and the answers by which we then live, think, and construct entire civilizations. In one sense, the overview above concerning Western Christianity's escalating capitulation of its Judeo-Christian worldview makes for rather depressing reading. The degree of human dysfunction that contemporary Western culture imposes on non-Western societies in order to maintain its own standards of living might well be perceived as the pathology of a worldview that does not correspond to creation and the law of neighbor love. And so, as a civilization we are at a crisis point—whether in the form of greenhouse gases and climate change (or not); or the epidemic of plastics polluting our seas; or diminishing fertility rates within Western industrialized nations; or immigration and the social, religious, political, and economic challenges that ensue; or relational pathologies; or dystopic social systems—there is perhaps reason to step outside the modernist/postmodernist boxes that evangelical theology has inhabited for the better part of the mid-twentieth century and continues to inhabit down to the present[72] and to recapitulate the gospel. To achieve this, we require a robust theological method, particularly in relation to reason and the possibility of knowing with any certainty, let alone understanding with integrity what we come to know.

Foundations

At this point, we remind ourselves that an evangelical theology is hallmarked by its own form of biblical reasoning, which is constructed upon its own biblical worldview perspective. In addition, we remind ourselves that our reasoning is not ours to preside over intellectually as we might wish, but rather it is to be located within the wider abundance of God's generosity, expressed most fully in the gospel yet grounded in three distinct dimensions:

1. *Creation.* Creation conforms to an intended way of being. Thus, in relation to reason, the doctrine of creation means that human beings think and reason according to certain principles. For example, each of us has what can be called a "learning style," which is determined not only by our external culture (we go to school to be taught to think in particular ways) but also by our own neural and cognitive development (inherited from our biological gene pool and developed by our habits). Yet there is more. Our understanding that all things come into existence by the

will of God and through the agency of the Son and are sustained by the Lord and the Giver of life, the Holy Spirit, allows us to make two further claims: first, that our thinking will at all times be bounded by the Creator's intentions and not ours, what Walter Brueggemann describes as *the self-giving generosity* of God. Second, this understanding offers us assurance that the triune God can indeed be known and that such knowledge is a consequence of personal generosity.[73]

2. *Covenant*. We think within specific relational contexts. Thus, in relation to reason, the doctrine of covenant means that people who have come to saving faith in Jesus Christ are renewed in their characters to the degree that their minds are renewed by the covenant relationship they have with God their Father by virtue of the redemptive work of the Son, as energized by the Spirit of God. Therefore, an evangelical understanding of covenant will resonate with Paul's perception laid out for us in 1 Corinthians 8:1–3—namely, that knowledge may well know something, but love actually sees it through to doing something about it.[74] This, of course, is the discombobulating nature of the gospel. As John Webster puts it, "What is scandalous about Christian theology is that it is a work of reason which can only fulfil its office if it bears the marks of God's destruction of the wisdom of the wise and the cleverness of the clever."[75] This, in turn, provides a specifically Christian assurance—namely, that the covenant we have with the triune God in and through the Lord Jesus Christ is what Brueggemann describes in terms of being "intimately and determinedly held in relation to God's governance."[76]

3. *Consummation*. Our focus—and therefore our attention, thinking, application, and desire—is driven by a hope that is fed by an increasingly informed and transformed understanding.[77] This hope of complete fulfillment echoes notes of Lesslie Newbigin's sense of *proper confidence* in being able to know God,[78] something we can indeed trust on the grounds, as Brueggemann put it, that the entirety of creation and covenant is contoured by God's *utterly reliable fidelity*.[79]

We can add to these three general criteria four additional distinctives regarding our reasoning:

1. Our foundation and authority are established by our understanding of Scripture.

2. Our understanding of Scripture is both apprehended and applied by faith.

3. Our entire being is one that is redeemed and sanctified as evidence of our salvation.

4. Our minds and intellects are christologically liberated from the bondage of sin and pneumatically empowered both to indwell and to live out our gospel identity by virtue of our reason.

The challenge facing the place of reason within a contemporary evangelical academic theology is one of integration. Historically, the task of academic theology has been premised on Enlightenment notions of objectivity and detachment from all external authorities over human reason or experience. The implications for Scripture, tradition, and the wider church have been put on the table, as it were, especially for any quest for truth. On the one hand, objective and verifiable knowledge was deemed suitable for public consumption. On the other, anything that failed this test of rationality was relegated to the realm of private and subjective opinion. Again, there were significant implications for the quest of faith seeking understanding. This dualism between public and private knowledge, in turn, enabled evangelical scholarship to participate in the academy on the latter's terms, in ways rather similar to women's experience in the workplace—namely, having to work twice as hard to receive the same recognition as their male counterparts. Evangelical theologians have indeed worked hard and as a result have made significant inroads into the academy, where they were once dismissed. However, it has been at the cost of an additional dualism: doing theology on the academy's terms and being a believer on the church's terms.

Jenson helpfully summarizes the big picture regarding reason's relation to Scripture in terms of marriage. First, the relation between pre-Enlightenment thinkers and Scripture can be likened to a marriage—a union between the two. Then, with the Enlightenment, the marriage between Scripture and reason is dissolved. Modernity, in turn, becomes the protracted divorce process of this marriage. I would add to this trajectory that postmodernity is the fallout from the divorce process once the marriage is annulled.[80] By and large, the evangelical theological academy accepted this trade-off for its place in the academy. It has succeeded in achieving acceptance and is now a major player. The cost of this trade-off, however, works itself out in the wider nonacademic, ordinary theological daily lives of the faithful.[81]

Toward a Reasonable Solution: Reason as Wisdom

We no longer inhabit a world that believes in absolutes, whether sovereignty, power, or truth. The cultural turn to a hermeneutic of suspicion and the postmodern realization that there can never be only one perspective, one interpretation, or one take coincides with the evangelical need to reframe the relationship of theology with reason, with the goal that theology would assume a more biblical, rather than modernist, focus.

This is where the notion of wisdom as the evidence of biblical reasoning helps us. We have seen that wisdom, or sapience, has been separated from reason. A line of thought does not require wise or beneficial consequences to make it true. This disconnect allows us to separate character from thought—the private life of a leader bearing no consequence on his or her public policies or actions. Of course, such a state of affairs could not be further removed from a biblical understanding of wisdom and reason. Scripture points to what we might describe as a cross-shaped kind of reason, one that is Holy Spirit resourced and driven. Put bluntly, if the cross is the wisdom of God that deconstructs the wisdom or reasoning of the world, then this same cross-shaped thinking should be evidenced in how we go about our theology, whether ordinary or academic. Of course, cross-shaped thinking is easier to do as ordinary theology, as the history of Christian spirituality reveals. The challenge for an evangelical theological method is met to the degree it is Holy Spirit driven and resourced: an evangelical theology will be hallmarked by the degree to which it bears fruit in our characters and expresses something of the nature of God the Father, Son, and Spirit. These markers are not separate from how we think but are intrinsic to our thinking. Such a task involves the learning of habits and skills that we will explore when we turn to our final methodological "tool"—community. These skills are the result of reason and wisdom, which result in practical codes of living that are universally acknowledged.[82]

Thus, an evangelical theological method will contour reason and wisdom with covenant. Why? Because only as we incorporate into our thinking the covenant expectations expressed by Jesus's summary of Jewish covenant—to love God with one's entire being and to love one's neighbor as oneself, as well as his command to take the gospel to the entire world—will we transform the pragmatic and practical into something that is capable of carrying the weight and force of the gospel. This reason-wisdom-covenant dynamic does not "just happen." Rather, it is living knowledge, living reasoning, such that not only *what* we think but also *how* we think is cross-shaped and results in pneumatic—that is, Spirit-empowered—living. Put this way, Athens has very little to do with Jerusalem if Jerusalem's work results only in an inward turn that produces a thinking self who alone is the judge of reason. However, when that work results in an outward turn that seeks to proclaim Jesus Christ as Truth and as the one who is the Wisdom of God and therefore the true judge of all things reasonable (and unreasonable), then we are moving in the right direction.

I hope by now you can see that an evangelical theology has its own plausibility. It is based on the prior credibility of the church, which in turn is founded on Scripture's own authority. This plausibility is both trinitarian and christological.

1. It is trinitarian in that we come to know God because of the faithfulness and righteousness of Jesus Christ. Jesus reveals to us that God is our Father. We see in Jesus Christ a life of filial obedience—faithful, trusting, and total obedience of the Son in the good will and love of his heavenly Father. This reveals Jesus Christ to be his true Son. In turn, this relationship is energized, like all personal relationships, by "spirit"—the life-energizing, relationship-empowering force field that "grows" friendship, relationship, and love. God the Father and Son are no different; their energy source is the Holy Spirit himself, whom Augustine describes as the "bond of love" between the Father and Son.[83] Theirs is a fully knowing relationship between Father, Son, and Spirit. There are various theological terms that describe this way of relating. One is *koinonia*: communion, or fellowship, of the deepest kind between persons.[84] Another is *perichoresis*: the mutual indwelling—permeation—of Father, Son, and Spirit in such a way that it is not possible to conceive of one without the other two.[85] In this relational knowing there is no autonomous self. Rather, the divine persons know in pure love as they are known in pure love. Were we to experience this quality of relationality in the here and now, we would most likely describe it in terms of absolute confidence—or proper confidence.

2. Our reasoning will also be christological in that an evangelical theological method knows that this kind of personal knowledge of God is only accessible through Jesus Christ and is very clearly given on Jesus Christ's own terms. Thus, we remind ourselves that Jesus does not call us to be theologians. He calls us to be disciples. This discipleship is contoured by the ability to reflect upon, desire, and worship the One we come to know through Jesus Christ and his gospel as it is revealed in Scripture and experienced in transformed lives. Therefore, to be a theologian is to be someone who follows Jesus Christ and who reflects on this relationship and seeks to make sense of it both individually and corporately. To be a follower of Jesus is to be someone who has taken up, and continually takes up, one's cross, dies to self, and is faithfully obedient to Jesus Christ. What happens, as a result, can only be described in terms of a change in gestalt—a change in our very way of being—so much so that it can be described in terms of having the very mind of Christ (1 Cor. 2:16). (What do you think it means to have the mind of Christ? How do you get it?)

All this is to say that the kind of reasoning and thinking that should drive an evangelical theological method is personal. It is personal both in that it is knowledge of the triune God—Father, Son, and Spirit—and because this kind of knowledge and form of reasoning bring about our own personal transformation. Thus, it is a way of thinking that does not conform to the rationalities of the world around us, despite there being significant or only slight points of overlap. In addition, evangelical reasoning is plausible in that it has its own form of rationality, both trinitarian and christological. None of this, however, allows us to sidestep the hard work involved in faith seeking understanding. While we live by faith and not by sight—in that we receive the gospel by faith and live in hopeful anticipation of its fulfillment—God remains a mystery and therefore worthy of significant thought and reflection in order that we might love God and neighbor more and respond in faithful obedience. Additionally, Jesus Christ presents to us profound tensions that require considerable and time-consuming thinking: he is fully human and also fully divine, and yet one person; he suffered an excruciating death, yet three days later broke out of death.

The history of Christian thought identifies magnificent moments in human thought when ideas and language were stretched to make sense of the divine mystery revealed to us in Scripture and to communicate it effectively. Our forefathers and foremothers thought and reasoned as a matter of firm conviction based on biblical knowledge and personal as well as corporate testimony. Their faith seeking understanding was one in which, as Alvin Plantinga puts it, faith was both revealed to the mind and sealed to the heart. As we have noted above, all this requires the right "affections"—of loving God, neighbor, and self. There is, according to Plantinga, "an intimate relation between revealing and sealing, knowledge and affection, intellect and will; they cooperate in a deep and complex and intimate way in the person of faith."[86] What matters, however, is that our modes of thinking and reasoning conform to Scripture and to the One we come to know through Jesus Christ.

I will let Parker Palmer do what he does best, describing and inspiring, this time in relation to how we might envisage the use of our minds in the search for truth as it is revealed to us in and through Jesus Christ:

> To know something or someone in truth is to enter troth with the known, to rejoin with new knowing what our minds have put asunder. To know is to become betrothed, to engage the known with one's whole self, an engagement one enters with attentiveness, care, and good will. To know in truth is to allow one's self to be known as well, to be vulnerable to the challenges and changes any true relationship brings. To know in truth is to enter into the life of that which we know and to allow it to enter into ours. Truthful knowing weds the knower

and the known; even in separation, the two become part of each other's life and fate. . . . Truth involves entering a relationship with someone or something genuinely other than us, but with whom we are intimately bound. . . . Truth requires the knower to become interdependent with the known. Both parties have their own integrity and otherness, and one party cannot be collapsed into the other. . . . We find truth by pledging our troth, and knowing becomes a reunion of separated beings whose primary bond is not of logic but love.[87]

SUGGESTED READING

Benson, Bruce Ellis. *Graven Ideologies: Nietzsche, Derrida, and Marion on Modern Idolatry*. Downers Grove, IL: IVP Academic, 2002.

Byerly, T. Ryan. *Introducing Critical Thinking: The Skills of Reasoning and the Virtues of Inquiry*. Grand Rapids: Baker Academic, 2017.

Charry, Ellen. *By the Renewing of Your Minds: The Pastoral Function of Christian Doctrine*. Oxford: Oxford University Press, 1997.

Clark, Kelly James. *God and the Brain: The Rationality of Belief*. Grand Rapids: Eerdmans, 2019.

Davies, William. *Nervous States: How Feeling Took Over the World*. London: Jonathan Cape, 2019.

Dew, James K., Jr., and Paul M. Gould. *Philosophy: A Christian Introduction*. Grand Rapids: Baker Academic, 2019.

Duby, Steven J. *God in Himself: Scripture, Metaphysics, and the Task of Christian Theology*. London: Apollos, 2019.

Green, Christopher C., and David I. Starling, eds. *Revelation and Reason in Christian Theology*. Bellingham, WA: Lexham, 2018.

McDermott, Gerald R. *Everyday Glory: The Revelation of God in All of Reality*. Grand Rapids: Baker Academic, 2018.

McGrath, Alister E. *A Passion for Truth: The Intellectual Coherence of Evangelicalism*. Downers Grove, IL: InterVarsity, 1996.

Meek, Esther Lightcap. *Loving to Know: Introducing Covenant Epistemology*. Eugene, OR: Cascade Books, 2011.

Moreland, J. P. *Love Your God with All Your Mind: The Role of Reason in the Life of the Soul*. Colorado Springs: NavPress, 2012.

Murray, Abdu. *Saving Truth: Finding Meaning and Clarity in a Post-Truth World*. Grand Rapids: Zondervan, 2018.

Newbigin, Lesslie. *Proper Confidence: Faith, Doubt, and Certainty in Christian Discipleship*. Grand Rapids: Eerdmans, 1995.

Smith, James K. A. *On the Road with Saint Augustine: A Real-World Spirituality for Restless Hearts*. Grand Rapids: Brazos, 2019 (see especially pp. 142–57).

eight

Experience

The Great Experiment

Tucked far into one of the most succinct, penetrating, and yet readable presentations of the Christian faith, C. S. Lewis's *Mere Christianity*, we encounter a brief but profound insight:

Theology is, in a sense, an experimental science.[1]

What Lewis means by this resonates with our earliest comments on the subject matter of theology—God—who can be known only if he chooses to be known. So, he goes on to say, "When you come to knowing God, the initiative lies on His side. If He does not show Himself, nothing you can do will enable you to find Him. And, in fact, He shows much more of Himself to some people than to others—not because He has favourites, but because it is impossible for Him to show Himself to a man whose whole mind and character are in the wrong condition."[2] In putting things this way, Lewis gives weight not only to the place of reason in our theological method in describing theology as a science.[3] He also prioritizes the place of human experience in our theological method—it is experimental. That is, in some sense, theology is what Christians produce as they "experiment" in the laboratories of their own transformed lives as well as in the corporate experience of the church in its universal and historical encounter with divine revelation.[4] In this sense, Lewis echoes John Wesley's earlier belief that "most religion was related to or based on experience."[5] Lewis's insight resonates on so many levels: first, the discipline of theology is to be as exacting of its own texts and subject, God, as any other discipline is of its own, including the sciences. Thus, the manner by which we approach God should conform to correct ways of knowing, as does any other academic discipline; otherwise nothing of any consequence can be said of God.

Second, our theology should entail some degree of "experiment"—if not simply in tasting and seeing that the LORD is good (Ps. 34:8). In making this point, Lewis rejects any notion of theology being abstracted from our own ability to test, reason, hypothesize, deduct, and conclude. Indeed, since, as we have already seen regarding reason, we are to *indwell* in order to *know*, the supposition follows that we are to *experiment*, to *engage*, and thus *experience* what this revelation means. The kind of reasoning proposed in the previous chapter suggests that to acquire sapience and thus to become a wise person—someone who flourishes in life, for whom knowledge becomes transformational and life-nourishing and sustaining—there must be some kind of "experiential" element to our theological method. And, as we will argue in the next chapter, both the experiential and the experimental take shape and form in the laboratory of life we call "church."

Third, if our subject matter, God, is known only to the extent that God reveals Godself—Father, Son, and Spirit—to us in the messy events of human dysfunctionality, history, and destiny, then this can hardly be described in terms of abstract theory. Rather, our knowledge of God comes about as we engage the gospel of our Lord Jesus Christ, respond to God the Father's gift of new life, and participate by means of the new life, the new breath, the new energy, the new Spirit in the altogether different polity and economics Jesus describes as the kingdom of God. Christian theology is drawn from this kind of engagement, which emerges from many different contexts, whether biblical or historical, each particular to a person or family or clan. Some encounters are particularly privileged and go on to be captured as narrative or dogma, whether the encounter of Noah, Moses, Miriam, the apostle John or Paul, Lydia, Priscilla, Ambrose of Milan, Augustine of Hippo, Basil the Great, Hilda of Whitby, John Damascene, Anselm of Canterbury, Clare of Assisi, Julian of Norwich, Martin Luther, Richard Hooker, Teresa of Avila, John Owen, Friedrich Schleiermacher, Phoebe Palmer, Karl Barth—the list is pregnant with giants of the faith, each with their own challenges, each with a specific context. Colin Gunton rightly comments that all our theologies emerge from specific contexts and that, therefore, "the context is one of the authorities to which the theologian must listen."[6]

Fourth, the notion of context is purely hypothetical until it is inhabited by agents—people like you and me—who encounter the God and Father of our Lord Jesus Christ as his Spirit brings life to us through the good news of the gospel. Encountering this God in this way through this proclamation results in what we might describe as "experience."

Fifth, as Ellen Charry points out, experience is a "disturbing" concept due to its ambiguity and awkwardness.[7] This is demonstrably obvious in the biblical narrative of Genesis 38, which describes the chaotic story of Judah's life in one of the most pivotal chapters of Genesis, where a wholly dysfunctional family group becomes the bedrock of a nation, a set of individuals whose lives would trump any contemporary TV sitcom in terms of believability, and yet whose experience of the living God is transformative and redemptive. This chapter expresses "experience" at its zenith. And yet it is also disturbing—it shatters our preconceived notions of order and merit and eschews any notion that the God of Israel and the Father of our Lord Jesus Christ is partial to the color-coordinated, perfect-smile, six-pack Kens or Barbies who bombard our senses each time we switch on the TV or buy groceries or sit in the dentist's waiting room or a hair salon. Divine choosing that translates into human experience disturbs us because it does not allow us to disengage from the gospel—it seeks out the unnoticed, the belittled, the broken, the messy, the time-consuming, the liminal, the not-quite-one-of-us. Its accusing romance with our sin and its transforming consummation engage the impurities of our lives at a deeply experiential level. It offers us a vision of the unseen, of what lies beyond our gaze and our boundaries, clear of our dysfunctions and past our disappointments. The experiential will always be metaphorical because it results from engagement with the divine—the no thing—and therefore is beyond the language we attribute to "things." Through the eyes of faith our theology maps not only past encounters but what is still to come. It gives expression to what already *is* because it has already been accomplished by Christ even though it does not appear to be: we are seated with Christ Jesus in heavenly places in our spirits (Eph. 2:6) and yet are firmly grounded by our physical bodies; our relational dysfunctions are already dealt with because of what Jesus Christ achieved on the cross (2 Cor. 5:21), and yet we still fall; we have been set free from the law of sin and death and been made alive by the Spirit of life in Christ Jesus (Rom. 8:2; 6:18)—and yet our physical bodies wear out and die.

Sixth, as Jeff Astley reminds us, "Experience is a good thing."[8] It signifies that we are alive! It demonstrates the power of the gospel as transformative and as engaging of both the mess and the hopes that make us who we are. It is expressed through our imaginations and erupts through the way we interpret what happens in and through our lives. It makes us wise rather than intellectually clever. It empowers us to discern the valuable from the insubstantial, the important from the interesting. And it enables us to see connections that otherwise would remain hidden.[9] For very positive reasons, an evangelical theological method resists anyone, past or present, who holds a somewhat "snooty" attitude to engaging experience in their theological quests.

Last, it is through the act of prayer and worship that we learn how to live. In old money, this is described as *lex orandi, lex credendi—how we pray and worship influences what we believe*. An evangelical theological method will, moreover, seek to extend this rule of faith to include *and what we believe influences how we live: lex orandi, lex credendi, lex vivendi*. Important in this insight is the fact that, for many of us, our experiences of prayer and worship are very much the starting point in our theology, in terms of what we believe—and in our theological method, in relation to how we go about what we believe. The equally important point here, however, is that this experience, as Anthony Thiselton puts it, should be "suitably *interpreted, qualified and constrained* in the light of biblical revelation."[10] Without the influence of our other tools—Scripture, tradition, and reason—basing our theological interpretation only on experience produces "unstable or diverse interpretation."[11]

There remains, however, a very real awkwardness and an ever-present possibility of stumbling in this divine-human encounter if only because while we are firmly rooted in the present, we are always pressing toward a better *we*, a more whole *me*, a more loving *us*, a clearer reflection of the triune God. Therefore, the notion of the experiential as a somewhat fluid "tool" in our theological method is perhaps, at the same time, the most significant, excepting the priority of Scripture. The reason for this is since God is revealed through human experience in such a way as to draw out faith and obedience, each of these revelatory experiences will at least challenge if not completely discombobulate the status quo. If you think about it, they must—they are revealing something hitherto hidden to us, as well as breaking up established patterns that have become possibly immured by repetition or familiarity. Either way, of all the tools we are looking at, experience is the "greasy pig" of our theological method. So, best to identify the animal we are engaging!

Defining Experience

It is perhaps a reflection of the banished state of experience, or of the influence experience has had and continues to have on how we go about our theology, that there is a sense in which to state that all theology is contextual is to state the obvious. Except that the contextual includes the experiential. As noted above, Gunton reminds us, "We must acknowledge the fact that all theologies belong in a particular context, and so are, to a degree, limited by the constraints of that context. To that extent the context is one of the authorities to which the theologian must listen."[12] A significant part of this "particular context" is the transforming response to the gospel we have experienced, our encounter with the God and Father of our Lord Jesus Christ and the life-changing energy of the Spirit, as well as how in reading Scripture we gain a sense of belonging to a body politic we know as "church." This experience as it relates to the ongoing task of theology, whether ordinary or academic, can be both individual, personal experience and corporate, community experience. Each dimension, whether personal or communal, embraces a wide range of human experience. The individual involves the subjective, inward-looking aspect of each of our lives, which embraces also the external aspects of the social, cultural, communal, and global village. When we consider this experience in relation to our own personal lives, we recognize that it includes all manner of things: conversion, baptism—in water and Spirit—guidance from both Scripture and church, words of previous knowledge, effective teaching, signs and wonders, healings, God-encounters, personal freedom from debilitating habits and addictions.

Scripture attests to the fact that human experience is one of the most powerful theological norms, whether it be Abram responding to the call of a very unknown yet extravagant Lord God, or Moses being enticed by a burning bush that was not consumed by the fire, or the paradigmatic exodus from Egypt and the crossing through the Sea of Reeds and divine provisions in the wilderness, or the establishing and flourishing, for a short period, of a royal dynasty, or experiencing the Lord God's presence in the temple, or being comforted and sustained while in Babylonian exile, or being on the receiving end of judgment. Again, we witness the experience of waiting for promises to be fulfilled, especially in unexpected places with insignificant people who are connected solely by the golden thread of obedient faith and trust in the God who speaks quietly but profoundly into different people's lives. This is true for everyone, as it was in the unassuming lives of Mary or Joseph, twelve searching disciples, an inquisitive tax-collector, a promiscuous Samaritan woman, blind beggars, ostracized lepers, condemned criminals, let alone the more extravagant experience of Paul on his way to kill more blasphemers claiming a cursed and crucified rabbi was Messiah, or John with his apocalyptic revelations on the island of Patmos. And these are only the records of a tiny percentage of people whose "lived-in-ness" in relation to the gospel catapulted them into an imperative to put into words, into song, into poetry what they had experienced. Then, of course, in the interplay of personal reflection and testimony, people discover that theirs is not an accident (a one-off experience), not even a coincidence ("Oh my—that happened to you too!") but a pattern (the normal experience of people caught up in the gospel's transformative power) that results in personal (experienced) transformation.

Pause

What are the various experiences of the triune God you have had that have influenced your theology? How would you describe their impact on what you believe?

Only when we become conscious of this "lived-in-ness" do we appreciate the sheer diversity of information and knowledge that experience supplies in our theological development. If we consider what we learned in part 1—that we are talking about the God who is not part of creation and therefore cannot be caught up in its cause-and-effect nature—it becomes more obvious that any experience of the triune God comes not by our own making but as a gift, as surprise, as encounter, as love seeking. Theologians of late have begun to make taxonomies of these various religious experiences in order to identify and understand them better. For example, Richard Swinburne, more philosopher than theologian, identifies five areas of spiritual experience:

1. Public—I see a beautiful sunset and sense the presence of God.
2. Private—A medical operation is canceled because the growth has disappeared.
3. Dreams or Visions—I put into words a deeply personal experience of the divine.
4. Numinous (concerning the spiritual realm)—I have mystical experiences that defy words.
5. Conversion—I am aware of God's presence bringing about transformation.[13]

I like the condensed focus Swinburne provides, and I think it would be helpful here to consider how each has affected how you view God. However, I am more attracted to the approach taken by Roger Olson, mainly because, first, he articulates his view of experience within his own experience, which I think is exactly where it should be located, and second, because of the sense of "lived-in-ness" that he brings to his theological method, as a result.[14] He identifies several aspects of experience that are worth exploring a little further:

1. *Common, universal human experience.* Olson identifies this as "a universal human experience if only a sense of something as sacred." I like this description, as it opens *the divine* to more than what happens on a Sunday or in a worship service. Rather, it allows God to speak to us through both the ecclesial (church) as well as the natural (the world).

2. *Cultural experience.* This operates through what we call the *aesthetic*: through music, architecture, and art. Thus, Gustav Mahler's *Resurrection Symphony* was the first piece of music that took me out of myself to another dimension of sound. Or my experience of Victorian architecture in my home city of Glasgow—where masons created red sandstone delights for the sheer sake of it. I remember one of the most striking moments in which I encountered what Swinburne calls "the numinous." It was in an art gallery in Paris, involving a relatively small painting of a vase of chrysanthemums by Claude Monet[15]—something of the beauty of the painting transported me into another realm, one where the goodness of something ordinary affected me so profoundly that I could not look at the world around me through the same eyes ever again. Of course, I could wax lyrical about London's Tate Modern and its contemporary expression of human meaning outside any belief of God or similar expressions in Minneapolis's Walker Art Center.[16] And then there are the architectural expressions, where human beings seek to dominate the landscape with buildings, whether cities around the world, like Philadelphia, where the architecture breaks up the massive flat horizon, or single edifices that capture the dominant worldview—Egyptian pyramids, Aztec pyramids such as the pyramid of Santa Cecilia Acatitlan, the Louvre's pyramid in Paris, St. Peter's Basilica in Rome, the Dome of the Rock in Jerusalem, the Kaaba in Mecca, or the Burj Khalifa in Dubai. Each speaks of its source of power, whether pharaoh; Aztec gods such as Huitzilopochtli and Tlaloc; the Christian triune God, Father, Son, and Spirit; Allah; or simply Mammon—the secular god of the financial world that dominates contemporary skylines. These are *my* encounters of God through culture—yours will be as individual to you as you are to anyone else. The important point is that you can identify them; interpret what they tell you about the triune God and the world that the divine will, desire, and execution have brought into being; and then decide what it means for you to live in the light of this experience.[17]

3. *Community experience.* Olson describes this as "smaller cultural experiences," which I very much appreciate.

    a. Like you, I have been influenced by the various communities to which I have belonged. One is my national and cultural influences as a Scot. They are rich in history and tradition. However, I have lived most of my adult life in an English culture. These are altogether different cultures and have very different theological traditions. Each of us needs to be clearly aware of how the various influences of our national cultures hold sway over us, many of which are often unspoken, deeply entrenched, and deeply influential.

b. There are also educational communities. Most contemporary Western theologians have had their theology formed by Enlightenment critical thinking.[18] This may not be the case for African, Asian, or other Majority World Christians. The privilege of engaging with a theological tradition outside our own affords us the lesson that our theology is influenced by various educational philosophies and agendas that differ from country to country. For instance, some educational communities hold their elders in higher esteem than we do in the West. Therefore, Christians from these cultures find it more difficult to take the critical stance in relation to esteemed and respected theologians that is required within the Western university system.

c. Then there are our ecclesial communities—the influence "church" has on each one of us. For example, womanist or feminist theologies can be very different from male theologies due to the silent positioning many women experience in church communities around the world. Other examples include black church experience in predominantly white neighborhoods, whether in South Africa or North America, or the Dalit church in the caste system of India. Without question, one of the main challenges for our contemporary church communities and their theology is going to occur around the increasing fluidity in sexual identity. On a more personal note, my theological development has been deeply influenced by the religion of my upbringing, a pietistic and profoundly biblically literate context. No matter how far I travel beyond my primary ecclesial community, this original influence permeates my theology for good and for ill.

4. *Personal, individual experience.* Olson nails his colors to the mast when he points out, "It is most evident when an individual breaks out of the molds of common, universal human experience, cultural experience, and communal experience and has a flash of insight, an 'Aha!' moment that cannot be explained (at least to his or her satisfaction) by cultural conditioning or common humanity." Of course, this requires some kind of authentication for it to count, as Ellen Charry puts it, "as a source of the knowledge of God."[19] William MacDonald offers the most precise standard when he identifies the kind of experience being referred to here as "Christ-centred, experience-certified theology."[20] For me, that moment came as I sat under an ancient cedar tree at L'Abri Fellowship, Greatham, England, when the reality of the gospel, the centrality of Jesus Christ, and the plausibility of God's existence and all that this

meant confronted me from without, and, as a result, I was able to submit to the lordship of Jesus Christ. This experience was to have far-reaching implications on the rest of my life.

Pause

What about you?

Does your personal experience influence your theology? If so, how?

How does experience—yours and others'—shape your theological method?

With Olson, then, we can agree that "theology has always been influenced by human experiences of all four types and should not attempt to exclude them from all theological criticism and construction."[21] In this sense, theology is simply our response to the questions in our human experience and situation that emerge when we are confronted with the gospel. If this is the case, then an evangelical theological method ensures that such experience is incorporated into how the method goes about its theology. I particularly like how Roman Catholic theologian Bernard Lonergan describes this process as "the real" that is "assembled from the perceived (the experienced), the understood, and the affirmed."[22]

In addition to the above, it is helpful to engage the criteria offered by Rodney Stark in relation to what he describes as the essential element that categorizes religious experience—namely, "*some sense of contact with a supernatural agency.*"[23] Although dated, Stark's point is as relevant today as it was in the mid-1960s. In particular, I like the focus Stark offers in stressing "divine agency"—that is, experience of God is always dynamic, not static. We could even say that it is essentially *agentic*—that is, it consists of some kind of "engagement" between God and ourselves that results in a reconfiguration of our perceived personal and collective wisdom about the triune God, Father, Son, and Holy Spirit. Stark distinguishes four criteria that define religious experience:

1. *A confirming experience*: when an individual feels an intensified awareness of the existence of divine agency.
2. *An experience of response*: when the divine is perceived as acknowledging the presence of the human individual.
3. *An ecstatic experience*: when the feeling of mutual presence gives way to a relationship like that of love or friendship.
4. *A revelational experience*: where the wishes or intentions of the divine are conveyed.[24]

What these various perspectives tell us is that when we refer to our "experience" as a component in our theological method, we are, in fact, referring to something that is multifaceted and not simply a one-dimensional event or occurrence. Given the complexity of the term, it might be helpful to engage in a little consciousness-raising at this point.

Pause

To become more aware of how you use experience in your own theological method and in your own thinking, take time to consider the following:

What do you understand the term "experience" to mean?

How do you use it in your own theological reflection?

How significant a tool is it in your own theological method?

For many Christians, the term "experience" means much more than the limited and very specific definition given by William James: "the feelings, acts, and experiences of individual men in their solitude, so far as they apprehend themselves to stand in relation to whatever they may consider the divine."[25] I think that Uche Anizor's description of religious experience helps move us to a clearer understanding of its all-embracing nature, in general. Anizor describes religious experience as

> encompassing knowledge arising from first- and secondhand personal and communal encounters with life, as well as perception and observations; it has to do with impression, insights, and information we receive from outside ourselves, that is from God, and the created world.[26]

Although this broad-brush description helps locate where we might identify the various life events that contribute to our experience of God, at the same time, this and many of the other definitions we have looked at in this section do not incorporate aspects of experience that are central to a specifically evangelical theological method. What this broad-brush description lacks is a final positioning in Scripture—that every divine encounter that we experience, whether individually or corporately, always occurs from outside ourselves. However, because these experiences are from and about the God and Father of our Lord Jesus Christ, they will never be *direct* experiences.

As we saw in part 1 regarding the nature of divine revelation, our knowledge of God the Father, Son, and Spirit is always indirect simply because the triune God is never known as object but always as subject. We know the Father because the Son has made him known. We know the Son because, on the one hand, our knowledge of him is *in carne*—that is, in the flesh. We know the Son in his humanity, not in his naked divinity. On the other hand, we know the Son because the Spirit makes him known to us through Scripture and the preaching of the gospel. But here is the rub! Increasingly, many evangelical Christians assumed that any experience of the Holy Spirit is direct—that is, Holy Spirit encounters are one-on-one experiences between the individual Christian and the Spirit of God. However, if this is true, two theological consequences occur. First, the Spirit is not like the Father and the Son, who are not known directly. If the Spirit is known directly in our charismatic experience, then he must be like everything else that can be known directly; that is, he is part of creation and is not Creator. Second, it means that we are not engaging the divine but at best some semidivine reality.

This being the case, how do we interpret charismatic or Holy Spirit experience? We do so through our knowledge of Scripture telling us that, as a result of our new birth, whether in baptism or conversion,[27] we are "in Christ."[28] By virtue of this new status, of being in Christ, we experience the Spirit—by virtue of being what Paul describes in Colossians 1 as being the body of Christ, of which Christ is the head. The Spirit of God engages those adopted into the family of God, not anyone else. Therefore, even the most intimate and powerful of experiences come about either by the preaching of the gospel, by the indwelling of Scripture, or by being in Christ.

What do we mean, then, when we talk about experience in relation to our theological method? We can put it this way. Experience as a theological tool refers to

- knowledge that is (a) derived from individual and collective encounter with the triune God through external media, whether creation, history, the arts, or human reality (positive and negative) and (b) discovered directly or indirectly via reflection;
- knowledge that does not contradict divine revelation in Scripture or the tenets of Christian orthodoxy;
- knowledge that results in personal and/or collective transformation that can be verified by the people of God.

The Problem of Experience

It Is Awkward

Even the briefest readings of subject indexes concerning contemporary theological literature reveal a paucity of references to religious experience. Its omission is startling[29] yet understanding, given that experience is a relatively late addition to contemporary theological methods. It should not surprise us, then, that experience brings with it what Charry describes as an "awkward fit" with more established aspects of our theological method—namely, Scripture, tradition, and reason.[30] We can illustrate this fact humorously with reference to a specific pondering of Ralph Waldo Emerson on the topic: "I knew a witty physician who found the creed in the biliary duct, and used to affirm that if there was disease in the liver, the man became a Calvinist, and if that organ was sound, he became a Unitarian."[31] No wonder it has been described as the "wax nose" of theology![32] The sheer ambiguity of human experience means that its application to our understanding of God has always been seen as a last resort and thus usually comes last in the tools or skills necessary for a theological method. Charry identifies several areas of concern:

- We have already mentioned the first: the formal acceptance of experience as a theological tool is relatively new to contemporary theological discourse.

- The second has to do with the slippery nature of experience, what Anizor describes as a "notoriously broad and slippery notion."[33] As Charry rightly points out, the slipperiness of experience makes it "the most destabilizing of the sources of authority because it cannot be easily controlled," although she does add this rejoinder: "Perhaps it is important precisely for this reason."[34] Clearly, we need some kind of demarcation in order to distinguish the kind of experience that tells us something about God from that which merely tells us something about ourselves.

- In addition, there is also the challenge of determining which "experience" has legitimacy. The rise in black, feminist, liberation, and gender theologies has expanded what we mean by experience from the purely personal into what Charry describes as "a political tool for advancing the agenda of special-interest groups who rewrite the Christian map along sociological, cultural, and bioethical lines."[35] After all, if the experience of every niche group, or of humanity as a whole, constitutes *divine* revelation, then it follows that there is no difference between the divine and the human and, therefore, no *divine illumination*.

- Fourth, there are the internal concerns that theology as a discipline raises. Charry identifies two. On the one hand, there is the very basic question concerning identifying which experiences, if any, should be used to resource our theology and theological method. If God is so "other," how can human experience tell us about God? How can we experience *no thing*? Alternatively, surely the belief that human beings are made in the image of God means that there must be some kind of correspondence that allows our experience of God to tell us something about God? On the other hand, if human experience can convey knowledge of the divine, is this common revelation for all, or special revelation only for a select few?[36] How do we safeguard against our semiprivate experiences being at odds with church teaching and tradition?

- Last, if we remind ourselves of the "hermeneutic of suspicion" we looked at earlier, it is hardly surprising that experience has had a particularly grueling run in the theological market. Whether private or collective, experience has had its full share of being derided and mocked. On the whole, our church services and gatherings historically have been much too controlled, and thus any excess of emotion, devotion, commitment, or spirituality has been dismissed as being too "enthusiastic." However, when explored more deeply, what undergirds such put-downs is the deeper fear of the status quo being destabilized.

A mature theological method already has the habits and skills necessary to engage such enthusiasm. These habits and skills may include a broad understanding of experience demonstrated in Scripture, or awareness of how the historical and universal church has engaged and discerned the validity of various experiences through the traditions to which it adheres. In addition, we can think critically, rather than naïvely, about an experience in order to discern its strengths and weaknesses as well as anticipate its effect longer term.

It Is Confusing

Experience can be awkward in that it has the potential to take us out of our comfort zones. It can throw googlies at us that unsettle the status quo. In addition, experience can confuse us because it requires some kind of interpretation and explanation. It is rarely self-explanatory. How, then, should we look at experience today, with this in mind? Alister McGrath identifies three possible theological perspectives from the past that we might adopt, rightly and wrongly, today for an evangelical theological method. The importance of the first two is that they provide us with solutions to the problem of confusion.[37]

- First, theology is a foundational resource in that it connects us with human experience. This is a helpful insight, primarily because of the "conversionist" aspect of evangelical identity; that is, evangelicals hold in common a shared experience of conversion, of moving from darkness to light. Interesting, too, in this regard, is the impact within the contemporary theological scene regarding the rise of charismatic evangelicalism and its own focus on experiencing God, as well as the wider impact of Pentecostalism and its influence on evangelicalism via broadcast media.

- Second, since experience is something "unfocused or ambiguous," theology provides us with a "framework" that enables us to interpret our experiences.[38] That is, theology enables us to interpret our own and others' experiences. McGrath's point is an important one: theology enables us to make sense of human experiences by offering plausible explanations for various human conditions. For instance, the universal sense of the divine, which is revealed in almost every religion, can be explained theologically. That is, humans are created to know God, they are incapable of meeting this need, and they remain restless until they find God, who alone is able to meet this need. An evangelical theological method will recognize the potency of experience and seek ways of incorporating questions that better enable us to recognize, engage, and understand our own experiences of God.

- Third, while the first two are foundational contributions, our theological method exposes itself to potential risk in engaging experience—namely, that theology may misinterpret human experience. Perhaps the most famous is the nineteenth-century German philosopher Ludwig Feuerbach, who argued that our experiences are evidence of nothing more than the human need to objectify our needs and experiences onto a "God-figure."[39] Hopefully, no evangelical theological method would fall foul of imputing the divine to purely human experience in this way. That said, this reductionist temptation remains potent today, nevertheless. For instance, the average contemporary Christian millennial has, at best, a very blunt and vague understanding of human identity,[40] let alone any meaningful understanding regarding how to distinguish *human* spirit from *Holy* Spirit, not to mention demonic or angelic spirit.[41] As a result, it is all too easy to misinterpret what happens when Christians gather to worship and create their own energy but confuse this phenomenon with God's Spirit. What is a human, albeit Christian, expression of collective worship is predicated to the Holy Spirit. In turn, all that the Spirit seeks to achieve is reduced to the purely experiential.[42] Again, an evangelical theological method will seek to ensure that this kind of reductionism will be difficult to fall into.

It Is Challenging

Experience on its own can never carry the weight of glory contained in the gospel of our Lord Jesus Christ, let alone the God and Father of our Lord

Jesus Christ. That said, some religious experiences are utterly transforming to the extent that they challenge the status quo. They act in a manner that philosopher of science Thomas Kuhn describes as a "paradigm shift."[43] That is, a normal scientific belief contains sufficient anomalies that it can no longer be held with assurance. This causes a state of crisis in which a scientist will suspend scientific "orthodoxy" and explore hitherto "heretical" assumptions and questions in order to discover a better framework and eventually a paradigm that explains things better. As a result, the latter becomes the new normal. Examples would be Copernicus's model, where the sun is the center of the universe, or Marie Curie's theory of radioactive decay, which proved the existence of subatomic particles, an event that completely undid the received understanding of atoms and opened the way for contemporary radiation therapy. These paradigm shifts are not restricted to the world of science. Since they are conceptual—they are "conjectures" waiting to be proved or unproved—they are present in all realms of knowledge.[44]

When we look at Paul's own dramatic conversion experience as narrated by Luke in Acts 9,[45] we see a similar paradigmatic shift at work. On his way to persecuting more followers of the Way, Saul—as he was then called—is confronted by some kind of Christophany, an appearance of the risen Christ so glorious that Christ appears as a brilliant light, reminiscent of the Shekinah glory of God. What happened to Paul was nothing short of what Kuhn describes as a paradigm shift, not simply because the new revelation turned Paul around but also because it resulted in altogether different responses to Christ, the most unique being that Jesus became the object of what Larry Hurtado describes as "full cultic devotion"—that is, the object of Christian worship.[46] Hurtado picks up on two points Rodney Stark makes: first, that certain powerful religious experiences can lead to significant changes in the religious tradition and, second, that these experiences do not confirm prior religious belief, nor are they signs of some kind of psychological pathology.[47] Rather, this Christ appearance caused a complete rethink on Paul's part that either there and then or later led him to know that his new calling was to take the gospel of this crucified and yet glorified Christ to the very people Paul's previous understanding of the Law had excluded from God's hospitality.

We are told in Acts 13–14 that after this experience, it was somewhere in the region of fourteen or fifteen years before Paul started his first missionary journey. This is a considerable amount of time for theological reflection on the significance and implications of what happened on that road. Paul was to rethink the place of Torah in relation to non-Jews. Whereas they had been previously excluded from direct cultic participation as the people of God, now they had direct access in and through Christ. Whereas cultic participation stood on the two cornerstones of Torah-keeping and sacrifice-observance, now gentiles had a similar privilege, only this time it was in following Jesus, not Torah, and having faith in his death as a redeeming sacrifice. Most significantly, while Jews worshiped the one God, the LORD, those who followed Jesus now had no problem, it would appear, in worshiping Jesus Christ alongside the LORD God of Israel.[48] This is nothing short of a complete paradigm shift for Paul to undergo.

This strongly suggests, in turn, a pattern for our own experience. On the one hand, experience is insufficient as a theological tool. The experience may well be completely valid—but it takes time for theological reflection. And, of course, the more powerful the experience in terms of undoing received norms, the more theological reflection is required. Without the latter, the former is nothing short of shallow sensationalism. It is easy to go with our experience, but it does not provide much staying power. Old Testament theologian Walter Brueggemann captures this dynamic in his usual excoriating way when he describes this very dynamic:

> It readily becomes obvious that when the church works from its experience—or worse, from the experience of the preacher—things very quickly become thin, boring, and predictable, perhaps too congenial or alternatively too angry and coercive, depending on the preacher's "experience." Any large vision of saving transcendence, moreover, devolves into the family or tribe, either in blasé comfort or in militant crusading, either way with a very low ceiling. The failure of such thinness makes clear that we need a text that addresses us inscrutably, from beyond us, beyond the low ceiling of the congregation and the short horizon of the preacher.[49]

Experience Raises Theological Questions and Issues

Without a doubt charismatic evangelicalism and Pentecostalism have catapulted the influence of experience on contemporary evangelical theology and theological method. This is a good reality. Any evangelical theological method that is grounded in the transforming power of the gospel and rooted in the sanctifying work of the Holy Spirit in bringing disciples of Jesus into deeper conformity with the Father's will should enable us, as his disciples, to listen to, engage with, ponder upon, interpret, and understand our personal and collective experience of the living God. This is also a challenging reality. As with other tensions that the historical and universal church has faced throughout its own faith seeking understanding, so too with experience: the place of experience in our theological method requires careful consideration of important questions.

- The first has to do with *authority*. What kind of authority should experience have in our theological method? Central to an evangelical theological method is Scripture. However, what comes next? Liturgically centered evangelicals will prefer tradition. Reformed evangelicals will default to reason as expressed through various edicts and dogma. Charismatic evangelicals will lean toward experience. If, in the past, the Spirit was subordinated to the Bible by many evangelicals, something quite perilous has superseded this—namely, that the Spirit of God is subordinated to our experience. That is, experience has now become the arbiter of our spiritual lives, not God's Word or Spirit. It may well be worth reflecting on where you place the influence of experience in relation to the other tools that we have been considering.

- The second has to do with *status*. What status does experience have in an evangelical theological method, especially given the breadth of experience and, often, its lack of depth? There are several issues to consider: experience can be thought of as the *starting point* of our theological inquiry—and for many, this is exactly what it is. For others, experience is the *touchstone* to which all theological suppositions defer—if any given theological statement does not concord with one's experience, it should be doubted. Then again, some accord to experience the status of being the *standard* for all things regarding their faith—whether a specific conversion experience or conscious response and commitment to Christ; speaking in tongues; healing and prosperity; baptism and confirmation; or a specific calling to ministry or mission.

- The third question concerns *innovation*. To what extent should our religious experience alter existing beliefs, let alone lead to new ones? As we have noted above, the latter implies that experience has taken on the role of revelation. The consequence is that too often our language and nomenclature suggest that what is experienced brings with it an authority that allows the influence of tradition and reason to wane. Of course, the history of the church reveals a very thin line between new understanding that equips the saints and new knowledge to which only a select few are privy, what might be identified as Gnosticism. An evangelical theological method will secure means that avoid this route.

- The last question has to do with *integrity*. We might locate this in two contexts. First, the personal: each one of us lives in multiple spaces. Integrity is how we allow our several spaces to engage with each other. However, as John Weaver puts it, "Many Christians have a surprising ability to live in two worlds: the private world of faith and the public world of work and daily life."[50] The problem with this, however, is that this kind of division often results in what we could describe as "schizophrenic" forms of questioning, where our personal life experiences are divided in such ways that we happily ask questions about work and life but rarely, if ever, about our faith. What I like about Weaver's approach—where he is at pains to lead the reader through various ways by which we can reflect better theologically—is an understanding of what it means to be a believer in the gospel of Jesus Christ that is similar to his understanding of what it means to be "church." "Yet to follow Christ in our daily lives involves asking God questions of each and every part of our lives. *Bringing the private and public world together is the main task facing the church as it seeks to engage with the whole of life in the mission of Christ.*"[51]

The second context concerns a more corporate integrity that comes from being citizens of the kingdom of God. The gospel is specifically oriented to those whose personal, physical, medical, mental, financial, relational, social, and ecclesial experiences have marginalized them from the public square, social intercourse, or any meaningful level of well-being. Undoubtedly, some of the greatest theologies have emerged from the furnace of profound suffering, persecution, solitude, and loss as well as heights of joy and overwhelming comfort. Any theological method centered on the good news of the kingdom of God is mandated to engage the reality that the gospel seeks to overturn. Citizenship, whether terrestrial or heavenly, is no abstraction. Rather, it is experienced in identity, responsibility, and accountability. For love and justice, mercy and righteousness to kiss, there must be relational structures in which they can be safely experienced. This is the kingdom of God, and it is embodied in the here and now in what we call "church." Its Magna Carta, its Declaration of Independence, its European Union Charter, is Scripture in general, and the gospel of our Lord Jesus Christ in particular. Its jurisprudence is worked out in our theology. Theological method is the system by which citizens of the kingdom live according to its polity and economy and by which constituents of the church abide by the will of its head, the Lord Jesus Christ. Given this fact, I like the way in which Murray Rae articulates what it means to reflect on an experience of God in terms of integrity with the gospel:

> Christianity concerns both the acts of God in drawing to himself a people to live in covenant relationship with him, and the call of the individual to respond in faith to the saving work of Christ. Unless these things become a matter of personal experience, transforming one's life and reshaping one's understanding of the world, the Christian gospel is but a dead letter.[52]

Theological Experience

Theological Experience and the Divine

Let's remind ourselves of a couple of things we have marked as fundamental axioms of Christian theology. We only know God to the extent that God makes Godself known to us. The Uncreated chooses to reveal to the created. This cognition is neither reciprocal nor causal. The other axiom is that this self-revealing is recorded for us in Scripture. Therefore, it should not surprise us that both Testaments overflow with examples—all rooted in the saving experience of the God of Abraham and our Lord Jesus Christ breaking into human history and lives. For instance, on the basis of national liberation from slavery in Egypt, Exodus 29:46 records the Israelite God declaring, "They will know that I am the LORD their God, who brought them out of Egypt so that I might dwell among them. I am the LORD their God." That is, as a result of personal experience, a particular people group come to a new understanding of the God who brings about their freedom. Of course, there is also the flip side of this positive experience of liberation—namely, the knowledge derived from being on the disciplining end of divine activity, as stated in Numbers 14:34: "For forty years—one year for each of the forty days you explored the land—you will suffer for your sins and know what it is like to have me against you." And again in 2 Chronicles 12:8: "They will, however, become subject to him, so that they may learn the difference between serving me and serving the kings of other lands." More personally, the psalmist creates liturgy for worship in Psalm 56:9 that seals this experiential aspect of trusting God in the midst of trouble:

> Then my enemies will turn back
>   when I call for help.
>   By this I will know that God is for me.

The cumulative effect of experiencing ongoing divine deliverance is additional, albeit altogether different, experiences and responses. Thus, the psalmist declares in Psalm 70:4:

> But may all who seek you
>   rejoice and be glad in you;
>   may those who long for your saving help always say,
>   "The LORD is great!"

These two texts encapsulate a biblical theme running throughout the Bible. They are neither unique nor uncommon in their declaration of what it means "to indwell" Scripture and the God who speaks therein. In what is perhaps one of the most famous psalms, Psalm 91, the psalmist declares with absolute confidence that when we choose to avail ourselves of divine hospitality—that is, when we dwell in the shelter of the Most High (v. 1)—the very experience of being at home with the Lord God results in additional benefits experienced as a consequence of being hosted by God: we rest securely within this divine hospitality; we are delivered from any schemes against us, any sickness, any threat of death; disaster and harm will not hit us, declares the psalmist.

The experience of divine hospitality brings with it tangible benefits that, in turn, reveal more of the nature and character of God to us. We can highlight two very distinct but complementary dynamics here. The first is one that is not peculiar to theology but is, rather, part of the DNA of all human relationships. That is, we influence each other, and in doing so we learn from and about each other. It is only when this interaction involves the One in and through whom all things were made and without whom nothing that exists exists (John 1:3; Col. 1:16) that we end up seeing or finding God *in and through* our divine-human as well as our human-to-human experiences, and as a result we end up seeing differently—experiencing "the world as God's world."[53] Second, this dynamic means that "Christian experience is 'saturated' in this sense by the triune God."[54] This is what the principle of *lex orandi, lex credendi* establishes—that the corporate "lived-in-ness" of the people of God with the triune God results in what Matthew Levering calls "not merely . . . a set of ideas, in an abstract vacuum, but . . . a way of life saturated by trinitarian presence,"[55] what Khaled Anatolios describes as an overwhelming "excess of presencing."[56]

What is being described in terms of "excess" or "overwhelming" is rather akin to what we have already noted in relation to Swinburne's fourth example of religious experience—namely, an experience that cannot be expressed by reason or words alone but, rather, transcends normal codes and conduct of understanding, what we might describe as *mystical*. Such an experience simply will not fit our normal theological conventions and language. It has to be expressed in language that can, in some way, both carry and give meaning to the experience. I like the simplicity of Mark McIntosh's explanation: the mystical is about the "hidden."[57] That is, there is a knowledge of God that is hidden in the entirety of creation. It is opaque—but still telling us something about God. It is liminal—and so insists on its own way of self-divulging. It is that ironic tension created when *no* thing self-discloses in *some* thing, when the *Creator* is discovered in the *created*. It means that in order for us to discover the Uncreated in the created, our way of knowing has to go the way of the negative, the *via negativa*: God is *not* this, God is *not* that. In essence, such knowledge can only be discovered not in what *is* but as it is hidden in what it is *not*.

Now, admittedly, this kind of knowledge is strange news from a distant star! We could very easily dismiss it as alien to evangelical sensibilities. After all, many contemporary evangelicals presume an immediacy and accessibility to God the Father, Son, and Spirit. In the consumerist Western church with its globally scattered franchises, there is little if any space for the hidden or mystical in the cluttered world of commercial worship or catchy self-help pep talks. However, we would be mistaken if this experiential but communicatively challenging knowledge of God were something alien to the evangelical gospel. It is present in the quiet pietism of early to late twentieth-century free churches such as the Brethren. It lies at the core of any Puritan spirituality, the embers of which could be found in the theologies of evangelical influencers of stature such as Arthur W. Tozer, Arthur W. Pink, and Watchman Nee as well as more contemporary interests.[58]

What they remind us, however, is that at the heart of evangelical theology is a historical tradition of personal piety and conviction conditioned by what Proverbs 9:10 calls "the fear of the Lord," which is, of course, the beginning of wisdom, of sapiental living. It means taking a stance, a position in relation to the triune God, not in quivering anxiety or fear but, rather, as Tremper Longman III puts it, in "the sense of standing before the God who created everything, including humans whose very continued existence depends on him."[59] We can say four things here about experience as it relates to a stance that "fears" God and seeks wisdom:

- To live in the fear of the Lord is to live in a state of openness to the new, and to do so requires some kind of space for this kind of encounter to happen—the space of prayer and worship, as well as reflection and study:

  > My world of experience should never be rigidly defined in advance. It is of the nature of experience to be open to the new, yet in such a manner that it is an integral part of my growth as a person and not an artificial parasitic growth, which disintegrates rather than integrates my personhood.[60]

- Living in the fear of the Lord causes us to "pay attention and listen" and "leads to obedience."[61]
- It means that our desire is both to seek and to discover God's truth and not merely to get information.[62]
- Since an evangelical theological method understands the purpose of experience in its overall scheme as contributing to personal lives and

communities hallmarked by sapiental transformation, it will look for a change in our emotional well-being. Given the power that various experiences can evoke emotionally, we recognize there to be some kind of upgrade in our emotional status. Matthew Elliott, after spending an entire book on the place of emotion in the New Testament, distills in one sentence what this means: "When Christians transfer allegiance from this world to the Kingdom of God, their emotions will be transformed."[63] And this is not a wishful desire to bridge the opposing camps of intellect and emotion. As Elliott deftly demonstrates, when the New Testament writers engage the realm of emotion, they do so from "a cognitive perspective." This cognitive perspective engages several perspectives: emotion is "freely and frequently commanded in the text"; particular emotions are prohibited; we are held responsible for our emotions, which are, in turn, judged right or wrong; there is a direct correlation between our emotions and our profession of faith; emotions "are regularly linked with thinking and beliefs"; emotions are a relation to objects; emotions may well be neutral, but they are deemed good or ill "depending on their object"; God has emotions; the solution to a person's bad emotions is through changed thinking; the most "predominant emotion" is love, which "motivates other feelings" in turn.[64]

What do we learn here? On the one hand, it reinforces what we discussed in part 1 regarding how we know God. Divine knowledge is not separate from theoretical supposition. Rather, it is mined from the rich layers of human experience of and engagement with the Creator God, the Covenant God of Abraham, the re-creating God and Father of our Lord Jesus Christ.[65] Therefore, an evangelical theological method will not dissociate experience in relation to the Divine as if it were something distinct from human experience of the Divine. Instead, we recognize the locations where God is revealed in human experience and seek to understand them in the light of Scripture, the wise traditions that our forebears in the faith willed to us for guidance and safekeeping, and the various ways in which the sages of the church have wrestled with the impossible possibility of the Unknown being known in the way he has—in Christ Jesus—a human like you and me, except that he had no dysfunctions in relation to his Father, to himself, or to his neighbors, and yet he was everything the Father is, "God of God, Light of Light, very God from very God; begotten, not made."[66]

Human theological experience of the Divine occurs in the messy business of the triune God's experience of breaking into our various worlds—of the Father seeking and finding us, in calling us out and inviting us to experience his hospitality and to take up our respective crosses to follow his Son, Jesus, in the power of the Spirit of love.

Theological Experience and Human Life

Those of us who know and love both the fiction and nonfiction of C. S. Lewis will not be surprised to hear that he spoke highly of human experience with his usual generosity and largesse of heart:

> What I like about experience is that it is such an honest thing. You may take any number of wrong turnings, but keep your eyes open and you will not be allowed to go very far before warning signs appear. You may have deceived yourself, but *experience* is not trying to deceive you. The universe rings true wherever you fairly test it.[67]

What Lewis does here is to locate our own human experience within the wider theater of creation—a creation that depends upon its Creator and therefore can be trusted, not because our experience is fail-safe but, rather, because creation conforms to its own rules and norms. It is with this confidence that we are then able to consider our own human experience as a criterion for developing our theology and theological method. That is, there is something about creation that corresponds to the Creator's goodwill and that allows us not only to see God in our own experience but, in addition, to have confidence in processing this experience through careful interpretation. Put differently, we can say with David Lamberth that "life is not so much made up of experiences as life is experiential. That is, experience is not something we have now and again, but rather something constitutively environmental, something we stand, think, and move both in and with."[68] The assurance we can derive from this specific foundation allows us to identify two further areas of interest: prayer and worship.

Experience, Theology, and First Principles

The genesis of our theological knowledge is the primary Christian human experience of God—namely, our encounters in prayer and worship. We have already discussed their place in an evangelical theological method. However, the point to highlight here is that in the intimate and personal as well as the corporate and ongoing activity of communicating with the Father, we discover the truth in Karl Barth's assertion that "it is peculiar and characteristic of theology that it can be performed only in the act of prayer."[69] We can identify various practical reasons and theological reasons in support of this starting point. The first practical reason is Godward—in the intimacy and habit of prayer we gain theological insight. The second is human—our prayers give much away concerning what we believe about God as well as how we think God relates to the world. Then, theologically, prayer helps position us in our theological endeavors—"God is God, and we are not!"

Next, liturgically, our worship prevents us from pushing our own ideas; that is, the liturgy of worship, whether credal or robust theological song, provides necessary "walls" within which our experience is "safe" or, better, "orthodox" as opposed to "heterodox," correct rather than false. Then, since prayer "is the liturgical act in which thinking of God is performed," it requires us to listen to God first and speak second. Last, prayerful worship serves to remind us that effective theology that facilitates human flourishing is contingent theology—that is, it is "dependent on God's grace from beginning to end."[70] In both senses, whether practical or theological, when the starting point of our theology is rooted in prayer and worship, we better see the place of experience in our theological method. We realize not only that our theology begins with experience but that the two—experience and theology—cannot be separated. Scot McKnight captures the essence of this truth succinctly: "Theology without experience is sterility, while experience without theology is emotionalism. True theology is something that also needs to be experienced, and experience needs to be theologically sound."[71]

Of course, on deeper reflection we discover that this is the dynamic of all relationships. As we relate to each other, we build up experiential knowledge that enables us better to understand each other, both the good and the bad. This knowledge, in turn, molds the kind of relationships we have with each other—some of them life-enhancing that lead to human flourishing and others life-diminishing that result in emaciation or dystopia. Therefore, when we bring to our theological method our own personal and collective experiences of God, whatever the context and the subsequent life events experienced, we take them and the contexts within which they occur seriously.

We do so, first, for hermeneutical reasons: while context—whether time, location, or history—locates experience, it also determines subsequent interpretation. That is, at high points in my own Christian walk, I have literally cried out to God in response to relational, financial, or medical challenges and experienced answers so detailed in their precision and provision that they have enabled me to trust the Faithful One more regularly as well as deepen my theological understanding of what it means to be in Christ and therefore teach more meaningfully.

This leads us into our second insight. If we are to bring our experience of God to bear on our theological method, that experience has to have the muscle to bear the weight of pain, brokenness, hope, and expectation that humans go through. Our method has to have earned its colors in the school of life. Its veracity will be seen in the extent to which it has weathered the tests of ordinary, everyday existence that no amount of money, talent, or cunning can somehow enable us to evade. If our theological method cannot add clarity and meaning to how we understand and engage the gospel, it is inadequate to the task.

Third, we respect our context with the desire for integrity. On the one hand, the quality of religious experience will be to the degree it resonates with other people's experience. "If theology is going to speak to human beings, its content must be relevant to the conditions faced by human beings."[72] In addition to this, what experience does is connect us with other people's humanity: we share something in common and can empathize more meaningfully. Not only so, but it "corroborates the teachings of Scripture and provides resources for better understanding it."[73] On the other hand, for this experience to have any credibility it must also conform to what we know of creation and its own norms.[74] Of course, this does not mean that human religious experience of the triune God merely apes what can already be seen in creation. Rather, although this may often be the case, it can also be that glimpses of the Divine are afforded where the norms of creation are suspended and thus catch our attention or arrest our imagination, whether this be a burning bush defying the second law of thermodynamics or a human corpse that defies biological laws through resurrection. Either way, whether in conformity or discontinuity with our understanding of creation, our experiences are potent for instructing how we go about our theology as well as other experiential forms of knowledge. Thus, Steven Porter writes,

> So it appears that experience as a source of knowledge can provide an experiential confirmation of the truth of what Scripture teaches, an inner assurance of our Christian beliefs, as well as a means of coming to empirical knowledge relevant to the doctrinal categories, content, and boundaries set by the Scriptures. It is this latter sense of experience that is most pertinent to integration, for in reflection on empirical experience we have the epistemological basis for the discipline of psychology.[75]

When we take these points and develop them in relation to our own evangelical theological model, we can make several comments:

- Theologians should be able to indwell not only Scripture as much as possible but also the contexts into which we communicate.[76]
- In turn, this kind of theological method demands of us the ability to identify the various geographical contexts of our global village: to be

relationally and spiritually aware of what is going on around and beyond us, whether in the context of our own Jerusalem, Judea, and Samaria, or at the ends of the earth (Acts 1:8).

- Then, to be able to respond effectively in these various contexts, a contemporary academic evangelical theological method will avoid falling into the trap of what is disparagingly described as "ivory tower" theology. That is, our responses will engage the questions, needs, hopes, and aspirations being articulated as well as the goals of theology itself. Miroslav Volf and Matthew Croasmun offer an excellent example of what this might look like in identifying the goal of theology as bringing about human flourishing.[77] Our doctrines of creation and re-creation support this understanding: human beings are created specifically to exercise dominion, be fruitful, and multiply; Jesus Christ himself identifies his ministry in terms of "abundant" life (Gen. 1:28; John 10:10).

- Being successful in these endeavors requires reflecting on how to go about communicating the gospel effectively in these very diverse contexts. This is where our faith seeking understanding requires a more reflective disposition. Edward Foley very helpfully provides a list of thirty-six goals of "reflective believing" that are worth listing if only to raise our level of awareness regarding what this task of theological engagement entails: integration, transformation, love of self, healing, discipleship, love of other, self-grounding, becoming more human, loving God, recreation/re-creation, problem solving, community building, apologetics, liberation, softening hearts, changing theology, character building, friendship, giving a religious account of one's life, self-knowledge, accompaniment, solidarity/connectedness, broadening perspectives, building hope, raising up voices of the marginalized, conversion of life, dialogue of life [nontheistic integration], strengthening faith, connecting people with the cosmos, eliminating religious privilege, promoting the common good, building respect, becoming a better practitioner of one's faith tradition, engaging significance in people's lives, making sense of suffering, and clarifying practice for the next challenge.[78] Of course, each of us will have different goals due to the different contexts and experiences that our faith seeking understanding throws at us, but it is worth acknowledging where we might be on this "reflective" scale, what we might call the practical outworking of faith seeking understanding. While this work is necessary, not all theologians have the skill to do it, unfortunately, and often the result is that ordinary theologians perceive academic theology to be irrelevant and unnecessary.

Pause

Perhaps at this moment you could pause and consider what this might mean for your own personal situation—what your experience whispers or shouts at you demanding some kind of practical and/or theological response. What is it? How might you respond in an integrated manner?

Experience, Theology, and Worldview

While our experience of the triune God is geographical and therefore contextual, it is also conceptual. Not only do we inhabit a certain space, time, and historical context, as we have already seen; we do so within the wider conceptual framework of a particular worldview. We have already noted that a worldview can be reduced to a set of questions, all of which seek to clarify the meaning of existence. One such question centers on the nature of reality, whether material or immaterial. The answer to this question will then influence how we live in this worldview.[79]

To a large extent, contemporary Western culture has undergone a seismic shift in terms of worldview, as we have noted, resulting in a movement away from notions of truth that are constant to those that are more fluid, more mercurial, sometimes downright fake. In addition, we can chart a reorientation from the rational to the affective or experiential. In a nutshell, as Michael Molloy puts it so deftly, "People are not content any longer simply to believe. They want to experience."[80] Now, this is a very important aspect of a contemporary evangelical theological method in that unless the method engages this particular reality and attempts to understand it and construct effective ways of communicating into it, the gospel cannot move forward with much success. Therefore, the present interest in experienced theology as well as the place that it has in our theological method offers us a platform upon which theological dialogue can develop regarding issues that concern contemporary inquirers and believers, whether climate change, sexual identity, poverty, nationalism, or globalism. This is because all these multitude forms of experience offer us a contemporary expression of what we have already seen happening in Scripture and how we know God—that is, through mediated forms of knowledge, never directly.

Therefore, our different experiences of the world and of one another (natural revelation) as well as of God (divine revelation) can act in a similar mediatorial manner. Thus, while in the outgoing worldview of the Enlightenment and modernity an appeal could be made to the truth of a text, event, or reality, and as a result people could respond *believingly*, in a postmodern worldview this simply does not wash. Rather, to some extent and somewhat ironically, our postmodern contemporaries have grasped this mediatorial understanding without realizing it. Jeff Astley captures the essence of this clearly when he comments that "people 'see' or 'find' God *in and through*" their experience of the world. "They experience *as*: seeing the world as God's world."[81] We can see here the reason why *imagination* is of importance: an effective theological method will be able to get into the other's perception in order to understand how she sees the world and why. It will also have the creativity of mind to construct the means by which the gospel can be understood from the other's perspective. Given the significance of this dynamic, I take seriously James D. G. Dunn's warning that we should never discount "the creative force of religious experience."[82] And given that the end of the gospel is that we are transformed from one degree of glory to another, the dynamic continues when, as a result of responding faithfully to the gospel, we experience the transformation of our affections and emotions.[83]

Experience, Theology, and Interpretation

By now it should be clear that experience is a powerful tool in our theological method. In many ways it is neutral—that is, in and of itself it is neither good nor ill. Indeed, from a specifically evangelical perspective, given that Scripture reminds us that the God and Father of our Lord Jesus Christ is able to bring good out of even the worst of our experiences and that the Spirit of God raises us, as he did Jesus Christ, from the worst-case human scenario—death—we have even more reason not to dismiss certain experiences out of hand (Rom. 6:10–11; 8:28). What appears to be bad can, with the eyes of faith, be a means of grace through which the transforming power of the gospel is able to regenerate or even resurrect what is intended for evil and bring about good.

However, experience in and of itself cannot be left as such. Bernard Cooke reminds us that the question is not "*whether* experience is a basic source of theology but *how* we can accurately and critically use it."[84] There needs to be some kind of interpretive tool, a reliable *hermeneutic*, if experience is to be understood meaningfully.

- In the first instance this is where our other methodological tools have significance. For example, an experience that contradicts Scripture should have little sway in our thinking; one that overrides the collective wisdom of the universal church as safeguarded in its creeds and traditions is unlikely to gain significant consensus; any experience that downright contradicts the core beliefs of the universal and historic church needs to be explored with caution. As Alister McGrath reminds us, even someone of the stature of Luther "argued that experience is important to theology, but it must be interpreted by theology because it is an unreliable source of theology alone."[85]

- Second, our individual experiences are personal to us. Astley comments that "experience is something you cannot have second hand; you have to undergo it yourself. Experience leaves an impression on you and often stirs your feeling in a unique way."[86] Yet our experiences are to be measured within the wider context of the people of God who know us and love us. In this John Wesley understands the human condition well. On the one hand, he insists, when we talk about Christian experience we are actually talking about moments when we experience assurance of the saving grace of God in our lives, when the fruits of the Spirit are evidence of the life of God in us. Yet, on the other hand, in such experiences, the individual is not the judge and jury who pass approval or reprobation. Rather, each of us is accountable to our community of faith. It is they who give witness to a work of grace in our lives. It is they who see the transformation in their brother and sister and who live better lives themselves as a result. For this reason Elaine Robinson, a Methodist, summarizes her tradition well when she adduces that "our individual experiences are accountable to the wider community of faith."[87]

- Amos Yong offers a taxonomy for identifying "spirit" and its value hermeneutically in relation to human experience. In some sense Yong, a Pentecostal, attests the Wesleyan point above, only this time from the perspective of how we go about discerning the veracity of any given religious experience. In the end, it is the words of Jesus Christ that provide us with the answer: the quality of the experience will be evidenced in the "fruit" produced (Matt. 7:15–20).

- If we can pick up on Foley's notion of reflective believing, we can apply it to our hermeneutic of Christian experience. Most of us spend little time reflecting on our experiences, especially if they are routine to our church gatherings. Indeed, in the consumerist social-media-savvy West, we are no more likely to reflect on these increasingly ubiquitous experiences than we would on our Sunday lunch. This would require the rediscovery of and the ability to enjoy what Thomas Merton describes as "meditation, silent prayer, and creative Christian silence."[88]

- That this is the case, however, does not mean it makes for good theological method. Rather, as Tremper Longman III points out, although we all have experiences, "not everyone is observant and self-reflective about those experiences in order to learn how to navigate life success-fully."[89] One way in which we can reflect toward a successful outcome is to engage our religious experience pragmatically—that is, in being able to identify what works not only for ourselves but for others. In this sense, there may well be a place for "How to . . ." theological responses. After all, we could say that the entire thirty-one chapters of Proverbs are an early Israelite publication in the same genre. Longman captures biblical humor and irony when he draws our attention to the fact that we can learn from the experience of ants:[90]

> Go to the ant, you sluggard;
>   consider its ways and be wise!
> It has no commander,
>   no overseer or ruler,
> yet it stores its provisions in summer
>   and gathers its food at harvest. (Prov. 6:6–8)

What Controls Experience?

I suggested in part 1,[91] citing Joel Green and Kevin Vanhoozer, that our rela-tion to Scripture—and therefore theology—is dynamic, not inert or static. It is to be performed (Green). It is a drama (Vanhoozer), a *theo*drama no less. Drama is helpful. It engages the body; it ignites the imagination. *Theo*drama is suggestive. The divine drama requires a theater within which the different acts and their respective scenes can be enacted. Scripture is the script. It con-tains the most expansive dramatic narrative we could imagine: the drama of God's relation to humanity and humanity's response. It is so vast that this drama can be understood in terms of worldview. It explains everything. And as with the great Shakespearean dramas, so dated in time yet so contempo-rary in their portrayal of the human condition, a sense of perspective and depth is often created by particularly significant scenes. I suggest that one of the most prominent scenes in the drama of Scripture of this genre occurs in chapter 10 of Luke's Gospel (10:25–37). It is the typical script followed by every wannabe Alpha male who must prove himself to his peers. He takes on the new kid in town and pushes for a showdown. Cue the slick city lawyer entering the set. Most certainly he has already eyed his opponent and goes for the jugular. After all, he is the legal expert in this scene. He goads the itinerant preacher, Jesus, with a sarcastic question the answer to which he is most certain of. "Teacher," he asks, "what must I do to inherit eternal life?" (v. 25). The simplicity of the question is intended to insult the rabbi,

Jesus. Just about every Jewish boy will have had the answer drilled into him at synagogue school. Jesus turns the question back on the lawyer and asks, "What is written in the Law? . . . How do you read it?" (v. 26). Clever! Jesus rises to the challenge in a manner that begins to show his own mettle. Here's a chance for the lawyer to be smug, thinking the bait has been taken and the trap is about to shut on Jesus. And so he responds correctly: "'Love the Lord your God with all your heart and with all your soul and with all your strength and with all your mind'; and, 'Love your neighbor as yourself'" (v. 27). Bait taken—now the trap door can shut. (You can almost feel the tension in the script as the drama intensifies. Horns are locked. What's the next line?) Jesus's reply is both wise and tempered with an almost tangible compassion: "You have answered correctly. Do this and you will live" (v. 28).

However, this is no comedic play. It is a tragedy, and so the antagonist does his worst. He asks a question intended to test Jesus and most likely uncover him for the charlatan and imposter the lawyer supposes him to be. It sets the scene up for one of the great high points of Scripture: "And who is my neighbor?" (Luke 10:29). The question was as divisive then as it is today: both contexts, the lawyer's and ours, are beset with the divisions created by nationalism, on the one hand, and globalism on the other. The dramatic tension is now set: if Jesus does not opt for the former, he fails the test. He is a dubious teacher at best, a bad one at worst. Bait taken, trap door about to shut—but which bait is it that has been taken? Whose is the trap that is going to close? Who is playing whom? The first hearers and readers would be aware of the different dramatic levels going on in this scene in a manner similar to those hearing *Hamlet* or *Macbeth* for the first time. Jesus tells a story.

A man was going down from Jerusalem to Jericho, when he was attacked by robbers. They stripped him of his clothes, beat him and went away, leaving him half dead. A priest happened to be going down the same road, and when he saw the man, he passed by on the other side. So too, a Levite, when he came to the place and saw him, passed by on the other side. But a Samaritan, as he traveled, came where the man was; and when he saw him, he took pity on him. He went to him and bandaged his wounds, pouring on oil and wine. Then he put the man on his own donkey, brought him to an inn and took care of him. The next day he took out two denarii and gave them to the innkeeper. "Look after him," he said, "and when I return, I will reimburse you for any extra expense you may have." (10:30–35)

Bait taken! The lawyer is drawn into the *theo*drama of the Torah. What will take priority? Torah (neighbor love) or expedience (temple regulations that forbid contamination from blood or corpse)? The trap shuts! Jesus asks a direct but rather gentle question: "Which of these three do you think was a neighbor to the man who fell into the hands of robbers?" (v. 36). Simple, really, even though the key actor in this scene is a despised Samaritan. Perhaps the lawyer's answer redeems him. Was it due to an underlying integrity? Or was it due to the genius of the narrator? Both? Either way, the scene's antagonist replies, "The one who had mercy on him" (v. 37). With this, the whole tone and energy of the scene is upturned: the initial self-righteousness of the lawyer at the beginning is upended by the compassion of Jesus, where an invitation is made to engage the drama—"Go and do likewise"—rather than an injurious put-down that excludes further engagement.

The significance of this example lies in two parts. First, it is a theological master-class. There is *form* in the shape of personal engagement as well as storytelling. There is *content* in how Jesus takes a scholarly, legal, and, yes, academic (rather than ordinary) question about the very heart of the Jewish faith and goes beyond the letter to the spirit of the Torah. Second, it has a *context*. It is a Jewish question from a Jewish lawyer to a Jewish teacher about the Jewish faith. The context provides the depth and perspective to the answer. It is the stage on which the scene is performed.

What has this to do with experience as a tool in our theological method? In this theological story-response the central light falls on the notion of covenant. The question is really about what it means to be Jewish. There is also a vision of the future, a re-creation where a new kind of relationality operates.[92] Enemies care for enemies. Neither the notion of covenant nor that of re-creation holds together, however, without a basic understanding of creation. I have already shown that experience on its own is inadequate to the task of theology. It is aided by tradition and reason in the task of making sense of Scripture. Yet, left even like this, is it enough? I propose not; otherwise such an understanding of experience remains abstract and open to incorrect interpretation. It is for this reason that P. T. Forsyth makes the point that "experience is a medium, not a matrix."[93] Since it is such, we can extrapolate from it "possibilities to theology but not solutions."[94] Our experience should never be the steering wheel or rudder driving the boat. In an evangelical theological method it will be, more helpfully, the sail that catches the breath of God's Spirit. And like a wind that can suddenly catch the sail at unexpected points on the journey, so our various experiences of God can intrude on us in ways that influence our understanding, our interpretation, and our reflection. Paul Hessert points out that all these different experiences require what he calls "a broad interpretation including all that is involved in one's contact with the world and with God."[95]

Hessert's point is important. We need a much bigger frame of reference regarding how we make sense of our experiences. What I am arguing here, in order both to establish the place of experience in an evangelical theological method and to identify a specifically evangelical understanding of experience, is that the only experiences relevant to our method are those whose "first content" is "God in a certain act, a certain giving, as giving Himself, as thus grasping, saving, new creating me."[96] Encapsulated in this astute sentence are the three realms required to elicit the very best theological understanding from our various experiences. With these realms, we conclude our exploration of experience's place in our theological method:

- The first should be relatively clear given our conversations above: creation. If ever there is a place where our doctrine of creation kicks in, it is in relation to how we make sense of our various religious experiences. It sets the agenda for human experience. After all, the entirety of our religious experiences are performed on the stage of creation and in the laboratory of church, and, as we have noted, this contextualizes all human experience. Without a robust understanding of creation (its origins, its purpose, its malfunctioning, and its end) as well as our own place in it (our identity, our purpose, our condition, our hope, and our end), we open ourselves to the temptation of making our experiences of God mean whatever we want.

- The second—covenant—"seals" our religious experience and reveals an intimate relationship to creation, rather than superseding it. Creation may well be the medium of our experience, but it is covenant that is the matrix within which we understand our experiences of the God and Father of our Lord Jesus Christ. Covenant sets the boundaries within which we make sense of relationship, and thus experience. The relationship between experience and covenant is further developed by Paul Williamson when he makes the very important sequence of biblical events as such: "Covenant is seen as framing or establishing . . . relationship. This, however, is not in fact what the biblical text suggests. Rather than establishing or framing such a divine-human relationship, a covenant seals or formalizes it. The biblical order is relationship, then covenant, rather than covenant, hence relationship."[97] That is, covenant is what brings plausibility to our religious experience. It articulates a particular way of life that is worth pursuing.[98] It sets our various experiences within this wider matrix of the relational expectations that equip us to understand a given experience. Covenant is the heuristic or interpretive key that enables us to identify an experience as revealing or telling us something about God. Covenant informs the practices that subsequently inform our theology, whether that be the influence of practiced experience or the way in which we hold each other together through our lived experience.

- Re-creation—If theology is exegesis of the gospel, then its purpose is only met to the extent that it engages the future hope about which the gospel speaks and to which the gospel points us. This has as much to do with the "now" and the degree to which we "get it," as Astley puts it, and he quite rightly locates this "getting" in relation to our "theology becoming redemptive for us."[99] We have addressed this at various points. Our experience of the triune God will always be redemptive. In its genesis and its ongoingness as well as its completion, the Christian experience of this God who loves the world so completely will always be in the service of our being re-created, redeemed, restored to all that our humanity was created to be and our living in the abundance of his covenant promises. This experience has, as N. T. Wright puts it, "never ceased to designate a living pact, a community of destiny, a bond with creation, which infinitely surpasses the relation of right."[100] Methodologically, this entails asking what understanding any given experience sheds on the gospel and what it means to engage faithfully with the gospel. It requires asking how the experience better enables us to be the people we were created to be—in exercising dominion, in being fruitful and multiplying, in loving the Lord God with our entire being, and in loving our neighbor in the same way we would want to be loved. And in addition to past and present, there is also a future or eschatological imperative. Whatever the experience, we should be able to see in some way how it serves in bringing nearer and fulfilling sooner the kingdom of God in all its social, political, and economic perfection.

SUGGESTED READING

Anizor, Uche. *How to Read Theology: Engaging Doctrine Critically and Charitably.* Grand Rapids: Baker Academic, 2018.

Chole, Alicia Britt. *The Sacred Slow: A Holy Departure from Fast Faith.* Nashville: W Publishing, 2017.

Dryden, J. de Waal. *A Hermeneutic of Wisdom: Recovering the Formative Agency of Scripture.* Grand Rapids: Baker Academic, 2018.

Elliott, Matthew. *Faithful Feelings: Emotion in the New Testament.* Leicester, UK: Inter-Varsity, 2005.

Keener, Craig. *Spirit Hermeneutics: Reading Scripture in Light of Pentecost.* Grand Rapids: Eerdmans, 2016.

Lewis, C. S. *Surprised by Joy: The Shape of My Early Life*. London: William Collins, 1955.

Okholm, Dennis. *Learning Theology through the Church's Worship*. Grand Rapids: Baker Academic, 2018.

Sanders, Fred. *The Triune God*. New Studies in Dogmatics. Grand Rapids: Zondervan, 2016.

Volf, Miroslav, and Matthew Croasmun. *For the Life of the World: Theology That Makes a Difference*. Grand Rapids: Brazos, 2019.

Weaver, John. *Outside-In: Theological Reflections on Life*. Macon, GA: Smyth & Helwys, 2006.

nine

Community

The Fifth Dimension

In the last four chapters we have looked at the more traditional "tools" in the theologian's tool bag: Scripture, tradition, reason, and experience. Generally, they are well used and widely accepted methodological norms for doing theology. In this chapter, however, I advocate an additional methodological tool that, on the whole, has been neglected in academic theology: community. This fifth dimension is an inclusive one in that with it we engage both the divine and the human. The gospel is the ultimate and most intimate invitation from the triune God to his human ambassadors, these image bearers, those to whom creation has been entrusted by its Creator. This gospel reveals that divine agency is trinitarian, not unitarian; social, not solitary. It reveals that the God who seeks us out is the Father who, in his good will, his love for creation, and his commitment to his covenant, sends his beloved Son to restore this creation, who does so in and through the enabling energy of the Holy Spirit. Therefore, it is right to identify the God of the gospel as triune. The God we meet in and through Jesus Christ is one who is an eternal communion between Father, Son, and Spirit.

Enough has been written on what it means to declare this "community" identity in relation to God.[1] However, my interest here is not so much in the doctrine of the Trinity. Rather, my concern is to advocate that the notion of community as an anthropological term is a necessary component of an evangelical theological method. Of course, the *theological* understanding is important in that human beings are made in the image of the triune God. It would be an inadequate theological method that extrapolated directly from the doctrine of the Trinity to our understanding either of human being or of the church. Rather, as we saw in part 1, our knowledge of God is mediated—most supremely in and through Jesus Christ. Therefore, an explicitly theological use of the doctrine of the Trinity will always be filtered through our understanding of the person and work of Christ and not from some abstracted theological interpretation, however much it be a cornerstone of our faith.[2] Rather, by "anthropological," I mean simply that our application of community, with regard to our theological method, can only be from a human perspective.

What, then, does this community perspective look like? I propose that two distinct aspects of church community are germane to an evangelical theological method. One is inward facing and concerns that community of believers who have responded to the call of the gospel and live under the lordship of Jesus Christ—what we call "church." The other is outward facing and is focused on the community of those who have not yet responded to the good news of the gospel of Jesus Christ—the rest of the world. Of course, both positions, the inward and the outward, really are the sine qua non of any *ordinary* evangelical theology. That is, they are standard and commonly assumed facets of normal Christian living: we are the church and we exist for others.

However, it should not be very surprising that, when we scrutinize evangelical *academic* theology more closely, the same cannot be said. There is a history here that has to be understood. As we have already noted in our chapter on reason, the Enlightenment imposed a great ditch between Christian belief and faith, on the one hand, and critical and empirical fact on the other. Theological education, which had once enjoyed a symbiotic relationship with the church, under the Enlightenment became estranged. In turn, the quest for pure knowledge demanded that all epistemic impurities be removed from the pursuit of secular wisdom. It took only a very short theological jump to arrive at the place where theology was removed from the arms of Mother Church and placed under the aegis of the increasingly secular university. Culturally and politically astute university institutions, particularly in Western Europe, were able to establish some degree of concord, especially those that were historically located in the state church or that were financially rich. North American theological education took a different tack, where denominational philanthropy permitted more amenable cohabitation. Evangelical theologians had very few, if any, academic options available to them. They had to accept either being ostracized to the theological leper community or remaining closeted on the whole and being an evangelical sheep in wolf's clothing. Evangelical theologians of the twentieth century had few choices open to them if they were to be salt and light within the academy. A few rose to the occasion, taking on the mores of the university and learning their craft with integrity. Many put in the decades of hard work required and earned the highest colors, influencing the direction in which academic theology could develop. It is on the shoulders of such giants—men and women of faith who shattered the theological ceiling—that contemporary evangelical theologians make their mark. This historical sketch, however, has come at a high cost. I think two costs are worth mentioning:

1. The content of academic theology, for many decades now, has had little to do with ordinary experience and the theological questions the messy reality of life throws at us. Let's face it—for many, the popular impression is that the content of academic theology bears little relation to the realities of life or ministry. Consequently, academic theologians and the theological education they offer has become more and more irrelevant to the many ordinary theologians whose faith seeking understanding is lived out in the ebb and flow of work, leisure, family, church, community, and the hard work of paying bills and keeping a roof over our heads.

2. Academic theology, by virtue of being detached from church and the needs of the faithful, as well as the unfaithful, has evolved into a self-oriented, self-perpetuating, and self-guided end in itself. It is, as Miroslav Volf and Matthew Croasmun state with real-life experience, "composed of specialists in an unrespected discipline who write for fellow specialists about topics that interest hardly anyone else." More seriously, they identify "the one complex illness that afflicts theology today, its most important crisis": that academic theology has, in reality, "forgotten its purpose: to critically discern, articulate, and commend visions of the true life in the light of the person, life, and teachings of Jesus Christ."[3]

It is fair to say that these two theological cancers have made their impact on the evangelical academic constituency too. Academic evangelical theologians are as prey to pride, whether intellectual or professional, as any other faculty. We, too, can be guilty of the sin of irrelevance in the quest for significance. Most professionals, given the chance, would prefer to be a big fish in a very small pond rather than suffer the ignominy of being a little fish in an ocean. Thus, academic evangelical theology, too, has suffered its own modicum of churchly irrelevance and professional hubris. We, too, are guilty of trading our birthright to another country for the immediate gratification of tenure, acceptance, publishing contracts, and elevated positions and titles. Many have not—by choice and calling—but the proof, at the end of the day, is in the eating: How much of our academic efforts engage the very people Jesus Christ spent most of his time hanging out with and dying for? On the whole, for understandable and unforeseeable reasons, evangelical theology has lost sight, to some extent, of the (gospel) forest for the sake of the (academic) trees.[4]

That's the bad news! Here's the good news! As a result of those who stood their ground theologically and faithfully and learned their craft excellently while remaining faithful to an evangelical gospel, the tide of general irrelevance of academic theology bequeathed to us by modernist as well as more contemporary postmodernist worldviews has turned. When I started my doctoral studies in the mid-1980s, I remember visiting a friend at an ancient Scottish university. I was introduced to two of his colleagues as they read their newspapers in the common room. They were told that I was doing research with Colin Gunton on some aspect of trinitarian Christology. This piqued their attention—obviously some strange breed worth taking a look at—and as their noses rose above the top of their respective newspapers, one said to the other, "Trinity? Don't think we have *anyone* who believes that stuff here." And with that, the noses proceeded in a southerly direction and they returned to their reading. Fortunately, this is no longer the case. Some form of mini-renaissance since then has occurred, built mainly on the legacy of Karl Barth, who made the case for a return to the more ancient paths.

This renaissance was developed through the likes of German Wolfhart Pannenberg, Scottish T. F. Torrance, North Americans Robert Jenson and Stanley Grenz, and English Colin Gunton. Through their influence an entire generation of theologians emerged who have proceeded to defend, support, and advance two of the most important Christian theological beliefs: the doctrine of the Trinity with its affirmation of the one God who is Father, Son, and Spirit and the doctrine of Christ that declares that the eternal Son of God became human and thus took to his own divine nature our human nature. Serendipitously, these theological developments were driven by a dissatisfaction with the modern worldview that collapsed in the late 1980s and a positive desire to construct something that corresponded better to the reality of the gospel.

Throughout this book, I have identified two nonnegotiables concerning evangelical theology. First, the discipline of theology has an ongoing relationship with the church. To be "in Christ" and to be baptized into the body of Christ is to be a theologian. For each one of us, our faith seeks understanding: of God, of the world, of ourselves and those around us, and supremely of what has happened in and through the life, death, resurrection, ascension, and glorification of Jesus Christ and the subsequent gifting of the Holy Spirit to those who follow Jesus Christ. Second, I have sought to establish a proper context for theology. It is the church. This community is formed and constituted by those who have exercised their faith and responded to the gospel of Jesus Christ. This social construct is the living *space* where theology is birthed. It is within this space that worship of God is embodied, breathed, and habituated. It is where we live and have our being. In this space, theology matures in understanding. And from this space theology provides the means to communicate with horizons beyond its ecclesial—flesh and brick—walls.

Pause

This is a good point to stop and think about your own community of faith and its relation to theology in general and academic theology in particular:

- Is it a positive or negative relationship?
- Would you say that much or little theological reflection takes place in your church or community? Why not give some "flesh" to your answer: What does the evidence look like for how you answered?
- Does church figure at all in your own theological method and reflection?

It should be clear by now that theology is the church's reflection on and exegesis of Scripture and the gospel with which it has been entrusted. That said, neither Scripture nor the gospel exists apart from the communities of faith that birthed them and into which they were birthed. Scripture is the Word of God, but it is the word of this God who has covenanted himself to a particular people: the called-out descendants of Abraham along with those met on the Way and who respond to the call to follow Jesus the Christ.

Theology is also a disciplined engagement with our experience of the Divine—that which remains unseen until its full unveiling. Such engagement requires habits and tools that release a mass of knowledge. Over time, patterns emerge, wisdom is unearthed, questions are asked, and traditions are crafted. This is no solitary, individualistic, let alone autonomous skill. Rather, like any other science, it has its own context.

> Theology is a scientific discipline, which like all scientific disciplines must answer to a community. The community to which theologians finally answer is the Church. . . . The Church receives the faith theology seeks to understand, forms individuals in it (including theologians), and hands it on to them. . . . Only a community that can't forget the truth, however great the failures and errors of her individual members—including those in authority—can be relied upon to recognize the truth. In this sort of community, but only here, one can responsibly suffer for the truth.[5]

This community is the church. In relation to theological method, two brief considerations should be stated concerning this fifth element in our evangelical theological method:

1. The church as a community is what happens, what gets produced, when people live faithfully with the triune God. It is where followers of Jesus learn the grammar of their faith, learn the habits necessary to reflect the family likeness, and learn politics and economics necessary for flourishing participation in the kingdom of God. It is the norm given in Scripture, proclaimed in the gospel, and taught in the apostolic tradition. Its DNA can be traced back to the earliest eyewitnesses who responded in faithful believing to the call of Jesus and his gospel.

2. The church as a community is also the context that most significantly molds our theology. I habitually remind my students that they—today's contemporary generation—are the ones called to prepare post-Christian communities for life in the third millennium. This is going to be a challenge—the mold has not been needed until now. It will make demands of Christian communities as they are increasingly marginalized from contemporary society. Equally demanding will be the need to learn new ways of taking the good news about Jesus Christ to those of different beliefs or no beliefs. The problem here is that most, if not all, of us have been molded by the theologies and ways of doing theology of the previous millennium, where discipleship and mission took forms that no longer enable us to flourish. We have been, as Robert Putnam describes it in his critique of late modernity, "bowling alone."[6] That is, late twentieth-century Western culture, and the Christendom it produced, developed a community form of individualism. People started to hibernate from people different from them—what sociologist Zygmunt Bauman describes as "mixophobia"[7]—and developed lifestyle enclaves established on lifestyle values. And our churches have followed a similar trend to the detriment of our character transformation, corporate witness, and public relevance. But it is as gathered communities—not as solitary individuals nor in tribal groups—that we best habituate the discipline of worship: where we extol but also lament, declare as well as contemplate, give thanks for a new life as well as for lives well lived. Let's remind ourselves of what we established in part 1—namely, that our theology arises from the context of worship. It does so for the simple reason that "it is in the process of being worshiped that God communicates His presence" to us.[8] And we do this as church. Douglas Farrow reminds us that it is the church that provides us with the necessary

theological constructions without which the task of theology would be rather difficult; it is the church that shapes our interpretive possibilities (and nonpossibilities); our theological interpretation "is conducted from within the church and under the conditions of the church militant"; and, last, the Spirit of God animates the body of Christ, the church, to become the place of possibility of knowing God.[9]

The community of the church exists for two constituencies: the internal and the external. An evangelical theological method will distinguish itself in these two particular aspects of community. To some extent, evangelical theologians have been shackled to a secondhand theological method, one caught in limbo between meeting the criteria of the academy and addressing the needs of the church. In drawing the idea of community into the toolbox of an evangelical theological method, I am not introducing something alien or innovative. Nor am I trying to reinvent the wheel. Our handling of Scripture and of the gospel are not private activities. They are profoundly public actions of the church. I am merely making explicit what has always been implicit in evangelicalism: that at the heart of an evangelical gospel lie two sensibilities that are encased in one Johannine verse: "For God so loved the world that he gave his one and only Son, that whoever believes in him shall not perish but have eternal life" (John 3:16). That is, the gospel is good news—it declares the love of God for each and every one of us—and it needs to be declared so that a believing response can be made. It is to the first sensibility, theology done under the reality of the presence of God demonstrated in the life, death, and resurrection of Jesus Christ, that we now turn: doing theology *coram Deo*—that is, *in the presence of God*.

Pause

Take time to reflect on this inward-outward dynamic. Where do you see this at work in your own theological method/theology? Where are the gaps, and how might you address them?

Doing Theology *Coram Deo*—in the Presence of the Triune God

Dear friends, let us love one another, for love comes from God. Everyone who loves has been born of God and knows God. Whoever does not love does not know God, because God is love. This is how God showed his love among us: He sent his one and only Son into the world that we might live through him.

This is love: not that we loved God, but that he loved us and sent his Son as an atoning sacrifice for our sins. Dear friends, since God so loved us, we also ought to love one another. No one has ever seen God; but if we love one another, God lives in us and his love is made complete in us.

This is how we know that we live in him and he in us: He has given us of his Spirit. And we have seen and testify that the Father has sent his Son to be the Savior of the world. If anyone acknowledges that Jesus is the Son of God, God lives in them and they in God. And so we know and rely on the love God has for us.

God is love. Whoever lives in love lives in God, and God in them. This is how love is made complete among us so that we will have confidence on the day of judgment: In this world we are like Jesus. There is no fear in love. But perfect love drives out fear, because fear has to do with punishment. The one who fears is not made perfect in love.

We love because he first loved us. Whoever claims to love God yet hates a brother or sister is a liar. For whoever does not love their brother and sister, whom they have seen, cannot love God, whom they have not seen. And he has given us this command: Anyone who loves God must also love their brother and sister.

Everyone who believes that Jesus is the Christ is born of God, and everyone who loves the father loves his child as well. This is how we know that we love the children of God: by loving God and carrying out his commands. In fact, this is love for God: to keep his commands. And his commands are not burdensome, for everyone born of God overcomes the world. This is the victory that has overcome the world, even our faith. Who is it that overcomes the world? Only the one who believes that Jesus is the Son of God. (1 John 4:7–5:5)

Thus writes the apostle John. He could equally be describing what life looks like if it is lived constantly in the presence of God. So let's dismiss a rather contemporary notion that we, in some way, "invite" God—usually the Holy Spirit on his own—to presence himself with us as though he had been away somewhere else. Rather, if we are "in Christ," we are already present to his energy and love, the Holy Spirit, and to the Father, whose will both the Son and the Spirit enjoy getting done. The use of such "invitational" terminology evidences a form of compartmentalism that suggests that we have not grasped the fact that to be "in Christ" is to live continually in the presence of God. The issue is, rather, the degree to which we habituate our lives accordingly. Not all of us will have read what is, probably, the most well-known book on the subject, written by a seventeenth-century Parisian Carmelite religious, Brother Lawrence of the Resurrection.[10] And most certainly, not many of us have perfected what it means to live as though we are constantly in the presence of God. However, an evangelical theological method has little option. Given that our theological method is the means by which we go about exegeting the gospel and that this method produces our theology, and given that we cannot separate the gospel from its originator, it follows that to be a theologian is to be someone who goes about his or her craft *coram Deo*—that is, in the constant presence of God. In what is one of the most succinct and readable introductions on what *coram Deo* means, R. C. Sproul explains it as signifying a life of integrity. I quote him at length since I think his definition best relates to what we should consider in achieving our theological method:

> This phrase literally refers to something that takes place in the presence of, or before the face of, God. To live *coram Deo* is to live one's entire life in the presence of God, under the authority of God, to the glory of God.
>
> To live in the presence of God is to understand that whatever we are doing and wherever we are doing it, we are acting under the gaze of God. God is omnipresent. There is no place so remote that we can escape His penetrating gaze.
>
> To live all of life *coram Deo* is to live a life of integrity. It is a life of wholeness that finds its unity and coherency in the majesty of God. A fragmented life is a life of disintegration. It is marked by inconsistency, disharmony, confusion, conflict, contradiction, and chaos.[11]

In part 1 we explored a couple of points that help us better understand what it means to do our theology *coram Deo*. One concerns the problem of how we know God. We established that such knowledge comes as a result of divine agency, not human effort. Our knowledge of God comes about as a result of "divine descent" reaching "into mundane reality."[12] That is, God takes the initiative, and as a result we are able to relate to and therefore know God. Otherwise, the mystery remains a mystery! The other issue engaged the means by which we relate to and therefore know God. We do so from the stance of faith. Only this posture double-clicks the divine icon and affords knowledge. These two points tell us that even when divine revelation has taken place and understanding has occurred, there is still a modicum of tension: the unknown remains, and knowledge is attained by faith. In the space between the two, there remains a place of tension where our theology is developed and performed in the presence of God. Trappist monk Thomas Merton describes beautifully what it means to live in this place of tension. He does so in a way that describes further what doing theology in the presence of God, before the face of God, looks like:

> Faith incorporates the unknown into our everyday life in a living, dynamic and actual manner. The unknown remains unknown, it is still a mystery, for it cannot cease to be one. The function of faith is not to reduce mystery to

rational clarity, but to integrate the unknown and the known together in a living whole, in which we are more and more able to transcend the limitations of our external self.

Hence the function of faith is not only to bring us into contact with the "authority of God" revealing; not only to teach us truths "about God," in so far as our unknown and undiscovered self actually lives in God, moving and acting only under the direct light of His merciful grace.

This is, to my mind, the crucially important aspect of faith which is too often ignored today. Faith is not just conformity, it is *life*. It embraces all the realms of life, penetrating into the most mysterious and inaccessible depths not only of our unknown spirit being but even of God's own hidden essence and love. Faith, then, is the only way of opening up the true depths of reality, even of our own reality.[13]

To do our theology *coram Deo* requires a theological method that can thrive in this tension. To do so, we must resist the temptation to resolve the tension in the name of "theological understanding" that provides certainty about the mystery. It must, rather, live between theological memory (of who God is) and human hope (of knowing God as we are known by God). To achieve this requires a particular disposition and specific habits.

Living under the sovereignty of God, methodologically, entails assuming a particular stance in relation to the triune God:

- *Always subject, never object.* We gladly accept that it is the God and Father of our Lord Jesus Christ who calls the shots, not we! We allow God to be God.

- *Cultivating silence.* In a world where human beings appear to have evolved into *homo smartphonicus*, the words of Old Testament prophets speak directly to us regarding what doing theology *coram Deo* means: "Be silent before the Sovereign LORD, for the day of the LORD is near. The LORD has prepared a sacrifice; he has consecrated those he has invited" (Zeph. 1:7).[14]

- *Living dangerously.* We have already noted that the Christian worldview challenges all others. Jesus—not Caesar, nor president, nor prime minister, nor queen—is Lord. This has dangerous implications. The biblical view of God is even more dangerous. Iain Provan draws our attention to six implications, all of which affect our methodology:[15]

  » The character of the triune God is dangerous in that it has implications for how we should live.

  » Abandoning any belief in God is not the solution to the problem of the human condition.

» The biblical God challenges every person who chooses to relate to their fellow humans as though they are not God's image bearers.

» This God offers an altogether different take on evil and suffering that does not allow for fatalism, alarming amorality, or perilous naïveté.

» It is dangerous for anyone who does not want to acknowledge their responsibility for the nonhuman creation.

» The character of the biblical God is politically dangerous for anyone who does not want to see societal change; it has a serious health warning for those who maintain the status quo, for political utopians and advocates of a naked public square that does not acknowledge other people's differences.

What does it mean, then, for an evangelical theological method to be constructed *coram Deo*, in the presence of God? After all, isn't God everywhere? Don't we acknowledge a basic theological given—namely, that since God is Spirit he is not constrained by material or chronological boundaries? To be divine is to have the capacity of being omnipresent. Indeed, this is the case—but to what extent do we bring this reality to bear on our theological method? I propose the following criteria to guide us in this quest of constructing an evangelical theological method *coram Deo*. So that this may not be an abstraction, I will seek to ground what we have discussed by locating this methodological task in two equally essential locations: love and fidelity.

Love and Fidelity

It may be somewhat trite to argue that love is the basis for doing theology—this is a theological ABC. However, in the light of what we discussed in part 1, it should be clear that this sine qua non of Christian faith has not necessarily been a driving force in theological method. This is hardly surprising given that once the discipline of theology was removed from the context of believing communities of faith, hope, and love, this "greasy pig" was removed from academic theological equations. The vacuum was replaced with reason, with disastrous consequences. That said, the challenge remains. How do we place love in our theological method?

For many, the term "love" is a dead theological metaphor. We are very familiar with the word but seldom bring it to bear on how we go about our theological tasks. Perhaps this is due to our having displaced it to a well-meaning sentiment or an act of goodwill. In doing so, we have severed the connection between our theology and our theological method. If this is the case, then let us remind ourselves that an evangelical theology, like every other Christian theology, takes its form and content from the gospel. The texts of Scripture provide the macropicture within which the gospel is best understood. The gospel is the good news of John 3:16: it is *all about love*! For this reason and because the very subject matter of Christian theology is the God who *is love*, our theology begins and ends, and is packed throughout, with this reality. The very essence of the divine toward human beings, according to Michael Rea, includes both "the desire for *the good* of the beloved" and the "desire for *union* with the beloved."[16] In addition, our theological method should enable us to articulate the all-embracing God of love with ease and focus. Of course, the Enlightenment influence on Western theology dislodged the Johannine connection within the academy. A contemporary evangelical theological method, however, seeks to undo this Gordian knot. I suggest it does so by means of its own understanding of the gospel: that Scripture with its grand narrative of creation, covenant, and re-creation/salvation contour the way forward.

Nicholas Wolterstorff helps us in this direction by reminding us that when we refer to the kind of love displayed in the gospel, we are not talking about attraction love, attachment love, or advantage love.[17] The kind of love we are talking about here is not some cuddly affection. Rather, it is to be identified within what Walter Brueggemann describes as "the narrative of emancipatory covenant-making"[18] and Wolterstorff as "covenant faithfulness."[19] It is a menacing and demanding kind of love. It is divine love demonstrated in the face of a dysfunctional creation, where human beings created to experience love have an altogether different reality living on the edges of society, family, physical and mental health, themselves, God, and neighbor. It cannot be reduced merely to the "saving of souls" in the sense of rescuing guilty sinners from the clutches of hell. Yes, this is a reality—any notion of a biblical understanding of human agency and responsibility takes this as a very real end point. However, the eternal life Jesus Christ offers us—the well-being, the flourishing, the exercising of dominion so that self and neighbor may live fruitfully—is a hope for the here and now.

Therefore, in a theological method that involves love in terms of emancipatory covenant making, covenant faithfulness will be unable to wander too far from its gospel center. It will be concerned with justice and the rule of kingdom law—because it is in the gospel of a crucified Savior that the triune God displays what divine justice looks like in taking ownership for our dysfunctions and breaking their power in order to enact, display, and guarantee his covenant relationship with us.[20] Thus, this covenant faithfulness is a love that understands what grace looks like, and therefore its theological method will be sensitive to the subterranean golden thread of divine and neighbor love that runs throughout Scripture. This method will humanize our theology in its recognition that a methodological imperative is involved here. Love is cognizant of its relational consequences. God is faithful to his Word, and so it can be trusted; the human condition cannot be reduced to rational fact but affects our entire gestalt; Scripture concerns the common good of the community and not merely our own private and individual concerns; fidelity to one's word, whether spoken or written, is a public affair, not private, because, as Brueggemann points out, fidelity "is grounded in unmocked holiness" that is worked out publicly.[21] I like his focus when he reminds us that

> the teaching of the holiness tradition is not in this or that rule; rather, the intent of the holiness tradition, taken in sum, is to fend off the reduction of public life into profanation that fails to respect, honor, or take seriously the deep mystery of the public good and the neighbors who inhabit it. When profanation is unchecked by a resolve to holiness, life becomes cheap, neighbors become dispensable, and the common good becomes subject to cynical distortion. In its practice of fidelity, Israel knew that the formation and maintenance of the common good was not simply an accident or a convenience. It was rather a common task. And the relentless reflection of the prophets is that this vocation of the common good had not been honored or taken seriously.[22]

Let me put it another way—I am not advocating that an evangelical theological method go about its business *coram Deo* because it is a trendy notion or because I want to be original. I have already stated that in promoting a theological method that embraces the notion of doing theology *coram Deo* I am merely bringing to the surface something that has always been a concern for every ordinary evangelical theologian. My gripe is with the evangelical academy, where theology has become so separated from this most essential and basic of theological tools that it will most likely raise the cringe factor for some readers within the academy, excepting most practical theologians, who have carried the flag faithfully and suffered the ignominy of not being taken so seriously within the academy until recently. My plea is that we do our theology *coram Deo* because we must, and we must because our theology is grounded in the narratives of creation, covenant, re-creation, and future hope. These are the various places where the God of love makes himself known. Therefore, theology *coram Deo* is not an add-on. It is a necessity. We do our theology *coram Deo* not because it reflects our relationship with the God and Father of our Lord Jesus Christ, our devotion to Christ, and our Spirit-renewed lives, corporate and individual. We do it because of "the joy of being in sync with the Lord of covenant, the sense of companionship in doing the things in which the partner delights. The delight in such obedience is not in its outcome but in its performance, because it is a gift to come down where you ought to be—namely, in sync with and in the presence of God."[23]

Pause

Reread the quotation from Brueggemann above and replace "Israel" with "church."

- How does your theological method empower you to take the gospel to your neighbors in the public square and enhance their opportunities to flourish?
- What are you being faithful to when you do your theology?
- How do you use love in your own theological reflection?
- How significant a tool is love in your own theological method?

Integration

When we undertake our theological method *coram Deo*, we do not prioritize our theology above Scripture or its gospel. Rather, our theology becomes reoriented around the law of love. Since our subject matter is the God who is love and since we are called to embody this law of God, neighbor, and self, we should reflect the same integrity in our theological method. In doing so, we must maintain covenant fidelity. As a result, we create a methodological dynamic that enables us to work out our theology with integrity. I believe that this is important since, as Robert Banks points out, "the very purpose of theology is to be found in the lives of people outside the profession of theology, in a way very different from, say, medicine or law."[24]

What we do as theologians should resonate with the daily reality of people who live out their lives in the ebb and flow of ordinary life. When it does not, the latter have little reason to listen to the former. Banks argues for a return to redeeming the routines of life that allow engagement between our ordinary lives and the realities each of us inhabits. I particularly like his declaration that if this discipline of life-enhancing routines "is forged into the warp and woof of everyday life it will also have vitality and relevance."[25] The point is as important for the way we go about our theological method as it is for any other aspect of Christian life. When theological education is reduced solely to the realm of *instruction*, there is less chance, if any necessarily, of *transformation*.[26] That is, it is only when we engage our body, our mind, our character, and our personality in the process that change happens: information on its own does not achieve this. As the apostle James reminds us, demonic reality knows quite a lot more than human reality concerning how the kingdom of

God functions, but this information brings about fear, not transformation. "You believe that there is one God. Good! Even the demons believe that—and shudder" (James 2:19).

I am making a methodological imperative once again. Our theology (what we understand of God), our theological method (how we go about the process of understanding), and theology's purpose (what we expect when understanding becomes practice) should mirror the integrity of our God. The degree to which these different perspectives of the one reality talk to one another, have their own ebb and flow, will affect the overall integrity of any contemporary evangelical theology. Otherwise, our theology will have no relevance, in relation either to the needs of the church or to its own internal structures. It is hardly surprising that much theological reflection carries little weight with ordinary theologians and believers, having been molded by theological and methodological factors contrary to its own DNA. In this, contemporary theology resonates more with the worldview it inhabits than that of Scripture.

If we can extend T. S. Eliot's poem quoted earlier, it is not merely that words crack and strain; it is that our contemporary postmodern take on the reality we daily receive has no integrity. Social media and newspapers move from the most gruesome of human atrocities on one page to inane speculations on the latest celebrity on the next. We can have the most eclectic music list on our smartphone, where the only factor in common is our own subjective approval and appreciation. The same goes for art, literature, architecture, fashion . . . The list is almost endless. Why? Because contemporary Western, postmodern culture celebrates diversity, pluralism, and relativism without consideration of their wider "fit." Holistic viewpoints are for dilettantes with their vegan and organic obsessions, or plant-based house paints and carbon-neutral footprints. There is no "big picture." Faddism now determines the zeitgeist and is made possible by post-truth truthiness.[27] Everything is "liquid."[28]

Of course, this state of affairs allows the lazy thinker to avoid the serious task of putting the various dots together to see the forest and the trees. In some sense, this is an understandable reaction to the place the Enlightenment gave to reason, thus enabling it to position meaning above covenant faithfulness. An evangelical theological method, however, is not allowed such a luxury if it is to do service to the gospel. If all it takes when we hit a theological difficulty is to press Delete and move on as we wish, then we have no need of any space for the hard work of thinking faith. There will be no need for a theological method premised on covenant values that require full participation of body, mind, and soul (i.e., our entire being), habituated effort, and a baptized imagination in order to achieve their goal. Think about it: we have hope and therefore grounds for trust solely because a covenant is in place.

This covenant has been documented for us in Scripture, and its veracity has been tested and utterly vindicated by the resurrection of Jesus from the dead, thus evidencing the trustworthiness of his message, which has been confirmed time and time again in the life of the church, past and present. Without these deeper grounds for trust, the gospel is a mere chimera, impotent to offer any future hope where the messy stuff of life can change and an altogether better existence become possible. The color-coordinated, lifestyle-balanced empty selves whose lives are determined by daily, weekly, or monthly journalistic holy writ amuse themselves to death in such a hope-less subculture. The gospel of Jesus Christ, on the other hand, offers evidence that change for the better is possible in *all* things for those who live *coram Deo*, the called ones who love God. It is because of the sheer anticipation of this kind of transformation that the followers of Jesus trade in everything, assume a cross-shaped life, and walk through the narrow gate onto the narrow Way that leads to abundant life.[29]

Methodologically, this challenge requires of us what Richard Hays describes as a "hermeneutics of trust."[30] This involves three things. First, if we are to read and understand Scripture correctly, "we must trust the God who speaks though scripture."[31] In the context of *coram Deo* this resonates deeply with regard to covenant faithfulness. Second, a hermeneutics of trust (trusting in the covenant God and therefore his Word) enables us to take a critical posture regarding ourselves. Here again the context of our theology hits home and demands that we take methodological recognition of the fact that our context is messy, we are messy, and our reading of the gospel can be messy. If we want to clean up, then "our minds must be transformed by grace, and that happens nowhere more powerfully than through reading scripture receptively and trustingly with the aid of the Holy Spirit."[32] Last, since hermeneutics is all about hearing the text rather than talking at it, we need to learn how to read and teach the text so that Scripture opens up to us and to others.[33] This is what a theological method *coram Deo* looks like: personal integration where we are addressed by God and then learn to listen, ponder, reflect, process, even digest, until trust is formed, faith is exercised, and mutual indwelling can occur.

When this kind of dynamic operates in our theological method—when we trust Scripture and when we commit ourselves to the incarnate Word— then integration can take place on several levels. By means of our theological method we can create spaces where theological understanding about the more difficult aspects of our faith can be listened to and engaged—aspects such as divine revelation and human understanding; expectation and fulfillment; faith in the unseen and certainty about the unknown; the personal and the communal; the haves and the have-nots; the "in" and the "out." A robust evangelical theological method enables us to act faithfully despite what is going on around us, not because we make a virtue out of "blind" faith but because the church historical and universal as well as each one of us have built a critical mass of experience where the truth of covenant love has been demonstrated. Out of this has emerged tradition that has been tested by serious reason only to find that once again the gospel and the God of the gospel pull through, and in this we know that God's Word is his bond. When we express the matter that way, then lines from the poem *In Memoriam*, by Alfred, Lord Tennyson, remind us of where our attention is best placed:

> Our little systems have their day;
>> They have their day and cease to be:
>> They are but broken lights of thee,
> And thou, O Lord, art more than they.[34]

Formative and Transformative

Our evangelical theological method will be effective to the degree it enables us to develop habits that nurture ways of integrating faith and thought, theory and praxis, hearing and responding, the personal and the communal, the visible and the liminal. I am proposing here that these various points of integration evidence the gospel, endorse the truthfulness of our theology, and confirm the relevance of our theological method. They are also necessary if how we do our theology is to facilitate its purpose: transformation. The necessary connection between what we believe concerning the triune God and how we live is clear in Ingolf Dalferth's summary:

> Theology is best understood and practiced not as a theoretical or speculative discipline that aims at knowledge of God and of everything in relation to God (*scientia speculativa*) but as a practical discipline that studies actions, acts, and activities that change human life . . . not, however, merely human actions . . . but the divine activity that changes human life from sin to salvation, from disregarding God's presence to orienting itself toward God's presence, from ignoring God to loving God and one's neighbour, from death to life.[35]

If theology is exegesis of the gospel, then its potency is seen to the degree it achieves the purpose of the gospel. This goal is intrinsically social in its construction. Faith in Christ—that he is Lord, that he was dead, that he is risen, and that he will come again—is an utterly formative event. It has to be seen as such because Scripture describes it as such. By virtue of what Jesus Christ achieved and our receiving the benefits of this by faith, we undergo a geographical change—from being foreigners to God's kingdom to being citizens who are now seated with Christ Jesus in heavenly places. In addition to this, we also experience ontological change—our very being is formed into something altogether new—we no longer walk according to the flesh but by the Spirit. Why? Because the gift of life we receive is the very breath and life force of God, the Holy Spirit. We are literally "re-birthed." As it is with our human birth in which new life is established only when we take the first breath on our own, so it is with the new life we receive when we are born "from above." We are new creations—the old disappears and something altogether new is formed.[36]

This formation brings into existence an altogether new *personal* identity in that it places us in a new set of relationships that constitute who we are (mother, father, daughter, son, twin, only child, wife, husband, friend, stranger, etc.). We are children of *this* God and thus have intimacy with the Father; we are coheirs with Christ and thus have his PIN, as it were, and can access his inheritance from the Father; and all this is possible because our life force is God's Spirit, not our own. This formation also brings about a new *corporate* identity. We belong to a new community with its own social structures, its own economy and political manifesto. Our newly formed identity is formed within the social structures of kingdom and church and takes its energy and vision from them. Our characters are formed not in isolation but in community, not independent of everyone else but in a very specific triangulation between God, neighbor, and self. It is community that provides each one of us with the support, the wherewithal, the necessary habits and routines that facilitate healthy growth of our new identity. A theological method that ignores this formative dynamic not only misses the entire point of the gospel; it renders itself impotent to engage what it takes to bring about a character that can flourish in the messiness of life. If it takes a whole village to raise a child, it takes a whole church community to raise similarly those born from above.

This formation does not "just happen." Human character does not simply appear from nowhere. There's something about human nature that requires ongoing transformation. Personal transformation—the power to change—evidences the strength of our own character and shows people what we are made of, the kind of grit, determination, and willpower we have. Put bluntly, transformation is where we show our true spirit. Similarly, with our new life: it is God's life force, the Holy Spirit, who gives us the energy. However, this only happens to the degree we change our thoughts and bring them into line with the good and perfect will of God (Rom. 12:2). The implications for ourselves and for our theological method are significant. Stanley Hauerwas captures just how much so when he narrates his own response to what transformation requires:

No! No! I don't want God to accept me the way I am. I want God to transform me, to make me perfect. Of course, the church rightly says to people, "We want you to know the joy of the life of what it means to worship God." But you're going to need a lot of transformation to be part of this kind of community because your life cannot remain the same when you become a member of the church of Jesus Christ. All your desires and loyalties must be directed to the worship of God, and that means, for example, you're not going to be a good American anymore. You're not going to believe that church and flag go easily together. And it may well change your friendship with some because their way of life is corrupting.

I don't believe in the "you're accepted" ideology. It is a way of our escaping the necessity of judgment on ourselves and a way to ensure we will have shallow souls. I am not for accepting people the way they are. As Mark Twain observed, "About the worst advice you can give anyone is to be themselves."[37]

To incorporate *coram Deo* into an evangelical theological method means the following:

- The method is formative in that it provides the means for understanding the new relationship that the gospel brings about. To some extent, this is where Western Enlightenment theology ends. It *in*forms minds with theological information for the practical application, usually, of an assessment.
- The method is transformative in that it understands that the purpose of theology and therefore of theological method is to enable us to go beyond information downloading to character upbuilding. An evangelical theological method will be as concerned as any other about its theological data. However, it should understand that this data is not information for information's sake but information for *trans*formation's sake.

Pause

Take a pause at this point for a consciousness-raising reflection on your own theological method.

- Is your theological method interested in formation or transformation or both?
- What takes up more of your focus: theology for information's or for transformation's sake?
- Identify where you need to improve and how you can go about this!

Neighborly Community

An evangelical theological method is a discipline that enables us to participate in the "final act," as it were, of the great drama of creation, covenant, and re-creation. To do theology *coram Deo* is to do theology aware of the drama of God's saving love for the whole world, about divine desire to reconcile all things to himself. Our theological method enables us better to speak the truth of the gospel so that others may flourish. These "others" are not abstracted from reality or from each one of us. They are you and me, they are "us"— people once "lost" but who now can "see."

Pushing the theater analogy further, the only difference between ourselves and others is that we find ourselves caught up on stage while the others watch from the stalls. Jesus Christ's preferred nomenclature for "others" was "neighbors," as we noted earlier. It rather goes without saying, then, that in order to be most effective and reach the most people, rather than having them come to the theater (not too dissimilar from contemporary church), the players have to take the performance out into the neighborhood, as it were. What makes this so incredible is that neighborhoods are where "stuff" happens, messy and flourishing. To achieve this, there have to be "laws"—in this case, "promises" since what we are talking about here are covenant laws. These promises, in turn, create neighborhoods—locations where these laws or promises are made good—neighbor*goods*! Government, whether local or national, makes promises (allocating resources, looking after infrastructure, supporting people, collecting refuse, maintaining law and order). In doing so, it creates neighborhoods. Good promises usually result in election to govern. Good governing produces good neighborhoods; bad governing, not so good.

Walter Brueggemann captures the essence of this dynamic well when he comments on the Ten Commandments, and on the last in particular: "These divine expectations and summons are about generative and sustainable neighborliness. We need not romanticize 'neighbor' as one with whom we share intimacy. Rather, the term refers to members who share a common destiny and so are ordered according to the common good, a commonality that requires that their relationship be other than that of rivals, competitors, or threats."[38] Even though I may not live on your turf, share your values, belong to your tribe or clan, or fit your profile, nevertheless, simply by virtue of being a fellow human being, someone created in the image of God, a creature just like you—in fact, just like a bird, cat, dog, mouse—as someone who lives *coram Deo*, I am your neighbor and you are mine.[39] What the gospel does is break down the "stuff" we put up in order to justify our nonneighborliness, the differences that act as relational cancers on the law of love. It does so because both Testaments, Old and New, make clear that love of God and love of neighbor (with a healthy dose of self-respect) are the right foundations for a flourishing life, for a life well lived.

In doing our theology *coram Deo* we are doing it *righteously*, or at least as righteously as we can, which means that we do it in a neighborly manner. To do this, we need to be in the neighborhood. In urban cultures where our churches are more and more out of reach for those on the edges of our neighborhoods, this is quite a challenge. To do our theology *coram Deo* means we take our place seriously: that we live and have our being as a gift, not an autonomous right; that our true human fulfillment is found in and through others, not on our own; that our reality is best articulated by the gospel—that abundant life, flourishing life is life grounded in neighborly community; that this kind of community does not exist to meet the needs of its own constituents but, rather, exists as a dynamic and flexible society always alert to those on its edges and those beyond. To do our theology *coram Deo* involves a radical repositioning of our own theological framing that reduces just about everything to one's own salvation, one's own individual life-plan, one's own fulfillment—all at the expense of neighbor, neighborliness, and neighborhood. This is not pie in the sky for when we die. This is the essence of covenant love supremely demonstrated in the gospel. It is the golden thread that runs throughout Scripture. Volf and Croasmun remind us, "Theology has a contribution to make, and theology *must make* that contribution if it is to remain true to its purpose."[40] Something has surely gone awry in our theological method if our theology is not exegesis of the gospel, if it is not in line with Jesus's mission. A gospel so extravagant in its love for the other, the neighbor in need, you and me, them and us, wandering blindly—the walking dead, dead in our trespasses and sins—aliens to the commonwealth of God, somehow has lost its true mission if it categorizes the neighbor to the realm of evangelism, mission, or patronizing support. The problem with this reductionist approach to the neighbor is that it mirrors the way in which the wider First World perceives its own "neighbors," best exemplified in the plight of contemporary refugees who are so easily perceived as "human waste, with no useful function to play in the land of their arrival . . . ; from their present place, the dumping site, there is no return and no road forward."[41]

The consequences for having removed the neighbor from our theological center—for having dumbed down the gospel in such a way that the "neighbor" is perceived generally as an evangelistic scalp or patronizingly as someone who needs help—have been damaging on so many levels. Our concern is that as a result, literally, evangelical theology takes its place among a myriad of other career choices. And when that career is chosen, all too easily the gospel it is meant to communicate becomes merely a means by which professional and career promotion is achieved. This has profound implications for our theological method: rather than how it might advance our career path as academic theologians, our theological method, when done *coram Deo*, should reflect the concerns of the gospel we are seeking to exegete in our theology. We should be asking, "How does this advance the gospel?" not "How does this advance my career?" And we will do so to the degree our theological method forces us to consider the wider neighborly community. I agree with D. H. Williams in his critique of evangelical churchmanship when he comments that "no amount of creative packaging and marketing of the gospel will rescue church ministry"—and we could replace that with "academic evangelical theology"—"if we lose the theological center which enables us to define the faith and prescribe the kinds of intellectual and practical relations it should have in the world. Given the centrifugal and atomistic forces already inherent among Free Church and evangelical forms of Christianity, the lack of an identifying center is theologically debilitating. Our unending search for a Spirit-filled and biblically refined faith has not paid off in enhanced clarity of ecclesiastical unity but in an increased fragmentation of the church."[42]

In advocating the inclusion of church community oriented toward neighbor, neighborliness, and neighborhood into our understanding of *coram Deo*, I'm contending that in doing so we can redress evangelicalism's drift from its center. The inclusion of "neighbor" into our theological method ensures not only that evangelical theology will necessarily engage the gospel (the triune God's response to our messy state) but also that we engage this gospel aware that to do our theology *coram Deo* makes demands of us that go far beyond our own self-awareness or self-aggrandizement. Samuel Wells pushes the point in describing being a neighbor as being someone who catches stones ("what Jesus did on the cross") and offers shoulders to cry on (what he does forever).[43] Since most if not all socially constructed relationships are the produce of hard work and require specific habits to maintain, and given, too, that we live in a global village with altogether different "neighbors," it follows that perhaps we need to develop habits up to the task. I cannot agree more with James Walters's proposal that two specific habits required if we are to be neighborly in the way we go about our theology are the habits of persuasion and of curiosity. Our theological method cannot assume the truth of our theology—neighborliness is all about the art of persuasion, after all. If our neighbors are convinced, we have won over an ally or made a new friend. If not, they still remain our neighbors and we are neighborly to each other. But perhaps the most challenging habit to form in a post-Christendom weary of Christian wordsmiths is curiosity about the gospel.[44] We must raise the bar of evangelism so that we cultivate curiosity in our neighbors. Rowan Williams offers a window into what this could look like and what it may take if our theology is to do justice to the gospel not merely intellectually but, much more importantly, relationally:

> God's love for the world is extraordinary, without cause, absolutely free, absolutely overwhelmingly unreasonable—and that's the kind of love we are invited to become part of. If the world hates God without cause, as it says in the reading, God in return loves without cause. There is the foundation laid for our Christian life and faith—that foundation, that tested stone, that precious cornerstone, that sure foundation on the basis of which we're instructed in the Old Testament reading not to panic. I like that translation! And of course, that foundation stone is identical with Jesus Christ because it is Jesus Christ who in every moment of his life, in every word he speaks, in every act he performs, in the death he dies and the life he reclaims, is the embodiment of that unreasonable, causeless love. The love for what doesn't belong, the love that spills over constantly from that little world of people like us and never acknowledges any stopping place, because there is absolutely no reason why God should ever stop loving.
>
> So, quite a challenge for the Church—rethinking love, rethinking belonging. Instead of saying "Well, these are the people who belong with us, these are the people we are like, so these are the people we shall like and who will like us," we are bound to say we've got to go out and create more and more belonging with the people who don't belong. We've got to go and unreasonably extend our welcome, our compassion, our joyful understanding to the entire world and live with the admittedly very awkward and messy consequences of that.[45]

Doing Theology *Missio Dei*: On the Mission of the Triune God

> I saw a stable, low and very bare,
> A little child in a manger.
> The oxen know him, had him in their care,
> To men he was a stranger.
> The safety of the world was lying there,
> And the world's danger.[46]

If the internal orientation of our community theological tool is doing our theology in the presence of God, *coram Deo*, then its external counterpart is doing our theology as participating in the mission of God, *missio Dei*. One takes its energy from the church's own existence as the people of God live out their faith before God. The other's energy comes from the church's understanding of who God is as well as the triune God's disposition toward his creation, the world, and those created to be his image bearers. Neither is an add-on only for the superspiritual, those who are more enthusiastic and better committed. In the same way that each of us lives our life in the presence of the God and Father of our Lord Jesus Christ, as we indwell the Son who indwells us by his Spirit, so, too, by virtue of this new relationship, do we participate in God's mission. In many ways, our being caught up in the mission of God grows out of our lives lived before God, *coram Deo*. However, while many of us are familiar with the words—living before God, in the presence of God—in reality, when we dig a little deeper, we see that we do not understand what they mean. The same can be said, too, with regard to being involved in God's mission. Before we define our terms, let's clear the ground, as it were, and identify some factors that need to be considered, as well as erroneous assumptions we need to dismiss concerning what doing theology *missio Dei* looks like.

1. Doing theology *missio Dei* requires that we step out of our various Christian comfort zones and enter more inhospitable terrain. The contemporary shift from a church-attending to nonattending Western culture means that to be Christian, let alone evangelical, is to be part of what William Willimon describes all too familiarly: "an outpost in a culture that is sometimes friendly, most often indifferent, and sometimes actively hostile to it."[47]

2. Theology done *missio Dei* involves the whole person and represents a loving movement toward others—one motivated by the gospel. It is love seeking simply because God is love. It requires a high view of the human body and the cultural body. That is, theology done *missio Dei* is an embodied theology. It won't reify one aspect of human existence at the expense of others. In terms of our theological method it means that intellectual knowledge is not prioritized over other forms of knowing, that our embodiedness is not something that gets in the way of the gospel, nor that the spiritual becomes detached from social expressions of the kingdom, whether political, relational, economic, or cultural.[48]

3. It requires a high view of culture for the single reason of the "so loved the world" principle of John 3:16. Rather than focusing on what is bad about culture, and thus legitimizing Christian forms of social construction, *missio Dei* recognizes that all cultures, Christian and non-Christian, exist under the sovereignty of God and can be redeemed.[49]

4. *Missio Dei* does not necessitate typical evangelical responses that it is highfalutin Christianese for a social gospel agenda, nor that it does not have a high view of Scripture and that it therefore opens the door to forms of syncretism.[50]

5. Doing our theology *missio Dei* means that we cannot participate in what Al Tizon describes as "theologies of Empire," where the churches'

resources are spent on the faithful for their own consumption or self-aggrandizement.[51]

6. A theological method driven by a concern for *missio Dei* will not reduce the missional to "soul saving." Rather, it will understand how the gospel is good news for God's entire creation, including for the nonhuman but equally dependent forms of creation.

All this means that when we do our theology *missio Dei*, we are tapping into, as it were, the narrative of God's own redemptive intentions, the work *God* has done toward and for us and through which *we* gain understanding—revelation—of God. In turn, this divine desire to see all men and women flourish becomes "the missional context of local communities of faith."[52] The problem here, however, is one of identification: Is this missional context something specific to particular people—evangelists, missionaries, global theologians—or is it something in which every follower of Jesus Christ is called to participate? Is the idea of *missio Dei* something we *do*, or is it something we *are*? That is, is it a function or a way of life? A. Scott Moreau briefly touches on the topic of *missio Dei* in the dictionary definition of "missiology" and advances the possibility of *missio Dei* as a lifestyle that prefers the poor, the marginalized, the downtrodden in such a way that the drive to evangelism and mission is inextricably intertwined with the cultural mandate that involves changing the worlds in which people live.[53]

Pause

- Without thinking too deeply, where do you identify on the *do-or-are* spectrum?
- Is a *missio Dei* perspective something that comes naturally to you, or is it an "add-on"? If the latter, identify two things you need to change to strengthen your own *missio Dei* perspective.

Once we acknowledge that theology is exegesis of the gospel, we understand better why we incorporate *missio Dei* into our theological method. However, at the same time, we need to clarify what we mean.

- Urging *missio Dei* is not the same as suggesting the idea of "mission" into our theological method. This would be an altogether backward step, first, because for most of us "mission" is something *we do*; second, it is something *done* most often by the most zealous among church

folks; and, last, for many Christians "mission" is perceived as an op-
tional dimension of Christian living. However, when we speak of *missio
Dei* we are referring, first, not to human action but to *divine* action,
the triune God revealing himself to us through what he does—in the
economies (the works of God) of creation and re-creation/salvation.
Missio Dei as a theological tool, therefore, is aware of its position in
the scheme of things and reminds us of the contingent nature of theological reflection.

- The gospel is God's greatest work, and in it we see the triune God at
  work. It is the grand drama of the God who spoke his will (by Word
  and Breath) and thereby brought creation into existence, the Father who
  sends his Son through the enabling of his Spirit. This is an important
  point: the method of *missio Dei*, as Moreau points out, "depends on
  its nature and goal."[54] If we see *missio Dei* as something we do rather
  than what God does, then there will be very different goals. The former
  invites God into our missional programs. The unintended consequence
  of this way of thinking has been to disconnect the church from divine
  presence and action in the world.[55] The latter reverses this dynamic,
  inviting us to participate in God's program.[56] And because it is *God's*
  program, it is a trinitarian program in which we are caught up in the
  perichoretic[57] unity of the Father, Son, and Spirit, and our theological
  method should reflect this dynamic relationship.

- Since the God of the gospel is Father, Son, and Spirit, it follows that our
  theological method *missio Dei* will have a *trinitarian* character. After
  all, if *missio Dei* is not something God does but who God is, then a
  similar dynamic exists regarding the church and how the church goes
  about doing its theology. Brian Harris applies this to how we should
  understand our worldview, but I think the three categories he suggests
  are equally pertinent to how we go about doing our theology *missio
  Dei*. Our theological method should allow for an element of *surprise*—it
  is faith seeking understanding of Mystery. In addition, an evangelical
  theological method will demonstrate an ability to *embrace* the other,
  the stranger, the foreigner, the immigrant (legal or not), and those on
  the margins for whom the gospel is good news. And, last, our theological method will demonstrate the power of *witness* as it engages and
  exegetes the gospel.[58] Daniel Migliore offers us a compact definition of
  what we are seeking to do when we approach our theology *missio Dei*:
  "The nature and mission of the church are grounded in the nature and
  missionary activity of the triune God. The mission of the church is to
  participate in the reconciling love of the triune God who reaches out

to the fallen world in Jesus Christ and by the power of the Holy Spirit brings strangers and enemies into God's new and abiding community."[59]

The notion of describing God as a "missionary" is rather strange, but this is exactly how Scripture presents the triune God: the Father sends the Son (John 3:16); the Father sends the Spirit (Gal. 4:6); the Son sends the Spirit (John 15:26); the Son sends the church (John 17:18), and the church sends its constituents (Rom. 10:15).[60] In this sense we can see that the *missionary* God is the *sending* God. We can summarize the trinitarian face of *missio Dei* thus: "Mission starts in the trinitarian activity of God; the Father sends the Son into the world through the enlivening power of the Spirit. The Church is brought into God's mission so that as the Father sent the Son, so too the Son sends the Church into the world in the life-giving power of the Spirit to participate in God's redemptive activity."[61]

- *Missio Dei* enlarges our theological method. It enables our theological method to extend beyond any theological restrictions imposed when we locate mission between human sin and human fall, on the one hand, and the death and resurrection of Jesus Christ, on the other. *Missio Dei* is not a response to human sin and the need for reconciliation: its cause is not human sin. Thus, our theological method is not subordinate to soteriology, as though the gospel is only interested in "saving" us. Rather, our theological method will be expansive enough to help us engage creation and re-creation.

- *Missio Dei* starts with the divine desire to create all that exists. Its foundations rest on what God has declared to be "good" and worth rescuing. This foundational goodness, in turn, extends through the mess of human dysfunctioning (sin) and creation's "fall" from all it can be—through covenant and Torah, which provide guidelines for flourishing—and extends even beyond the death and resurrection of our Lord Jesus Christ. Its reach extends beyond these to the very consummation of all things and the final establishing of God's reign within his creation.[62] Some, like John Piper, argue that at this point *missio Dei* will come to an end. It will have achieved its purpose and will no longer be required in the new heaven and new earth. That is, the mission of God in creating and bringing about the redemption of this creation will have succeeded.[63] I think otherwise: doing our theology *missio Dei* reminds us that when we do our theology from the perspective of God's mission, it cannot be singularly focused on human redemption but must be focused on creation's restoration. Yes, we participate in the redemptive activity of God in the world.[64] However, we engage, too, in the ongoing creational activity of the triune God in creation. This starts with the triune actions of Father, Son, and Spirit in creation, through covenant, and ultimately in Christ, and flows beyond with the participation of the church as Father, Son, and Spirit seek the redemption and perfection of creation.[65]

- Since divine action cannot be separated from divine being, and since Jesus Christ himself tells us that God is love, when we do our theology *missio Dei*, we do so with an eye on the love God has for his creation and for his image bearers, however messed up. I think we can identify two very significant implications from this for our theological method when it is done *missio Dei*. First, the externally facing dimension of our methodological tool is energized by love. It means we do our theology from a disposition of goodwill, from a position of hope and faith, and from a perspective of respect and love. It means the gospel is unpacked theologically in ways that resonate with these dispositions in such a way that the lost, the lame, and the lonely not only hear good news but understand the degree to which we are all loved. It means that when we do our theology in this manner, the outward-facing posture of *missio Dei* should stop us from doing theology in ways that prefer those who are safely embedded within church walls. Rather, it means that theological method done *missio Dei* enables us to be with the excluded: the disadvantaged, the oppressed, the afflicted, and the isolated.[66]

- Last, when our theological method is done *missio Dei*, it means that the community aspect of our theological method occurs from a particular position and a specific disposition.

  » In terms of *position*, we do our theology from a position of confidence in the gospel. An evangelical theological method will have a confidence to be *missio Dei* not because it is superior to others, nor because of any misplaced belief that it has any special privilege in relation to truth. The confidence will be grounded in the tried and tested testimony of the people of God about their own experience of the gospel. It really does work! The transforming power of the gospel is a living reality. More than that, the quality of the gospel's power to change is such that the "transformed"—those who have met the risen Christ and are in touch with his energy, his breath, his Spirit—cannot do anything but want to tell others. Lovers are the most effective and contagious communicators.[67] It is the mean-spirited, mealy-mouthed, tight-lipped who are the least motivated to see someone happier than their own Uriah Heep attitude.[68] A theological method done *missio Dei* will be one that reaches out to the communities around them who have not yet tasted and seen that the gospel of the Lord God, the God and Father of our Lord Jesus Christ, the One who promised us abundant lives—lives that flourish in the energy, power, and love of the Holy Spirit—is good.

» In terms of *disposition*, when theology is done *missio Dei*, it will always be focused outward to the world, not inward. It will be concerned for the gospel to be understood in order that it draw a response. From the lost, lame, and lonely, that response is often positive; from those whom the gospel threatens in politics, economics, society, and ego, the historical response has rarely been positive. Theological method, like the gospel it structures, never operates within a vacuum. Faith seeking understanding does not always take place in smooth, gentle, cool waters. Often, theology done *missio Dei* is forged on the anvil of sacrifice, suffering, and martyrdom. Those readers who live where a minority Christian witness exists know only too well what this means. Presently, Christians are the most persecuted religious people group worldwide. I am particularly grateful for the way in which Scott Sunquist apportions significant focus to *suffering love* in his own statement of mission. What he advocates in relation to missiology is equally relevant for theological method—namely, that it is "rooted in the life, teaching, and ministry of Jesus Christ that the mission of God, the *missio Dei*, is a matter of *our participating with Jesus Christ in his suffering love for the greater glory of God to be revealed*."[69]

When we go about our theology *missio Dei*, it is driven by our desire that others might share in and enjoy what we have already come to know. Lovers are the most effective communicators because they say what they say and do what they do for the sheer joy of it! As Darrell Guder puts it, "The gospel is about news that is so urgently good that it must be shared."[70] We have known what it is like not to enjoy the benefits of being citizens of the kingdom of God. We have experienced the bondage of sin, the brokenness of our own humanity, and dystopic relationships corroded by addiction, lack of integrity, despair, and deferred hope. All that differs for us is that the gospel bumped into us and we have gotten to know Jesus. We are no longer in bondage to sin or afraid of death but have been made alive by the Spirit of life in Christ Jesus; we are now seated with Christ Jesus in heavenly places far above the powers that mess up human life and society—these powers are now Christ's footstool! We were lost—now we are found. We were nobody, now we are Somebody's. Our testimony is that the gospel is not "theory" or "pie in the sky for when we die." Rather, it is a countertestimony to our previous way of living: it delivers what it says on the label, as it were. Our experience endorses Scripture; it confirms Christian tradition and corresponds to millennia of thinking. There is something almost infectious in the way Patrick Franklin captures the spirit of theologian Lesslie Newbigin when he describes this attitude:

> Primarily, mission results from an explosion of joy in the church community, which overflows into the world. It is the manifestation of the church's experience of the presence and power of the Holy Spirit. When the church has been granted a taste of God's presence, God's power, God's grace, and God's reconciliatory and unifying love, it is transformed into a living testimony to the gospel. When it exhibits the selfless and sacrificial love of Christ, living not for itself but for the sake of its neighbours, it lives provocatively as a sign and foretaste of the kingdom of God.[71]

I used to think that anything to do with mission was a specialist field and calling. The thought that it had anything to do with the task of theology rarely occurred to me. On reflection, I think this is a commonly held perception by many Christians, evangelical or not. Perhaps there is such confusion regarding the identity and character of the God of the gospel because what the triune God is most passionate about is often relegated to a theological ghetto. We have established in part 1 that our knowledge of God is given to the degree God chooses to reveal Godself. What God *does* reveals *who* God is. We have also seen that this knowledge is a result of God the Father seeking out creation and re-creation through the Son and doing so through the empowering agency of the Holy Spirit. Our theology, then, which is exegesis of this gospel, seeks to portray this *sending* God. Consequently, our theological method should consist of this intrinsic aspect of the God of the gospel. It is ironic that, according to Guder, contemporary theological training has often omitted mission and *missio Dei* (it is an option or a custom-made program).[72] It is even more ironic that theological method is missing in so many contemporary expressions of *missio Dei*.[73]

To do our theology *missio Dei* is to bring together, on the one hand, our worship of God as well as any theological reflection arising from our worship and, on the other, the praxis that emerges in response to both our worship and reflection. This involves what Stephen Bevans describes as a "missiological imagination"—a theological method that "would be a sustained and serious effort to 'listen to all the voices' in the doing of theology"[74] rather than existing solely for the internal consumption of those living *coram Deo*.[75] Such a method cannot be reduced to a personal and private salvation package but, rather, involves the entire communion of the saints.[76] This, of course, is a real problem today given that the problem facing an evangelical theological method is that historically it has reduced the gospel to purely individual categories and has understood only second, if at all, that the gospel "transforms individuals, but it also redeems communities of faith."[77]

If I can (mis)appropriate sociologist Zygmunt Bauman's description of societies as "factories of meaning" or, better still, as "nurseries of *meaningful life*,"[78] and couple this with the notion of flourishing, then in similar manner, our theological method can be perceived as the means by which we go about articulating life in all its abundance. To achieve this in terms of how our theological method reaches out to others beyond the community of faith who live *coram Deo* yet in a manner that has integrity with our theological method, I find it helpful to do this through the lens offered by Theo Sundermeier in relation to Christian mission:[79]

1. Doing theology *missio Dei* involves *mystery*—a mystery revealed in Jesus Christ that continues through the ministry of the Holy Spirit. The community of the faithful—church—recognizes that it understands and experiences the gospel "through a glass dimly." Its knowledge of the Truth who is God is secondhand. When our theology becomes firsthand knowledge—the thing in itself—then we have opted for our own forms of security rather than put the priorities of the triune God first.[80]

2. For our theology *missio Dei* to be a dynamic rather than a static and therefore fundamentalist process, those who hear our message must be able to respond to the gospel in a free manner, rather than coerced or manipulated. At the heart of the gospel is a message of love. Love requires freedom if it is to thrive. In a practical sense, we see this at work on the day of Pentecost. Here we have a model of freedom where everyone heard the gospel in their own tongue. Concerning our theological method, it cannot straitjacket the gospel to fit a particular or preferred theological agenda or tradition. We do not confuse our own cultural or denominational or even theological norms with the gospel's norms. Rather, theology done *missio Dei* allows the community of the have-not-yet-heard to hear and to respond in their own way.

3. This diversity of hearers means, in turn, that theology done *missio Dei* allows for pluralism (not relativism). Guder summarizes the point nicely: "Because of the mystery and freedom of God's mission, cultural pluralism means intercultural encounter, crossing boundaries, changing and being changed."[81] One of the very clear consequences of an evangelical theological method developing in terms of God's *missio Dei* will be that it will instinctually approach other religions in similar manner, *missio Dei*.[82]

4. Perhaps the most potent element in this lens is that theology done *missio Dei* will be characterized by thick hope. This notion of thick hope has several layers. Our hope is "thick" because the gospel lies embedded in its own culture and history, which have been relocated into different contexts. For our theology to speak anew the gospel hope, it has to be retranslated out of its original context, as well as its "thick" history of theological interpretation, in order to be communicated anew without it getting lost in translation. We have already noted that the church reads Scripture as the story of God's mission to the world. If I can put a twist on N. T. Wright, I would argue that the task of an evangelical theological method is to allow us "to read Scripture today to help us discern God's ongoing mission and ours within it."[83] Second, our hope is thick because in being incorporated into our theological method, it helps us refuse to reduce our theology to our own community reality. It refuses a liminal, or thin, take on what it means to be part of the communion of saints and exposes the gospel to the thickness of hope embodied and lived out in different communities, past and present. For this to be possible, we need to incorporate a high view of culture—including other cultures—into our theological method.[84] After all, every culture, whether good or ill, exists under the sovereignty of God. Third, our hope is thick—and not superficial—because it ensures that our theological method asks the right questions concerning the relevance and meaning of the gospel to those for whom it is good news. The gospel offers thick hope to those at the margins—the lame, the lonely, and the lost, those who have yet to experience being found, being free, and being fulfilled. And, last, this thick hope will be set within the context of God's reign—not ours—where true hope, in all its abundance, in all its thickness, exists and critiques all false and alternative gospels.

> The reclamation of the central New Testament theme of the "reign of God" and the thick hope of the church shaped by that reign, both present and coming, is the most powerful force to confront the many-faceted reductionism of the Christendom legacy. Nothing less sweeping than "conversion" will orient the Western church to hear and respond to the unexpected fullness of the gospel.[85]

Only as the community of faithful theologians does theology *coram Deo* will we understand the hope offered in participating in God's reign. Only as we understand this hope will we be able, in turn, to look outward and undertake our theology *missio Dei*.

> ### Pause
>
> - Where do you recognize in your own faith seeking understanding the notions of *coram Deo* and *missio Dei*?
> - What structures do you need to construct in how you go about your theology so that your theology will facilitate a theological method that lives *coram Deo* and *missio Dei*?

Concluding Remarks

In proposing a fifth dimension—community—to our evangelical theological method, I am not advocating something new. Rather, I am bringing to the surface a social construct that lies beneath just about everything else that we do as followers of Christ and as academic theologians. It is naming the theological elephant and giving due respect to what, for many, has been the Cinderella discipline within the academy. By advocating community *coram Deo* and *missio Dei*, we are seeking to address hitherto neglected or marginalized aspects of our faith seeking understanding. Let me summarize them as such:

- We are making space in our theological method for this theological binary to breathe and to have an identity of its own rather than be shunted to the margins as an add-on.
- We are allowing our contemporary understanding of community to resonate with both the old and new covenant communities. Elaine Robinson helps us identify three from the former that have parallels with the latter:
  - » It is the nature of faith communities to adapt as well as "respond to changing circumstances."
  - » We have the opportunity to see how the faith community maintained a separate existence from the "sociopolitical scheme of things" that established the status quo.
  - » Most importantly, we give priority to Scripture as a form of identity formation as well as a "source of ongoing interpretation and reinterpretation of our faithfulness to God and how that faithfulness is expressed in communal ways and through institutions."[86]
- Perhaps, in conclusion, the notion of doing our theology through the lens of community *coram Deo* and *missio Dei* is best summarized in Donald Opitz's pithy statement, "Connect Up, Connect Out."[87] We

do our theology *coram Deo* as we "connect up" with the triune God in worship, faithful obedience, loving reflection, and hopeful thinking. We do our theology *missio Dei* as we "connect out," with baptized missional imaginations, to tell others about the God of love who sends his Son into the messy business of the world with the sole aim of seeing his creation flourish.[88]

SUGGESTED READING

Ashford, Bruce Riley, and Heath A. Thomas. *The Gospel of Our King: Bible, Worldview, and the Mission of Every Christian*. Grand Rapids: Baker Academic, 2019.

Banks, Robert. *Redeeming the Routines: Bringing Theology to Life*. Grand Rapids: Baker Academic, 1993.

Bevans Stephen B. *An Introduction to Theology in Global Perspective*. Maryknoll, NY: Orbis Books, 2009.

Brueggemann, Walter. *God, Neighbor, Empire: The Excess of Divine Fidelity and the Command of Common Good*. Waco: Baylor University Press, 2016.

Comfort, Ray. *Faith Is for Weak People: Responding to the Top 20 Objections to the Gospel*. Grand Rapids: Baker Books, 2019.

Dawn Marva, J. *A Royal "Waste" of Time: The Splendor of Worshiping God and Being Church for the World*. Grand Rapids: Eerdmans, 1999.

Harshaw, Jill. *God beyond Words: Christian Theology and the Spiritual Experiences of People with Profound Intellectual Disabilities*. London: Jessica Kingsley, 2016.

Meador, Jake. *In Search of the Common Good: Christian Fidelity in a Fractured World*. Downers Grove, IL: InterVarsity, 2019.

Nehrbass, Kenneth. *God's Image and Global Cultures: Integrating Faith and Culture in the Twenty-First Century*. Eugene, OR: Cascade Books, 2016.

Opitz, Donald. *Learning for the Love of God: A Student's Guide to Academic Faithfulness*. 2nd ed. Grand Rapids: Brazos, 2014.

Provan, Iain. *Seriously Dangerous Religion: What the Old Testament Really Says and Why It Matters*. Waco: Baylor University Press, 2016.

Schirrmacher, Thomas. *Missio Dei: God's Missional Nature*. Eugene, OR: Wipf & Stock, 2018.

Sennett, Richard. *Together: The Rituals, Pleasures and Politics of Cooperation*. London: Allen Lane, 2012.

Smith, Amos. *Be Still and Listen*. Orleans, MA: Paraclete, 2019.

Smith, James K. A. *On the Road with Saint Augustine: A Real-World Spirituality for Restless Hearts*. Grand Rapids: Brazos, 2019.

Sunquist, Scott W. *Understanding Christian Mission: Participation in Suffering and Glory*. Grand Rapids: Baker Academic, 2018.

Tizon, Al. *Whole and Reconciled: Gospel, Church, and Mission in a Fractured World*. Grand Rapids: Baker Academic, 2018.

Wells, Samuel. *Incarnational Mission: Being with the World*. Grand Rapids: Eerdmans, 2018.

Wright, Christopher J. H. *The Mission of God: Unlocking the Bible's Grand Narrative*. Leicester, UK: Inter-Varsity, 2006.

Conclusion

The Quintilateral as a Dynamic Theological Method

We now approach the conclusion of our introduction to an evangelical theological method. It has been a journey from the Unknowable God who is the Revealed through our faith seeking understanding. The process has been a necessary baptism into the discipline of theology itself. In many senses the various chapters can be likened to a much more ancient discussion—by Aristotle—concerning the skills human beings need in order to live well together. Aristotle called these skills *technē*—techniques necessary to make flourishing possible. In our own day Richard Sennett develops this need when talking about the kind of rituals necessary if we are to live and work together, a particularly appropriate expectation for Christian theologians, whether ordinary or academic.[1] Like rituals, theological method makes it possible for the guild of Christian theologians, ordinary and academic, to make what Sennett describes as "expressive cooperation" work. That is, these rituals enable "expressive cooperation in religion, in the workplace, in politics, and in community."[2] More helpfully, Sennett points out that "ritual"—and for us, theological method—becomes second-nature activity. These actions—mental or physical—become so much a part of us that we are not even aware that we are doing them. As Sennett puts it, the ritual "seems to be behaviour coming from outside ourselves, which relieves us of self-consciousness; we focus on just doing the ritual right."[3]

The same can be said for theological method. It functions in a similar manner, enabling us to focus on being gospel exegetes and making the journey of faith seeking understanding less self-conscious and more gospel conscious. New Testament scholar John Barclay speaks similarly, employing an

Aristotelian term used by anthropologist Pierre Bourdieu, only this time the term is *habitus*—that is, habits of mind or action and practice that we take for granted.[4] Although it is something akin to muscle memory, the use of this term is more properly understood in terms of *technē*. The apostle Paul uses the term in relation to our bodies in each of us offering our body to God as an instrument of righteousness (Rom. 6:12–13) or bringing our minds under the influence of God's Spirit (8:6)—that is, habits of the body that not only parallel the renewed mind but also "embody and act out the new alignment of the self before God."[5]

All of this underscores the foundational and necessary function that theological method holds in our theological development, understanding, and growth. The more our theology is done in this way—as ritual and habit—the more it becomes part of not only our theological endeavors but our very selves. Admittedly, to some this will sound mechanistic and lacking in the extemporaneity and freedom that the Spirit brings. However, I would like to address this criticism and contend that without such a ritual, habit, or method, it is not possible to engage in the task of faith seeking understanding with any consistency or success. The reason for this is correct practice in theological method, like everything else, makes perfect. Let me use a tennis analogy. Why do you think Serena Williams, Roger Federer, Novak Djokovic, Rafael Nadal, Martina Navratilova, and Billie Jean King made it to the top of their sport? Sure, their personalities played a huge part in it, as well as their physical and genetic makeup. Of late, Malcolm Gladwell[6] has popularized the ten-thousand-hours theory, by which success is predicated on putting in ten thousand hours of work. Unfortunately, on its own this theory lacks credibility. Practice results in creating bad as well as good habits! Rather, the many hours of practice should be *quality* hours. Quality comes from the habit of implementing the correct techniques so that actions become second nature and work with the body, the physical and genetic constitution, and a personality that does not give up because of the mental agility to stay with each point and not let the score determine the outcome. Similarly, with theological method: the habits and techniques honed in the apprentice years go on to sustain in maturity.

So, here's a question: Do you want to be a dynamic, relevant, and potent theologian? Then put in the quality hours and develop the techniques, the habits, and the skills. Without proper theological method it is impossible to be an effective communicator of the gospel. It is possible to communicate the gospel—but not to the best of our ability. Human beings are created in such a way that very rarely does the Holy Spirit turn a person into a mature theologian overnight. We have already looked at the apostle Paul's habits, rituals, and *technē* and seen that they do not fall on us unawares. Christian history is replete with similar examples. Rather, an evangelical theological method will be successful to the degree it is consistent, and the better the method, the more effective the consistency will be.

Throughout this book I have repeated what theologians have been saying since the time of Moses: we have knowledge of God because God chooses to make that possible. It is God who reveals God. What we do is seek to understand this revelation, which is safeguarded for us in Scripture. Scripture, for this reason, always takes primacy. This is a fundamental and absolute technique—always put Scripture first. The technique, in turn, takes on a life of its own once we have made it a habit. It is an automatic response, one that offers us the flexibility to respond to any question or problem: *What does Scripture have to say on this matter?* Of course, to be able to answer with any quality, we must be, on the one hand, familiar enough with Scripture that we can speak it out and, on the other hand, so indwelled by Scripture ourselves that our ongoing responses draw us stage by stage more closely into its world and orbit.

We also familiarize ourselves with the *success* of tradition: that body of knowledge that has stood the test of time and human experience to the extent that it has become such a thing of worth that the church deems it important to pass on to each new generation. Tradition helps us avoid partisan theological positions in that it realigns our theology with the ancient tradition of the universal church, whether it be that God is Trinity or that Christ is the God-Human of the Niceno-Constantinopolitan Creed. By means of tradition, Christian theologians have successfully passed on from generation to generation teachings and practices that are silent in Scripture but whose authority safeguarded Christian faith and thought. Using the Nicene Creed as an example, Stephen Holmes offers four criteria that drive this sense of authority and that we can use to assess tradition: exegetical (it is a reading of Scripture); logical (the creed is a logical outcome of Scripture); experiential (the creed corresponds to human experience); and authoritative (it appeals to theological authority).[7] As we have seen, tradition safeguards our theology from being hijacked by "the tyranny of experience."[8] Rather, it should serve "as a resource for theology, not as a final arbiter of theological issues or concerns."[9]

This process, of course, requires the rigor of reason, which equips us to engage the knotty issues of faith that at first glance appear to defy understanding and equips us to unravel the complicated dysfunctions that human beings can cultivate. Looking through this prism, we can affirm that when evangelical theology is done properly, it will not be perceived as "the intellectual justification of the faith, apart from the practice of Christian life."[10] Rather, as we have noted earlier, faith seeking understanding is thinking faith.

Therefore, the rigor of reason will always be grounded in the practical reality of Christian faith lived out in the here and now that each of us inhabits. Christian reasoning is a form of reasoning that rests not in intellectual knowledge alone but in *shalom*—in the common grace that each of us has received from God and that enables human flourishing. It is a relational form of reason—one deeply rooted in gospel relationships and nourished by ecclesial support and fellowship. Of course faith seeking understanding involves reason, but it is a particular kind of reason—"not neutral, universal, or disinterested, but engaged, public, and (self)-critical."[11] It is a faith-seeking-understanding kind of reason. Ingolf Dalferth identifies four "rules" for how we perceive this coupling of reason and faith:

- Reason helps us distinguish between God and our own understanding of God.

- Reason enables us to know God as we keep company with God since God is not known in abstraction but in our worship of God.

- Reason makes it possible to understand our lives and the world in which we live *coram Deo*, as we live "in the light of the effective presence of God."

- With our reason we are able to move our theology from naïve to critical thinking—that is, it enables us to expose our theological perception to criticism and thus prevents us from straying off the path, as it were, in a movement away from divine to human reality.[12]

To guard our theology from abstraction, we anchor it in the testimony of experience. Experience bears witness to the veracity and truth of Scripture, to the tradition that has grown out of millennia of faithful obedience, and to the reasoning that has been undertaken in order to birth such tradition. As we have noted already, the kind of experience we are talking about here is one that is particular to the gospel—it is personal and transformational experience. On the one hand, it is inward facing: in the words of P. T. Forsyth, it is "obedient experience."[13] On the other, it has an outward-facing disposition: through our experience of God's world and human cultures, what David Ford describes as "good possibilities" open to us wherein our experience of the gospel of the living God connects us to diverse and sometimes very different disciplines, communities of faith, and cultures.[14] What we have discovered about experience as a theological tool is, in Forsyth's words, that "Christianity is nothing if it [does] not end in experience. But it is nothing if it only begins there."[15]

Finally, an evangelical theological method requires the groundedness of community where the reign of God demonstrates its own politico-economic reality in which the lame, the lost, and the lonely, those living on the edges, experience the gospel and learn to live flourishing lives. This is done by living both before the face of God—*coram Deo*—and in light of God's mission to the world and the church's participation in it—*missio Dei*. Our theological method *coram Deo* grows out of our ongoing understanding of ourselves, our lives, and our worlds as they are lived under the reign of God. Therefore, theology *coram Deo* will always "speak from the perspective of the participants,"[16] which we have already identified in terms of worship. This is neither a philosophical nor a social justice community. It is neither tribal nor partisan. It is not the community of lifestyle enclaves that hibernate from all others different from them[17] or cynical collectives whose denizens are ill disposed to cooperate.[18]

Our theological method *missio Dei* grows out of the people of God's understanding that in every action of the economy, whether creation or re-creation, the triune God is revealed to be the sending God. In speaking creation into existence, the Creator commissioned his Word and Spirit into creative action, sending them on a mission to create all things. In obedience to the loving will of the Father, the Son is sent into the same but distorted creation and empowered to be heard in his actions and words through the enabling agency of the Holy Spirit. And with the Son's ascension to his glorious enthronement with the Father on high, it is now the Spirit who animates the church in the same manner that he breathed life into the spoken words of creation and the incarnate Word of re-creation and who continues to breathe life into Scripture and the gospel it proclaims.

As the Western church moves from modernity, which resulted in theological insularism and secularism, through the relativism and pluralism of postmodernity, which tries to reduce Christian theology to just another narrative, the same church faces a new context and challenge, neither of which it has before had to face: the antagonism of post-Christendom. This crisis the Western church is undergoing is one that lies at the very center of its calling to proclaim the gospel of our Lord Jesus Christ. The challenge the Western church faces is that it has lost its center and as a result suffers from a form of theological amnesia. The result is a church that has a weak sense of identity both corporately and individually.

Consequently, the temptation arises for contemporary churches simply to chase anything that "works." This tends to take the form of seeking to redress the crisis by appealing to one "technique" after another, most of which are not premised on the gospel, saturated in Scripture, endorsed by tradition, examined by reason, let alone ratified by experience and most certainly not lived out with any organic sense of awareness of living under the presence of God or of participating in his missional love for his broken creation. In addition to this dystopic state of ecclesial affairs, Western culture suffers from a profound sense of identity crisis: Westerners have no commonly agreed-on concept of "person." Rather, our modern inheritance has left us with a profound hiatus between the individual and the collective—hence our deep tribalism. Forget "What has Jerusalem to do with Athens?" Our tribalism manifests itself profoundly in terms of "What have Republicans to do with Democrats? Conservatives with socialists?" Similarly, with modern theological counterparts: "What has Calvin to do with Wesley? Bible-believing Christians with Spirit-filled Christians?" The binaries are almost endless.

This lack of personal identity, which regresses to various forms of political, cultural, or denominational tribes, is only a symptom of a deeper malaise— namely, the collective Western ignorance concerning the true identity of God as it is revealed to us in creation, covenant, and supremely in Christ. The solution is not another guru's best-selling ten ways to have perfect teeth or twelve steps to celibacy, or . . . ! Rather, the solution is located in the gospel—the good news that if you sit on the edges of society, your family, or even yourself,[19] that there is space to flourish at the King's table, in the Lord's land, in the Father's kingdom. It is our honor and destiny as theologians, ordinary and academic, to be caught up in being partakers in the greatest cultural revolution, the reign of God—first, in and through the descendants of Abraham, and second, with those who respond to the gospel of our Lord Jesus Christ in obedient faith. It involves being caught up in what Philip Edgcumbe Hughes describes as "the creative task of theology," one that can be done only by those "who have been put in tune with the mind of Christ."[20]

It is my belief that the evangelical expression of the Western church will only ever reverse its current spiral of irrelevance, in relation to both the triune God who calls it into being and the world for which it exists, to the degree it brings its house into gospel order—that is, as it lives out its calling to be a visible demonstration of this gospel as the sociopolitical construct we call church. It is a church that

- is birthed as a result of our response to the gospel declared in Scripture;
- finds its energy and sustenance from the Holy Spirit, who is gifted to us in response to the gospel; and
- lives in faithful obedience to the triune God of the gospel.

It is equally my belief that this goal is not possible without adequate tools. It does not "just happen." I am proposing, rather, that an evangelical theological method is an essential requisite to the task of evangelical theology. My hope is that in rediscovering the primacy of Scripture, the success of tradition, the rigor of reason, the testimony of experience, and the groundedness of community as both *coram Deo* and *missio Dei*, you will be given the skills that will enable you to take your place in the grand company of believers in Christ whose faith, like yours and mine, is a faith that is seeking understanding and that lives in hopeful and joyful anticipation of no longer needing to live by faith because we shall see as we are seen, know as we are known, and flourish as only the triune God, Father, Son, and Holy Spirit, flourishes. To God be the glory!

Notes

Preface

1. Hans Urs von Balthasar, *Love Alone Is Credible*, trans. D. C. Schindler (San Francisco: Ignatius, 2004), 12.

Chapter 1: Framing the Skill of Being a Theologian

1. The answer is 90.

2. Daniel L. Migliore, *Faith Seeking Understanding: An Introduction to Christian Theology*, 3rd ed. (Grand Rapids: Eerdmans, 2014), 6.

3. John Webster, *Holy Scripture: A Dogmatic Sketch* (Cambridge: Cambridge University Press, 2003), 43.

4. See Kevin J. Vanhoozer and Daniel J. Treier, *Theology and the Mirror of Scripture: A Mere Evangelical Account* (Downers Grove, IL: IVP Academic, 2015), 87–95, for a useful extended summary of what "gospel" includes.

5. For the distinction between good and bad "fundamentals," see Graham McFarlane, "Fundamentalism and Fundamentals," *Franciscan* 15, no. 3 (September 2003): 1–2.

6. Stephen W. Sykes, "Theological Study: The Nineteenth Century and After," in *The Philosophical Frontiers of Christian Theology: Essays Presented to D. M. MacKinnon*, ed. Brian Hebblethwaite and Stewart R. Sutherland (Cambridge: Cambridge University Press, 1982), 97.

7. Gareth Jones, *Christian Theology* (Oxford: Polity, 1999), 23.

8. Jones, *Christian Theology*, 23. Jones insightfully reminds us that "messy" is "something good, because it is something natural."

9. Colin E. Gunton, "Creation and Mediation in the Theology of Robert W. Jenson: An Encounter and a Convergence," in *Trinity, Time, and Church: A Response to the Theology of Robert W. Jenson*, ed. Colin E. Gunton (Grand Rapids: Eerdmans, 2000), 81.

10. Robert W. Jenson, *A Theology in Outline: Can These Bones Live?*, ed. Adam Eitel (Oxford: Oxford University Press, 2016), 6.

11. Umberto Eco, *The Name of the Rose* (London: Picador, Pan Books, 1984), 399.

12. Peter L. Berger, *A Far Glory: The Quest for Faith in an Age of Credulity* (New York: Free Press, 1992), 9.

13. James W. Sire, *Naming the Elephant: Worldview as a Concept* (Nottingham, UK: InterVarsity, 2004), 122.

14. Sire, *Naming the Elephant*, 20.

15. David Burnett, *Clash of Worlds* (London: Monarch Books, 2002), 13.

16. Nancy R. Pearcey, *Total Truth: Liberating Christianity from Its Cultural Captivity* (Wheaton: Crossway, 2004), 23.

17. N. T. Wright, *The New Testament and the People of God* (London: SPCK, 1993), 123–24. Tawa J. Anderson, W. Michael Clark, and David K. Naugle identify the following as their own core worldview questions: "What is our nature? What is our world? What is our problem? What is our end?" See Anderson, Clark, and Naugle, *An Introduction to Christian Worldview: Pursuing God's Perspective in a Pluralistic World* (London: Apollos, 2017), 97–179.

18. For a contemporary critique of modern technology and its place in our worldview, see Craig M. Gay, "The Technological Worldview," chap. 3 in *Modern Technology and the Human Future: A Christian Appraisal* (Downers Grove, IL: IVP Academic, 2018).

19. Anderson, Clark, and Naugle, *Introduction to Christian Worldview*, 143.

20. Vanhoozer and Treier, *Theology and the Mirror of Scripture*, 57.

21. For instance, the Spanish language is wonderfully straightforward to learn, as its grammar is almost entirely "regular" and thus has a consistency that makes learning easier. In contrast, Polish and Russian are languages with highly complex grammatical rules.

22. Jenson, *Theology in Outline*, 6.

23. Craig S. Keener, *Spirit Hermeneutics: Reading Scripture in Light of Pentecost* (Grand Rapids: Eerdmans, 2016), 201.

24. Marva J. Dawn, *A Royal "Waste" of Time: The Splendor of Worshiping God and Being Church for the World* (Grand Rapids: Eerdmans, 1999), esp. 21–57, quoted in Carol M. Bechtel, "Teaching the 'Strange New World' of the Bible," *Interpretation* 56, no. 4 (October 2002): 369.

25. This point, perhaps, serves as a critique to faddism in the contemporary church. The commercialization of worship and the resultant focus on "the new" in order to keep royalties buoyant deconstructs this basic building block of theological education, where the language of the church, its theology, was mastered through creed and liturgy as well as psalm and hymn over the church year.

26. Karl Barth, *The Word of God and the Word of Man* (London: Hodder & Stoughton, 1935), 28–50.

27. Throughout, "spiritual" is understood to incorporate "relational"—that is, to be spiritual is to have the capacity to relate beyond one's own physical existence and relate to others.

28. This can also be translated "for as he thinks within himself, so he is."

29. See Matthew Lee Anderson, *Earthen Vessels: Why Our Bodies Matter to Our Faith* (Bloomington, MN: Bethany House, 2011) for a fuller commentary on the important part our bodies play in Christian faith.

30. Lance J. Peeler, "Thinking Bodily," in *Thinking Theologically*, ed. Eric D. Barreto (Minneapolis: Fortress, 2015), 23.

31. The opening verses of the Hebrew Bible declare that the genesis of everything that exists came about linguistically and imperatively—that is, the Lord God spoke a command, "Light be," and light became! John the Apostle grasps the soteriological parallel to the creational in Genesis when he writes about the Word becoming human—not by command but by personal volition—in order to bring about a new creation. See Jonathan Sacks, *Covenant and Conversation: A Weekly Reading of the Jewish Bible*, vol. 3, *Leviticus: The Book of Holiness* (Jerusalem: Maggid Books, 2015), 202–5.

32. Trevor Hart, *Regarding Karl Barth: Toward a Reading of His Theology* (Carlisle, UK: Paternoster, 1999), 174–75.

33. See Colin E. Gunton, *Enlightenment and Alienation: An Essay towards a Trinitarian Theology* (Basingstoke, UK: Marshall Morgan & Scott, 1985), 137.

34. Emil Brunner, *The Divine-Human Encounter*, trans. Amandus W. Loos (London: SCM, 1944), 31.

35. Webster, *Holy Scripture*, 6.

36. Colin E. Gunton, "Using and Being Used: Scripture and Systematic Theology," *Theology Today* 47, no. 3 (October 1990): 253.

37. See Brendan Sweetman, "The Failure of Modernism," in *The Failure of Modernism: The Cartesian Legacy and Contemporary Pluralism*, ed. Brendan Sweetman (Washington, DC: Catholic University of America Press, 1999), 1–9.

38. For a fuller explanation, see Graham McFarlane, *Why Do You Believe What You Believe about Jesus?* (Eugene, OR: Wipf & Stock, 2009).

39. Philip Schaff, ed., *Creeds of Christendom, with a History and Critical Notes*, vol. 1, *The History of Creeds*, rev. David S. Schaff (Grand Rapids: Baker, 1983), 27–28.

40. Migliore, *Faith Seeking Understanding*, 2.

41. Mark A. McIntosh, *Divine Teaching: An Introduction to Christian Theology* (Oxford: Blackwell, 2008), 12.

42. McIntosh, *Divine Teaching*, 12.

43. Ingolf U. Dalferth, *Theology and Philosophy* (Oxford: Basil Blackwell, 1988), 8.

44. Migliore goes so far as to argue that historical consideration should be a criterion for "faith seeking understanding" since theology does not occur in a vacuum but, rather, is the product of people who "live in their particular historical contexts that have their own distinctive problems and possibilities." *Faith Seeking Understanding*, 4.

45. John 3:16 in Inuit, available at GospelGo, http://gospelgo.com/e/john316.htm.

46. Galatians 3:13–14 in Spanish, available at BibleGateway, https://www.biblegateway.com/passage/?search=G%C3%A1latas+3%3A13-14&version=NVI.

47. Psalm 23:1–4 in Dutch, available at BibleGateway, https://www.biblegateway.com/passage/?search=Psalm+23%3A+1-4&version=HTB.

48. Romans 1:16–17 in Romanian, available at BibleGateway, https://www.biblegateway.com/passage/?search=romans+1%3A+16-17&version=RMNN.

49. Veli-Matti Kärkkäinen, *Christology: A Global Introduction; An Ecumenical, International, and Contextual Perspective* (Grand Rapids: Baker Academic, 2005), 6.

50. "You cannot love God and hate human beings. You cannot bring sacrifices at the Temple and then oppress your fellow. God will not hear your prayers if you fail to hear the cries of those around you." Sacks, *Leviticus*, 38.

51. McIntosh puts it nicely: "If you thought that the doctrines of Christian theology were in fact communal expressions of the divine teaching, you might pause . . . to reflect that you were not simply having a few interesting ideas but rather that the ideas might be having you!" McIntosh, *Divine Teaching*, 36.

52. Schubert M. Ogden, *The Point of Christology* (London: SCM, 1982), 4.

53. Craig S. Keener, *The Mind of the Spirit: Paul's Approach to Transformed Thinking* (Grand Rapids: Baker Academic, 2016), 29.

54. Ellen T. Charry, *By the Renewing of Your Minds: The Pastoral Function of Christian Doctrine* (Oxford: Oxford University Press, 1997), 19. Charry particularly emphasizes "the virtue-shaping function of the divine pedagogy of theological treatises"—that is, it is God who forms our character, and "theological treatises" draw us into God's life (19).

55. Charry, *By the Renewing of Your Minds*, vii.

56. John H. Newman, "Faith leads the mind to communion with the universal God." See Newman, "Sermon 12," sec. 29, in *Fifteen Sermons Preached before the University of Oxford*, 3rd ed. (Notre Dame, IN: University of Notre Dame Press, 1997), 242, cited in McIntosh, *Divine Teaching*, 52.

57. Gunton gives an example of the dynamic nature of metaphor and an insight into how language works. "The word 'muscle' is, technically, a dead metaphor. Originally, the word in Latin meant 'mouse'—*musculus*. How did it change to mean muscle? To answer, imagine yourself belonging to a tribe of very skinny, thin-armed people. You meet a soldier from another tribe with huge, bulging arms and need to describe what he looks like. You raise your skinny arm, flex it pathetically and say that he has a huge *musculus* on his arm: the shape of a mouse translates over to the shape of a well-built arm!" Colin E. Gunton, *The Actuality of Atonement: A Study of Metaphor, Rationality and the Christian Tradition* (Edinburgh: T&T Clark, 1988), 34.

58. Webster, *Holy Scripture*, 123.

59. See Anselm, *Cur Deus Homo?*, in *Works of St. Anselm*, trans. Sidney Norton Deane (Chicago, 1903), Internet Sacred Text Archive, accessed March 1, 2020, https://www.sacred-texts.com/chr/ans/ans117.htm, and in our own day, Migliore, *Faith Seeking Understanding*.

60. Faith is "confidence in what we hope for and assurance about what we do not see" (Heb. 11:1). It is an action of the human spirit in that it is a relational (distinct from physical or mental) action on our part in response to God's promise and word to us.

61. I use the word "obedience" and its cognates throughout the book as a positive reference to the deepest and most personal response one person can make to another—namely, love. As such, the act of obedience is not to be located in the impersonal realm of an employee who is employed to do a job, or a dog that is trained to obey, but rather it is to be understood within the deepest bonds of human relations and camaraderie, where it signifies the richness of personal relations of a marriage or family in which trust, respect, and mutual giving operate, or when soldiers demonstrate the deep bonds of camaraderie when they obey their leader for love of country. Obedience, therefore, is an act of will, driven by the desire for the other's well-being.

62. Jeff Astley, *Studying God: Doing Theology* (London: SCM, 2014), 23.

63. McIntosh summarizes well: "Christians believe that because God is the Creator God of everything that exists, God cannot be *one of* those things: God is, rather, the reason why there is anything at all rather than simply nothing." McIntosh, *Divine Teaching*, 32. Gunton's *The Triune Creator* can be understood as a systematic and theological answer to the question he asks in the opening sentence of the book, illustrating his depth of knowledge of both theological and philosophical inquiry: "Why is there something rather than nothing?" Colin E. Gunton, *The Triune Creator: A Historical and Systematic Study* (Edinburgh: Edinburgh University Press, 1998), 1. Martin Heidegger rather beautifully argues that this is *the* metaphysical question; see *Introduction to Metaphysics* (New Haven: Yale University Press, 1959), 7–8.

64. Ingolf Dalferth, *Crucified and Resurrected: Restructuring the Grammar of Christology* (Grand Rapids: Baker Academic, 2015), xi–xiii.

65. Dalferth, *Crucified and Resurrected*, xiii.

66. Augustine, "Sermon 52," sec. 16, in *Sermons 51–94*, trans. Edmund Hill, The Works of Saint Augustine III/3 (New York: New City Press, 1991), 57: "For if thou hast been able to comprehend what thou wouldest say, it is not God; if in original thou hast been able to comprehend it, thou hast comprehended something else instead of God. If thou hast been able to comprehend Him as thou thinkest, by so thinking thou hast deceived thyself. This then is not God, if thou hast comprehended it; but if it be God, thou hast not comprehended it. How therefore wouldest thou speak of that which thou canst not comprehend?"

67. Gabriel Marcel, *The Mystery of Being* (Chicago: Henry Regnery, 1969), 1:260–61.

68. Migliore makes this important distinction in *Faith Seeking Understanding*, 3n6.

69. Exodus 3:6, to which Jesus refers in Matt. 22:32, where he affirms that God is the God of the living, not of the dead.

70. Since the second or third century BC, observant Jews have not spoken the divine name—YHWH in Hebrew or JHVH (Jehovah) in Greek—since they understand God to be so "other" and holy that even the divine name cannot be uttered on human lips. Whenever they refer to God, they use what is called the Tetragrammaton (meaning "the four letters" that make up the divine name, YHWH or JHVH) or use the term *Adonai*, Hebrew for "Lord." In many English translations, whenever the divine name occurs, small capitals are used—Lord—in order to distinguish a use of YHWH, the covenant name of God, from the Hebrew (*Adonai*) and Greek (*Kyrios*) words for "Lord," as in "Lord Jesus." Pious orthodox Jews today use the term *Hashem* (The Name) when referring to YHWH in conversation. The significant point here is that these various terms signify linguistically that the subject matter of theology is not to be treated as though it is like any other topic. Of course, this raises a further question for you to consider: Where in *your* theology do you signify the same kind of distinction—or does the incarnation and the gospel mean that this is now no longer necessary?

71. Genesis 1:1–25, obviously, but throughout Scripture too: Neh. 9:6; Isa. 45:18; Rev. 4:11.

72. Isaiah 40:25. *Hakkadosh* in Hebrew—"The Holy One, blessed is He"—is a commonly used term today for God among orthodox Jews.

73. Jesus's name for God: Abba, "Father" (Matt. 6:9; Mark 14:36; Luke 11:2). See also, for Paul, Rom. 8:15; Gal. 4:6.

74. Galatians 3:13–14. See Deut. 21:23 for the Old Testament source for Paul's theological statement to the churches in Galatia (modern-day central Turkey, the highlands of central Anatolia, to be precise).

75. Robert K. Johnston, *God's Wider Presence: Reconsidering General Revelation* (Grand Rapids: Baker Academic, 2014), 39. See also Robin Lovin, Peter Danchin, Agustín Fuentes, Friederike Nüssel, and Stephen Pope, "Introduction: Theology as Interdisciplinary Inquiry," in *Theology as Interdisciplinary Inquiry: Learning with and from the Natural and Human Sciences*, ed. Robin W. Lovin and Joshua Mauldin (Grand Rapids: Eerdmans, 2017), xxix.

76. Donald G. Bloesch, *A Theology of Word and Spirit: Authority and Method in Theology* (Downers Grove, IL: InterVarsity, 1992), 22.

Chapter 2: Working Definition

1. Mark A. McIntosh, *Divine Teaching: An Introduction to Christian Theology* (Oxford: Blackwell, 2008), 16–17.

2. Emil Brunner, *Dogmatics*, vol. 1, *The Christian Doctrine of God* (Cambridge: J. Clark, 2002), 3, cited in Cynthia Bennett Brown, *Believing Thinking, Bounded Theology: The Theological Methodology of Emil Brunner* (Eugene, OR: Pickwick, 2015), 16.

3. Thanks to Julie Canlis, *A Theology of the Ordinary* (Wenatchee, WA: Godspeed, 2017), 2–3, for making the connection with Peterson. See also Helmut Thielicke, *A Little Exercise for Young Theologians* (Grand Rapids: Eerdmans, 2016), for an accessible read on the challenge of theology for the ordinary believer. See also Charles Octavius Boothe, *Plain Theology for Plain People* (Bellingham, WA: Lexham, 2017), for a classic but accessible theology for "ordinary" people. See also Amy Plantinga Pauw, *Church in Ordinary Time: A Wisdom Ecclesiology* (Grand Rapids: Eerdmans, 2017).

4. Canlis, *Theology of the Ordinary*, 2–3. See also Tish Harrison Warren, *Liturgy of the Ordinary: Sacred Practices in Everyday Life* (Downers Grove, IL: InterVarsity, 2016). A similar sentiment is expressed by the Polish poet Czeslaw Milosz in "By the Peonies" when he concludes, "The charms of the ordinariness soothe the threat of anxiety." Available at PoemHunter.com, https://www.poemhunter.com/poem/by-the-peonies.

5. Alicia Britt Chole, *The Sacred Slow: A Holy Departure from Fast Faith* (Nashville: W Publishing, 2017).

6. Chole, *Sacred Slow*, 9.

7. You might also be interested in Stephen Cherry, *God-Curious: Exploring Eternal Questions* (London: Jessica Kingsley, 2017), 77–98, where Cherry offers an additional perspective on how we can express our *ordinary* theology in the form of fifteen tweet-length quotes that summarize his own theological Western Christian tradition. He helpfully provides a short commentary for each.

8. C. S. Lewis describes himself as a "very ordinary layman." Lewis, *Mere Christianity* (Glasgow, UK: Fontana, 1978), 6. And he says, "I write as one amateur to another." Lewis, *Reflections on the Psalms* (New York: Harcourt Brace Jovanovich, 1958), 9. Cited by Andrew G. Walker, *Notes from a Wayward Son: A Miscellany*, ed. Andrew D. Kinsey (Eugene, OR: Cascade Books, 2015), 125.

9. See Jeff Astley, *Ordinary Theology: Looking, Listening and Learning in Theology* (London: Routledge, 2002), chaps. 3–5. Astley explores the distinction between the two forms of theology in Jeff Astley, *Studying God: Doing Theology* (London: SCM, 2014), chaps. 3–4. Helen Cameron offers an alternate but equally helpful fourfold perspective: *normative* theology—which includes Scripture, creeds, and official church teaching and its liturgies; *formal* theology—the academic theology of theologians and the academy along with its dialogue with other

disciplines; *espoused* theology—the theology we find in particular denominational settings; and *operant* theology—theology as it is practiced by a group of Christians. See Helen Cameron, Deborah Bhatti, Catherine Duce, James Sweeney, and Clare Watkins, *Talking about God in Practice: Theological Action Research and Practical Theology* (London: SCM, 2010), 54, esp. fig. 4.2. See also Howard W. Stone and James O. Duke, *How to Think Theologically*, 3rd ed. (Minneapolis: Fortress, 2013), who make a similar distinction, only they use the terms "embedded" and "deliberative," the former being unprocessed and uncritical belief about God, and the latter signifying more critical and structured belief about God:

> Embedded theology is often known as *first-order theology* or *the language of witness*, being made up of the most immediate and direct testimonies to the meaning of faith. It is rooted (embedded) in the preaching and practices of the church and its members. It is the implicit theology that Christians live out in their daily lives. . . . Embedded theology is what devoted Christians have in mind when they say things like, "My faith and my church mean a lot to me." . . . *Deliberative theology* is the understanding of faith that emerges from the process of carefully reflecting upon embedded theological convictions. This sort of reflection is sometimes called *second-order theology*, in that it follows upon and looks back over the implicit understandings embedded in the life of faith. (15)

10. Peter J. Leithart, *Against Christianity* (Moscow, ID: Canon Press, 2003), 91.

11. Astley, *Studying God*, chap. 3.

12. Hans Urs von Balthasar, "Theology and Sanctity," in *Word and Redemption: Essays in Theology 2* (New York: Herder and Herder, 1965), 49–86. See also Astley, *Ordinary Theology*, 74–76; Astley, *Studying God*, 3–4.

13. Astley, *Studying God*, 3.

14. Edward Schillebeeckx, preface to *Interim Report on the Books Jesus and Christ* (New York: Crossroad, 1981), cited in Daniel L. Migliore, *Faith Seeking Understanding: An Introduction to Christian Theology*, 3rd ed. (Grand Rapids: Eerdmans, 2014), 4.

15. Astley, *Studying God*, 28.

16. Craig Ott, "Maps, Improvisation, and Games: Retaining Biblical Authority in Local Theology," *Evangelical Quarterly* 89, no. 3 (July 2018): 200.

17. Ott, "Maps, Improvisation, and Games," 202.

18. Maurice Merleau-Ponty, *Signs*, trans. Richard C. McCleary (Evanston, IL: Northwestern University Press, 1964), 12.

19. Ott, "Maps, Improvisation, and Games," 206–7.

20. Elaine A. Robinson, *Exploring Theology* (Minneapolis: Fortress, 2014), 9, 28–31.

21. Robinson, *Exploring Theology*, 28–31. Alister E. McGrath talks of "theory" in such a way that it parallels the task of doctrine. Theories are "not free creations of the human mind but are rather constructed in response to an encounter with an existing reality." As such, theory is both "a considered *response* to reality, and . . . it is *accountable* to the community of faith for the manner in which its corporate vision of reality is depicted." Alister E. McGrath, *The Science of God: An Introduction to Scientific Theology* (Grand Rapids: Eerdmans, 2004), 171.

22. Colin E. Gunton, "Dogma, the Church and the Task of Theology," in *The Task of Theology Today*, ed. Victor Pfitzner and Hilary Regan (Edinburgh: T&T Clark, 1998), 2.

23. David K. Clark, *To Know and Love God: Method of Theology* (Wheaton: Crossway, 2003), 196–200, summarizes specific challenges to evangelical theologians in the university. Increasingly, the conflict between the academy's emphasis on critical thinking, on the one hand, and upholding the church's posture regarding the authority of the Bible, on the other, is weakening with the rise of the Majority World church (the growing number of churches of the Southern Hemisphere) as well as of evangelical theologians within the academy. Majority World church is best here.

24. Colin E. Gunton, "General Introduction," in *The Practice of Theology: A Reader*, ed. Colin Gunton, Stephen R. Holmes, and Murray A. Rae (London: SCM, 2001), 1.

25. Tradition has it that Karl Barth said this in Chicago. However, Fred Sanders, having listened to all the recordings of the Q&A sessions, could not find it. In addition, Stanley Hauerwas

claims it was said at Union Theological Seminary, Richmond (now named Union Presbyterian Seminary). See Fred Sanders, "Jesus Loves Karl Barth," *The Scriptorium Daily*, August 3, 2012, http://scriptoriumdaily.com/jesus-loves-karl-barth-2/.

26. John R. Franke, *The Character of Theology: An Introduction to Its Nature, Task, and Purpose* (Grand Rapids: Baker Academic, 2005), 84, 104–5.

27. Franke, *Character of Theology*, 44.

28. Franke, *Character of Theology*, 44. The three components are expanded in chaps. 3–5.

29. Genesis 3:9; 32:28; Pss. 137:1, 4; 103:1; Isa. 40:3; John 1:1; Matt. 6:9.

30. Migliore, *Faith Seeking Understanding*, 36–39.

31. Karl Barth, *Church Dogmatics* I/1, ed. and trans. G. W. Bromiley and T. F. Torrance (Edinburgh: T&T Clark, 1957–75), 11, cited in Colin Gunton, "The Truth . . . and the Spirit of Truth: The Trinitarian Shape of Christian Theology," in *Loving God with Our Minds: The Pastor as Theologian; Essays in Honor of Wallace M. Alston*, ed. Michael Welker and Cynthia A. Jarvis (Grand Rapids: Eerdmans, 2004), 341n1. Gunton paraphrases Barth describing theology "as the church's self-examination as to the truth of her message" (341).

32. See Clark, *To Know and Love God*, 424. See Kelly M. Kapic, *A Little Book for New Theologians: Why and How to Study Theology* (Downers Grove, IL: InterVarsity, 2012), esp. chap. 2, for an accessible introduction to similar sentiments.

Chapter 3: The Relational and the Revelational

1. I am grateful to a former research student, Daniel Cooling, for pointing out what he identifies as some basic coordinates for a theology of language to emerge: (1) it must be part of creation; (2) it finds its basis in the doctrine of the *imago Dei*, of humans made in the image of the God who speaks; (3) it takes into account the fall, incarnation, Pentecost, and the new creation; (4) it understands that the doctrine of the Trinity accounts for the complex nature of language as a social construct; (5) it has an expressive dimension; (6) it addresses the problem of presence and therefore employs the concepts of mediation and absence.

2. Daniel L. Migliore, *Faith Seeking Understanding: An Introduction to Christian Theology*, 3rd ed. (Grand Rapids: Eerdmans, 2014), 5.

3. For fuller details in relation to Emil Brunner's theology, see Cynthia Bennett Brown, *Believing Thinking, Bounded Theology: The Theological Methodology of Emil Brunner* (Eugene, OR: Pickwick, 2015).

4. David Reichenbach, "Divine Revelation: Discernment and Interpretation," in *For Faith and Clarity: Philosophical Contributions to Christian Theology*, ed. James K. Beilby (Grand Rapids: Baker Academic, 2006), 85–86.

5. Jonathan Sacks, *Covenant and Conversation: A Weekly Reading of the Jewish Bible*, vol. 3, *Leviticus: The Book of Holiness* (Jerusalem: Maggid Books, 2015), 34.

6. Avery Dulles, *Models of Revelation* (New York: Orbis Books, 1992). René Latourelle offers ten forms of revelation: word, testimony, encounter, creation, history, incarnation, light of faith, miracle, church, vision. See Latourelle, *Theology of Revelation* (New York: Alba House, 1967), cited in Balázs M. Mezei, *Radical Revelation* (London: Bloomsbury, 2017), 79.

7. Robert K. Johnston, *God's Wider Presence: Reconsidering General Revelation* (Grand Rapids: Baker Academic, 2014), 6.

8. Mezei, *Radical Revelation*, 88–97.

9. William J. Abraham, "The Offense of Divine Revelation," *Harvard Theological Review* 95, no. 3 (July 2002): 258, 259. See also William J. Abraham, *Crossing the Threshold of Divine Revelation* (Grand Rapids: Eerdmans, 2007).

10. Jan Meyer and Ray Land, *Threshold Concepts and Troublesome Knowledge: Linkages to Ways of Thinking and Practising within the Disciplines*, ETL Project Occasional Report 4 (Edinburgh: ETL Project, University of Edinburgh, 2003), 1, http://www.etl.tla.ed.ac.uk/docs /ETLreport4.pdf. See also Jan H. F. Meyer, Ray Land, and Caroline Baillie, eds., *Threshold Concepts and Transformational Learning* (Rotterdam: Sense, 2010).

11. See "Threshold Concepts: Undergraduate Teaching, Postgraduate Training, Professional Development and School Education; A Short Introduction and a Bibliography from 2003 to 2018," Department of Electronic and Electrical Engineering of University College London, last updated September 27, 2019, https://www.ee.ucl.ac.uk/~mflanaga/thresholds.html#ML2003.

12. Migliore identifies six aspects of revelation as the term is used in Christian theology: (1) it refers to God's own self-disclosure; (2) it points to particular events and people through whom God communicates; (3) it is paradoxically also the veiling of God; (4) it elicits personal response; (5) it is always a disturbing, and sometimes a shocking, event; (6) it becomes the new interpretive focus for how we understand God, ourselves, and the world. See Migliore, *Faith Seeking Understanding*, 29–30.

13. Colin E. Gunton, *Enlightenment and Alienation: An Essay toward a Trinitarian Theology* (Basingstoke, UK: Marshall Morgan & Scott, 1985), 141.

14. Bennett Brown puts it beautifully: "The something we come to know about in divine revelation directly corresponds to the person of God that we know through faith-obedience." *Believing Thinking*, 22.

15. John Webster, *Holy Scripture: A Dogmatic Sketch* (Cambridge: Cambridge University Press, 2003), 17.

16. Jeff Astley, *Studying God: Doing Theology* (London: SCM, 2014), 15. See John M. G. Barclay, *Paul and the Gift* (Grand Rapids: Eerdmans, 2015), for a magisterial presentation of the notion of gift. The implications for arguing that revelation is gift are significant in that the gift of revelation is not given freely but comes with conditions—namely, transformational response.

17. Colin E. Gunton, *A Brief Theology of Revelation* (Edinburgh: T&T Clark, 1995), 24.

18. P. T. Forsyth, *The Principle of Authority*, 2nd ed. (1913; repr., London: Independent Press, 1952), cited in Gunton, *Brief Theology of Revelation*, 24.

19. Gunton, *Brief Theology of Revelation*, 24.

20. See Mezei, *Radical Revelation*, chap. 3, for a fuller presentation of self-revelation.

21. Esther Lightcap Meek, *Loving to Know: Introducing Covenant Epistemology* (Eugene, OR: Cascade Books, 2011), 200.

22. F. D. E. Schleiermacher, *The Christian Faith*, trans. and ed. H. R. Mackintosh and J. S. Stewart (Edinburgh: T&T Clark, 1986).

23. Colin E. Gunton, *The Christian Faith: An Introduction to Christian Doctrine* (Oxford: Blackwell, 2002), 176.

24. Isaac Massey Haldeman, *The Signs of the Times*, 5th ed. (New York: Charles C. Cook, 1914), 69, 72.

25. Gunton points out that we need to rediscover "the mediatedness of revelation" since the revelation only comes to us through creation. Gunton, *Brief Theology of Revelation*, 5, cited in Matthew Levering, *Engaging the Doctrine of Revelation: The Mediation of the Gospel through Church and Scripture* (Grand Rapids: Baker Academic, 2014), 32.

26. Gerard Manley Hopkins, "God's Grandeur," in *The Poems of Gerard Manley Hopkins*, ed. W. H. Gardner and N. H. MacKenzie (Oxford: Oxford University Press, 1970), 66. Reproduced with permission of Oxford Publishing Ltd. through PLSclear.

27. Astley, *Studying God*, 15.

28. I am grateful to my research student Youngsung Han for alerting me to this warning. See Colin E. Gunton, *The Promise of Trinitarian Theology*, 2nd ed. (Edinburgh: T&T Clark, 1997), 193. See also Bruce Ellis Benson, *Graven Ideologies: Nietzsche, Derrida, and Marion on Modern Idolatry* (Downers Grove, IL: IVP Academic, 2002), for the way in which our thinking can become conceptual idolatry and for a biblical response to this problem. Knowledge of God is indeed possible; the question is how it comes about (21–24).

29. Bennett Brown, *Believing Thinking*, 14.

30. As Mark A. McIntosh puts it, "Following Jesus, as opposed to following someone else, gives a very definite form to life and thought." McIntosh, *Divine Teaching: An Introduction to Christian Theology* (Oxford: Blackwell, 2008), 12.

31. Donald G. Bloesch, *A Theology of Word and Spirit: Authority and Method in Theology* (Downers Grove, IL: InterVarsity, 1992), 22.

Chapter 4: Theological Method

1. David F. Ford, *Theology: A Very Short Introduction* (Oxford: Oxford University Press, 1999), 152.

2. J. L. Segundo, *Liberation of Theology* (Maryknoll, NY: Orbis Books, 1975), 39, cited in Stephen B. Bevans, *Models of Contextual Theology* (Maryknoll, NY: Orbis Books, 1992), 129n10.

3. There are evangelical Methodists, Anglicans, Presbyterians, charismatics, Baptists—among others—who are united not necessarily by dogma or doctrine but by a common allegiance to these four norms: Protestant, conversionist, high regard for Scripture, centered on the gospel.

4. Martin E. Marty, *The Public Church: Mainline, Evangelical, Catholic* (New York: Cross-road, 1981), 13.

5. Kevin J. Vanhoozer and Daniel J. Treier, *Theology and the Mirror of Scripture* (Downers Grove, IL: IVP Academic, 2015), 11–12.

6. "Scripture alone," "grace alone," "faith alone," "Christ alone," and "to God alone be glory."

7. Vanhoozer and Treier, *Theology and the Mirror of Scripture*, 52.

8. Roger E. Olson, "The Future of Evangelical Theology," *Christianity Today*, February 9, 1998, 40–50, cited in David K. Clark, *To Know and Love God: Method of Theology* (Wheaton: Crossway, 2003), xxvii.

9. See Jeff Astley, *Ordinary Theology: Looking, Listening and Learning in Theology* (London: Routledge, 2002), chap. 4, where his focus on practical theology could be describing a specifically evangelical theology.

10. David W. Bebbington, *Evangelicalism in Modern Britain: A History from the 1730s to the 1980s* (London: Unwin Hyman, 1989), 1–17. See also Derek J. Tidball, *Who Are the Evangelicals?* (London: Marshall Pickering, 1994). Tidball confirms that Bebbington's fourfold definition "has quickly established itself as near to a consensus as we might ever expect to reach" (14). John G. Stackhouse adds a fifth criterion to Bebbington's four—namely, transdenominationalism. Stackhouse, "Evangelical Theology Should Be Evangelical," in *Evangelical Futures: A Conversation on Theological Method*, ed. John G. Stackhouse Jr. (Grand Rapids: Baker Books, 2000), 42. For a more historical contemporary analysis, see Thomas S. Kidd, *Who Is an Evangelical? The History of a Movement in Crisis* (New Haven: Yale University Press, 2019).

11. Douglas J. Ottati, "Conclusion: A Collaborative Manner of Theological Reflection," in *Theology as Interdisciplinary Inquiry*, ed. Robin W. Lovin and Joshua Mauldin (Grand Rapids: Eerdmans, 2017), 144.

12. Mary M. Veeneman, *Introducing Theological Method: A Survey of Contemporary Theologians and Approaches* (Grand Rapids: Baker Academic, 2017), 4.

13. Simon Oliver, "Introducing Radical Orthodoxy," in *The Radical Orthodoxy Reader*, ed. John Milbank and Simon Oliver (London: Routledge, 2009), 20–21.

14. Gordon R. Lewis and Bruce A. Demarest, *Integrative Theology*, 3 vols. (Grand Rapids: Academie, 1987).

15. Gordon R. Lewis and Bruce A. Demarest, *Integrative Theology*, vol. 1, *Knowing Ultimate Reality: The Living God* (Grand Rapids: Academie, 1987), 37–40.

16. Richard Hooker, *The Laws of Ecclesiastical Polity*, vol. 1 of *The Works of That Learned and Judicious Divine Mr. Richard Hooker with an Account of His Life and Death by Isaac Walton*, arranged by John Keble, 7th ed. revised by R. W. Church and F. Paget (Oxford, 1888), available at http://oll.libertyfund.org/titles/hooker-the-works-of-richard-hooker-vol-1.

17. See *The Theologian*, http://www.theologian.org.uk/about.html.

18. "H. Jurgens Hendriks," Africa Leadership Study, accessed March 1, 2020, https://africa leadershipstudy.org/team/jurgens-hendriks.

19. F. LeRon Shults and Steven J. Sandage, *Transforming Spirituality: Integrating Theology and Psychology* (Grand Rapids: Baker Academic, 2006).

20. This approach to theological method is to be distinguished from one that is "interdisciplinary." For this, see Robin W. Lovin and Joshua Mauldin, eds., *Theology as Interdisciplinary Inquiry* (Grand Rapids: Eerdmans, 2017).

21. James I. Packer, "Maintaining Evangelical Theology," in Stackhouse, *Evangelical Futures*, 186–89.

22. Stanley J. Grenz and Roger E. Olson, *Who Needs Theology? An Invitation to the Study of God* (Leicester, UK: Inter-Varsity, 1996), 91–102.

23. Alister E. McGrath, *Christian Theology: An Introduction*, 6th ed. (Oxford: Wiley & Sons, 2017), 104. Interestingly, earlier in the same book McGrath states, "Throughout its long history, Christian theology has made an appeal to three fundamental resources: the Bible, tradition, and reason" (xv).

24. Albert C. Outler, ed., *John Wesley* (Oxford: Oxford University Press, 1964).

25. Don Thorsen, *The Wesleyan Quadrilateral: Scripture, Tradition, Reason, and Experience as a Model of Evangelical Theology* (1990; repr., Lexington: Emeth, 2005).

26. Veeneman, *Introducing Theological Method*, 13.

Chapter 5: Scripture

1. Trevor Hart, "Tradition, Authority, and a Christian Approach to the Bible as Scripture," in *Between Two Horizons: Spanning New Testament Studies and Systematic Theology*, ed. Joel Green and Max Turner (Grand Rapids: Eerdmans, 1999), 184.

2. John Franke, *The Character of Theology: An Introduction to Its Nature, Task, and Purpose* (Grand Rapids: Baker Academic, 2005), 135.

3. R. W. L. Moberly, "In God We Trust?," *Ex Auditu* 24 (2008): 31.

4. Franke, *Character of Theology*, 135.

5. Robert W. Jenson, *A Theology in Outline: Can These Bones Live?*, ed. Adam Eitel (Oxford: Oxford University Press, 2016), 3.

6. Martin B. Copenhaver, Anthony B. Robinson, and William H. Willimon, "Scripture: Our Home in Exile," in *Good News in Exile: Three Pastors Offer a Hopeful Vision for the Church* (Grand Rapids: Eerdmans, 1999), 36.

7. Do look at N. T. Wright, *Scripture and the Authority of God: How to Read the Bible Today* (London: SPCK, 2011), esp. 139, for a helpful and expanded reflection on this topic.

8. Gerhard F. Hasel, "Divine Inspiration and the Canon of the Bible," *Journal of the Adventist Theological Society* 5, no. 1 (1994): 68–105, quoted in John C. Peckham, *Canonical Theology: The Biblical Canon, Sola Scriptura, and Theological Method* (Grand Rapids: Eerdmans, 2016), 32.

9. See Peckham, *Canonical Theology*, 41–47, for a helpful unpacking of this point.

10. Colin E. Gunton, "The Bible," in *Theology through Preaching* (Edinburgh: T&T Clark, 2001), 28.

11. Peter L. Berger, "Different Gospels: The Social Sources of Apostasy," in *Different Gospels*, ed. Andrew Walker (London: Hodder & Stoughton, 1988), 117 (emphasis original).

12. Metropolitan Anthony of Sourozh, quoted in Andrew Walker, *Notes from a Wayward Son: A Miscellany*, ed. Andrew D. Kinsey (Eugene, OR: Cascade Books, 2015), 176. Walker comments in his chapter "Harmful Religion" that "misshapen theology can itself cause harm" (246–47).

13. Bruce Ellis Benson, *Graven Ideologies: Nietzsche, Derrida, and Marion on Modern Idolatry* (Downers Grove, IL: IVP Academic, 2002), 11, 19.

14. Daniel L. Migliore, *Faith Seeking Understanding: An Introduction to Christian Theology*, 3rd ed. (Grand Rapids: Eerdmans, 2014), 46–47.

15. Migliore, *Faith Seeking Understanding*, 52.

16. Wright, *Scripture and the Authority of God*, 17, 22. See also William Lamb, *Scripture: A Guide for the Perplexed* (London: Bloomsbury T&T Clark, 2013), 158–80.

17. John Webster, *Holy Scripture: A Dogmatic Sketch* (Cambridge: Cambridge University Press, 2003), argues that Scripture too "is a shorthand term for the nature and function of the biblical writings in a set of communicative acts which stretch from God's merciful self-manifestation to the obedient hearing of the community of faith" (5).

18. Peckham, *Canonical Theology*, 32; see 28–47 for fuller discussion.

19. Peckham, *Canonical Theology*, 33.

20. John Goldingay, *Models for Scripture* (Grand Rapids: Eerdmans, 1994), chaps. 10–11.

21. See John Douglas Morrison, *Has God Said? Scripture, the Word of God, and the Crisis of Theological Authority* (Eugene, OR: Pickwick, 2006), 253–54.

22. Peckham offers a very concise and helpful summary of the issues involved (*Canonical Theology*, 41–44).

23. Craig Keener, "A Common Objection to Studying in Context," CraigKeener.com, April 20, 2012, http://www.craigkeener.com/tag/special-revelation.

24. John Barton, *People of the Book? The Authority of the Bible in Christianity* (London: SPCK, 1988), 43–44.

25. Henry Chadwick, ed., *Lessing's Theological Writings* (London: A. & C. Black, 1956), 53, 55.

26. C. S. Lewis, *Surprised by Joy: The Shape of My Early Life* (London: William Collins, 1955), 207–8. This "snobbery" also excludes how Christians have previously interpreted Scripture, prior to the Enlightenment. See Ian Christopher Levy, *Introducing Medieval Biblical Interpretation: The Senses of Scripture in Premodern Exegesis* (Grand Rapids: Baker Academic, 2018), as well as Craig A. Carter, *Interpreting Scripture with the Great Tradition: Recovering the Genius of Premodern Exegesis* (Grand Rapids: Baker Academic, 2018), and Keith D. Stanglin, *The Letter and Spirit of Biblical Interpretation: From the Early Church to Modern Practice* (Grand Rapids: Baker Academic, 2018).

27. Richard B. Hays, "Can the Gospels Teach Us How to Read the Old Testament?," *Pro Ecclesia* 11, no. 4 (2002): 402.

28. Joel B. Green, "Scripture and Theology: Uniting the Two So Long Divided," in Green and Turner, *Between Two Horizons*, 25.

29. R. W. L. Moberly, *The Bible, Theology, and Faith: A Study of Abraham and Jesus* (Cambridge: Cambridge University Press, 2000), 180.

30. C. S. Lewis, *The Weight of Glory, and Other Addresses: A Collection of Lewis's Most Moving Addresses* (London: William Collins, 2013), 58–59.

31. Green, "Scripture and Theology," 31. Green references Umberto Eco, *The Role of The Reader: Explorations in the Semiotics of Texts* (Bloomington: Indiana University Press, 1979).

32. Donald G. Bloesch, *A Theology of Word and Spirit: Authority and Method in Theology* (Downers Grove, IL: InterVarsity, 1992), 279n17.

33. Bloesch, *Theology of Word and Spirit*, 21.

34. See Michael Polanyi, *Personal Knowledge: Towards a Post Critical Philosophy* (1958; repr., London: Routledge, 1998).

35. Michael Polanyi, *The Tacit Dimension* (New York: Anchor Books, 1967), 4.

36. Esther Lightcap Meek, *Loving to Know: Introducing Covenant Epistemology* (Eugene, OR: Cascade Books, 2011), 200.

37. Wolfhart Pannenberg, *Toward a Theology of Nature: Essays on Science and Faith* (Louisville: Westminster John Knox, 1993); Alister E. McGrath, *The Science of God: An Introduction to Scientific Theology* (Grand Rapids: Eerdmans, 2004).

38. Polanyi, *Tacit Dimension*, 24–25.

39. Green, "Scripture and Theology," 32.

40. Kevin J. Vanhoozer, *The Drama of Doctrine: A Canonical-Linguistic Approach to Christian Theology* (Louisville: Westminster John Knox, 2005), 362. See also Kevin J. Vanhoozer and

Daniel J. Treier, *Theology and the Mirror of Scripture* (Downers Grove, IL: IVP Academic, 2015), 226–30.

41. William Lamb offers nine "patterns" for construing Scripture: proof, history, memory, narrative, canon, testimony, tradition, resistance, and performance. *Scripture: A Guide*, 102–46.

42. Craig S. Keener, *Spirit Hermeneutics: Reading Scripture in Light of Pentecost* (Grand Rapids: Eerdmans, 2016), 192, points out that the Bible is not like the Qur'an, to be memorized, but is to be approached in terms of obedience.

43. Keener, *Spirit Hermeneutics*, 189.

44. See Trevor Hart, "Tradition, Authority, and a Christian Approach to the Bible as Scripture," in Green and Turner, *Between Two Horizons*, esp. 184.

45. Bloesch, *Theology of Word and Spirit*, 185.

46. Keener, *Spirit Hermeneutics*, 202.

47. Katherine Sonderegger, *Systematic Theology*, vol. 1, *The Doctrine of God* (Minneapolis: Fortress, 2015), 264–65.

48. Lamb, *Scripture: A Guide*, 147–48.

49. Peter Leithart, "Biblical Truth," *Leithart* (blog), June 1, 2016, https://www.patheos.com/blogs/leithart/2016/06/biblical-truth.

50. See 2 Sam. 22:16; Job 26:13; 32:8; 33:4; Ps. 33:6; Isa. 11:2, 4; 61:1; Joel 2:28–29; John 16:13–15.

51. Roger Olson, "Scripture and Tradition Again: What John Calvin Said," *My Evangelical Arminian Theological Musings* (blog), October 30, 2013, http://www.patheos.com/blogs/roger eolson/2013/10/scripture-and-tradition-again-what-john-calvin-said/.

52. Stanley S. Harakas, "Doing Theology Today: An Orthodox and Evangelical Dialogue on Theological Method," *Pro Ecclesia* 11, no. 4 (Fall 2002): 435.

53. Clement of Rome, *The First Epistle of Clement to the Corinthians* 42.1–4, trans. J. B. Lightfoot, Early Christian Writings, http://www.earlychristianwritings.com/text/1clement-light foot.html.

Chapter 6: Tradition

1. Marmite has its own international family members—Vegemite (Australia), Cenovis (Switzerland), Vitam-R (Germany).

2. The word used by the soldiers from Gilead in Judges 12:5–6 to identify the conquered Ephraimite soldiers, who were unable to pronounce the sound represented in English by *sh* and thus said "sibboleth" rather than "shibboleth" and thereby revealed their ethnicity.

3. You might want to dip into Walter Brueggemann and Hans Walter Wolff, *The Vitality of Old Testament Traditions*, rev. ed. (Louisville: Westminster John Knox, 1985), for more on a static understanding of tradition.

4. Alister McGrath, "Faith and Tradition," in *The Oxford Handbook of Evangelical Theology*, ed. Gerald R. McDermott (Oxford: Oxford University Press, 2010), 91.

5. Jaroslav Pelikan, *The Vindication of Tradition* (New Haven: Yale University Press, 1984), 65. For an up-to-date unpacking of Pelikan's aphorism, see Edith M. Humphrey, *Scripture and Tradition: What the Bible Really Says* (Grand Rapids: Baker Academic, 2013), where Humphrey critiques dead traditionalism and argues that we cannot live without the gift of living tradition.

6. One very good example of this is UK Christian songwriter Graham Kendrick's "We Believe," YouTube audio recording, 4:54, uploaded April 23, 2015, by Graham Kendrick Music, https://www.youtube.com/watch?v=8OhjvKHNKb0.

7. See Andrei Rublev's *The Holy Trinity*, Russia, fifteenth century, Christianity Art: Icons, Murals, and Mosaics, http://www.icon-art.info/masterpiece.php?lng=en&mst_id=161.

8. See Ed Stetzer, "Trends in Church Architecture, Part 1," The Exchange, July 18, 2016, https://www.christianitytoday.com/edstetzer/2016/july/trends-in-church-architecture-part-1 .html, for a helpful article on how church architecture seeks to reflect Christian belief.

9. An excellent example of this is the Oberammergau Passion play produced every ten years in the town of Oberammergau, Germany. See the website of Ammergau Alps, https://www .ammergauer-alpen.de/oberammergau/en/Discover-History-and-stories/Passion-Play/History -of-the-Passion-Play.

10. For example, whether you believe that the word "day" in Genesis 1 refers to a literal twenty-four-hour day and that creation came into being in six literal days, or whether the word signifies an undetermined length of time meaning that creation came into being over a much longer time, Christians are united in their belief that God is Creator of all things, no matter how they might have come into being.

11. The game, once known as Russian Scandal or Russian Gossip, is now known as Telephone in the USA and other English-speaking contexts and as Chinese Whispers in the UK.

12. See Alasdair MacIntyre, *Whose Justice? Which Rationality?* (Notre Dame, IN: University of Notre Dame Press, 1988).

13. There is agreement that Job is probably the oldest book in the Bible, but less agreement as to when it was written. The majority of scholars believe it was written around 1500 BC, with the Pentateuch being written around 1446–1406 BC. The youngest book in the Bible is Revelation, which is dated around either AD 65 or AD 95. Scripture has over forty authors and was written on three continents and in three different languages.

14. Kenneth E. Bailey, "Informal Controlled Oral Tradition and the Synoptic Gospels," *Themelios* 20, no. 2 (January 1995): 4–11. See also Richard Bauckham, *Jesus and the Eyewitnesses: The Gospels as Eyewitness Testimony*, 2nd ed. (Grand Rapids: Eerdmans, 2017), chaps. 10–13. Marva J. Dawn identifies the shift that has occurred as premodern cultures have moved through modernity into postmodernity. Dawn, *A Royal "Waste" of Time: The Splendor of Worshiping God and Being Church for the World* (Grand Rapids: Eerdmans, 1999), 41–45.

15. Neil Postman, *Amusing Ourselves to Death* (London: Methuen, 1997).

16. Bailey describes how the meter of seven syllables per line developed by Saint Ephraim in the fourth century is alive and well today in the Middle East, in the Syrian Orthodox Church. "Informal Controlled Oral Tradition," 5.

17. Bailey, "Informal Controlled Oral Tradition," 6–9.

18. Bailey, "Informal Controlled Oral Tradition," 10.

19. Bauckham, *Jesus and the Eyewitnesses*, 288, 278.

20. Bryan Stone, *Evangelism after Pluralism: The Ethics of Christian Witness* (Grand Rapids: Baker Academic, 2018), 83–105, critiques contemporary consumerist approaches to Christian faith in similar fashion. Mark Noll, Cornelius Plantinga Jr., and David Wells describe it more colorfully: "Not surprisingly one can find in conservative settings altogether too much by way of what Marty calls 'Christian bodybuilding and beautyqueening,' rock music 'with a Jesus gloss on it,' and entrepreneurs 'hawking a complete line of Christian celebrity cosmetics and panty-hose'—all this in combination with considerable suspicion of the Synoptic problem." "Evangelical Theology Today," *Theology Today* 51, no. 4 (January 1995): 501.

21. See 1 Cor. 11:23–26 for the entire tradition. Emphasis added.

22. Bauckham, *Jesus and the Eyewitnesses*, chap. 11.

23. Bauckham, *Jesus and the Eyewitnesses*, 269.

24. Bauckham, *Jesus and the Eyewitnesses*, 270.

25. Bauckham, *Jesus and the Eyewitnesses*, 269.

26. Cited by Richard Bauckham, "Tradition in Relation to Scripture and Reason," in *Scripture, Tradition and Reason: A Study in the Criteria of Christian Doctrine* (Edinburgh: T&T Clark, 1988), 118.

27. Bauckham, "Tradition in Relation to Scripture and Reason," 124. Anthony Lane identifies four descriptions of how Scripture, tradition, and the teaching office of the church relate to each other: (1) the *coincidence* view; (2) the *supplementary* view of the medieval church (tradition supplements Scripture—e.g., veneration of the Virgin Mary); (3) the *ancillary* view of the Reformers, who rejected the teaching of the Roman church, not tradition itself, which they understood as being subordinate or ancillary to Scripture; and (4) the *solitary* view (*sola*

Scriptura). Lane, "Tradition," in *Dictionary for Theological Interpretation of the Bible*, ed. Kevin J. Vanhoozer (Grand Rapids: Baker Academic, 2005), 809–12. See also A. N. S. Lane, "Scripture, Tradition and Church: An Historical Survey," *Vox Evangelica* 9 (1975): 37–55, where Lane's original fourth position is the *unfolding* view, which understands tradition "as the process by which the full meaning of the apostolic message is gradually unfolded" (cited by Bauckham, "Tradition in Relation to Scripture and Reason," 124).

28. Andrew Walker, *Notes from a Wayward Son: A Miscellany*, ed. Andrew D. Kinsey (Eugene, OR: Cascade Books, 2015), 165.

29. William Lamb, *Scripture: A Guide for the Perplexed* (London: Bloomsbury T&T Clark, 2013), 265.

30. John Douglas Morrison, *Has God Said? Scripture, the Word of God, and the Crisis of Theological Authority* (Eugene, OR: Pickwick, 2006), 265 (emphasis original).

31. Morrison, *Has God Said?*, 266n70.

32. F. F. Bruce, *The Canon of Scripture*, new ed. (Downers Grove, IL: InterVarsity, 1988), 117.

33. Irenaeus, *Against Heresies* 3.4, New Advent, http://www.newadvent.org/fathers/010 3304.htm.

34. Alister E. McGrath, *Historical Theology: An Introduction to the History of Christian Thought* (London: Blackwell, 1998), 43.

35. McGrath, "Faith and Tradition," 85.

36. See J. N. D. Kelly, *Early Christian Doctrines*, 5th ed. (London: Adam & Charles Black, 1977), 101, 413.

37. "The Apostles' Creed," Anglicans Online, last updated May 23, 2017, http://www.ang licansonline.org/basics/apostles.html.

38. Cynthia Bennett Brown, *Believing Thinking, Bounded Theology: The Theological Methodology of Emil Brunner* (Eugene, OR: Pickwick, 2015), 19, quoting Emil Brunner, *The Divine-Human Encounter*, trans. Amandus W. Loos (London: SCM, 1944), 83.

39. Walker, *Notes from a Wayward Son*, 175.

40. Except the boundary imposed by relativists, who insist there are no boundaries!

41. Stanley S. Harakas, "Doing Theology Today: An Orthodox and Evangelical Dialogue on Theological Method," *Pro Ecclesia* 11, no. 4 (Fall 2002): 435–62.

42. Morrison, *Has God Said?*, 251. For an accessible introduction to the Apostolic Fathers and their theology, see Clayton N. Jefford, *Reading the Apostolic Fathers: A Student's Introduction*, 2nd ed. (Grand Rapids: Baker Academic, 2012).

43. Robert Burns, "A Red, Red Rose," Burns Country, accessed March 1, 2020, http://www .robertburns.org/works/444.shtml.

44. Alasdair MacIntyre, *After Virtue: A Study in Moral Theology*, 3rd ed. (Notre Dame, IN: University of Notre Dame Press, 2007), 221–22.

45. Georges Florovsky, "The Catholicity of the Church," in *Bible, Church, Tradition: An Eastern Orthodox View*, vol. 1 of *The Collected Works of Georges Florovsky* (Belmont, MA: Nordland, 1972), 47 (emphasis added).

46. John of Damascus, *On Icons* 11, 12, cited in Timothy Ware, *The Orthodox Church*, rev. ed. (London: Penguin, 1993), 196.

47. Steven D. Cone, *Theology from the Great Tradition* (London: Bloomsbury T&T Clark, 2018), 112 (emphasis original).

48. For a church-based understanding of interpretation, see Daniel Castelo and Robert W. Wall, *The Marks of Scripture: Rethinking the Nature of the Bible* (Grand Rapids: Baker Academic, 2018); for a practical how-to understanding, see Robbie F. Castleman, *Interpreting the God-Breathed Word: How to Read and Study the Bible* (Grand Rapids: Baker Academic, 2018); for a more systematic approach, see Joseph K. Gordon, *Divine Scripture in Human Understanding: A Systematic Theology of the Christian Bible* (Notre Dame, IN: University of Notre Dame Press, 2019).

49. D. H. Williams, *Retrieving the Tradition and Renewing Evangelicalism* (Grand Rapids: Eerdmans, 1999), 18, 19.

50. Williams, *Retrieving the Tradition*, 278.

51. T. F. Torrance, "The Deposit of Faith," *Scottish Journal of Theology* 36, no. 1 (1983): 6.

52. D. H. Williams, *Evangelicals and Tradition: The Formative Influence of the Early Church* (Grand Rapids: Baker Academic, 2005), 183.

53. Timothy George, "A Theology to Die For," *Christianity Today*, February 9, 1998, https://www.christianitytoday.com/ct/1998/february9/8t2049.html.

54. James I. Packer, *"Fundamentalism" and the Word of God* (Grand Rapids: Eerdmans, 1958), 48, cited in McGrath, "Faith and Tradition," 91.

55. Ellen Charry, *By the Renewing of Your Minds: The Pastoral Function of Christian Doctrine* (Oxford: Oxford University Press, 1997), 234.

56. Walter Brueggemann, *Hopeful Imagination: Prophetic Voices in Exile* (Philadelphia: Fortress, 1987), 102.

57. Williams, *Retrieving the Tradition*, 14.

Chapter 7: Reason

1. Trevor Hart, *Faith Thinking: The Dynamics of Christian Theology* (London: SPCK, 1995), 94.

2. Colin Gunton, "The Truth . . . and the Spirit of Truth: The Trinitarian Shape of Christian Theology," in *Loving God with Our Minds: The Pastor as Theologian; Essays in Honor of Wallace M. Alston*, ed. Michael Welker and Cynthia A. Jarvis (Grand Rapids: Eerdmans, 2004), 341.

3. The actual Hebrew is better expressed as "Light, be!" (and so on)—a command rather than a whimsical possibility suggested by the English translation "Let there be light."

4. J. P. Moreland, *Kingdom Triangle: Recover the Christian Mind, Renovate the Soul, Restore the Spirit's Power* (Grand Rapids: Zondervan, 2007), 127 (emphasis original).

5. Ellen T. Charry, *By the Renewing of Your Minds: The Pastoral Function of Christian Doctrine* (Oxford: Oxford University Press, 1997), 4.

6. David B. Lott, ed., *Douglas John Hall: Collected Readings* (Minneapolis: Fortress, 2013).

7. See chap. 3 above, under "The Relational."

8. John M. Frame, *A History of Western Philosophy and Theology* (Phillipsburg, NJ: P&R, 2015), 129.

9. Ian Stackhouse, *Praying Psalms: A Personal Journey through the Psalter* (Eugene, OR: Cascade Books, 2018), 131.

10. For instance, the application of Shari'a law within a specific Islamic community that exists within a wider non-Muslim context.

11. Daniel J. Treier, "The Personal and Cultural Character of Reason," in *Revelation and Reason in Christian Theology*, ed. Christopher C. Green and David I. Starling (Bellingham, WA: Lexham, 2018), 41–44.

12. Treier, "Personal and Cultural Character of Reason," 42–43.

13. Treier, "Personal and Cultural Character of Reason," 43.

14. Treier, "Personal and Cultural Character of Reason," 44.

15. Ingolf U. Dalferth, *Theology and Philosophy* (Oxford: Basil Blackwell, 1988), 63.

16. Dalferth, *Theology and Philosophy*, 64–66.

17. Peter Hicks, *Evangelicals and Truth: A Creative Proposal for a Postmodern Age* (Leicester, UK: Apollos, 1998), chaps. 20–21. It is of interest to note Don Thorsen's qualification of Wesley's understanding of "experimental" religion—namely, that it makes use of both empirical and experiential knowledge. Don Thorsen, *The Wesleyan Quadrilateral: Scripture, Tradition, Reason, and Experience as a Model of Evangelical Theology* (1990; repr., Lexington: Emeth, 2005), 129–34.

18. Edward Foley, *Theological Reflection across Religious Traditions: The Turn to Reflective Believing* (Lanham, MD: Rowman & Littlefield, 2015), 71. For a helpful diagram of the relationship between all three, see Steven Liss, "Orthodoxy, Orthopraxy, and Orthopathy: Series

on Sanctification (Part Two)," *Christian Paradoxes* (blog), February 24, 2016, https://christian paradoxes.blogspot.com/2016/02/orthodoxy-orthopraxy-and-orthopathy.html.

19. J. P. Moreland, *Love Your God with All Your Mind: The Role of Reason in the Life of the Soul* (Colorado Springs: NavPress, 2012), 19–26.

20. Moreland, *Love Your God with All Your Mind*, 19.

21. Arius proposed that, in order to maintain that Christ did indeed die for our sins and that his sufferings were real, we must also admit that he was not fully God but was, instead, the most exalted of God's creation. The unintended consequence was that, in so arguing, he undermined the good news that in Christ God is fully with us. Apollinaris's gospel was the opposite—to establish the Son's humanity, Apollinaris contended that the divine Logos took the place of the human logos (soul/mind). The unintended consequence here is that, in so arguing, Apollinaris rendered the humanity of the Savior incomplete. The church fathers argued that if that which makes us most human is missing in Christ, especially if it is the center of dysfunctioning, our humanity has not been redeemed. Contemporary distortions manifest in "Christian" cults—Mormons, Jehovah's Witnesses, Christadelphians, etc.—as well as in current expressions that separate the work of the Spirit from the ongoing application of the cross, as though Christians can "have" the Holy Spirit without the cost of the cross and obedience to Christ and his gospel.

22. For a helpful time line of Paul's life and ministry, see Janet Meyers Everts, "The Apostle Paul and His Times: Christian History Timeline," *Christianity Today*, accessed March 1, 2020, https://www.christianitytoday.com/history/issues/issue-47/apostle-paul-and-his-times-christian -history-timeline.html.

23. After his conversion, Paul first spent three years in Damascus (Acts 9:19; Gal. 1:18) and then went to Arabia. It is unlikely that Paul was on a three-year retreat in Arabia; most likely he was indeed preaching the new gospel he had encountered on the Damascus-Jerusalem road (Acts 9–12). However, it was also undoubtedly a time of serious theological reflection: Torah stated unequivocally that anyone "hung on a tree" was cursed. "If someone guilty of a capital offense is put to death and their body is exposed on a pole, you must not leave the body hanging on the pole overnight. Be sure to bury it that same day, because anyone who is hung on a pole is under God's curse. You must not desecrate the land the LORD your God is giving you as an inheritance" (Deut. 21:22–23). The theological challenge for Paul, a highly trained and experienced Pharisee, was getting his head around the unequivocal authority of Torah while having personally encountered the risen Jesus Christ, who had been publicly crucified (hung, hung on a pole, hung on a tree). It is remarkable that Paul does not question in any way the Christophany on the Damascus-Jerusalem road. Thus, he had to think very seriously in order to understand his newfound faith—perhaps one of the most excellent examples of faith seeking understanding. In the end, it was clear: if God vindicated Jesus by resurrection, it means Jesus has a unique relationship to Torah, to the Law, to the way in which the God of Abraham relates not only to his own people but also to non-Jews (Gal. 3:6–14, esp. 13–14).

24. Treier, "Personal and Cultural Character of Reason," 39.

25. Treier, "Personal and Cultural Character of Reason," 40.

26. Treier, "Personal and Cultural Character of Reason," 41.

27. Mark Noll, Cornelius Plantinga Jr., and David Wells, "Evangelical Theology Today," *Theology Today* 51, no. 4 (January 1995): 503.

28. Esther Lightcap Meek, *Loving to Know: Introducing Covenant Epistemology* (Eugene, OR: Cascade Books, 2011), 8–11.

29. Meek, *Loving to Know*, 9 (emphasis original).

30. Meek, *Loving to Know*, 8–9.

31. Meek, *Loving to Know*, 13. See Treier, "Personal and Cultural Character of Reason," 41, where he, too, describes the same skepticism as a result of confusion and of overconfidence in the plain meaning of the Bible.

32. John Owen, *The Works of John Owen*, vol. 3, *The Holy Spirit* (Edinburgh: Banner of Truth Trust, 1965), 540. Admittedly, there are exceptions. Hong Kong–based Jackie Pullinger testifies to addicts being set free from the power of their addictions through strategic prayer and

fasting—something that does not bypass the power of reason but rather constitutes a partnering of Spirit and will in accordance with Scripture and the power of the gospel. See Jackie Pullinger and Andrew Quicke, *Chasing the Dragon*, rev. ed. (London: Hodder & Stoughton, 2006).

33. See Alexandra Carstensen and Caren M. Walker, "The Paradox of Relational Development Is Not Universal: Abstract Reasoning Develops Differently across Cultures," COGSCI: The Annual Meeting of the Congnitive Science Society, accessed March 1, 2020, https://mind modeling.org/cogsci2017/papers/0335/paper0335.pdf. See, too, Todd David Whitmore, *Imitating Christ in Magwi: An Anthropological Theology* (London: Bloomsbury T&T Clark, 2019).

34. "Truthiness," Lexico.com, accessed March 1, 2020, https://www.lexico.com/definition /truthiness.

35. Stephen B. Bevans, *An Introduction to Theology in Global Perspective* (Maryknoll, NY: Orbis Books, 2009), 39.

36. Hicks, *Evangelicals and Truth*, 193–94.

37. Tertullian, a second-century theologian. The original context is: "Whence spring those 'fables and endless genealogies,' and 'unprofitable questions,' and 'words which spread like a cancer'? From all these, when the apostle would restrain us, he expressly names *philosophy* as that which he would have us be on our guard against. Writing to the Colossians, he says, 'See that no one beguile you through philosophy and vain deceit, after the tradition of men, and contrary to the wisdom of the Holy Ghost.' He had been at Athens, and had in his interviews (with its philosophers) become acquainted with that human wisdom which pretends to know the truth, whilst it only corrupts it, and is itself divided into its own manifold heresies, by the variety of its mutually repugnant sects. What indeed has Athens to do with Jerusalem? What concord is there between the Academy and the Church? what between heretics and Christians? Our instruction comes from 'the porch of Solomon,' who had himself taught that 'the Lord should be sought in simplicity of heart.' Away with all attempts to produce a mottled Christianity of Stoic, Platonic, and dialectic composition! We want no curious disputation after possessing Christ Jesus, no inquisition after enjoying the gospel! With our faith, we desire no further belief." Tertullian, *Prescription against Heretics* 7, trans. Peter Holmes, in *Latin Christianity: Its Founder, Tertullian*, ed. Alexander Roberts and James Donaldson, vol. 3 of *The Ante-Nicene Fathers: Translations of the Writings of the Fathers Down to A.D. 325* (Peabody, MA: Hendrickson, 1994), 246.

38. Indeed, the entire history of Western civilization could be mapped in 500- to 1,000-year blocks that are dominated and determined by the way in which reason, and how we come to know, has been understood.

39. Gregory of Nyssa (*Life of Moses* 2.39–40) typologically draws from the story of the Israelites "spoiling" the Egyptians on the night of Passover as an example of how Christians might engage non-Christian wisdom. Thus, human reason, or philosophy, is to be used only if it is "circumcised" of anything that is not in concord with the spirit of Christianity. See Gregory of Nyssa, *Life of Moses*, trans. Abraham J. Malherbe and Everett Ferguson, Classics of Western Spirituality (New York: Paulist Press, 1978), 337, cited in Donald L. Ross, "Gregory of Nyssa (c. 335–c. 395 C.E.)," in *Internet Encyclopedia of Philosophy*, accessed March 1, 2020, https:// www.iep.utm.edu/gregoryn/#H6.

40. Lesslie Newbigin, "What Kind of Certainty?," *Tyndale Bulletin* 44, no. 2 (1993): 339–50.

41. Colin E. Gunton, "'The Place of Reason in Theology," in *The Practice of Theology*, ed. Colin Gunton, Stephen R. Holmes, and Murray A. Rae (London: SCM, 2001), 150 (emphasis added).

42. "Catholic" as in "universal"—or, to be more precise, pertaining, by and large, to the entire Western church, as distinguished from "Orthodox," referring, on the whole, to the Eastern church.

43. Bruce Ellis Benson, *Graven Ideologies: Nietzsche, Derrida, and Marion on Modern Idolatry* (Downers Grove, IL: IVP Academic, 2002), 47.

44. This desire does not evidence a lack of personal faith on Descartes's part. Rather, it was concomitant with the worldview perspective that emerged in which the union between faith and reason was gradually divorced.

45. See Nancey Murphy, *Beyond Liberalism and Fundamentalism: How Modern and Post-modern Philosophy Set the Theological Agenda* (Harrisburg, PA: Trinity Press International, 1996), 29, 64, and esp. 91: "Descartes's strategy has been rejected by most philosophers simply because, in the passage of time, it has turned out that what is indubitable in one intellectual context is all too questionable in another." Stephen Toulmin deconstructs the place modernity gave to rationalism in *Cosmopolis: The Hidden Agenda of Modernity* (Chicago: University of Chicago Press, 1992).

46. Murphy, *Beyond Liberalism and Fundamentalism*, 14.

47. Benson, *Graven Ideologies*, 44.

48. Hicks, *Evangelicals and Truth*, 30.

49. Charry, *By the Renewing of Your Minds*, 5.

50. Robert W. Jenson, *A Theology in Outline: Can These Bones Live?*, ed. Adam Eitel (Oxford: Oxford University Press, 2016), 107.

51. Jenson, *Theology in Outline*, 108.

52. Jenson, *Theology in Outline*, 109–10.

53. Jenson, *Theology in Outline*, 111.

54. Jenson, *Theology in Outline*, 112.

55. Benson, *Graven Ideologies*, 46.

56. Brian McNair, *Fake News: Falsehood, Fabrication and Fantasy in Journalism* (London: Routledge, 2018), x.

57. McNair, *Fake News*, 11. If you are interested in what this power might look like in Christian ministry, a good place to start is Bob Burns, Tasha D. Chapman, and Donald C. Guthrie, *The Politics of Ministry: Navigating Power Dynamics and Negotiating Interests* (Downers Grove, IL: InterVarsity, 2019).

58. American Dialect Society, "*Truthiness* Voted 2005 Word of the Year by American Dialect Society," https://www.americandialect.org/Words_of_the_Year_2005.pdf. Defined by the Oxford Dictionary as "The quality of seeming or being felt to be true, even if not necessarily true," https://en.oxforddictionaries.com/definition/truthiness.

59. "The Oxford Word of the Year is a word or expression . . . that is judged to reflect the ethos, mood, or preoccupations of that particular year and to have lasting potential as a term of cultural significance." See "Word of the Year 2016," Oxford Languages, accessed March 1, 2020, https://languages.oup.com/word-of-the-year/2016. See also Lee McIntyre, *Post-Truth* (Cambridge, MA: MIT Press, 2018); Julian Baggini, *A Short History of Truth: Consolations in a Post-Truth World* (London: Quercus, 2018); and the more popular Matthew D'Ancona, *Post-Truth: The New War on Truth and How to Fight Back* (London: Ebury Press, 2017). For a specifically Christian apologetic, see Abdu Murray, *Saving Truth: Finding Meaning and Clarity in a Post-Truth World* (Grand Rapids: Zondervan, 2018).

60. Sam Browse, "Between Truth, Sincerity and Satire: Post-Truth Politics and the Rhetoric of Authenticity," in *Metamodernism: Historicity, Affect and Depth after Postmodernism*, ed. Robert van den Akker, Alison Gibbons, and Timotheus Vermeulen (London: Rowman & Littlefield, 2017), 167–81.

61. John Thornhill, *Christianity's Estranged Child Reconstructed* (Grand Rapids: Eerdmans, 2000), 5.

62. T. S. Eliot, "Four Quartets," in *The Complete Plays and Poems of T. S. Eliot* (London: Faber and Faber, 1969), 175.

63. D'Ancona, *Post-Truth*, 112.

64. Graham Ward, ed., *The Blackwell Companion to Postmodern Theology* (Oxford: Blackwell, 2001), xv.

65. Linda Hutcheon, *A Poetics of Postmodernism: History, Theory, Fiction* (New York: Routledge, 1980), 3.

66. Hans Bertrens, *The Idea of the Postmodern: A History* (Abingdon, UK: Routledge, 1995), 83.

67. Ingolf Dalferth, "'I Determine What God Is!' Theology in the Age of 'Cafeteria Religion,'" *Theology Today* 57, no. 1 (April 2000): 8.

68. Craig A. Carter, *Interpreting Scripture with the Great Tradition: Recovering the Genius of Premodern Exegesis* (Grand Rapids: Baker Academic, 2018), 27.

69. David Tracy, "Fragments: The Spiritual Situation of Our Times," in *God, the Gift, and Postmodernism*, ed. John D. Caputo and Michael J. Scanlon (Bloomington: Indiana University Press, 1999), 171.

70. Almost every major world city houses collections of art that offer instant visual entrance into the worldview of the artist. The city of London hosts the National Gallery (https://www.nationalgallery.org.uk), which affords, in one visit, a visual tour through early Renaissance art, which was wholly religious, through Enlightenment art, which reified the successes of the self-made (usually) man, through to the Impressionism of Romantic thinking. Interestingly, there is little fragmentation on show here since each period subscribes, overall, to one form or other of an integrated Judeo-Christian worldview. This all changes, however, with a short ride over to the Tate Modern; its website, https://www.tate.org.uk/visit/tate-modern, offers a contemporary visual feast.

71. Take, for example, the 2019 Oscar contender *The Favourite*, portraying female political and sexual power in the court of late seventeenth- and early eighteenth-century Queen Anne of Great Britain. Both the ahistoricity of the film (history portrays Queen Anne as an astute politician as well as a devout Christian) and its politico-sexual presentation of an all-women ménage à trois exemplifies the worldview shift in contemporary popular culture.

72. See Alister McGrath, *A Passion for Truth: The Intellectual Coherence of Evangelicalism* (Downers Grove, IL: InterVarsity, 1996), 166–79, cited in David K. Clark, "Postmodern Evangelical Apologetics?," in *Alister E. McGrath and Evangelical Theology: A Dynamic Engagement*, ed. Sung Wook Chung (Carlisle, UK: Paternoster, 2003), 313.

73. Walter Brueggemann, "A Text That Redescribes," *Theology Today* 58, no. 4 (January 2002): 530.

74. I am grateful to John Leaf for making this point so inspiringly clear in a sermon, thus demonstrating the power of another of our theological tools—doing theology *coram Deo*.

75. John Webster, *Holy Scripture: A Dogmatic Sketch* (Cambridge: Cambridge University Press, 2003), 134.

76. Brueggemann, "Text That Redescribes," 531.

77. We could add that evangelicalism's understanding of *covenant* in terms of conversionism or salvation has been at the deeper cost of its appreciation of *creation* and *consummation*. That is, its understanding of salvation (covenant) is divorced from creation (and so Jesus saves us to be something not necessarily connected with God's mandate for human beings or Israel) and from consummation (that is, that we are brought into covenant relationship with the triune God in order to bring about the Creator's intentions for creation and church, not simply for our own fulfillment and destiny).

78. Lesslie Newbigin, *Proper Confidence: Faith, Doubt, and Certainty in Christian Discipleship* (Grand Rapids: Eerdmans, 1995).

79. Walter Brueggemann, *God, Neighbor, Empire: The Excess of Divine Fidelity and the Command of Common Good* (Waco: Baylor University Press, 2016), 9–38.

80. Jenson, *Theology in Outline*, 114. In this, Jenson echoes Charry's point that the Enlightenment was also a divorce between *sapientia* and *scientia*, or Hicks's point concerning the relation between *reality* and *goodness*. Of course, once the notion came about that creation was an intentional act of an all-beneficent Creator, the connection between reality and goodness could be perceived only by sight—that creation is a magnificent but cruel and often ugly reality, depending on how fortunate one is in one's locale.

81. It will be argued in the final chapter, on *community*, that this can be rectified.

82. See Treier, "Personal and Cultural Character of Reason," 42, who rightly points out that "much of what passes for 'wisdom' is a matter of skill—of learned and/or calculated behavior."

83. Alister E. McGrath, *Christian Theology: An Introduction* (Oxford: Wiley & Sons, 2017), 312–13.

84. See Jerry Bridges, *True Community: The Biblical Practice of Koinonia* (Colorado Springs: NavPress, 2012).

85. Gerald R. McDermott, *Everyday Glory: The Revelation of God in All of Reality* (Grand Rapids: Baker Academic, 2018), 59–61.

86. Alvin Plantinga, *Warranted Christian Belief* (New York: Oxford University Press, 2000), 323.

87. Parker Palmer, *To Know as We Are Known: Education as a Spiritual Journey* (San Francisco: HarperSanFrancisco, 1966), 31–32, cited in Meek, *Loving to Know*, 40–41. Meek reminds us that "*Troth* is an old word for *pledge*" (*Loving to Know*, 40).

Chapter 8: Experience

1. C. S. Lewis, *Mere Christianity* (Glasgow, UK: Fontana, 1978), 140.

2. Lewis, *Mere Christianity*, 140.

3. Several theologians argue for what we might call the "scientificity" of theology. See, in particular, Iain G. Barbour, *Issues in Science and Religion*, 2nd ed. (New York: Harper Collins, 1971); Niels H. Gregersen and Wentzel van Huyssteen, eds., *Rethinking Theology and Science: Six Models for the Current Dialogue* (Grand Rapids: Eerdmans, 1998); Alister McGrath, *The Science of God* (London: T&T Clark, 2004); Wolfhart Pannenberg, *Theology and the Philosophy of Science* (London: Darton, Longman & Todd, 1976); Arthur R. Peacocke, *The Sciences and Theology in the Twentieth Century* (Stocksfield, UK: Oriel, 1981); John Polkinghorne, *Science and Christian Belief* (London: SPCK, 1994); Jim B. Stump and Alan G. Padgett, eds., *The Blackwell Companion to Science and Christianity* (Malden, MA: Blackwell, 2012); Thomas F. Torrance, *Theological Science* (Edinburgh: T&T Clark, 1996).

4. Alternatively, Miroslav Volf and Matthew Croasmun, in *For the Life of the World: Theology That Makes a Difference* (Grand Rapids: Brazos, 2019), 48–51, negatively view the idea of theology as a science. When theology is divorced from any transformative context and becomes an end in itself—knowledge for the sake of knowledge divorced from any context other than the university—it results in three "significant consequences": (1) A lack of unity: like many other academic disciplines, theology generates a lot of data. This is done with little concern for the big picture and how the particular fits into the greater whole. (2) A lack of relevance: "The questions of life are now more or less absent from the academy entirely" (49). (3) A lack of purpose: the purpose of theology is, according to Volf and Croasmun, "to discern with intellectual integrity the shape of genuinely flourishing life" (51) that centers on Jesus Christ. The incremental increase of knowledge acquired in academic theology fails this purpose.

By relocating the term "scientific" within the transformative power of the gospel and the sanctifying and ongoing work of God's Spirit within the body politic of those who have responded to the call of the gospel, we are able to give the term a more positive meaning, in line with Volf and Croasmun's critique.

5. See Don Thorsen, *The Wesleyan Quadrilateral: Scripture, Tradition, Reason, and Experience as a Model of Evangelical Theology* (1990; repr., Lexington: Emeth, 2005), 129–30.

6. Colin E. Gunton, "Using and Being Used: Scripture and Systematic Theology," *Theology Today* 47, no. 3 (October 1990): 253.

7. Ellen T. Charry, "Experience," in *Dictionary of Systematic Theology*, ed. John Webster, Kathryn Tanner, and Iain Torrance (Oxford: Oxford University Press, 2007), 413.

8. Jeff Astley, *Studying God: Doing Theology* (London: SCM, 2014), 33.

9. Astley, *Studying God*, 34–35.

10. Anthony C. Thiselton, *Hermeneutics of Doctrine* (Grand Rapids: Eerdmans, 2007), 452 (emphasis original).

11. Thiselton, *Hermeneutics of Doctrine*, 253.

12. Gunton, "Using and Being Used," 253.

13. Richard Swinburne, *The Existence of God* (Oxford: Clarendon, 1979), 25–51.

14. Roger Olson, "Thoughts about the Role of Experience in Theology: Part One," *My Evangelical Arminian Theological Musings* (blog), November 28, 2014, www.patheos.com/blogs/rogereolson/.2014/11/thoughts-about-the-role-of-experience-in-theology-part-one. See also Olson, "Thoughts about the Role of Experience in Theology: Part Two (with Special Reference to Friedrich Schleiermacher and Stanley J. Grenz," *My Evangelical Arminian Theological Musings* (blog), November 30, 2014, http://www.patheos.com/blogs/rogereolson/2014/11/thoughts-about-the-role-of-experience-in-theology-part-two-with-special-reference-to-friedrich-schleiermacher-and-stanley-j-grenz.

15. See an image of Monet's *Chrysanthèmes* on the website of the Musée d'Orsay, accessed March 1, 2020, https://www.musee-orsay.fr/en/collections/index-of-works/notice.html?no_cache=1&nnumid=001299&cHash=459109a0ce.

16. Tate Modern, https://www.tate.org.uk/visit/tate-modern; https://walkerart.org/visit.

17. For a concise and contemporary view of culture sympathetic to Judeo-Christian faith, see Roger Scruton, *Culture Counts: Faith and Feeling in a World Besieged* (New York: Encounter Books, 2007).

18. For an accessible and user-friendly introduction to critical thinking, see T. Ryan Byerly, *Introducing Critical Thinking: The Skills of Reasoning and the Virtues of Inquiry* (Grand Rapids: Baker Academic, 2017).

19. Charry, "Experience," 417.

20. William G. MacDonald, "Pentecostal Theology: A Classical Viewpoint," in *Perspectives on the New Pentecostalism*, ed. Russell P. Spittler (Grand Rapids: Baker, 1976), 63–65, cited in Stephen E. Parker, *Led by the Spirit: Toward a Practical Theology of Pentecostal Discernment and Decision Making*, expanded ed. (Cleveland, TN: CPT Press, 2015), 18.

21. Olson, "Thoughts about the Role of Experience in Theology: Part One."

22. Bernard Lonergan, *Early Works on Theological Method 1*, vol. 22 of *Collected Works of Bernard Lonergan* (Toronto: University of Toronto Press, 2010), 36.

23. Rodney Stark, "A Taxonomy of Religious Experience," *Journal for the Scientific Study of Religion* 5, no. 1 (1965): 98.

24. Stark, "Taxonomy of Religious Experience," 85.

25. William James, *The Varieties of Religious Experience: A Study in Human Nature*, Gifford Lectures on Natural Religion Delivered in Edinburgh, 1901–2 (London: Longmans, Green, & Co., 1935), 42.

26. Uche Anizor, *How to Read Theology: Engaging Doctrine Critically and Charitably* (Grand Rapids: Baker Academic, 2018), 154.

27. While evangelicals are uniform in their insistence of new birth and conversion, historically they are not uniform in their understanding of the *how* of this new birth and conversion. Evangelicals can be either paedo-baptist or conversion-baptist.

28. The notion of being "in Christ" dominates Paul's theology. Take time to reflect upon and consider the following biblical texts: Rom. 6:23; 8:38–39; 1 Cor. 1:2; 15:22; 2 Cor. 1:20; 5:17, 21; Gal. 3:26; Eph. 1:7; 2:6; Phil. 4:7, 19; 2 Tim. 1:9. For a scholarly summary of New Testament and systematic theology scholarship on the subject, see Kevin J. Vanhoozer, "From 'Blessed in Christ' to 'Being in Christ': The State of Union and the Place of Participation in Paul's Discourse, New Testament Exegesis, and Systematic Theology Today," in *"In Christ" in Paul: Explorations in Paul's Theology of Union and Participation*, ed. Michael J. Thate, Kevin J. Vanhoozer, and Constantine R. Campbell (Tübingen: Mohr Siebeck, 2014).

29. For instance, excellent resources on evangelical theology and theological method omit any reference to the topic of experience; see Stanley E. Porter and Steven M. Studebaker, eds., *Evangelical Theological Method: Five Views* (Downers Grove, IL: IVP Academic, 2018); Daniel J. Treier and Walter A. Elwell, eds., *Evangelical Dictionary of Theology*, 3rd ed. (Grand Rapids: Baker Academic, 2017).

30. Charry, "Experience," 414.

31. Ralph Waldo Emerson, "Experience," in *The Collected Works of Ralph Waldo Emerson*, vol. 3, *Essays: Second Series*, ed. Joseph Slater, Alfred R. Ferguson, and Jean Ferguson Carr (Cambridge, MA: Belknap, 1983), 30.

32. Anizor, *How to Read Theology*, 153.

33. Anizor, *How to Read Theology*, 148.

34. Charry, "Experience," 429.

35. Charry, "Experience," 416.

36. Charry, "Experience," 417.

37. Alister E. McGrath, *Christian Theology: An Introduction*, 6th ed. (Oxford: Wiley & Sons, 2017), 131–34.

38. McGrath, *Christian Theology*, 132.

39. For an accessible reading of Ludwig Feuerbach and others, see Robert Banks, *And Man Created God: Is God a Human Invention?* (Oxford: Lion Books, 2011).

40. Thirty years of teaching theological anthropology convinces me that the average seminarian lacks any significant understanding of what Scripture describes as "spirit" or "soul." They may well be shibboleths about which we assume meaning, but when pushed, there is little consensus regarding their meaning, let alone how they are understood to relate to each other, let alone to the mind or body.

41. If you are interested in how one might distinguish or discern spirits/Spirit, see Amos Yong, *Discerning the Spirit(s): A Pentecostal-Charismatic Contribution to Christian Theology of Religions* (Sheffield, UK: Sheffield Academic, 2000); Yong, *Beyond the Impasse: Toward a Pneumatological Theology of Religions* (Grand Rapids: Baker Academic, 2003).

42. The contemporary commodification of the Spirit in worship, whether commercial or not, along with the notion that we "invite" the Holy Spirit to join us once the sound check is complete, evidences this kind of theological veneer.

43. Thomas Kuhn, *The Structure of Scientific Revolutions*, 2nd ed. (Chicago: University of Chicago Press, 1970).

44. See the Freiburg Institute for Advanced Studies website for examples: https://www.frias.uni-freiburg.de/en/events/lunch-lectures/former-lectures/paradigm-shifts-in-science-1.

45. Paul further elaborates on his own experience in Acts 26:12–18; 1 Cor. 9:1; 15:8.

46. Larry W. Hurtado, *How on Earth Did Jesus Become a God? Historical Questions about Earliest Devotion to Jesus* (Grand Rapids: Eerdmans, 2005), 197.

47. Hurtado, *How on Earth Did Jesus Become a God?*, 192.

48. See Graham McFarlane, *Why Do You Believe What You Believe about Jesus?* (Eugene, OR: Wipf & Stock, 2009), chap. 7.

49. Walter Brueggemann, "A Text That Redescribes," *Theology Today* 58, no. 4 (January 2002): 526.

50. John Weaver, *Outside-In: Theological Reflections on Life* (Macon, GA: Smyth & Helwys, 2006), 7. This publication is an excellent resource for anyone interested in exploring more fully what theological reflection looks like practically and in an accessible form.

51. Weaver, *Outside-In*, 7 (emphasis added).

52. Murray Rae, "Reflecting on Experience of God," in *The Practice of Theology: A Reader*, ed. Colin E. Gunton, Stephen R. Holmes, and Murray Rae (London: SCM, 2001), 185.

53. Astley, *Studying God*, 35.

54. Matthew Levering, *Engaging the Doctrine of Revelation: The Mediation of the Gospel through Church and Scripture* (Grand Rapids: Baker Academic, 2014), 206. Levering is engaging here with Orthodox theologian Khaled Anatolios, *Retrieving Nicaea: The Development and Meaning of Trinitarian Doctrine* (Grand Rapids: Baker Academic, 2011), 10.

55. Levering, *Engaging the Doctrine of Revelation*, 206.

56. Anatolios, *Retrieving Nicaea*, 10.

57. Mark A. McIntosh, *Divine Teaching: An Introduction to Christian Theology* (Oxford: Blackwell, 2008), 24.

58. See Christopher Gertz and Mark Pattie III, *The Pietist Option: Hope for the Renewal of the Church* (Downers Grove, IL: IVP Academic, 2017).

59. Tremper Longman III, *The Fear of the Lord Is Wisdom: A Theological Introduction to Wisdom in Israel* (Grand Rapids: Baker Academic, 2017), 12.

60. C. D. Batson, J. C. Becker, and W. M. Clark, *Commitment without Ideology* (London: SCM, 1973), 35.

61. Longman, *Fear of the Lord Is Wisdom*, 13.

62. Craig Keener, *Spirit Hermeneutics: Reading Scripture in Light of Pentecost* (Grand Rapids: Eerdmans, 2016), 189.

63. Matthew Elliott, *Faithful Feelings: Emotion in the New Testament* (Leicester, UK: Inter-Varsity, 2005), 268.

64. Elliott, *Faithful Feelings*, 238.

65. J. de Waal Dryden, in *A Hermeneutic of Wisdom: Recovering the Formative Agency of Scripture* (Grand Rapids: Baker Academic, 2018), argues that Christians are called to see Scripture as God's revealed wisdom and that by engaging faithfully with Scripture we grow in our spiritual formation.

66. Nicene Creed. See https://www.ccel.org/creeds/nicene.creed.html.

67. C. S. Lewis, *Surprised by Joy: The Shape of My Early Life* (London: William Collins, 1955), 205.

68. David M. Lamberth, "Putting 'Experience' to the Test in Theological Reflection," *Harvard Theological Review* 1 (2000): 73.

69. Karl Barth, *Evangelical Theology: An Introduction* (London: Weidenfield and Nicolson, 1963), 160, cited in Dennis Okholm, *Learning Theology through the Church's Worship* (Grand Rapids: Baker Academic, 2018), 21.

70. Okholm, *Learning Theology through the Church's Worship*, 22–24.

71. Scot McKnight, *Galatians*, NIV Application Commentary (Grand Rapids: Zondervan, 1995).

72. Mary M. Veeneman, *Introducing Theological Method: A Survey of Contemporary Theologians and Approaches* (Grand Rapids: Baker Academic, 2017), 135.

73. Anizor, *How to Read Theology*, 164. Anizor offers very helpful reflections and principles regarding the relationship between theology and experience. (1) Experience is not the starting point for theology and should be tempered by Scripture and sound theology. (2) Experience will not always agree with theological documents. (3) Experience can confirm individual and corporate theologies. (4) There is a place for culture in our assessment of experience. (5) Theology should be tested culturally, first, in how it "fits" a particular culture, and, second, we should be able to translate our own cultural theologies in order to engage other cultures and "address universal concerns." (6) If our theology is "good," it should produce "good" people. Anizor, *How to Read Theology*, 170–71.

74. For a good example of what this looks like in relation to other academic disciplines, see Deane D. Downey and Stanley E. Porter, *Christian Worldview and the Academic Disciplines* (Eugene, OR: Pickwick, 2009).

75. Steven L. Porter, "Wesleyan Theological Methodology as a Theory of Integration," *Journal of Psychology and Theology* 32, no. 3 (2004): 197.

76. We will pick up on this imperative in the next chapter.

77. Volf and Croasmun, *For the Life of the World*, esp. chap. 6, "A Vision of Flourishing Life."

78. Edward Foley, *Theological Reflection across Religious Traditions: The Turn to Reflective Believing* (Lanham, MD: Rowman & Littlefield, 2015), 64.

79. For a helpful and concise, if slightly dated, read on this topic, see Francis A. Schaeffer, *How Should We Then Live?*, 50th L'Abri anniversary edition (Wheaton: Crossway, 2005).

80. Michael Molloy, *The Christian Experience: An Introduction to Christianity* (London: Bloomsbury Academic, 2017), 461.

81. Astley, *Studying God*, 35.

82. James D. G. Dunn, *Jesus and the Spirit: A Study of the Religious and Charismatic Experience of Jesus and the First Christians as Reflected in the New Testament* (Grand Rapids: Eerdmans, 1997), 3–4.

83. Elliott, *Faithful Feelings*, 252.

84. Bernard Cooke, "The Experiential 'Word of God,'" in *Consensus in Theology? A Dialogue with Hans Küng and Edward Schillebeeckx*, ed. Leonard Swidler (Philadelphia: Westminster, 1980), 72.

85. McGrath, *Christian Theology*, 193.

86. Astley, *Studying God*, 33.

87. Elaine A. Robinson, *Exploring Theology* (Minneapolis: Fortress, 2014), 87.

88. Thomas Merton, *Love and Living* (London: Sheldon, 1979), cited in Matthew Knell, "Lessons for An Evangelical Spirituality from Bernard of Clairvaux and Thomas Merton," 230–31, in *Learning from the Past: Essays on Reception, Catholicity, and Dialogue in Honour of Anthony N. S. Lane*, ed. Jon Balserak and Richard Snoddy (London: Bloomsbury T&T Clark, 2015).

89. Longman, *Fear of the Lord Is Wisdom*, 118.

90. Longman, *Fear of the Lord Is Wisdom*, 117.

91. See Kevin Vanhoozer, *The Drama of Doctrine: A Canonical-Linguistic Approach to Christian Theology* (Louisville: Westminster John Knox, 2005), 362; Kevin J. Vanhoozer and Daniel J. Treier, *Theology and the Mirror of Scripture* (Downers Grove, IL: IVP Academic, 2015), 226–30; and William Lamb, *Scripture: A Guide for the Perplexed* (London: Bloomsbury T&T Clark, 2013), 102–46.

92. If Jesus were to give a contemporary and contextual example today, I wonder if he might illustrate the plight of the refugee. See Donatella Di Cesare, *Resident Foreigners: A Philosophy of Migration*, trans. David Broder (Medford, MA: Polity, 2019).

93. Colin E. Gunton, *Theology through the Theologians: Selected Essays 1972–1995* (London: Bloomsbury, 2003), 230, summarizing Forsyth.

94. Gareth Jones, *Christian Theology* (Oxford: Polity, 1999), 56. Jones establishes an important criterion here. He adds later, "Experience in itself does not offer solutions to theology, it simply provides an environment of possibility" (57). That environment, as he points out, is always "*in* the world" (55). The significance of these points should not be missed in contemporary Western Christian culture, where experience increasingly takes center stage with little if any theological or biblical constraints.

95. Paul Hessert, *Introduction to Christianity* (Englewood Cliffs, NJ: Prentice-Hall, 1958), 28.

96. P. T. Forsyth, *The Principle of Authority*, 2nd ed. (London: Independent Press, 1952), 372, cited in Gunton, *Theology through the Theologians*, 230.

97. Paul R. Williamson, "Covenant: The Beginning of a Biblical Idea," *Reformed Theological Review* 65, no. 1 (2006): 10–11.

98. See Miroslav Volf, "Theology for a Way of Life," in *Practicing Theology: Beliefs and Practices in Christian Life*, ed. Miroslav Volf and Dorothy C. Bass (Grand Rapids: Eerdmans, 2002), 245–63, as well as Volf and Croasmun, *For the Life of the World*, 13–20, 76–83, 180–82.

99. Astley, *Studying God*, 37.

100. N. T. Wright, *Paul and the Faithfulness of God* (Minneapolis: Fortress, 2013), 369, cited in Thomas Andrew Bennett, *Labor of God: The Agony of the Cross as the Birth of the Church* (Waco: Baylor University Press, 2017), 85.

Chapter 9: Community

1. Recent and contemporary examples include Stanley J. Grenz and Roger E. Olson, *Twentieth Century Theology: God and the World in a Transitional Age* (Downers Grove, IL: InterVarsity, 1992); Stanley J. Grenz, *Rediscovering the Triune God: The Trinity in Contemporary Theology* (Minneapolis: Fortress, 2004); Grenz, *The Social God and the Relational Self: A Trinitarian Theology of the Imago Dei* (Louisville: Westminster John Knox, 2001); Fred Sanders,

The Deep Things of God: How the Trinity Changes Everything (Wheaton: Crossway, 2010); Sanders, *Embracing the Trinity: Life with God in the Gospel* (Downers Grove, IL: InterVarsity, 2010); Sanders, *The Triune God*, New Studies in Dogmatics (Grand Rapids: Zondervan, 2016); Alan J. Torrance, *Persons in Communion: Trinitarian Description and Human Participation* (Edinburgh: T&T Clark, 1996); Thomas F. Torrance, *The Christian Doctrine of God: One Being Three Persons* (1996; repr., New York: Bloomsbury T&T Clark, 2017); Thomas F. Torrance, *The Trinitarian Faith: The Evangelical Theology of the Ancient Catholic Church*, 2nd ed. (1991; repr., New York: T&T Clark, 2006); John D. Zizioulas, *Being as Communion: Studies in Personhood and the Church* (Crestwood, NY: St. Vladimir's Seminary Press, 1985); Zizioulas, "On Being a Person: Towards an Ontology of Personhood," in *Persons, Divine and Human*, ed. Christoph Schwöbel and Colin E. Gunton (Edinburgh: T&T Clark, 1999), 33–46. For a critical but readable response to the above "trinitarian revival," see Stephen R. Holmes, *The Quest for the Trinity: The Doctrine of God in Scripture, History, and Modernity* (Downers Grove, IL: InterVarsity, 2012).

2. Friedrich Schleiermacher, a great theologian whose passion for the gospel led him to appeal not to God but to something on which his "cultural despisers" audience might agree—the human sense of the divine—made the point that the doctrine of the Trinity is the "coping stone" of the Christian faith. That is, it is a foundational article of faith. However, because his theological method centered on the human sense of the divine, although this "feeling" and "sense of absolute dependence" tells us that there must be a God, it cannot divulge the deity's identity. For this reason, Schleiermacher put the doctrine of God as Trinity at the end of his theological treatise, *The Christian Faith*, as an appendix. In doing so, Schleiermacher repositioned theological inquiry from a divine enterprise to a thoroughly human one, thus introducing the seedbed in which the later "liberal" theology would grow. For this reason, Schleiermacher is referred to as the father of liberalism, although, to be fair to Schleiermacher, he would eschew the very movement he spawned on the basis of his passion for the gospel.

3. Miroslav Volf and Matthew Croasmun, *For the Life of the World: Theology That Makes a Difference* (Grand Rapids: Brazos, 2019), 44–45. Thomas Oden, *Requiem: A Lament in Three Movements* (Nashville: Abingdon, 1995), similarly critiques the inward-facing nature of seminary theological education. See also John G. Stackhouse Jr., "Evangelical Theology Should Be Evangelical," in *Evangelical Futures: A Conversation on Theological Method*, ed. John G. Stackhouse Jr. (Grand Rapids: Baker Books, 2000), 39–58. Kevin Vanhoozer aptly describes the end result: "Scripture dwindles into human history; tradition shrivelled into human experience." *The Drama of Doctrine: A Canonical-Linguistic Approach to Christian Theology* (Louisville: Westminster John Knox, 2005), 8n21.

4. Volf and Croasmun, *For the Life of the World*, 33–59, provide a readable and penetrating critique of both the challenges facing contemporary academic theology and the crisis in which it finds iself. This should be essential reading for every student thinking of embarking on any form of theological education and training.

5. Bruce D. Marshall, "The Theologian's Ecclesial Vocation: Explaining the Difference between Loyal and Disloyal Dissent," *First Things*, October 2013, https://www.firstthings.com /article/2013/10/the-theologians-ecclesial-vocation.

6. Robert D. Putnam, *Bowling Alone: The Collapse and Revival of American Community*, new ed. (New York: Simon & Schuster, 2001).

7. Zygmunt Bauman, *Liquid Love* (Cambridge: Polity, 2003), 115. For Bauman, mixophobia is "the allergic, febrile insensitivity to strangers and the strange."

8. C. S. Lewis, *Reflections on the Psalms* (New York: Harcourt Brace Jovanovich, 1958), 92–93.

9. Douglas Farrow, "Church, Doctrine of the," in *Dictionary for Theological Interpretation of the Bible*, ed. Kevin J. Vanhoozer (Grand Rapids: Baker Academic, 2005), 115–19.

10. Brother Lawrence, *The Practice of the Presence of God: Conversations and Letters of Brother Lawrence* (Oxford: Oneworld, 1999).

11. R. C. Sproul, "What Does 'coram Deo' Mean?," Ligonier Ministries, November 13, 2017, https://www.ligonier.org/blog/what-does-coram-deo-mean/.

12. Walter Brueggemann, *God, Neighbor, Empire: The Excess of Divine Fidelity and the Command of Common Good* (Waco: Baylor University Press, 2016), 105.

13. Thomas Merton, *New Seeds of Contemplation* (Boston: Shambhala, 1961), 139–40. I like Andrew Louth's perception that similarly echoes Merton's sentiment:

> Theology is not simply a matter of learning, though we risk losing much of the wealth of theological tradition if we despise learning: rather theology is the apprehension of the believing mind combined with a right state of the heart. . . . It is tested and manifest in a life that lives close to the mystery of God in Christ, that preserves for all men a testimony to that mystery which is the object of our faith, and, so far as it is discerned, awakens in the heart a sense of wondering awe which is the light in which we see light.
> (Louth, *Discerning the Mystery* [Oxford: Clarendon, 1983], 147)

On a more practical front, see Amos Smith, *Be Still and Listen* (Orleans, MA: Paraclete, 2019).

14. In addition to Zeph. 1:7, consider Lam. 3:26, "It is good to wait quietly / for the salvation of the Lord," and Hab. 2:20, "The Lord is in his holy temple; / let all the earth be silent before him." I am grateful to Bobby Grow for this insight: "Silence, Suffering, and Worship Coram Deo with Reference to Sonderegger," *The Evangelical Calvinist* (blog), July 11, 2015, https://growrag.wordpress.com/2015/07/11/silence-suffering-and-worship-coram-deo-with-reference-to-sonderegger.

15. Iain Provan, *Seriously Dangerous Religion: What the Old Testament Really Says and Why It Matters* (Waco: Baylor University Press, 2016), 380–405.

16. Michael C. Rea, "Divine Love and Personality," in *Love, Divine and Human: Contemporary Essays in Systematic and Philosophical Theology*, ed. Oliver D. Crisp, James M. Arcadi, and Jordan Wessling (London: T&T Clark, 2020), 44–45.

17. Nicholas Wolterstorff, *Justice in Love* (Grand Rapids: Eerdmans, 2011), 38–40. See 40n21, where, in relation to C. S. Lewis's four loves (affection, friendship, eros, and charity), Wolterstorff identifies four additional loves that mirror the four Lewis offers: "These other four are need-love, gift-love, appreciation, and affection. Lewis's need-love is the same as what I call love of advantage, his gift-love is the same as what I call benevolence, his appreciation is the same as what I call attraction, and his affection is the same as what I call attachment."

18. Brueggemann, *God, Neighbor, Empire*, 6.

19. Wolterstorff, *Justice in Love*, 250.

20. Both Brueggemann and Wolterstorff draw out the Old Testament foundations for justice, its content, and its meaning in the light of the gospel. In doing so, they highlight the essential place of the Old Testament for a New Testament understanding of love: it is covenantal.

21. Breuggemann, *God, Neighbor, Empire*, 26.

22. Brueggemann, *God, Neighbor, Empire*, 27.

23. Brueggemann, *God, Neighbor, Empire*, 137.

24. Robert Banks, *Redeeming the Routines: Bringing Theology to Life* (Grand Rapids: Baker Academic, 1993), 7.

25. Banks, *Redeeming the Routines*, 135.

26. Banks, *Redeeming the Routines*, 134.

27. The turn against Christian orthodoxy being experienced in the West is paralleled by an equal turn against any form of scientific orthodoxy that might undermine or refute the views of the zeitgeist. For example, while the scientific community, on the whole, has defended centuries of scientific orthodoxy regarding male and female sexual identity, this orthodoxy no longer applies to juridical, political, or social orthodoxy. Rather, contemporary sexuality is perceived, mainly, as a personal or social construction determined by affections—how one feels—or neurons—how one thinks—about one's sexuality.

28. Zygmunt Bauman, *Culture in a Liquid Modern World* (Cambridge: Polity, 2011).

29. John 10:9; Matt. 7:13–14; John 14:6. See Provan, *Seriously Dangerous Religion*, 287–307.

30. Richard B. Hays, "Salvation by Trust? Reading the Bible Faithfully," *Christian Century*, February 26, 1997, 218–23.

31. Hays, "Salvation by Trust?," 221.

32. Hays, "Salvation by Trust?," 221.

33. Hays, "Salvation by Trust?," 222.

34. Alfred, Lord Tennyson, *In Memoriam A. H. H. OBIIT MDCCCXXXIII*: [Prelude], Poetry Foundation, https://www.poetryfoundation.org/poems/45328/in-memoriam-a-h-h -obiit-mdcccxxxiii-prelude.

35. Ingolf Dalferth, *Crucified and Resurrected: Restructuring the Grammar of Christology* (Grand Rapids: Baker Academic, 2015), xv.

36. John 3:3; Rom. 8:2; 2 Cor. 5:17; Gal. 5:16; Eph. 2:6, 19.

37. Stanley Hauerwas and William H. Willimon, *Where Resident Aliens Live: Exercises for Christian Practice* (Nashville: Abingdon, 1996), 88. See also Hauerwas and Willimon, "Why *Resident Aliens* Struck a Chord," *Missiology: An International Review* 19, no. 4 (October 1991): 419–29.

38. Brueggemann, *God, Neighbor, Empire*, 121.

39. Ingolf Dalferth makes the point even more strongly: "To describe men, mice, or mistletoe as *creatures* is not to describe them more precisely or better than the sciences, but to express the way one ought to approach them appropriately in light of God's presence." Dalferth, "'I Determine What God Is!': Theology in the Age of 'Cafeteria Religion,'" *Theology Today* 57, no. 1 (April 2000): 16.

40. Volf and Croasmun, *For the Life of the World*, 33.

41. Zygmunt Bauman, *Wasted Lives: Modernity and Its Outcasts* (Cambridge: Polity, 2004), 77. OT outsider (the poor, foreigner, widow, orphan, chronically ill) or NT outsider (Samaritan, foreigner, medically or mentally ill), we encounter the similar phenomenon of "societal human waste." Bauman unpacks this tragic dynamic further: "Refugees, the human waste of the global frontier-land, are 'the outsiders incarnate,' the absolute outsiders, outsiders everywhere and out of place everywhere except in places that are themselves out of place—the 'nowhere places' that appear on no maps used by ordinary humans on their travels. Once outside, indefinitely outside, a secure fence with watching towers is the only contraption needed to make the 'indefiniteness' of the out-of-the-place hold forever" (80).

42. D. H. Williams, *Retrieving the Tradition and Renewing Evangelicalism* (Grand Rapids: Eerdmans, 1999), 15.

43. Samuel Wells, *Incarnational Mission: Being with the World* (Grand Rapids: Eerdmans, 2018).

44. James Walters, *Loving Your Neighbour in an Age of Religious Conflict: A New Agenda for Interfaith Relations* (London: Jessica Kingsley, 2019), 111–36.

45. Rowan Williams, "Archbishop of Canterbury's Sermon at the Opening Service of the 15th Meeting of the Anglican Consultative Council," Auckland, New Zealand, October 28, 2012, http://aoc2013.brix.fatbeehive.com/articles.php/2669/archbishops-sermon-at-acc-15-on -the-reckless-love-of-god.

46. Mary Coleridge, "I Saw a Stable," in *The Lion Christian Poetry Collection*, ed. Mary Batchelor (Oxford: Lion, 1995), 260, also available at Poetry Explorer, http://poetryexplorer .net/poem.php?id=10024525.

47. William H. Willimon, "Up from Liberalism," in *Good News in Exile: Three Pastors Offer a Hopeful Vision for the Church*, ed. Martin B. Copenhaver, Anthony B. Robinson, and William H. Willimon (Grand Rapids: Eerdmans, 1998), 81.

48. Elizabeth Kent, "Embodied Evangelicalism: The Body of Christ and the Christian Body," in *New Perspectives for Evangelical Theology: Engaging with God, Scripture and the World*, ed. Tom Greggs (London: Routledge, 2010), 108.

49. Kenneth Nehrbass, *God's Image and Global Cultures: Integrating Faith and Culture in the Twenty-First Century* (Eugene, OR: Cascade Books, 2016), 141.

50. David E. Fitch, *The End of Evangelicalism? Discerning a New Faithfulness for Mission; Towards an Evangelical Political Theology* (Eugene, OR: Cascade Books, 2011), esp. chap. 10.

51. Al Tizon, *Whole and Reconciled: Gospel, Church, and Mission in a Fractured World* (Grand Rapids: Baker Academic, 2018).

52. Stanley E. Porter and Steven M. Studebaker, eds., *Evangelical Theological Method: Five Views* (Downers Grove, IL: IVP Academic, 2018), 63.

53. A. Scott Moreau, "Missiology," in *Evangelical Dictionary of Theology*, ed. Daniel J. Treier and Walter A. Elwell, 3rd ed. (Grand Rapids: Baker Academic, 2017), 554.

54. Moreau, "Missiology," 554.

55. Timothy C. Tennent, *Invitation to World Missions: A Trinitarian Missiology for the Twenty-First Century* (Grand Rapids: Kregel Academic, 2010), 2.

56. "*Mission* is far more about *God* and *who He is* than about *us* and *what we do*." Tennent, *Invitation to World Missions*, 55 (emphasis original).

57. As noted near the end of chapter 7, *perichoresis* is a theological term that helps us understand the Trinity as "the mutual indwelling—permeation—of Father, Son, and Spirit in such a way that it is not possible to conceive of one without the other two."

58. Brian Harris, *The Big Picture: Building Blocks of a Christian Worldview* (Milton Keynes, UK: Paternoster, 2015), 137–42.

59. Daniel Migliore, "The Missionary God and the Missing Church," *Princeton Seminary Bulletin*, n.s., 19, no. 1 (1998): 14–15, cited in Darrell L. Guder, *Called to Witness: Doing Missional Theology* (Grand Rapids: Eerdmans, 2015), 30.

60. Thomas Schirrmacher, *Missio Dei: God's Missional Nature* (Eugene, OR: Wipf & Stock, 2018), 33.

61. Michael P. Knowles, "Cross-Cultural Preaching: Proclaiming a Global Faith," in *The Globalization of Christianity: Implications for Christian Ministry and Theology*, ed. Gordon L. Heath and Steven M. Studebaker (Eugene, OR: Pickwick, 2015), 97.

62. Douglas McConnell, *Cultural Insights for Christian Leaders: New Directions for Organizations Serving God's Mission* (Grand Rapids: Baker Academic, 2018), 2.

63. Cited by Moreau, "Missiology," 554.

64. Christopher J. H. Wright, *The Mission of God: Unlocking the Bible's Grand Narrative* (Leicester, UK: Inter-Varsity, 2006), 61.

65. John G. Flett provides an excellent definition of *missio Dei* in this sense: "It is, first, a call for the Christian community to worship God as he is, and it belongs to God from and to all eternity to come to us in creation, reconciliation and redemption." Flett, "A Theology of Missio Dei," *Theology in Scotland* 21, no. 1 (June 2014): 75, https://ojs.st-andrews.ac.uk/index.php/TIS/article/view/1230.

66. Wells, *Incarnational Mission*, 217. See also Jill Harshaw's excellent theology of disability, *God beyond Words: Christian Theology and the Spiritual Experiences of People with Profound Intellectual Disabilities* (London: Jessica Kingsley, 2016).

67. See James K. A. Smith, *You Are What You Love: The Spiritual Power of Habit* (Grand Rapids: Brazos, 2016), 5–25.

68. Uriah Heep is a fictional character in Charles Dickens's *David Copperfield*, renowned for his fawning, obsequious, and somewhat crawling character.

69. Scott W. Sunquist, *Understanding Christian Mission: Participation in the Suffering and Glory* (Grand Rapids: Baker Academic, 2018), 172 (emphasis original).

70. Darrell L. Guder, *Called to Witness: Doing Missional Theology* (Grand Rapids: Eerdmans, 2015), 155.

71. Patrick S. Franklin, *Being Human, Being Church: The Significance of Theological Anthropology for Ecclesiology* (Milton Keynes, UK: Paternoster, 2016), 259. See also Lesslie Newbigin, *The Gospel in a Pluralist Society* (London: SPCK, 1989), 116, 242–44. Newbigin is at his best in *Proper Confidence: Faith, Doubt and Certainty in Christian Discipleship* (Grand Rapids: Eerdmans, 1995).

72. Guder, *Called to Witness*, 152.

73. See, e.g., Andrew Walls and Cathy Ross, *Mission in the Twenty-First Century: Exploring the Five Marks of Global Mission* (Maryknoll, NY: Orbis Books, 2008). The authors offer five criteria for global mission but do so without reference to the theological method necessary to establish their excellent proposal.

74. Stephen B. Bevans, *An Introduction to Theology in Global Perspective* (Maryknoll, NY: Orbis Books, 2009), 57. The immediate paragraph quoted is a masterful summary of what systematic theology looks like when it is *missio Dei*.

75. Al Tizon gives the example of the contemporary megachurch as evidence of a "gospel of empire" that serves its own purposes. *Whole and Reconciled*, 69–71.

76. Matthew Levering, *Engaging the Doctrine of Revelation: The Mediation of the Gospel through Church and Scripture* (Grand Rapids: Baker Academic, 2014), 300.

77. Porter and Studebaker, *Evangelical Theological Method*, 62.

78. Zygmunt Bauman, *The Individualized Society* (Cambridge: Polity, 2005), 2.

79. Theo Sundermeier, "*Missio Dei* Today: On the Identity of Christian Mission," *International Review of Mission* 92, no. 367 (October 2003): 560–78.

80. R. C. Hubbard, "Response to Moberly," *Ex Auditu* 24 (2008): 35.

81. Guder, *Called to Witness*, 43.

82. See Keith E. Johnson, *Rethinking the Trinity and Religious Pluralism: An Augustinian Assessment* (Downers Grove, IL: IVP Academic, 2011), 194.

83. N. T. Wright, "The Bible and Christian Mission," in *Scripture and Its Interpretation: A Global, Ecumenical Introduction to the Bible*, ed. Michael J. Gorman (Grand Rapids: Baker Academic, 2017), 389.

84. Point made by Nehrbass, *God's Image and Global Cultures*, 141.

85. Sundermeier, "*Missio Dei* Today," 28.

86. Elaine A. Robinson, *Exploring Theology* (Minneapolis: Fortress, 2014), 129.

87. Donald Opitz, *Learning for the Love of God: A Student's Guide to Academic Faithfulness*, 2nd. ed. (Grand Rapids: Brazos, 2014), 73.

88. Opitz, *Learning for the Love of God*, 74, highlights seven weekly habits of community that ensure our health in connecting up and connecting out: (1) congregational confession of faith, (2) congregational confession of sin, (3) congregational sacramental celebration of our union with Christ, (4) worship of Jesus Christ, (5) prayer to God, (6) reading of Scripture, and (7) hearing exposition.

Conclusion

1. Richard Sennett, *Together: The Rituals, Pleasures and Politics of Cooperation* (London: Allen Lane, 2012).

2. Sennett, *Together*, 17.

3. Sennett, *Together*, 88.

4. John M. G. Barclay, *Paul and the Gift* (Grand Rapids: Eerdmans, 2015), 506–8.

5. Ben Witherington, "John Barclay's *Paul and the Gift*—Part Twenty," *The Bible and Culture* (blog), November 21, 2015, https://www.patheos.com/blogs/bibleandculture/2015/11/21/john-barclays-paul-and-the-gift-part-twenty/.

6. Malcolm Gladwell, *Outliers: The Story of Success* (London: Penguin, 2008).

7. Stephen R. Holmes, *Listening to the Past: The Place of Tradition in Theology* (Grand Rapids: Baker Academic, 2003), 158–59.

8. John Douglas Morrison, *Has God Said? Scripture, the Word of God, and the Crisis of Theological Authority* (Eugene, OR: Pickwick, 2006), 278.

9. John Franke, *The Character of Theology: An Introduction to Its Nature, Task, and Purpose* (Grand Rapids: Baker Academic, 2005), 156.

10. Ellen Charry, *By the Renewing of Your Minds: The Pastoral Function of Christian Doctrine* (Oxford: Oxford University Press, 1997), 5.

11. Ingolf Dalferth, "'I Determine What God Is!' Theology in the Age of 'Cafeteria Religion,'" *Theology Today* 57, no. 1 (April 2000): 21–22.

12. Dalferth, "'I Determine What God Is!,'" 22.

13. P. T. Forsyth, *Revelation Old and New: Sermons and Addresses* (London: Independent Press, 1962).

14. David F. Ford, *Theology: A Very Short Introduction* (Oxford: Oxford University Press, 1999), 10.

15. Forsyth, *Revelation Old and New*, 80.

16. Dalferth, "'I Determine What God Is!,'" 16.

17. Robert D. Putnam, *Bowling Alone: The Collapse and Revival of American Community* (New York: Simon & Schuster, 2001).

18. Jeffrey C. Goldfarb, *The Cynical Society: The Culture of Politics and the Politics of Culture in American Life* (Chicago: University of Chicago Press, 1991).

19. Contemporary health professionals engage on a daily basis with those who live on the edge of their "self" whether in terms of the "embodied" self (body dysmorphia, anorexia, bulimia, morbid obesity, etc.) or the embodied "self" (various mental health disorders).

20. Philip E. Hughes, ed., *Creative Minds in Contemporary Theology* (Grand Rapids: Eerdmans, 1969), 25.

Bibliography

Abraham, William J. *Crossing the Threshold of Divine Revelation*. Grand Rapids: Eerdmans, 2007.

———. "The Offense of Divine Revelation." *Harvard Theological Review* 95, no. 3 (July 2002): 251–64.

Anatolios, Khaled. *Retrieving Nicaea: The Development and Meaning of Trinitarian Doctrine*. Grand Rapids: Baker Academic, 2011.

Anderson, Matthew Lee. *Earthen Vessels: Why Our Bodies Matter to Our Faith*. Bloomington, MN: Bethany House, 2011.

Anderson, Tawa J., W. Michael Clark, and David K. Naugle. *An Introduction to Christian Worldview: Pursuing God's Perspective in a Pluralistic World*. London: Apollos, 2017.

Anizor, Uche. *How to Read Theology: Engaging Doctrine Critically and Charitably*. Grand Rapids: Baker Academic, 2018.

Anselm. *Cur Deus Homo?* In *Works of St. Anselm*, translated by Sidney Norton Deane. Chicago, 1903. Internet Sacred Text Archive. https://www.sacred-texts .com/chr/ans/ans117.htm.

Ashford, Bruce Riley, and Heath A. Thomas. *The Gospel of Our King: Bible, Worldview, and the Mission of Every Christian*. Grand Rapids: Baker Academic, 2019.

Astley, Jeff. *Ordinary Theology: Looking, Listening and Learning in Theology*. London: Routledge, 2002.

———. *Studying God: Doing Theology*. London: SCM, 2014.

Augustine. *Sermons 51–94*. Translated by Edmund Hill. The Works of Saint Augustine III/3. New York: New City Press, 1991.

Baggini, Julian. *A Short History of Truth: Consolations in a Post-Truth World*. London: Quercus, 2018.

Bailey, Kenneth E. "Informal Controlled Oral Tradition and the Synoptic Gospels." *Themelios* 20, no. 2 (January 1995): 4–11.

———. *"Poet and Peasant" and "Through Peasant Eyes": A Literary-Cultural Approach to the Parables in Luke.* Grand Rapids: Eerdmans, 1983.

Balthasar, Hans Urs von. *Love Alone Is Credible.* Translated by D. C. Schindler. San Francisco: Ignatius, 2004.

———. *Word and Redemption: Essays in Theology 2.* Translated by A. V. Littledale in cooperation with Alexander Dru. New York: Herder and Herder, 1965.

Banks, Robert. *And Man Created God: Is God a Human Invention?* Oxford: Lion Books, 2011.

———. *Redeeming the Routines: Bringing Theology to Life.* Grand Rapids: Baker, 1993.

Barbour, Iain G. *Issues in Science and Religion.* 2nd ed. New York: Harper & Row, 1971.

Barclay, John M. G. *Paul and the Gift.* Grand Rapids: Eerdmans, 2015.

Barreto, Eric D., ed. *Thinking Theologically.* Minneapolis: Fortress, 2015.

Barth, Karl. *Church Dogmatics* I/1. Edited and translated by G. W. Bromiley and T. F. Torrance. Edinburgh: T&T Clark, 1975.

———. *Evangelical Theology: An Introduction.* Translated by Grover Foley. London: Weidenfield and Nicolson, 1963.

———. *The Word of God and the Word of Man.* London: Hodder & Stoughton, 1935.

Barton, John. *People of the Book? The Authority of the Bible in Christianity.* London: SPCK, 1988.

Batson, C. D., J. C. Becker, and W. M. Clark. *Commitment without Ideology.* London: SCM, 1973.

Bauckham, Richard. *Jesus and the Eyewitnesses: The Gospels as Eyewitness Testimony.* 2nd ed. Grand Rapids: Eerdmans, 2017.

———. *Scripture, Tradition and Reason: A Study in the Criteria of Christian Doctrine.* Edinburgh: T&T Clark, 1988.

Bauman, Zygmunt. *Culture in a Liquid Modern World.* Cambridge: Polity, 2011.

———. *The Individualized Society.* Cambridge: Polity, 2005.

———. *Liquid Love.* Cambridge: Polity, 2003.

———. *Wasted Lives: Modernity and Its Outcasts.* Cambridge: Polity, 2004.

Bebbington, David W. *Evangelicalism in Modern Britain: A History from the 1730s to the 1980s.* London: Unwin Hyman, 1989.

Bechtel, Carol M. "Teaching the 'Strange New World' of the Bible." *Interpretation* 56, no. 4 (October 2002): 368–77.

Bennett, Thomas Andrew. *Labor of God: The Agony of the Cross as the Birth of the Church.* Waco: Baylor University Press, 2017.

Bennett Brown, Cynthia. *Believing Thinking, Bounded Theology: The Theological Methodology of Emil Brunner*. Eugene, OR: Pickwick, 2015.

Benson, Bruce Ellis. *Graven Ideologies: Nietzsche, Derrida, and Marion on Modern Idolatry*. Downers Grove, IL: IVP Academic, 2002.

Berger, Peter L. *A Far Glory: The Quest for Faith in an Age of Credulity*. New York: Free Press, 1992.

Bertrens, Hans. *The Idea of the Postmodern: A History*. Abingdon, UK: Routledge, 1995.

Bevans, Stephen B. *An Introduction to Theology in Global Perspective*. Maryknoll, NY: Orbis Books, 2009.

———. *Models of Contextual Theology*. Maryknoll, NY: Orbis Books, 1976.

Bloesch, Donald G. *A Theology of Word and Spirit: Authority and Method in Theology*. Downers Grove, IL: InterVarsity, 1992.

Boothe, Charles Octavius. *Plain Theology for Plain People*. Bellingham, WA: Lexham, 2017.

Bridges, Jerry. *True Community: The Biblical Practice of Koinonia*. Colorado Springs: NavPress, 2012.

Brother Lawrence. *The Practice of the Presence of God: Conversations and Letters of Brother Lawrence*. Oxford: Oneworld, 1999.

Browse, Sam. "Between Truth, Sincerity and Satire: Post-Truth Politics and the Rhetoric of Authenticity." In *Metamodernism: Historicity, Affect and Depth after Postmodernism*, edited by Robert van den Akker, Alison Gibbons, and Timotheus Vermeulen, 167–81. London: Rowman & Littlefield, 2017.

Bruce, F. F. *The Canon of Scripture*. New ed. Downers Grove, IL: InterVarsity, 1988.

Brueggemann, Walter. *God, Neighbor, Empire: The Excess of Divine Fidelity and the Command of Common Good*. Waco: Baylor University Press, 2016.

———. *Hopeful Imagination: Prophetic Voices in Exile*. Philadelphia: Fortress, 1987.

———. "A Text That Redescribes." *Theology Today* 58, no. 4 (January 2002): 526–40.

Brueggemann, Walter, and Hans Walter Wolff. *The Vitality of Old Testament Traditions*. Revised ed. Louisville: Westminster John Knox, 1985.

Brunner, Emil. *The Divine-Human Encounter*. Translated by Amandus W. Loos. London: SCM, 1944.

———. *Dogmatics*. Vol. 1, *The Christian Doctrine of God*. Cambridge: J. Clark, 2002.

Burnett, David. *Clash of Worlds*. London: Monarch Books, 2002.

Burns, Bob, Tasha D. Chapman, and Donald C. Guthrie. *The Politics of Ministry: Navigating Power Dynamics and Negotiating Interests*. Downers Grove, IL: InterVarsity, 2019.

Burns, Robert. "A Red, Red Rose." Burns Country. http://www.robertburns.org /works/444.shtml.

Byerly, T. Ryan. *Introducing Critical Thinking: The Skills of Reasoning and the Virtues of Inquiry*. Grand Rapids: Baker Academic, 2017.

Cameron, Helen, Deborah Bhatti, Catherine Duce, James Sweeney, and Clare Watkins. *Talking about God in Practice: Theological Action Research and Practical Theology*. London: SCM, 2010.

Canlis, Julie. *A Theology of the Ordinary*. Wenatchee, WA: Godspeed, 2017.

Caputo, John D., and Michael J. Scanlon, eds. *God, the Gift, and Postmodernism*. Bloomington: Indiana University Press, 1999.

Carstensen, Alexandra, and Caren M. Walker. "The Paradox of Relational Development Is Not Universal: Abstract Reasoning Develops Differently across Cultures." COGSCI: The Annual Meeting of the Cognitive Science Society. https://mindmodeling.org/cogsci2017/papers/0335/paper0335.pdf.

Carter, Craig A. *Interpreting Scripture with the Great Tradition: Recovering the Genius of Premodern Exegesis*. Grand Rapids: Baker Academic, 2018.

Castelo, Daniel, and Robert W. Wall. *The Marks of Scripture: Rethinking the Nature of the Bible*. Grand Rapids: Baker Academic, 2018.

Castleman, Robbie F. *Interpreting the God-Breathed Word: How to Read and Study the Bible*. Grand Rapids: Baker Academic, 2018.

Chadwick, Henry, ed. *Lessing's Theological Writings*. London: A. and C. Black, 1956.

Charry, Ellen T. *By the Renewing of Your Minds: The Pastoral Function of Christian Doctrine*. Oxford: Oxford University Press, 1997.

———. "Experience." In *Dictionary of Systematic Theology*, edited by John Webster, Kathryn Tanner, and Iain Torrance, 413–31. Oxford: Oxford University Press, 2007.

Cherry, Stephen. *God-Curious: Exploring Eternal Questions*. London: Jessica Kingsley, 2017.

Chole, Alicia Britt. *The Sacred Slow: A Holy Departure from Fast Faith*. Nashville: W Publishing, 2017.

Chung, Sung Wook, ed. *Alister E. McGrath and Evangelical Theology: A Dynamic Engagement*. Carlisle, UK: Paternoster, 2003.

Clark, David K. "Postmodern Evangelical Apologetics?" In Chung, *Alister E. McGrath and Evangelical Theology*, 310–32.

———. *To Know and Love God*. Wheaton: Crossway, 2003.

Clark, Kelly James. *God and the Brain: The Rationality of Belief.* Grand Rapids: Eerdmans, 2019.

Clement of Rome. *The First Epistle of Clement to the Corinthians*. Translated by J. B. Lightfoot. Early Christians Writings. http://www.earlychristianwritings.com/text/1clement-lightfoot.html.

Cole, Graham A. *Faithful Theology: An Introduction*. Wheaton: Crossway, 2020.

Coleridge, Mary. "I Saw a Stable." In *The Lion Christian Poetry Collection*, edited by Mary Batchelor. Oxford: Lion, 1995. Also available at PoetryExplorer, http://poetryexplorer.net/poem.php?id=10024525.

Comer, John Mark. *The Ruthless Elimination of Hurry: How to Stay Emotionally Healthy and Spiritually Alive in the Chaos of the Modern World*. London: Hodder & Stoughton, 2019.

Comfort, Ray. *Faith Is for Weak People: Responding to the Top 20 Objections to the Gospel*. Grand Rapids: Baker Books, 2019.

Cone, Steven D. *Theology from the Great Tradition*. London: Bloomsbury T&T Clark, 2018.

Cooke, Bernard. "The Experiential 'Word of God.'" In *Consensus in Theology? A Dialogue with Hans Küng and Edward Schillebeeckx*, edited by Leonard Swidler, 69–74. Philadelphia: Westminster, 1980.

Copenhaver, Martin B., Anthony B. Robinson, and William H. Willimon. *Good News in Exile: Three Pastors Offer a Hopeful Vision for the Church*. Grand Rapids: Eerdmans, 1999.

Dalferth, Ingolf U. *Crucified and Resurrected: Restructuring the Grammar of Christology*. Grand Rapids: Baker Academic, 2015.

———. "'I Determine What God Is!' Theology in the Age of 'Cafeteria Religion.'" *Theology Today* 57, no. 1 (April 2000): 5–23.

———. *Theology and Philosophy*. Oxford: Basil Blackwell, 1988.

D'Ancona, Matthew. *Post-Truth: The New War on Truth and How to Fight Back*. London: Ebury, 2017.

Davies, William. *Nervous States: How Feeling Took Over the World*. London: Jonathan Cape, 2019.

Dawn, Marva J. *A Royal "Waste" of Time: The Splendor of Worshiping God and Being Church for the World*. Grand Rapids: Eerdmans, 1999.

Dew, James K., Jr., and Paul M. Gould. *Philosophy: A Christian Introduction*. Grand Rapids: Baker Academic, 2019.

Downey, Deane D., and Stanley E. Porter. *Christian Worldview and the Academic Disciplines*. Eugene, OR: Pickwick, 2009.

Dryden, J. de Waal. *A Hermeneutic of Wisdom: Recovering the Formative Agency of Scripture*. Grand Rapids: Baker Academic, 2018.

Duby, Steven J. *God in Himself: Scripture, Metaphysics, and the Task of Christian Theology*. London: Apollos, 2019.

Dulles, Avery. *Models of Revelation*. New York: Orbis Books, 1992.

Dunn, James D. G. *Jesus and the Spirit: A Study of the Religious and Charismatic Experience of Jesus and the First Christians as Reflected in the New Testament*. Grand Rapids: Eerdmans, 1997.

Eco, Umberto. *The Name of the Rose*. London: Picador, Pan Books, 1984.

———. *The Role of the Reader: Explorations in the Semiotics of Texts*. Bloomington: Indiana University Press, 1979.

Eliot, T. S. *The Complete Plays and Poems of T. S. Eliot*. London: Faber and Faber, 1969.

Elliott, Matthew. *Faithful Feelings: Emotion in the New Testament*. Leicester, UK: Inter-Varsity, 2005.

Emerson, Ralph Waldo. "Experience." In *The Collected Works of Ralph Waldo Emerson*. Vol. 3, *Essays: Second Series*, edited by Joseph Slater, Alfred R. Ferguson, and Jean Ferguson Carr, 25–50. Cambridge, MA: Belknap, 1983.

Everts, Janet Meyers. "The Apostle Paul and His Times: Christian History Timeline." *Christianity Today*. https://www.christianitytoday.com/history/issues/issue-47 /apostle-paul-and-his-times-christian-history-timeline.html.

Fairbairn, Douglas, and Ryan M. Reeves. *The Story of Creeds and Confessions*. Grand Rapids: Baker Academic, 2019.

Farrow, Douglas. "Church, Doctrine of the." In Vanhoozer, *Dictionary for Theological Interpretation of the Bible*, 115–19.

Fitch, David E. *The End of Evangelicalism? Discerning a New Faithfulness for Mission; Towards an Evangelical Political Theology*. Eugene, OR: Cascade Books, 2011.

Flett, John G. "A Theology of Missio Dei." *Theology in Scotland* 21, no. 1 (June 2014): 69–78. https://ojs.st-andrews.ac.uk/index.php/TIS/article/view/1230.

Florovsky, Georges. *Bible, Church, Tradition: An Eastern Orthodox View*. Vol. 1 of *The Collected Works of Georges Florovsky*. Belmont, MA: Nordland, 1972.

Foley, Edward. *Theological Reflection across Religious Traditions: The Turn to Reflective Believing*. Lanham, MD: Rowman & Littlefield, 2015.

Ford, David F. *Theology: A Very Short Introduction*. Oxford: Oxford University Press, 1999.

Forsyth, P. T. *The Principle of Authority*. 2nd ed. London: Independent, 1952. First published 1913.

———. *Revelation Old and New: Sermons and Addresses*. London: Independent, 1962.

Frame, John M. *A History of Western Philosophy and Theology*. Phillipsburg, NJ: P&R, 2015.

Franke, John. *The Character of Theology: An Introduction to Its Nature, Task, and Purpose*. Grand Rapids: Baker Academic, 2005.

———. "Missional Theology." In *Evangelical Dictionary of Theology*, edited by Daniel J. Treier and Walter A. Elwell, 555. 3rd ed. Grand Rapids: Baker Academic, 2017.

Franklin, Patrick S. *Being Human, Being Church: The Significance of Theological Anthropology for Ecclesiology*. Milton Keynes, UK: Paternoster, 2016.

Gardner, W. H., and N. H. MacKenzie, eds. *The Poems of Gerard Manley Hopkins*. Oxford: Oxford University Press, 1970.

Gay, Craig M. *Modern Technology and the Human Future: A Christian Appraisal*. Downers Grove, IL: IVP Academic, 2018.

George, Timothy. "A Theology to Die For." *Christianity Today*, February 9, 1998. https://www.christianitytoday.com/ct/1998/february9/8t2049.html.

Gertz, Christopher, and Mark Pattie III. *The Pietist Option: Hope for the Renewal of the Church*. Downers Grove, IL: IVP Academic, 2017.

Gladwell, Malcolm. *Outliers: The Story of Success*. London: Penguin, 2008.

Goldfarb, Jeffrey C. *The Cynical Society: The Culture of Politics and the Politics of Culture in American Life*. Chicago: University of Chicago Press, 1991.

Goldingay, John. *Models for Scripture*. Grand Rapids: Eerdmans, 1994.

Gordon, Joseph K. *Divine Scripture in Human Understanding: A Systematic Theology of the Christian Bible*. Notre Dame, IN: University of Notre Dame Press, 2019.

Gorman, Michael J., ed. *Scripture and Its Interpretation: A Global, Ecumenical Introduction to the Bible*. Grand Rapids: Baker Academic, 2017.

Green, Christopher C., and David I. Starling, eds. *Revelation and Reason in Christian Theology*. Bellingham, WA: Lexham, 2018.

Green, Joel B. "Scripture and Theology: Uniting the Two So Long Divided." In Green and Turner, *Between Two Horizons*, 23–43.

Green, Joel B., and Max Turner, eds. *Between Two Horizons: Spanning New Testament Studies and Systematic Theology*. Grand Rapids: Eerdmans, 2000.

Gregersen, Niels H., and Wentzel van Huyssteen, eds. *Rethinking Theology and Science: Six Models for the Current Dialogue*. Grand Rapids: Eerdmans, 1998.

Greggs, Tom, ed. *New Perspectives for Evangelical Theology: Engaging with God, Scripture and the World*. London: Routledge, 2010.

Gregory of Nyssa. *Life of Moses*. Translated by Abraham J. Malherbe and Everett Ferguson. Classics of Western Spirituality. New York: Paulist Press, 1978.

Grenz, Stanley J. *Rediscovering the Triune God: The Trinity in Contemporary Theology*. Minneapolis: Fortress, 2004.

———. *The Social God and the Relational Self: A Trinitarian Theology of the Imago Dei*. Louisville: Westminster John Knox, 2001.

Grenz, Stanley J., and Roger E. Olson. *Twentieth-Century Theology: God and the World in a Transitional Age*. Downers Grove, IL: InterVarsity, 1992.

———. *Who Needs Theology? An Invitation to the Study of God*. Leicester, UK: Inter-Varsity, 1996.

Grow, Bobby. "Silence, Suffering, and Worship Coram Deo with Reference to Sonderegger." *The Evangelical Calvinist* (blog), July 11, 2015. https://growrag.word press.com/2015/07/11/silence-suffering-and-worship-coram-deo-with-reference -to-sonderegger/.

Guder, Darrell L. *Called to Witness: Doing Missional Theology*. Grand Rapids: Eerdmans, 2015.

Gunton, Colin. *The Actuality of Atonement: A Study of Metaphor, Rationality and the Christian Tradition*. Edinburgh: T&T Clark, 1988.

———. *A Brief Theology of Revelation*. Edinburgh: T&T Clark, 1995.

———. *The Christian Faith: An Introduction to Christian Doctrine*. Oxford: Blackwell, 2002.

———. "Creation and Mediation in the Theology of Robert W. Jenson: An Encounter and a Convergence." In *Trinity, Time, and Church: A Response to the Theology of Robert W. Jenson*, edited by Colin E. Gunton, 80–93. Grand Rapids: Eerdmans, 2000.

———. "Dogma, the Church and the Task of Theology." In *Doctrines and Dogmas*, edited by Victor Pfitzner and Hilary Regan, 1–22. Edinburgh: T&T Clark, 1999.

———. *Enlightenment and Alienation: An Essay toward a Trinitarian Theology*. Basingstoke, UK: Marshall Morgan & Scott, 1985.

———. *The Promise of Trinitarian Theology*. 2nd ed. Edinburgh: T&T Clark, 1997.

———. *Theology through Preaching*. Edinburgh: T&T Clark, 2001.

———. *Theology through the Theologians: Selected Essays, 1972–1995*. London: Bloomsbury, 2003.

———. *The Triune Creator: A Historical and Systematic Study*. Edinburgh: Edinburgh University Press, 1998.

———. "The Truth . . . and the Spirit of Truth: The Trinitarian Shape of Christian Theology." In *Loving God with Our Minds: The Pastor as Theologian; Essays in Honor of Wallace M. Alston*, edited by Michael Welker and Cynthia A. Jarvis, 341–51. Grand Rapids: Eerdmans, 2005.

———. "Using and Being Used: Scripture and Systematic Theology." *Theology Today* 47, no. 3 (October 1990): 248–59.

Gunton, Colin, Stephen R. Holmes, and Murray A. Rae, eds. *The Practice of Theology: A Reader*. London: SCM, 2001.

Haldeman, Isaac Massey. *Signs of the Times*. 5th ed. New York: Charles C. Cook, 1914.

Harakas, Stanley S. "Doing Theology Today: An Orthodox and Evangelical Dialog on Theological Method." *Pro Ecclesia* 11, no. 4 (Fall 2002): 435–62.

Harris, Brian. *The Big Picture: Building Blocks of a Christian Worldview*. Milton Keynes, UK: Paternoster, 2015.

Harshaw, Jill. *God beyond Words: Christian Theology and the Spiritual Experiences of People with Profound Intellectual Disabilities*. London: Jessica Kingsley, 2016.

Hart, Trevor. *Faith Thinking: The Dynamics of Christian Theology*. London: SPCK, 1995.

———. *Regarding Karl Barth: Essays toward a Reading of His Theology*. Carlisle, UK: Paternoster, 1999.

———. "Tradition, Authority, and a Christian Approach to the Bible as Scripture." In Green and Turner, *Between Two Horizons*, 183–204.

Hasel, Gerhard F. "Divine Inspiration and the Canon of the Bible." *Journal of the Adventist Theological Society* 5, no. 1 (1994): 68–105.

Hauerwas, Stanley, and William H. Willimon. *Where Resident Aliens Live: Exercises for Christian Practice*. Nashville: Abingdon, 1996.

———. "Why *Resident Aliens* Struck a Chord." *Missiology: An International Review* 19, no. 4 (October 1991): 419–29.

Hays, Richard B. "Can the Gospels Teach Us How to Read the Old Testament?" *Pro Ecclesia* 11, no. 4 (2002): 402–18.

———. "Salvation by Trust? Reading the Bible Faithfully." *Christian Century*, February 26, 1997, 218–23.

Heath, Gordon L., and Steven M. Studebaker. *The Globalization of Christianity: Implications for Christian Ministry and Theology.* Eugene, OR: Pickwick, 2015.

Heidegger, Martin. *Introduction to Metaphysics.* New Haven: Yale University Press, 1959.

Hessert, Paul. *Introduction to Christianity.* Englewood Cliffs, NJ: Prentice-Hall, 1958.

Hicks, Peter. *The Journey So Far: Philosophy through the Ages.* Grand Rapids: Zondervan, 2003.

Holmes, Stephen R. *Listening to the Past: The Place of Tradition in Theology.* Grand Rapids: Baker Academic, 2003.

———. *The Quest for the Trinity: The Doctrine of God in Scripture, History, and Modernity.* Downers Grove, IL: InterVarsity, 2012.

Hooker, Richard. *The Laws of Ecclesiastical Polity.* Vol. 1 of *The Works of That Learned and Judicious Divine Mr. Richard Hooker with an Account of His Life and Death by Isaac Walton,* arranged by John Keble, 7th ed. revised by R. W. Church and F. Paget. Oxford, 1888. Available at http://oll.libertyfund.org/titles /hooker-the-works-of-richard-hooker-vol-1.

Hopkins, Gerard Manley. "God's Grandeur." In *The Poems of Gerard Manley Hopkins,* edited by W. H. Gardner and N. H. MacKenzie, 66. Oxford: Oxford University Press, 1970.

Hubbard, R. C. "Response to Moberly." *Ex Auditu* 24 (2008): 34–36.

Hughes, Philip E. *Creative Minds in Contemporary Theology.* Grand Rapids: Eerdmans, 1969.

Humphrey, Edith M. *Scripture and Tradition: What the Bible Really Says.* Grand Rapids: Baker Academic, 2013.

Hurtado, Larry W. *How on Earth Did Jesus Become a God? Historical Questions about Earliest Devotion to Jesus.* Grand Rapids: Eerdmans, 2005.

Hutcheon, Linda. *A Poetics of Postmodernism: History, Theory, Fiction.* New York: Routledge, 1980.

Irenaeus. *Against Heresies,* book 3. In *The Early Church Fathers and Other Works.* Grand Rapids: Eerdmans, 1867. Available at CatholicCulture.org, https://www .catholicculture.org/culture/library/view.cfm?recnum=3830.

James, William. *The Varieties of Religious Experience: A Study in Human Nature.* Gifford Lectures on Natural Religion, Delivered in Edinburgh, 1901–1902. London: Longmans, Green, 1935.

Jefford, Clayton N. *Reading the Apostolic Fathers: A Student's Introduction.* 2nd ed. Grand Rapids: Baker Academic, 2012.

Jenson, Robert W. *A Theology in Outline: Can These Bones Live?* Transcribed, edited, and introduced by Adam Eitel. Oxford: Oxford University Press, 2016.

Johnson, Keith E. *Rethinking the Trinity and Religious Pluralism: An Augustinian Assessment*. Downers Grove, IL: IVP Academic, 2011.

Johnston, Robert K. *God's Wider Presence: Reconsidering General Revelation*. Grand Rapids: Baker Academic, 2014.

Jones, Gareth. *Christian Theology*. Oxford: Polity, 1999.

Kapic, Kelly M. *A Little Book for New Theologians: Why and How to Study Theology*. Downers Grove, IL: InterVarsity, 2012.

Kärkkäinen, Veli-Matti. *Christology: A Global Introduction; An Ecumenical, International, and Contextual Perspective*. Grand Rapids: Baker Academic, 2003.

Keener, Craig S. "A Common Objection to Studying in Context." CraigKeener.com, April 20, 2012. http://www.craigkeener.com/tag/special-revelation.

———. *The Mind of the Spirit: Paul's Approach to Transformed Thinking*. Grand Rapids: Baker Academic, 2016.

———. *Spirit Hermeneutics: Reading Scripture in Light of Pentecost*. Grand Rapids: Eerdmans, 2016.

Kelly, J. N. D. *Early Christian Doctrines*. 5th ed. London: Adam & Charles Black, 1977.

Kent, Elizabeth. "Embodied Evangelicalism: The Body of Christ and the Christian Body." In Greggs, *New Perspectives for Evangelical Theology*, 108–22.

Kidd, Thomas S. *Who Is an Evangelical? The History of a Movement in Crisis*. New Haven: Yale University Press, 2019.

Knell, Matthew. "Lessons for an Evangelical Spirituality from Bernard of Clairvaux and Thomas Merton." In *Learning from the Past: Essays on Reception, Catholicity, and Dialogue in Honour of Anthony N. S. Lane*, edited by Jon Balserak and Richard Snoddy, 230–31. London: Bloomsbury T&T Clark, 2015.

Knowles, Michael P. "Cross-Cultural Preaching: Proclaiming a Global Faith." In *The Globalization of Christianity: Implications for Christian Ministry and Theology*, edited by Gordon L. Heath and Steven M. Studebaker, 69–84. Eugene, OR: Pickwick, 2015.

Kreider, Glenn R., and Michael J. Svigel. *A Practical Primer on Theological Method*. Grand Rapids: Zondervan Academic, 2019.

Kuhn, Thomas. *The Structure of Scientific Revolutions*. 2nd ed. Chicago: University of Chicago Press, 1970.

Lamb, William. *Scripture: A Guide for the Perplexed*. London: Bloomsbury T&T Clark, 2013.

Lamberth, David M. "Putting 'Experience' to the Test in Theological Reflection." *Harvard Theological Review* 93, no. 1 (2000): 67–77.

Lane, A. N. S. "Scripture, Tradition and Church: An Historical Survey." *Vox Evangelica* 9 (1975): 37–55.

Latourelle, René. *Theology of Revelation*. New York: Alba House, 1967.

Leithart, Peter J. *Against Christianity*. Moscow, ID: Canon, 2003.

———. "Biblical Truth." *Leithart* (blog), June 1, 2016. https://www.patheos.com/blogs/leithart/2016/06/biblical-truth.

Levering, Matthew. *Engaging the Doctrine of Revelation: The Mediation of the Gospel through Church and Scripture*. Grand Rapids: Baker Academic, 2014.

Levy, Ian Christopher. *Introducing Medieval Biblical Interpretation: The Senses of Scripture in Premodern Exegesis*. Grand Rapids: Baker Academic, 2018.

Lewis, C. S. *Mere Christianity*. Glasgow, UK: Fontana, 1978.

———. *Reflections on the Psalms*. New York: Harcourt Brace Jovanovich, 1958.

———. *Surprised by Joy: The Shape of My Early Life*. London: William Collins, 1955.

———. *The Weight of Glory, and Other Addresses: A Collection of Lewis's Most Moving Addresses*. London: William Collins, 2013.

Lewis, Gordon R., and Bruce A. Demarest. *Integrative Theology*. 3 vols. Grand Rapids: Academie, 1987.

Liss, Steven. "Orthodoxy, Orthopraxy, and Orthopathy: Series on Sanctification (Part Two)." *Christian Paradoxes* (blog), February 24, 2016. https://christianparadoxes.blogspot.com/2016/02/orthodoxy-orthopraxy-and-orthopathy.html.

Lonergan, Bernard. *Early Works on Theological Method 1*. Vol. 22 of *Collected Works of Bernard Lonergan*. Toronto: University of Toronto Press, 2010.

Longman, Tremper, III. *The Fear of the Lord Is Wisdom: A Theological Introduction to Wisdom in Israel*. Grand Rapids: Baker Academic, 2017.

Lott, David B., ed. *Douglas John Hall: Collected Readings*. Minneapolis: Fortress, 2013.

Louth, Andrew. *Discerning the Mystery*. Oxford: Clarendon, 1983.

Lovin, Robin W., and Joshua Mauldin, eds. *Theology as Interdisciplinary Inquiry: Learning with and from the Natural and Human Sciences*. Grand Rapids: Eerdmans, 2017.

MacIntyre, Alasdair. *After Virtue: A Study in Moral Theology*. 3rd ed. Notre Dame, IN: University of Notre Dame Press, 2007.

———. *Whose Justice? Which Rationality?* Notre Dame, IN: University of Notre Dame Press, 1988.

Marcel, Gabriel. *The Mystery of Being*. Chicago: Henry Regnery, 1969.

Marshall, Bruce D. "The Theologian's Ecclesial Vocation: Explaining the Difference between Loyal and Disloyal Dissent." *First Things*, October 2013. https://www.firstthings.com/article/2013/10/the-theologians-ecclesial-vocation.

Marty, Martin E. *The Public Church: Mainline, Evangelical, Catholic*. New York: Crossroad, 1981.

McConnell, Douglas. *Cultural Insights for Christian Leaders: New Directions for Organizations Serving God's Mission*. Grand Rapids: Baker Academic, 2018.

McDermott, Gerald R. *Everyday Glory: The Revelation of God in All of Reality*. Grand Rapids: Baker Academic, 2018.

———, ed. *The Oxford Handbook of Evangelical Theology*. Oxford: Oxford University Press, 2010.

McFarlane, Graham W. P. "Fundamentalism and Fundamentals." *Franciscan* 15, no. 3 (September 2003): 1–2.

———. *Why Do You Believe What You Believe about Jesus?* Eugene, OR: Wipf & Stock, 2009.

McGrath, Alister E. *Christian Theology: An Introduction*. 6th ed. Oxford: Wiley & Sons, 2017.

———. "Faith and Tradition." In McDermott, *Oxford Handbook of Evangelical Theology*, 81–95.

———. *Historical Theology*. London: Blackwell, 1998.

———. *A Passion for Truth: The Intellectual Coherence of Evangelicalism*. Downers Grove, IL: InterVarsity, 1996.

———. *The Science of God: An Introduction to Scientific Theology*. London: T&T Clark, 2004.

McIntosh, Mark A. *Divine Teaching: An Introduction to Christian Theology*. Oxford: Blackwell, 2008.

McIntyre, Lee. *Post-Truth*. Cambridge, MA: MIT Press, 2018.

McKnight, Scot. *Galatians*. Grand Rapids: Zondervan, 1995.

McNair, Brian. *Fake News: Falsehood, Fabrication and Fantasy in Journalism*. London: Routledge, 2018.

Meador, Jake. *In Search of the Common Good: Christian Fidelity in a Fractured World*. Downers Grove, IL: InterVarsity, 2019.

Meek, Esther Lightcap. *Loving to Know: Introducing Covenant Epistemology*. Eugene, OR: Cascade Books, 2011.

Merleau-Ponty, Maurice. *Signs*. Translated by Richard C. McCleary. Evanston, IL: Northwestern University Press, 1964.

Merton, Thomas. *Love and Living*. London: Sheldon, 1979.

———. *New Seeds of Contemplation*. Boston: Shambhala, 1961.

Meyer, Jan H. F., and Ray Land. *Threshold Concepts and Troublesome Knowledge: Linkages to Ways of Thinking and Practising within the Disciplines*. ETL Project Occasional Report 4. Edinburgh: ETL Project, University of Edinburgh, 2003. http://www.etl.tla.ed.ac.uk/docs/ETLreport4.pdf.

Meyer, Jan H. F., Ray Land, and Caroline Baillie, eds. *Threshold Concepts and Transformational Learning*. Rotterdam: Sense, 2010.

Mezei, Balázs. *Radical Revelation*. London: Bloomsbury, 2017.

Migliore, Daniel L. *Faith Seeking Understanding: An Introduction to Christian Theology*. 3rd ed. Grand Rapids: Eerdmans, 2014.

———. "The Missionary God and the Missing Church." *Princeton Seminary Bulletin*, n.s., 19, no. 1 (1998): 14–15.

Moberly, R. W. L. *The Bible, Theology, and Faith: A Study of Abraham and Jesus.* Cambridge: Cambridge University Press, 2000.

———. "In God We Trust?" *Ex Auditu* 24 (2008): 18–33.

Molloy, Michael. *The Christian Experience: An Introduction to Christianity.* London: Bloomsbury Academic, 2017.

Moreau, A. Scott. "Missiology." In Treier and Elwell, *Evangelical Dictionary of Theology,* 552–55.

Moreland, J. P. *Kingdom Triangle: Recover the Christian Mind, Renovate the Soul, Restore the Spirit's Power.* Grand Rapids: Zondervan, 2007.

———. *Love Your God with All Your Mind: The Role of Reason in the Life of the Soul.* Colorado Springs: NavPress, 2012.

Morrison, John Douglas. *Has God Said? Scripture, the Word of God, and the Crisis of Theological Authority.* Eugene, OR: Pickwick, 2006.

Mouw, Richard J. *Restless Faith: Holding Evangelical Beliefs in a World of Contested Labels.* Grand Rapids: Brazos, 2019.

Murphy, Nancey. *Beyond Liberalism and Fundamentalism: How Modern and Postmodern Philosophy Set the Theological Agenda.* Harrisburg, PA: Trinity Press International, 1996.

Murray, Abdu. *Saving Truth: Finding Meaning and Clarity in a Post-Truth World.* Grand Rapids: Zondervan, 2018.

Neder, Adam. *Theology as a Way of Life: On Teaching and Learning the Christian Faith.* Grand Rapids: Baker Academic, 2019.

Nehrbass, Kenneth. *God's Image and Global Cultures: Integrating Faith and Culture in the Twenty-First Century.* Eugene, OR: Cascade Books, 2016.

Newbigin, Lesslie. *The Gospel in a Pluralist Society.* London: SPCK, 1989.

———. *Proper Confidence: Faith, Doubt, and Certainty in Christian Discipleship.* Grand Rapids: Eerdmans, 1995.

———. "What Kind of Certainty?" *Tyndale Bulletin* 44, no. 2 (1993): 339–50.

Newman, John H. *Fifteen Sermons Preached before the University of Oxford.* 3rd ed. Notre Dame, IN: University of Notre Dame Press, 1997.

Noll, Mark, Cornelius Plantinga Jr., and David Wells. "Evangelical Theology Today." *Theology Today* 51, no. 4 (January 1995): 495–507.

Oden, Thomas. *Requiem: A Lament in Three Movements.* Nashville: Abingdon, 1995.

Ogden, Schubert M. *The Point of Christology.* London: SCM, 1982.

Okholm, Dennis. *Learning Theology through the Church's Worship.* Grand Rapids: Baker Academic, 2018.

Oliver, Simon. "Introducing Radical Orthodoxy." In *The Radical Orthodoxy Reader,* edited by John Milbank and Simon Oliver, 3–27. London: Routledge, 2009.

Olson, Roger E. "The Future of Evangelical Theology." *Christianity Today,* February 9, 1998, 40–48.

————. "Thoughts about the Role of Experience in Theology: Part One." *My Evangelical Arminian Theological Musings* (blog), November 28, 2014. www.patheos
.com/blogs/rogereolson/.2014/11/thoughts-about-the-role-of-experience-in-theol
ogy-part-one/.

————. "Thoughts about the Role of Experience in Theology: Part Two (with Special
Reference to Friedrich Schleiermacher and Stanley J. Grenz." *My Evangelical Arminian Theological Musings* (blog), November 30, 2014. https://www.patheos.com/blogs
/rogereolson/2014/11/thoughts-about-the-role-of-experience-in-theology-part-two
-with-special-reference-to-friedrich-schleiermacher-and-stanley-j-grenz/.

Opitz, Donald. *Learning for the Love of God: A Student's Guide to Academic Faithfulness*. 2nd ed. Grand Rapids: Brazos, 2014.

Ortlund, Gavin. *Theological Retrieval for Evangelicals: Why We Need Our Past to Have a Future*. Wheaton: Crossway, 2019.

Ott, Craig. "Maps, Improvisation, and Games: Retaining Biblical Authority in Local Theology." *Evangelical Quarterly* 89, no. 3 (July 2018): 195–208.

Ottati, Douglas J. "Conclusion: A Collaborative Manner of Theological Reflection." In Lovin and Mauldin, *Theology as Interdisciplinary Inquiry*, 132–60.

Outler, Albert C., ed. *John Wesley*. Oxford: Oxford University Press, 1964.

Owen, John. *The Works of John Owen*. Vol. 3, *The Holy Spirit*. Edinburgh: Banner of Truth Trust, 1965.

Packer, James I. *Fundamentalism and the Word of God*. Grand Rapids: Eerdmans, 1958.

————. "Maintaining Evangelical Theology." In Stackhouse, *Evangelical Futures*, 186–89.

Palmer, Parker. *To Know as We Are Known: Education as a Spiritual Journey*. San Francisco: HarperSanFrancisco, 1966.

Pannenberg, Wolfhart. *Theology and the Philosophy of Science*. London: Darton, Longman & Todd, 1976.

————. *Toward a Theology of Nature: Essays on Science and Faith*. Louisville: Westminster John Knox, 1993.

Parker, Stephen E. *Led by the Spirit: Toward a Practical Theology of Pentecostal Discernment and Decision Making*. Expanded ed. Cleveland, TN: CPT Press, 2015.

Pauw, Amy Plantinga. *Church in Ordinary Time: A Wisdom Ecclesiology*. Grand Rapids: Eerdmans, 2017.

Peacocke, Arthur R. *The Sciences and Theology in the Twentieth Century*. Stocksfield, UK: Oriel, 1981.

Pearcey, Nancy R. *Total Truth: Liberating Christianity from Its Cultural Captivity*. Wheaton: Crossway, 2004.

Peckham, John C. *Canonical Theology: The Biblical Canon, Sola Scriptura, and Theological Method*. Grand Rapids: Eerdmans, 2016.

Peeler, Lance J. "Thinking Bodily." In *Thinking Theologically*, ed. Eric D. Barreto, 23–34. Minneapolis: Fortress, 2015.

Pelikan, Jaroslav. *The Vindication of Tradition*. New Haven: Yale University Press, 1984.

Pfitzner, Victor, and Hilary Regan, eds. *The Task of Theology Today*. Edinburgh: T&T Clark, 1998.

Plantinga, Alvin. *Warranted Christian Belief*. New York: Oxford University Press, 2000.

Polanyi, Michael. *Personal Knowledge: Towards a Post-Critical Philosophy*. London: Routledge, 1998. First published 1958.

———. *The Tacit Dimension*. New York: Anchor Books, 1967.

Polkinghorne, John. *Science and Christian Belief*. London: SPCK, 1994.

Porter, Stanley E., and Steven M. Studebaker, eds. *Evangelical Theological Method: Five Views*. Downers Grove, IL: IVP Academic, 2018.

Porter, Steven L. "Wesleyan Theological Methodology as a Theory of Integration." *Journal of Psychology and Theology* 32, no. 3 (2004): 190–99.

Postman, Neil. *Amusing Ourselves to Death*. London: Methuen, 1997.

Provan, Iain. *Seriously Dangerous Religion: What the Old Testament Really Says and Why It Matters*. Waco: Baylor University Press, 2016.

Pullinger, Jackie, and Andrew Quicke. *Chasing the Dragon*. Rev. ed. London: Hodder & Stoughton, 2006.

Putnam, Robert D. *Bowling Alone: The Collapse and Revival of American Community*. New York: Simon & Schuster, 2001.

Rae, Murray. "Reflecting on Experience of God." In *The Practice of Theology: A Reader*, edited by Colin E. Gunton, Stephen R. Holmes, and Murray Rae, 185–89. London: SCM, 2001.

Rea, Michael C. "Divine Love and Personality." In *Love, Divine and Human: Contemporary Essays in Systematic and Philosophical Theology*, edited by Oliver D. Crisp, James M. Arcadi, and Jordan Wessling, 43–61. London: T&T Clark, 2020.

Reichenbach, David. "Divine Revelation: Discernment and Interpretation." In *For Faith and Clarity: Philosophical Contributions to Christian Theology*, edited by James K. Beilby, 85–112. Grand Rapids: Baker Academic, 2006.

Robinson, Elaine A. *Exploring Theology*. Minneapolis: Fortress, 2014.

Sacks, Jonathan. *Covenant and Conversation: A Weekly Reading of the Jewish Bible*. Vol. 3, *Leviticus: The Book of Holiness*. Jerusalem: Maggid Books, 2015.

Samples, Kenneth Richard. *A World of Difference: Putting Christian Truth-Claims to the Worldview Test*. Grand Rapids: Baker Books, 2007.

Sanders, Fred. *The Deep Things of God: How the Trinity Changes Everything*. Wheaton: Crossway, 2010.

———. *Embracing the Trinity: Life with God in the Gospel*. Downers Grove, IL: InterVarsity, 2010.

———. "Jesus Loves Karl Barth." *Scriptorium Daily*, August 3, 2012. http://scriptoriumdaily.com/jesus-loves-karl-barth-2.

————. *The Triune God*. New Studies in Dogmatics. Grand Rapids: Zondervan, 2016.

Schaeffer, Francis A. *How Should We Then Live?* 50th L'Abri anniversary edition. Wheaton: Crossway, 2005.

Schaff, Philip, ed. *Creeds of Christendom, with a History and Critical Notes*. Vol. 1, *The History of Creeds*. Revised by David S. Schaff. Grand Rapids: Baker, 1983. First published 1877.

Schillebeeckx, Edward. *Interim Report on the Books "Jesus" and "Christ."* New York: Crossroad, 1981.

Schirrmacher, Thomas. *Missio Dei: God's Missional Nature*. Eugene, OR: Wipf & Stock, 2018.

Schleiermacher, F. D. E. *The Christian Faith*. Edited and translated by H. R. Mackintosh and J. S. Stewart. Edinburgh: T&T Clark, 1986.

Segundo, J. L. *The Liberation of Theology*. Maryknoll, NY: Orbis Books, 1976.

Sennett, Richard. *Together: The Rituals, Pleasures and Politics of Cooperation*. London: Allen Lane, 2012.

Shults, F. LeRon, and Steven J. Sandage. *Transforming Spirituality: Integrating Theology and Psychology*. Grand Rapids: Baker Academic, 2006.

Sire, James. *Naming the Elephant: Worldview as a Concept*. Nottingham, UK: InterVarsity, 2004.

Smith, Amos. *Be Still and Listen*. Orleans, MA: Paraclete, 2019.

Smith, James K. A. *On the Road with Saint Augustine: A Real-World Spirituality for Restless Hearts*. Grand Rapids: Brazos, 2019.

Sonderegger, Katherine. *Systematic Theology*. Vol. 1, *The Doctrine of God*. Minneapolis: Fortress, 2015.

Sproul, R. C. "What Does 'Coram Deo' Mean?" Ligonier Ministries, November 13, 2017. https://www.ligonier.org/blog/what-does-coram-deo-mean.

Stackhouse, Ian. *Praying Psalms: A Personal Journey through the Psalter*. Eugene, OR: Cascade Books, 2018.

Stackhouse, John G., Jr., ed. *Evangelical Futures: A Conversation on Theological Method*. Grand Rapids: Baker Books, 2000.

————. "Evangelical Theology Should Be Evangelical." In Stackhouse, *Evangelical Futures*, 39–58.

Stanglin, Keith D. *The Letter and Spirit of Biblical Interpretation: From the Early Church to Modern Practice*. Grand Rapids: Baker Academic, 2018.

Stark, Rodney. "A Taxonomy of Religious Experience." *Journal for the Scientific Study of Religion* 5, no. 1 (1965): 97–116.

Stetzer, Ed. "Trends in Church Architecture, Part 1." The Exchange, July 18, 2016. https://www.christianitytoday.com/edstetzer/2016/july/trends-in-church-architecture-part-1.html.

Stone, Bryan. *Evangelism after Pluralism: The Ethics of Christian Witness*. Grand Rapids: Baker Academic, 2018.

Stone, Howard W., and James O. Duke. *How to Think Theologically*. 3rd ed. Minneapolis: Fortress, 2013.

Stump, Jim B., and Alan G. Padgett, eds. *The Blackwell Companion to Science and Christianity*. Malden: Blackwell, 2012.

Sundermeier, Theo. "*Missio Dei* Today: On the Identity of Christian Mission." *International Review of Mission* 92, no. 367 (October 2003): 560–78.

Sunquist, Scott W. *Understanding Christian Mission: Participation in Suffering and Glory*. Grand Rapids: Baker Academic, 2018.

Sweetman, Brendan, ed. *The Failure of Modernism: The Cartesian Legacy and Contemporary Pluralism*. Washington, DC: Catholic University of America Press, 1999.

Swinburne, Richard. *The Existence of God*. Oxford: Clarendon, 1979.

Sykes, Stephen W. "Theological Study: The Nineteenth Century and After." In *The Philosophical Frontiers of Christian Theology: Essays Presented to D. M. MacKinnon*, edited by Brian Hebblethwaite and Stewart R. Sutherland, 95–118. Cambridge: Cambridge University Press, 1982.

Tennent, Timothy C. *Invitation to World Missions: A Trinitarian Missiology for the Twenty-First Century*. Grand Rapids: Kregel Academic, 2010.

Tennyson, Alfred, Lord. *In Memoriam A. H. H. OBIIT MDCCCXXXIII*: [Prelude]. Poetry Foundation, https://www.poetryfoundation.org/poems/45328/in-memoriam-a-h-h-obiit-mdcccxxxiii-prelude.

Tertullian. *Prescription against Heretics*. Translated by Peter Holmes. In *Latin Christianity: Its Founder, Tertullian*, 243–65. Vol. 3 of *The Ante-Nicene Fathers: Translations of the Writings of the Fathers Down to A.D. 325*. Edited by Alexander Roberts and James Donaldson. 10 vols. New York: Christian Literature, 1885–87. Reprint, Peabody, MA: Hendrickson, 1994.

Thielicke, Helmut. *A Little Exercise for Young Theologians*. Grand Rapids: Eerdmans, 2016.

Thiselton, Anthony C. *The Hermeneutics of Doctrine*. Grand Rapids: Eerdmans, 2007.

Thornhill, John. *Christianity's Estranged Child Reconstructed*. Grand Rapids: Eerdmans, 2000.

Thorsen, Don. *The Wesleyan Quadrilateral: Scripture, Tradition, Reason, and Experience as a Model of Evangelical Theology*. Lexington: Emeth, 2005. First published 1990.

Tidball, Derek J. *Who Are the Evangelicals?* London: Marshall Pickering, 1994.

Tizon, Al. *Whole and Reconciled: Gospel, Church, and Mission in a Fractured World*. Grand Rapids: Baker Academic, 2018.

Torrance, Alan J. *Persons in Communion: Trinitarian Description and Human Participation*. Edinburgh: T&T Clark, 1996.

Torrance, Thomas F. *The Christian Doctrine of God: One Being Three Persons*. New York: Bloomsbury T&T Clark, 2017. First published 1996 by A&C Black (Oxford).

———. "The Deposit of Faith." *Scottish Journal of Theology* 36, no. 1 (1983): 1–28.

———. *Theological Science*. Edinburgh: T&T Clark, 1996.

———. *The Trinitarian Faith: The Evangelical Theology of the Ancient Catholic Church*. 2nd ed. New York: T&T Clark, 1991. Reprinted 2006.

Toulmin, Stephen. *Cosmopolis: The Hidden Agenda of Modernity*. Chicago: University of Chicago Press, 1992.

Tracy, David. "Fragments: The Spiritual Situation of Our Times." In *God, the Gift, and Postmodernism*, edited by John D. Caputo and Michael J. Scanlon, 170–84. Bloomington: Indiana University Press, 1999.

Treier, Daniel J. *Introducing Evangelical Theology*. Grand Rapids: Baker Academic, 2019.

———. "The Personal and Cultural Character of Reason: Christ's Triumph over Modern Technique." In *Revelation and Reason in Christian Theology: Proceedings of the 2016 Theology Connect Conference*, edited by Christopher C. Green and David I. Starling, 37–62. Bellingham, WA: Lexham, 2018.

Treier, Daniel J., and Walter A. Elwell, eds. *Evangelical Dictionary of Theology*. 3rd ed. Grand Rapids: Baker Academic, 2017.

Vanhoozer, Kevin J., ed. *Dictionary for Theological Interpretation of the Bible*. Grand Rapids: Baker Academic, 2005.

———. *The Drama of Doctrine: A Canonical-Linguistic Approach to Christian Theology*. Louisville: Westminster John Knox, 2005.

———. "From 'Blessed in Christ' to 'Being in Christ': The State of Union and the Place of Participation in Paul's Discourse, New Testament Exegesis, and Systematic Theology Today." In *"In Christ" in Paul: Explorations in Paul's Theology of Union and Participation*, edited by Michael J. Thate, Kevin J. Vanhoozer, and Constantine R. Campbell, 3–33. Tübingen: Mohr Siebeck, 2014.

Vanhoozer, Kevin J., and Daniel J. Treier. *Theology and the Mirror of Scripture: A Mere Evangelical Account*. Downers Grove, IL: IVP Academic, 2015.

Veeneman, Mary M. *Introducing Theological Method: A Survey of Contemporary Theologians and Approaches*. Grand Rapids: Baker Academic, 2017.

Volf, Miroslav. "Theology for a Way of Life." In Volf and Bass, *Practicing Theology*, 245–63.

Volf, Miroslav, and Dorothy C. Bass, eds. *Practicing Theology: Beliefs and Practices in Christian Life*. Grand Rapids: Eerdmans, 2002.

Volf, Miroslav, and Matthew Croasmun. *For the Life of the World: Theology That Makes a Difference*. Grand Rapids: Brazos, 2019.

Walker, Andrew. *Different Gospels*. London: Hodder & Stoughton, 1988.

———. *Notes from a Wayward Son: A Miscellany*. Edited by Andrew D. Kinsey. Eugene, OR: Cascade Books, 2015.

Walls, Andrew, and Cathy Ross, eds. *Mission in the Twenty-First Century: Exploring the Five Marks of Global Mission*. Maryknoll, NY: Orbis Books, 2008.

Walters, James. *Loving Your Neighbour in an Age of Religious Conflict: A New Agenda for Interfaith Relations*. London: Jessica Kingsley, 2019.

Ward, Graham, ed. *The Blackwell Companion to Postmodern Theology*. Oxford: Blackwell, 2001.

Ware, Timothy. *The Orthodox Church*. Rev. ed. London: Penguin, 1993.

Warren, Tish Harrison. *Liturgy of the Ordinary: Sacred Practices in Everyday Life*. Downers Grove, IL: InterVarsity, 2016.

Weaver, John. *Outside-In: Theological Reflections on Life*. Macon, GA: Smyth & Helwys, 2006.

Webster, John. *The Culture of Theology*. Edited by Ivor J. Davidson and Alden C. McCray. Grand Rapids: Baker Academic, 2019.

———. *Holy Scripture: A Dogmatic Sketch*. Cambridge: Cambridge University Press, 2003.

Welker, Michael, and Cynthia A. Jarvis, eds. *Loving God with Our Minds: The Pastor as Theologian; Essays in Honor of Wallace M. Alston*. Grand Rapids: Eerdmans, 2005.

Wells, Samuel. *Incarnational Mission: Being with the World*. Grand Rapids: Eerdmans, 2018.

Whitmore, Todd David. *Imitating Christ in Magwi: An Anthropological Theology*. London: Bloomsbury T&T Clark, 2019.

Williams, D. H. *Evangelicals and Tradition: The Formative Influence of the Early Church*. Grand Rapids: Baker Academic, 2005.

———. *Retrieving the Tradition and Renewing Evangelicalism*. Grand Rapids: Eerdmans, 1999.

Williams, Rowan. "Archbishop of Canterbury's Sermon at the Opening Service of the 15th Meeting of the Anglican Consultative Council." Auckland, New Zealand, October 28, 2012. http://aoc2013.brix.fatbeehive.com/articles.php/2669/archbish ops-sermon-at-acc-15-on-the-reckless-love-of-god.

Williamson, Paul R. "Covenant: The Beginning of a Biblical Idea." *Reformed Theological Review* 65, no. 1 (2006): 1–14.

Willimon, William H. "Up from Liberalism." In *Good News in Exile: Three Pastors Offer a Hopeful Vision for the Church*, edited by Martin B. Copenhaver, Anthony B. Robinson, and William H. Willimon, 27–32. Grand Rapids: Eerdmans, 1998.

Witherington, Ben. "John Barclay's *Paul and the Gift*—Part Twenty." *The Bible and Culture* (blog), November 21, 2015. https://www.patheos.com/blogs/bibleandcult ure/2015/11/21/john-barclays-paul-and-the-gift-part-twenty/.

Wolterstorff, Nicholas. *Justice in Love*. Grand Rapids: Eerdmans, 2011.

Wright, Christopher J. H. *The Mission of God: Unlocking the Bible's Grand Narrative*. Leicester, UK: Inter-Varsity, 2006.

Wright, N. T. "The Bible and Christian Mission." In Gorman, *Scripture and Its Interpretation*, 388–400.

———. *The New Testament and the People of God*. London: SPCK, 1993.

———. *Paul and the Faithfulness of God*. Minneapolis: Fortress, 2013.

———. *Scripture and the Authority of God: How to Read the Bible Today*. London: SPCK, 2011.

Yong, Amos. *Beyond the Impasse: Toward a Pneumatological Theology of Religions*. Grand Rapids: Baker Academic, 2003.

———. *Discerning the Spirit(s): A Pentecostal-Charismatic Contribution to Christian Theology of Religions*. Sheffield, UK: Sheffield Academic, 2000.

Zizioulas, John D. *Being as Communion: Studies in Personhood and the Church*. Crestwood, NY: St. Vladimir's Seminary Press, 1985.

———. "On Being a Person: Towards an Ontology of Personhood." In *Persons, Divine and Human*, edited by Christoph Schwöbel and Colin E. Gunton, 33–46. Edinburgh: T&T Clark, 1999.

Index